EMIL AND KATHLEEN SICK SERIES IN WESTERN HISTORY AND BIOGRAPHY

With support from the Center for the Study of the Pacific Northwest at the University of Washington, the Sick Series in Western History and Biography features scholarly books on the peoples and issues that have defined and shaped the American West. Through intellectually challenging and engaging books of general interest, the series seeks to deepen and expand our understanding of the American West as a region and its role in the making of the United States and the modern world.

# PIONEERING DEATH

• ——————— •

## THE VIOLENCE OF BOYHOOD IN TURN-OF-THE-CENTURY OREGON

PETER BOAG

CENTER FOR THE STUDY
OF THE PACIFIC NORTHWEST

in association with

UNIVERSITY OF WASHINGTON PRESS
*Seattle*

*Pioneering Death* was made possible in part by a grant from the Emil and Kathleen Sick Fund of the University of Washington's Department of History.

Copyright © 2022 by the University of Washington Press

Composed in Minion Pro typeface designed by Robert Slimbach
Maps and chart by Pease Press Cartography, https://peasepress.com

26  25  24  23  22      5  4  3  2  1

Printed and bound in the United States of America

All rights reserved. No part of this publication may be reproduced or transmitted in any form or by any means, electronic or mechanical, including photocopy, recording, or any information storage or retrieval system, without permission in writing from the publisher.

CENTER FOR THE STUDY
OF THE PACIFIC NORTHWEST
http://cspn.uw.edu

UNIVERSITY OF WASHINGTON PRESS
www.washington.edu/uwpress

LIBRARY OF CONGRESS CATALOGING-IN-PUBLICATION DATA
Names: Boag, Peter, author.
Title: Pioneering death : the violence of boyhood in turn-of-the-century Oregon / Peter Boag.
Description: Seattle : Center for the Study of the Pacific Northwest in association with University of Washington Press, [2022] | Series: Emil and Kathleen Sick book series in western history and biography | Includes bibliographical references and index.
Identifiers: LCCN 2021032009 (print) | LCCN 2021032010 (ebook) |
  ISBN 9780295749983 (hardcover) | ISBN 9780295749990 (ebook)
Subjects: LCSH: Montgomery, Loyd, 1877–1896. | Parricide—Oregon—History—19th century—Case studies. | Boyhood—Oregon—History—19th century | Oregon—Rural conditions—19th century.
Classification: LCC HV6542 .B63 2022 (print) | LCC HV6542 (ebook) |
  DDC 364.152/30979509034—dc23
LC record available at https://lccn.loc.gov/2021032009
LC ebook record available at https://lccn.loc.gov/2021032010

♾ This paper meets the requirements of ANSI/NISO Z39.48-1992 (Permanence of Paper).

*For Brent*

# CONTENTS

In Small and Large Things Remembered . . . . . . . . . . . . . . . . . . ix

**PROLOGUE.** "A Scene of Wholesale Butchery":
A Document of Rural Ethnology . . . . . . . . . . . . . . . . . . . . . . . 1

**PART 1.** "Aided by Boys upon Horseback, Who Carried Lanterns":
Boyhood in Rural Oregon

**CHAPTER 1.** "The Hope and Life of the Nation":
Boys and Families on the Republican Landscape . . . . . . . . . . . . 25

**CHAPTER 2.** "A Child, Sick with Scarlet Fever":
The Traumas and Violence of Rural Childhood . . . . . . . . . . . . . 44

**CHAPTER 3.** "Spare the Rod and Spoil the Child":
The Bad-Boy Problem and the Montgomery Parricide . . . . . . . . . . 61

**PART 2.** "One by One They Are Dropping Like the Autumn Leaves":
Agricultural Decline, Dying Pioneers, and Parricide

**CHAPTER 4.** "The Pinching Economies of Life":
The Agrarian Crisis and the Murder of Parents . . . . . . . . . . . . . 95

**CHAPTER 5.** "His People Being Pioneers":
Parricide in an Age of Death and an Era That Celebrated Killing . . . . 123

**PART 3.** "We're Going to Hang Him Right Here, on This Tree": Killing Loyd Montgomery

**CHAPTER 6.** "The Scaffold Is All Framed and Ready to Be Put in Place": Executing a Boy on an Altar of Global Capitalism . . . . . . . 156

**CHAPTER 7.** "At 14½ Minutes His Heart Ceased to Beat": A Boy's Life from 4:30 p.m., 19 November 1895, to 7:26 a.m., 31 January 1896 . . . . . 169

**EPILOGUE.** "The Case of Loyd Montgomery Does Not End with His Death": Burying a Boy and Digging Up the Past . . . . . . . . . . . . . . . 213

Notes . . . . . . . . . . . . . . . . . . . . . . . . . . . . 223
Bibliography . . . . . . . . . . . . . . . . . . . . . . . 265
Index . . . . . . . . . . . . . . . . . . . . . . . . . . . . 285

# IN SMALL AND LARGE
# THINGS REMEMBERED

This project began with a scrap of paper. I came across it on 10 January 1987, while doing research at the Linn County Historical Museum (LCHM) in Brownsville, Oregon. It was a cool, dark, rainy Saturday, and the staff let me sit in their institution's windowless vault, done up like a bank teller's office of long ago. It was located in one of the museum's boxcars, a series of which are ingeniously strung together to provide a good portion of the exhibit space; the main entry to the museum is through a building that replicates an old train station. Practically no one else was in the museum that wintry day. As I sifted through odds and ends that might provide material for my doctoral dissertation, I chanced upon a photocopy of a portion of the *Brownsville Times*'s supplemental issue of 20 November 1895. It was the first news account about, and the one published most proximate to, a triple murder committed by Loyd Montgomery. It was also a chance find: that newspaper for those years has not otherwise been preserved, except for some very random issues. That someone had a copy of this fragment of the local past and that it ended up with a variety of other materials in a box at the museum constituted something of a miracle.

Loyd's story was beyond both my dissertation's timeframe and focus. It so haunted me, though, that I made a copy of that scrap from the past, tucked it away in a file, and promised myself that one day I would do something with it. Over the years, I occasionally collected research on Loyd and the triple murder when I happened to find myself in an appropriate archive or library. As my folder of materials slowly grew, the story only disturbed me more. I wondered all the more about what must have happened behind the scenes of what the newspaper described—matters involving boyhood, violence, trauma, and how all that fit into the broader history of that place.

It was not until the 2010s that I wrote a few article- and chapter-length pieces on the topic and spoke about it to audiences, in places ranging from the LCHM's theater, also located in a boxcar, to Oxford University. But mostly in these recent years I found myself more often setting the project aside, being either frustrated in trying to write a book that I imagined or frustrated that I could not imagine the book I was trying to write. It came together for me just as the horrors of the COVID-19 pandemic enveloped the world and I found myself confined to my home office.

Because the research for and my discussions with others about this project are scattered over so many years, I have no doubt forgotten some of the people who have contributed to it. To them I offer my deepest apology. But I certainly do remember many who gave their time to listen (willingly or otherwise), who provided insight and ideas, who shared their own research and expertise, and who helped gather and organize documents and information for me. They each made this book much better than it would have been had it been left in my hands alone.

During my years at Washington State University (WSU), I had three marvelous research assistants, each of whom touched this project in special ways: Laura Arata, Jacki Hedlund Tyler, and Brian Stack. They spent a great deal of time with old newspapers and data about human death and agricultural produce. WSU, in both Pullman and Vancouver, also provided funding that I utilized for research and to produce the maps—the work of Ben Pease—contained herein.

The Oregon Historical Society (OHS) provided me the Donald J. Sterling Jr. Memorial Senior Research Fellowship at one point; it supported my research in OHS's wonderful collections. Erin Brasell of the OHS's *Oregon Historical Quarterly* gave generously of her time, assisting me with genealogical materials and illustrations. The *Quarterly*'s editor, Eliza Canty-Jones, included me in a public program, "Death and the Settling and Unsettling of Oregon," and offered me encouragement on a couple of articles that she published in the journal. She also provided other sorts of help to me in all things OHS.

Louise Parker, Lynn Machen, and Todd and Chris Cooper, all descendants or relations of various people included in this book, provided useful genealogical and family-history materials that cannot be found elsewhere. Gina Bardi with the National Park Service in San Francisco looked through old Portland Cordage Company records for me during COVID-19 closures.

Paul Rohde and Linda Hatzenbuehler shared their knowledge on matters of psychology and their knowledge of relevant psychological literature. David Peterson del Mar, Sterling Evans, and Matthew A. Sutton each lent their expertise on matters relevant to their own research that informed my writing. Elliott West and Clayton Koppes both provided moral support and encouragement.

Keith Lohse at the Albany Regional Museum, as well as Joni Nelson, Mandy Cole, and Barbara Anderson at the LCHM, helped me with their collections and photographs. The staff at the LCHM and the Brownsville Community Library were also instrumental in my early research into this project. Layne Sawyer, now retired from the Oregon State Archives in Salem, helped open many research doors for me at what is now her former institutional employer.

I am very much indebted to my friends and the gifted historians Ronald L. Hatzenbuehler and Lori Ann Lahlum. They each read major portions of my manuscript and provided thoughts and recommendations that improved this book considerably. Lori also lent a good deal of moral support as I labored over my writing. Melinda Marie Jetté and Ryan Dearinger, both accomplished historians, each read the entire manuscript. Their recommendations on historiography and myriad other suggestions about conceptualization had a significant impact on this book. I also thank my editor, Mike Baccam. He has been enthusiastic about this project throughout and also provided useful feedback on the book's content. The rest of those who work for the University of Washington Press, including freelance copyeditor Maureen Bemko, have been a pleasure to work with. Kim McKaig at the *Pacific Northwest Quarterly*, as well as Joshua Reid, who is at the University of Washington's Center for the Study of the Pacific Northwest and serves as editor of the Emil and Kathleen Sick Series in Western History and Biography, provided additional editorial assistance and support in the later stages of this book's production.

Finally, four people deserve special recognition. Over the years, as I thought about this project, I gathered a great deal of inspiration from my doctoral advisor, Richard Maxwell Brown. He made a career of the history of violence. He passed away in 2014, unable to see my endeavors finally come to fruition—though we had talked about it, even long ago while I worked on my dissertation. Over these years, I also lost my parents. I am thankful that while they were living, I had the occasion to dedicate another book to them, something in which they took great pride. While they found this project captivating, it would have been a bit awkward dedicating a book about parricide to Mom and Dad. But being the people they were, they would have appreciated the morbid humor in that. I miss them greatly for that and for many other reasons. I dedicate this book, however, to my life partner and husband of many, many years, Brent Owens. He loves murder-mystery thrillers. He was also once an Oregon boy and was one (I am sure he would appreciate me saying) not so terribly long ago.

# PIONEERING DEATH

PROLOGUE

# "A Scene of Wholesale Butchery"

*A Document of Rural Ethnology*

AT ABOUT 4:15 IN THE AFTERNOON, ROUGHLY A HALF hour before sunset on Tuesday, 19 November 1895, several rifle shots cracked the cool autumn air in rural Linn County, Oregon, about three miles east of the small town of Brownsville. There the forested foothills of the Cascade Range gently rise from the softly sloping agricultural lands of the southern Willamette Valley (map P.1). Sound traveled exceptionally well that late afternoon; the fog of earlier in the day had evaporated into fair skies that, at most, produced only the slightest of breezes. Since it was late autumn, when local men and youths regularly turned to hunting, no one might have taken special notice of these blasts, except that alarming screams of "Oh don't, don't!" and "Oh, God, don't, don't!" punctuated them. And then, after a few minutes of dead silence, from the same direction coursed the distinct wailing of young children. Just returning from school, they were the first to discover the aftermath of a murderous rampage that had transformed their home into a scene of "wholesale butchery," as a local newspaper described it the next day.[1]

The children were fourteen-year-old Eva, twelve-year-old Robert, and nine-year-old John Montgomery, all siblings. Accompanying them was their cousin Clyde Templeton. He lived on a neighboring farm and was marking his thirteenth birthday that very day. The Montgomery children's modest home, where the events transpired, was actually one they shared

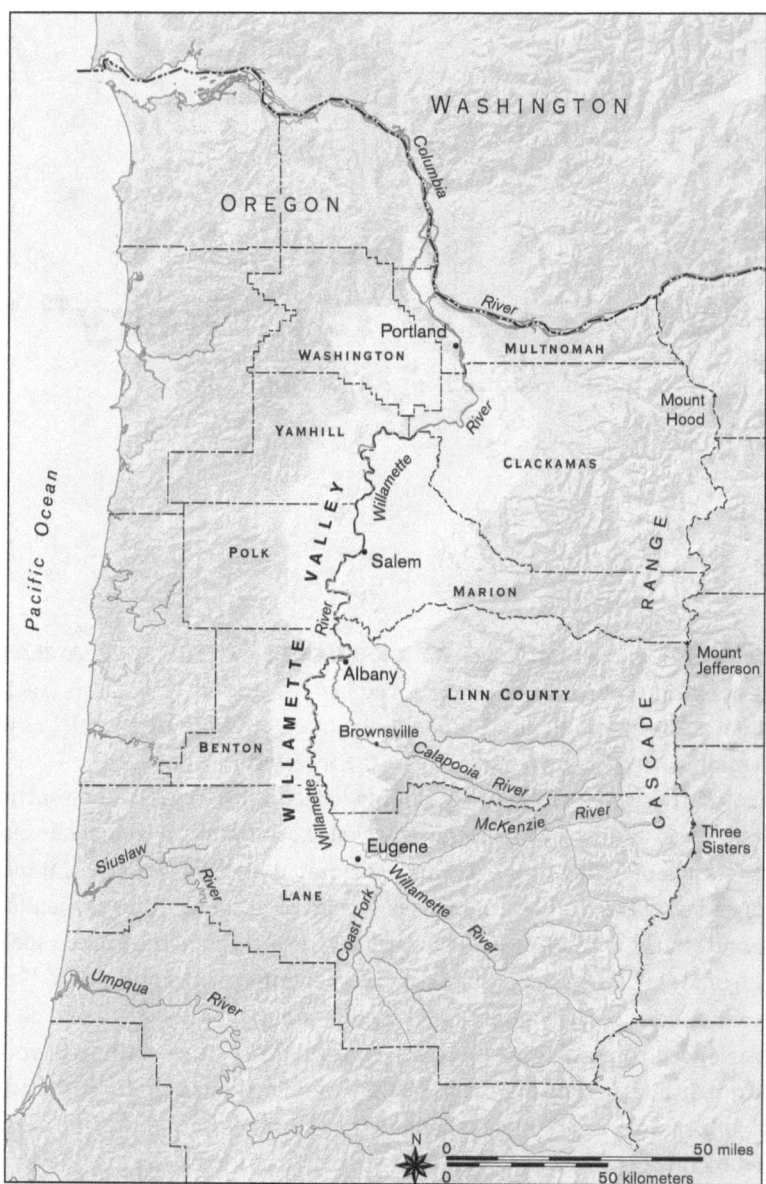

Map P.1. The Willamette Valley. This small slice of northwestern Oregon, because of its gentle climate and topography, was the goal for most of the early American migrants who headed west on the overland trails to the Pacific Northwest. Once there, they went about creating a republican landscape that included taking the land from its first people, the Kalapuya. The ancestors of Loyd Montgomery settled in Linn County (center of the map) beginning in 1846. There they founded the town of Brownsville, not far from which Loyd committed his triple murder forty-nine years later.

Figure P.1. Loyal "Loyd" Bryson Montgomery. Born on 26 August 1877, Loyd lived his entire life in the vicinity of where he was residing on 19 November 1895, when he murdered both his parents and a neighbor who happened to be visiting. The triple murder became a local and regional sensation, and news of it spread across the nation. Source: *Weekly Herald-Disseminator* (Albany, OR), 6 February 1896.

with its owner, Samuel Templeton. He was the brother-in-law to two paternal aunts of the children: Sarah and Orpha. These Montgomery sisters had married Samuel's brothers Albert and Robert. Orpha and Robert were the parents of Clyde. In 1895, Samuel, who never married, was in his early sixties. His home sat amid his modest farm of about ninety acres, of which thirty were planted in hops. The Montgomery children's parents, John (born 1851) and Elizabeth (born 1856), had moved their struggling family onto Sam's farm the year before, during the depths of the 1890s depression. There they sharecropped.[2]

There were two more Montgomery children. Sixteen-year-old Orville was well known in the community as a dutiful son. At the time of the disturbance, which he had not heard, he was out plowing a nearby field. The other Montgomery child, eighteen-year-old Loyal, known simply as Loyd, was the oldest of them all (figure P.1). Loyd had a history of challenging behaviors; just one day earlier he had disappeared without telling his parents where he was going, what he was doing, or if he would return. He had done such things before. This time, he had absconded to go hunting, taking his father's Winchester .40-82 with him. He did, in fact, return—around 3:15 p.m. on 19 November. At that time his widowed grandmother, Eveline (Brown) Montgomery, his aunt Orpha, and Orpha's four-year-old daughter, Bessie, were visiting from their own nearby farms, helping Loyd's mother in the garden. The women had harvested cabbage, which they planned to put up as sauerkraut the next day. The visitors left just before 4:00 p.m.[3]

About then, Edgar Gilkey, a hop buyer who was traveling the neighborhood, arrived by wagon. He met John Sr. under the immense maple tree that stood at the corner of the yard. There, the men faced each other on either side of the rough and weathered picket fence that bounded the family's domicile, separating it from the larger world beyond. The fence was, at best, nothing more than a dilapidated cordon between the two overlapping realms. Over it, Gilkey transmitted to John the very public information about the shockingly low price he could expect for his recent hop harvest—information that connected the penury of the Montgomery household to the larger depression then raging beyond the picket fence, across the land, and even around the globe.[4]

Just as Gilkey headed off to convey the same bad news to the next struggling farm, thirty-four-year-old Daniel McKercher, proprietor with his brother of a small gristmill located a couple of miles farther up the road to the east, near the hamlet of Crawfordsville, rode up on horseback with his black-and-white dog trotting alongside. He dismounted, met John, who remained on the household side of the fence, and engaged him in conversation. They also spoke of matters related to depression and scarcity—namely, John's mounting debt to the mill for flour. Loyd happened to be close at hand. With news of the outside world bearing down hard on the farmer, as well as being annoyed with his son, who seemed to come and go as he pleased, John began quarreling with Loyd. McKercher voiced his opinion on the matter, supporting John, who then slapped the boy across the face and commanded him to tend his chores.

John no doubt thought that was the end of it when he turned back to look outward to the world and into Daniel's face. It would be the last thing he saw. For, violently angered, seething with humiliation, and tormented by a darker side, Loyd had marched into the house. There he grabbed his father's rifle—the very weapon he had taken with him the day before on his hunting excursion. He reemerged at the kitchen door. With deadly accuracy, the youth fired a single bullet into the back of his father's head, above and behind the left ear. John was grasping the fence at the time. As he collapsed backward, his grip locked, and the weight of his fall snapped some of the rotting pickets. After hitting the ground, his brains flowed from the cavern in his skull (maps P.2 and P.3).

Loyd turned his father's rifle on his mother, Elizabeth, who also happened to be in the yard. He fired. The bullet entered her back at the left

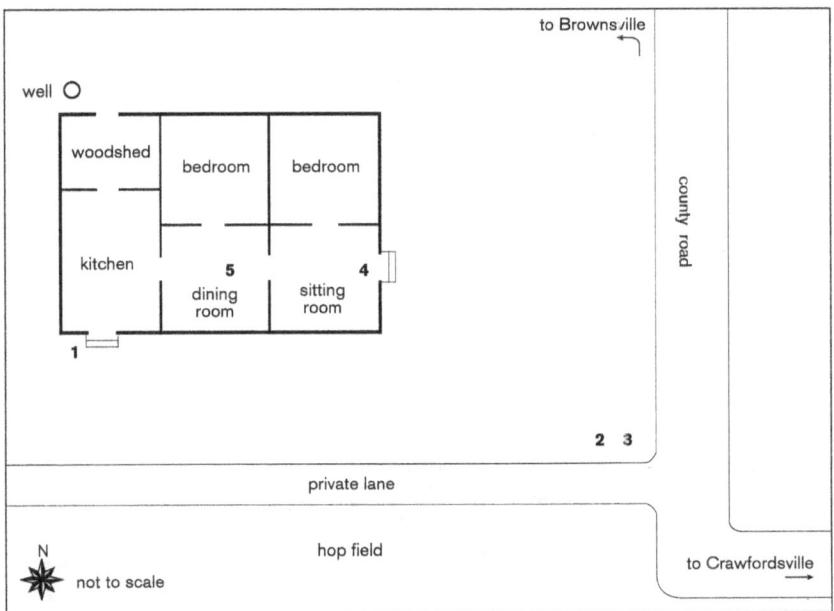

Map P.2. The Montgomery-Templeton home and scene of the murders. Position number 1 indicates where Loyd stood when he shot his father, John (position number 2), in the back of the head, killing him instantly. At the time, John was talking to Daniel McKercher (position number 3), who then ran for the house's front door. Loyd caught up with him and shot him from behind (number 4). Loyd then shot and killed his mother (number 5). This was his second shot at her; he initially fired at her after he killed his father and when she was also in the yard. Sources: *State Rights Democrat* (Albany, OR), 29 November 1895; *Oregonian* (Portland), 26 November and 1 December 1895; "A Triple Murder," *Brownsville (OR) Times*, supplement, 20 November 1895.

shoulder and exited through her left breast. This did not kill her. Loyd quickly turned to take aim at McKercher, who by then was desperately running to the house, seeking refuge. Loyd again fired but missed. Just as McKercher entered the front door, however, the youth came quickly behind him from around the corner of the house and shot once again. The miller, like the farmer seconds before, took a bullet behind his left ear. The projectile shredded the back of McKercher's skull before exiting through the front of his head, spraying brains profusely about the sitting room. Meanwhile, Elizabeth had made it into the house through the kitchen door. As McKercher tumbled before him, Loyd spotted his mother crossing through

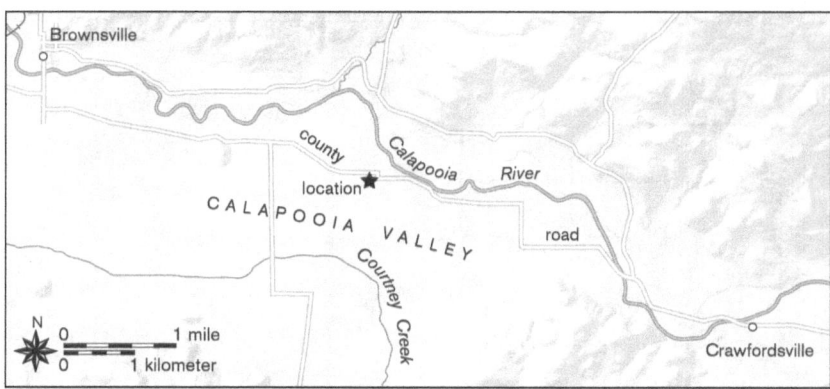

Map P.3. Location of the murder scene. In 1895, the county road between Brownsville and Crawfordsville followed a slightly different path from what it does today. Back then it made sharp turns around the northern and eastern edges of the yard around the Templeton-Montgomery home, the location of which is near the center of the map and halfway between Brownsville and Crawfordsville.

the dining room beyond. He shot one final round; it hit below her right eye and passed through the base of her brain before exiting. As she slumped to the floor, Elizabeth somehow managed to lift herself slightly, or perhaps she had caught herself on the way down. Her body froze there—her face angling downward but not touching the floor.

Loyd released his weapon. It fell across McKercher's legs. As the youth withdrew, the miller's dog slunk in from behind and took up vigil next to his master's body. "Faithful to the last," a later news account reported. The dog crouched there for hours, unyielding to the dozens of later arrivals who tried to coax him away. But well before those onlookers came onto the premises, Loyd headed out into the nearby country lane and in the direction of Brownsville. Where he planned to go, or if he had any plans at all, is impossible to know. But there on the road he ran smack into his three siblings and cousin returning from school. One can hardly imagine what he thought and felt. The youngsters asked if he had been shooting. He told them no but that he had heard the gunfire and thought that his father was likely taking aim at a hawk. Robert broke away and raced to the house. The others followed, though Loyd lagged somewhat behind.[5]

So began a stunning story that consumed the attention of Brownsville and Crawfordsville locals, residents of Linn County, and citizens of Oregon for the next several weeks and beyond. Reports spread up and down the West Coast and even across the nation. From the local to the national level, the Montgomery parricide and McKercher murder attracted morbid curiosity and generated considerable discussion about matters of childhood, the wayward and even murderous boys and youths of America, parental failings and responsibilities, the troubles of contemporary rural life, and the supposed limitations of the Oregon legal system. Central to all this was the query that burned most intensely of all: why did Loyd Montgomery kill his parents?

Why do some children kill their parents? The search for the answer to that question has a history as long as that of humankind. Tales of matricide and patricide—collectively referred to, along with the killing of any close relative, as parricide—exist in the foundational myths of varied cultures. In Western civilization, names such as Oedipus, Orestes, and Pelias are well known. The first committed patricide. The second killed his mother. The last fell victim to his murderous daughters. In addition to commandments that proscribe murder and prescribe honoring fathers and mothers, the Bible tells the tale of the Assyrian king Sennacherib, whose sons slew him with a sword. In the Western world, Sigmund Freud, often drawing on ancient mythology, based a good part of his indelibly influential psychodynamic theories and explanations of Western culture on tales of and allusions to patricide and matricide.

In recent years, shocking stories of children who have killed their parents have competed for column space and air time in news outlets and have provided "entertainment" on both big and small screens. The perennially best-known parricide, at least in the American context, comes from the time of Loyd Montgomery but from the side of the continent opposite his: the case involving Lizzie Borden. Although found innocent of the brutal ax murder of her father and stepmother in 1892 in Fall River, Massachusetts, many believed then and have believed since in her guilt. A popular and fittingly gruesome rhyme, long popular with young children (of all people), is evidence of that.[6]

There were, in fact, many especially alarming parricides in the 1890s that beset rural America. Just a handful of samples includes Pennsylvania's twenty-six-year-old Ralph Crossmeier, who in 1892 brutally attacked his mother with a club while she was milking a cow in the barn. In an attempt to cover his crime, Ralph hanged her lifeless body to make it appear a suicide. The next year in Illinois, brothers John and Ernest Swarthout shot their widowed father, a wealthy farmer, in the head and then attempted to burn his remains on a pile of hay. Failing to dispose of the body that way, they then mutilated his face in an attempt to render it unidentifiable. In a case with some similarities to the Montgomery parricide, in December 1892 a sixty-year-old farmer near Novi, Michigan, reprimanded his twenty-year-old son for going hunting. During the quarrel, the enraged youth shot and killed his father. And then, in the same year as the Montgomery killings, a thirty-year-old woman near Summerfield, Kansas, crushed her mother's skull with an ax while the older woman slept. That same day she also tried but failed to poison her brother.[7]

But other than the Lizzie Borden sensation, which was no more brutal than any of these and has generated libraries full of prose (and the Borden house serves today as a bed-and-breakfast museum), relatively few academic historical analyses of parricide exist.[8] This is also in contrast to the avalanche of historical studies on interpersonal violence, not to mention serial murder, lynching, war, and genocide. On the history of the causes of murder in the United States, historians have explored every angle imaginable. This includes examining the types of weapons used, the judicial and political systems' choices to prosecute or not prosecute murderers, the role honor plays in self-defense, and the nation's frontier heritage as contributing to a murder culture. Scholars have also parsed homicide in light of race, gender, biological determinism, migration patterns and mobility, and long-term social forces such as the "civilizing process."[9]

The study of murder in the form of parricide, on the other hand, has been primarily left to psychologists and criminologists. They have also tended to focus their attention on more recent times. That is partly because of the purposes and goals of those disciplines and partly due to sources: it was only in the mid-1970s that the Federal Bureau of Investigation began collecting and reporting data on this type of crime. Working with this information, as well as clinical case studies, social scientists who focus on juvenile perpetrators of parricide have identified basically three types of children who commit most parricides: the severely abused child, the severely mentally ill child, and the child who is dangerously antisocial. Moreover, such studies have determined that most perpetrators of parricide are male, most victims are fathers, and most offenders use firearms to commit their act.[10] Although there is some disagreement, this research has also determined that through the late twentieth century, the rate of parricide has remained relatively stable. In the United States it has lingered at around 2 percent of all homicides. While in the overall scheme of things parricide is a relatively rare occurrence, criminologist Kathleen M. Heide has determined that for the years from 1976 to 2007, an average of 248 parricides of biological parents occurred annually in the United States.[11]

Various of the aforementioned conclusions have explanatory relevance for the Montgomery parricide and suggest its typicality. Yet, I am aware that such factors and determinations that come from our times do not necessarily translate wholesale into explanations or predictions for parricide that occurred long ago, when people lived differently from how they do today. The criminologist Phillip Chong Ho Shon, unusual among social scientists in that he sees history as a factor in parricide, has pointed out one of the problems with his discipline's approach to explaining that act. Ascribing the offense to personality types and mental illness ignores a variety of temporal matters. In a series of studies on nineteenth-century American parricides, Shon has demonstrated the role of historically contingent factors in the crime, such as what types of weapons were available and thus used, how different forms of socializing and residential arrangements in an earlier era provided venues for disagreements that escalated into killings, and the availability and role of alcohol in parricide.[12]

I take seriously Shon's observations, but in *Pioneering Death*, I proceed somewhat differently. In doing so, I take to heart an overlooked observation that the philosopher, theoretician, and historian Michel Foucault made in 1975 in the foreword to a collaborative study that he and his students produced on one nineteenth-century French parricide. The case they considered took place on 3 June 1835, in the small village of Faucterie in Lower Normandy. There, the twenty-year-old peasant Pierre Rivière murdered his mother, a sister, and a brother. Foucault and his students interested themselves mostly in the varied legal, medical, and confessional texts that the case generated. Although the team provided critical commentary, "the main point for us," Foucault explained, "was to have the documents published." Then he noted, merely in passing, that while his coauthors eschewed the texts for such an examination, their diverse narratives provide a "marvelous document of peasant ethnology."[13]

I maintain that it is within the very exploration of the ethnology of parricide—that is, an examination not only of the people involved and their relations with each other but also of the community, the society, and indeed the history that they were part of—where we can best find answers to why a rural Oregon lad murdered his farming parents on a cool autumn day long ago. The Montgomery parricide was an event with a *longue durée* that no psychological analysis of the perpetrator can fully explain.[14] My argument is that the fifteen or so minutes that commenced at about four o'clock in the afternoon of 19 November 1895, on an out-of-the-way Oregon farm, were the climax to developments, events, and relationships long in the making in the Montgomery family, on the farm where they lived, in the community that surrounded them, in the broader Pacific Northwest, and in even the nation and the world beyond. At the same time, the climactic moment was hardly its denouement; the parricide is also the story of how the survivors integrated that numbing event into the history of their community and even into the history of the larger Pacific Northwest. The rifle shots that rang out at about 4:15 p.m. halfway between Brownsville and Crawfordsville on 19 November 1895 publicly announced a story that had been in the making for years. Their reverberation through the valley continued long after the Winchester fell silent.

In the pages that follow I narrate that story, and I do so from multiple historical perspectives—the westward expansion of the United States, rural and agricultural decline, the consolidation of market capitalism, political change, environmental transformation, race and labor, penal reform and the evolution of justice, religion and the meaning of death, and the especially intimate matters of childhood, family, gender relations, and memory. But before sending readers down darkened lanes into a deathly past, I wish to offer a few guideposts about history, setting, victims, and the perpetrator to assist them in that journey.

TIME AND PLACE

The Montgomery parricide took place during the most forbidding moments of the worst worldwide depression up to that point in modern history. American agrarians like the Montgomery family suffered especially so, given that a general slump in prices for their produce had begun two decades earlier. By the 1890s the situation had reached its most desperate, and the social and cultural implications extended far and wide. The late historian Warren Susman summed it up well in the foreword to Michael Lesy's unsettling and unconventional *Wisconsin Death Trip*, which explores the darkness of the 1890s in the Upper Midwest. By then, Susman explains, there existed "a growing awareness of awesome problems of death, decline, delinquency, and even degeneracy," not just in the city, as traditionally thought, but in rural and agrarian America, too.[15] These very concepts—death, decline, delinquency, and degeneracy—shaped the contemporary conceptualization of the Montgomery parricide. They did so certainly from the perspective of urban people, but—and although they at times argued forcefully against such views of their lives and ideals—rural folk in Linn County could also not entirely escape these concepts' explanatory usefulness when making sense of the tragedy that had befallen them.

The later years of the nineteenth century posed special challenges for Willamette Valley farmers. Wheat, long the staple of their livelihoods, not only experienced the aforementioned decline in prices, but the western Oregon climate was never ideal for its cultivation. Unable to compete with newly opening and superior wheat-growing regions in the interior Northwest, Willamette Valley farmers began a painful search for replacement crops. One that they turned to was hops. The Templetons pioneered hop cultivation in Linn County. Samuel's hopyard, among the oldest, was already steeped in history by the time the Montgomery-McKercher murders happened there. But that they happened there was partly a product of that hopyard's history, which provides a darker and forgotten side to that crop's blood-soaked roots in the region.

Samuel Templeton's farm was situated halfway along the east-west country lane stretching six miles or so between the small towns of Brownsville and Crawfordsville. The former, composed of separate north and south villages until 1895, traced its founding to the 1850s (figure P.2). Founders of Crawfordsville incorporated it in 1870. Located close to the eastern margin of the southern Willamette Valley's arable lands, the towns lay some ninety miles south of Portland and thirty miles north of Eugene. Just north of the Templeton hopyard, the smallish Calapooia River, which brushed the northern limits of the larger Templeton farmstead and at that time powered McKercher's gristmill, tumbles westward out of the Cascade Range through Crawfordsville and then, just beyond Brownsville, turns and meanders in a northerly course. It enters the Willamette River at the town of Albany, the seat of Linn County, where much of the drama of the Montgomery case would play out in the weeks following Loyd's murderous act.

Figure P.2. Brownsville in about 1890. Founded in 1853, Brownsville was named in honor of Hugh Brown, Loyd Montgomery's great-grandfather and one of the most highly regarded Oregon "pioneers." Joseph H. Templeton, whose brother's house outside of town became the scene of the murders, took this photograph just a few years before the crime. It looks toward the southwest over the main part of what was then North Brownsville. Courtesy of the Oregon Historical Society Research Library, Portland. Digital image no. bc004764.

PEOPLE

The Montgomerys, Templetons, and related families were among the earliest Americans to occupy Linn County (map P.4). As part of the southern half of the original Oregon Country, the region only became US territory in 1846. It was in that year that Loyd's paternal grandmother, Eveline Brown, who was twelve at the time, came to the Calapooia with her parents, Hugh and Clarissa, and an adult cousin, James Blakely. The following year, Loyd's grandfather, Robert Montgomery, who was twenty, arrived with his brother Canada and his sister Sarah, who was married to James McHargue. These Montgomery siblings' parents, John and Ellen, followed in 1851.

The Templetons also reached the Calapooia in 1847, and the next year Loyd's mother's maternal grandparents, Elisha and Elizabeth Griffith, arrived, though they had already been in Oregon for a few years, working for the Hudson's Bay Company. Elizabeth Griffith's two brothers, John and William Findley (the latter married a Templeton), and in-law Agnes

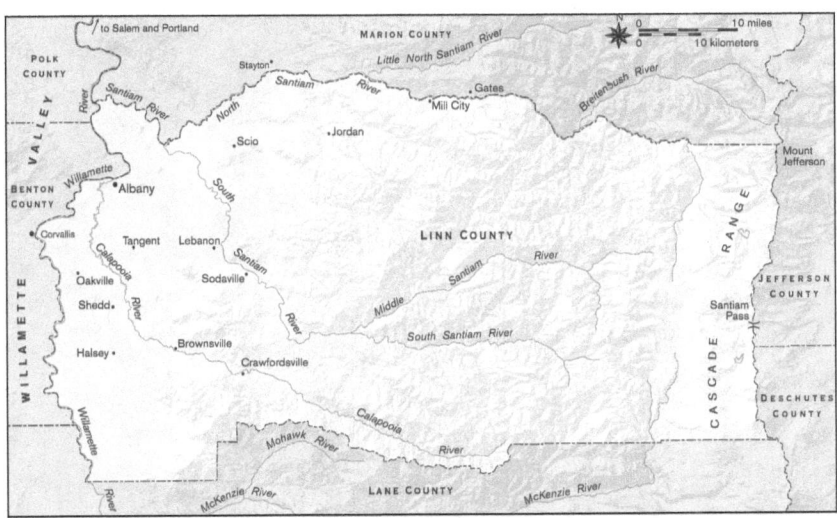

Map P.4. Linn County. The Montgomery-McKercher murders took place midway between Brownsville and Crawfordsville. Much of the story thereafter centered on Albany, the county seat, which served as host to the county jail, Loyd's trial, and then the boy's execution. The map also includes the locations of other towns and landmarks referred to in this story.

Courtney also came to the Calapooia and were thus among the earliest of its settlers. The year 1847 also marked the appearance of Richard Finley, a millwright, who settled near what later became Crawfordsville. The gristmill that he built there in 1848 became the property of the McKercher family in the late 1880s, though by then it had been rebuilt and expanded.[16]

These people were part of the vast migration of largely white Americans who took to the Oregon Trail in the 1840s and 1850s. Some eighteen thousand of them had arrived in the Pacific Northwest before 1851, when the US government first began negotiating with the Willamette Valley's indigenous Kalapuya people for cession of their lands.[17] The Kalapuya people had suffered a demographic collapse in the 1830s, when fur traders entering the valley brought diseases with which the indigenous people had previously had little or no contact.[18] And yet many of the Kalapuya continued to live and to follow, as best they could, traditional patterns of life into the years when white Americans began moving onto their land. Those remaining experienced horrific treatment, and most found themselves forced into resettlement on reservations in the 1850s, though a few would live apart

PROLOGUE 13

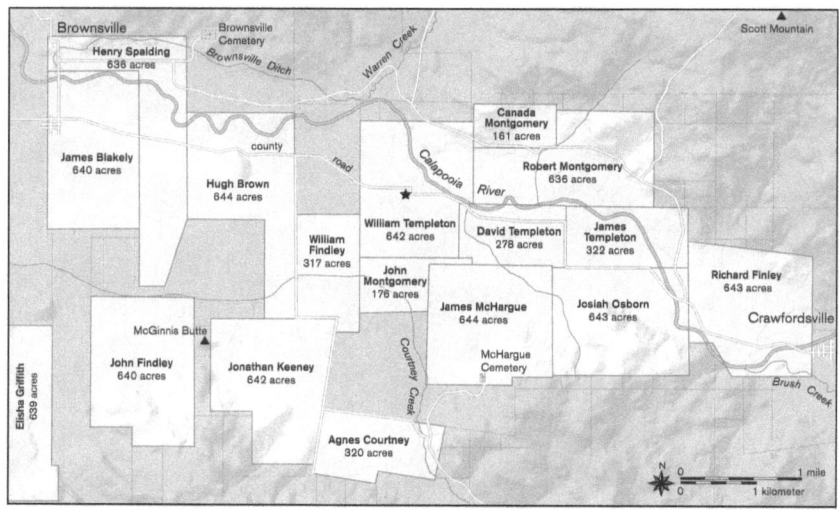

Map P.5. Donation Land Claims southeast of Brownsville. The grandparents, great-grandparents, and other relatives of Loyd Montgomery settled in the vicinity of Brownsville beginning in 1846. Highlighted here are the lands of a few of these people, lands they gained through the largesse of the Oregon Donation Land Claim Act. Near the center of the map, marked by a star, is where the murders took place in 1895. Toward the upper left is Brownsville Cemetery. Near the lower-center right is McHargue Cemetery. Both of these locations played roles in the story of Loyd Montgomery.

from their people by residing in Willamette Valley villages and town, such as Brownsville and Albany. In 1880, the census found thirty-eight there. Ten years later, the number had dropped to eight.[19]

The land that the Americans seized was only some years later federally recognized as the settlers' property, under the terms of the Donation Land Claim Act (DLCA) (map P.5). DLCA provisos for those who might be eligible claimants turned principally on white male American citizenship. Those who fit that bill could receive title to parcels, which varied in size depending on the migrant's time of arrival prior to 1 December 1855. Unique in American history to that point was that women could also receive land under the DLCA, though only if married to (or widowed by) an eligible male; the wife's land was to be held in her name. The sole exception to the racial exclusiveness of the law was an allowance to the sons of the early fur trappers who had Native American wives. Called "American half-breed Indians" in the legislation, they could make claims only if they were the sons of white men, at least eighteen years old, and had occupied and cultivated their land for four years prior to 1 December 1850. These criteria ensured that Oregon's foundational wealth flowed into the hands of white people. Through the DLCA, the aforementioned families gained ownership of thousands of acres along the upper Calapooia River, thus securing the origins of their wealth and their subsequent influence and lingering memory in the region. The DLCA's racial barriers also helped make the later population of the state primarily white. As late as 1890, the population of Linn County was composed of 16,112 white, 20 African American, 124 Chinese, 1 Japanese, and 8 Native American residents.[20]

If not already related to each other when arriving in 1846 and 1847, the varied families mentioned above intermarried with each other and newer arrivals over the years, creating a large, extended-family network spreading up and down the banks of the Calapooia River. Many, many of these Montgomery relations played a role in the unfolding story of parricide. This study refers to any number of them repeatedly and thus provides a genealogical table for reference to the more central figures (chart P.1).

AFTER LOYD'S ARREST

On 20 November 1895, a day after Loyd Montgomery slew his parents and Daniel McKercher, a coroner's jury pointed to him as the primary suspect. The county sheriff arrested him, and a deputy soon transported him to the county jail in Albany. At first, Loyd denied that he had committed the crimes but then confessed to them on 25 November. A few days later, however, he retracted this admission and then claimed to have killed only Daniel McKercher, in defense of himself and his parents. Indicted on the charge of murder in all three cases, he was tried on 17 and 18 December, but only for the murder of McKercher. Found guilty, the judge sentenced Loyd to death by hanging. The execution went forward on the north side of the county jail early on the morning of 31 January 1896.

THIS STUDY

I have divided this study into three parts, each composed of an introduction and two to three chapters. In part 1, I explore boyhood in the late nineteenth-century Willamette Valley. At the time Loyd Montgomery committed his

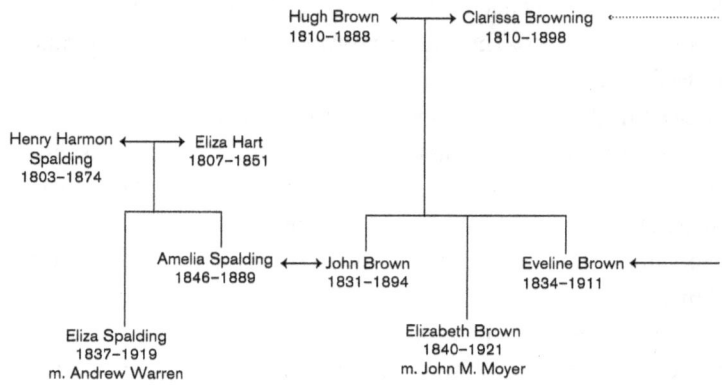

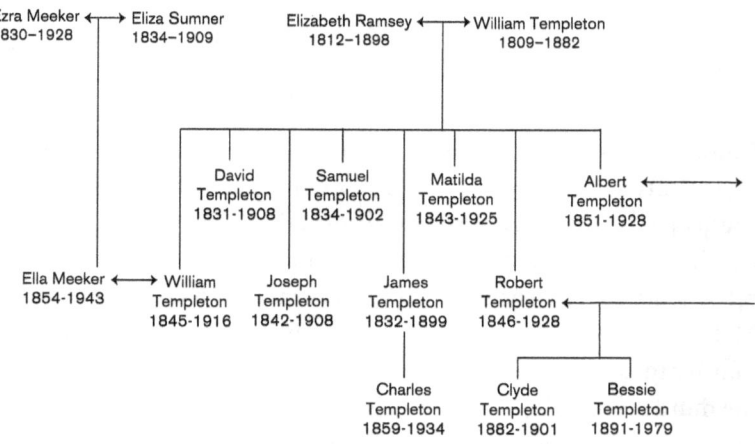

Chart P.1. Loyd Montgomery's relations. Loyd Montgomery, appearing in the lower right part of this genealogical table, was related through blood and marriage to many individuals and families who were significant in the early history of Brownsville, Crawfordsville, Linn County, and the larger Pacific Northwest. The names and personages of many of these also played a role in the unfolding parricide.

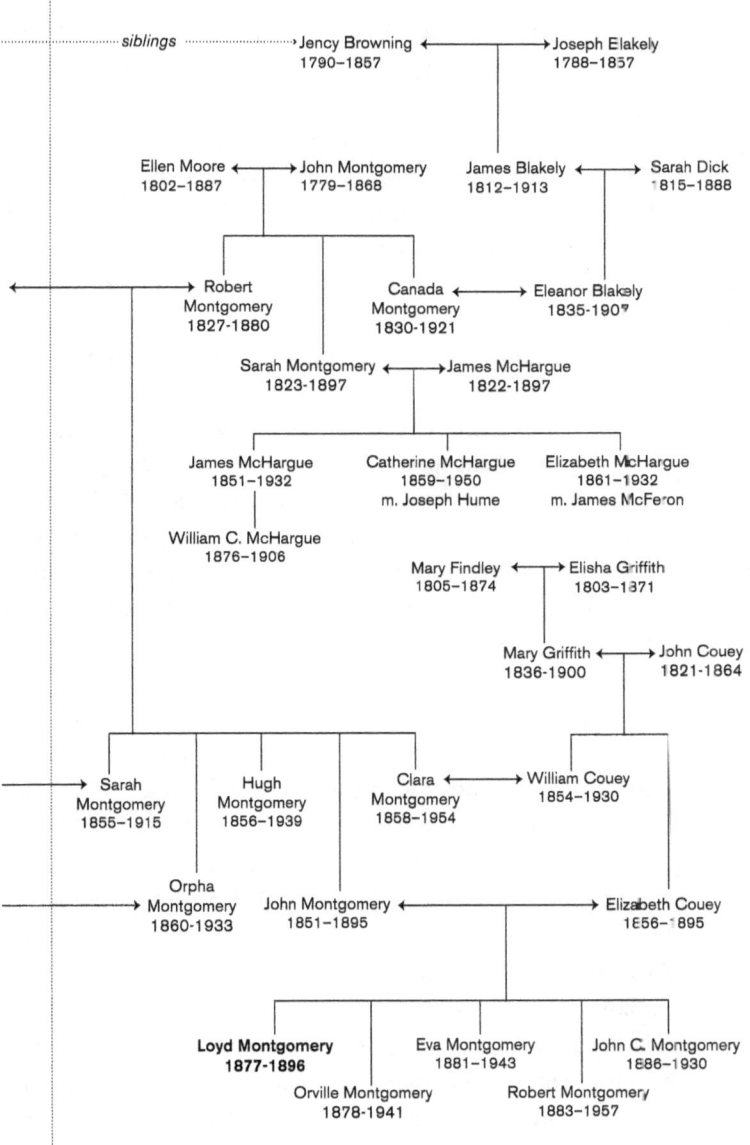

deed, he was eighteen and lived with his natal family. As such, he was culturally, officially, and legally still a boy. In chapter 1, I consider the romanticized view of farming life and farming boys, captured at the time in the descriptive phrase "republican landscape." Newspapers and literature publicly promoted this romantic image of rural life in the Pacific Northwest and elsewhere in America during this era. The myth of the republican landscape, something that wholly elided the darkness of events that made that landscape possible, helps provide us with a better understanding of the broader social reactions to Loyd, a boy who so sundered expectations about children and their proper relationship to parents, community, and polity.

Leaving behind the romanticized landscape, chapter 2 reconnoiters the reality of childhood, especially the traumas and violence that boys experienced in the late nineteenth-century Willamette Valley. In our times, psychologists and child-development specialists explain that suffering in early life can have serious effects on people's personalities, their relationships with others, and behaviors, whether when they are still young or when they become adults. Because of sources and the gap in time since the events, I can only suggest here the sorts of experiences that rural boys like Loyd had, how and why society at that time was blind to the effects that trauma might have had on youths, and how the violence of childhood might offer insight into Loyd's personality and why he behaved as he did.

Chapter 3 investigates Loyd's biography in relationship to family, parents, and community. It searches more thoroughly for reasons for his murderous actions, but it also juxtaposes him with the so-called bad-boy problem then gripping America. More typically associated at that time with urban life, the bad-boy problem enveloped rural America as well, and it specifically related to the challenges that society faced on the republican landscape and amid the decline of the agrarian ideal.

In part 2, I explore the larger social and cultural contexts of the Montgomery parricides. Chapter 4 looks at the downward political and economic spiral that farmers faced after the panic of 1873, the very years when Loyd's father, John, became an adult, became a father, and attempted to succeed as both. Using this atmosphere as a departure point, I then consider the poverty that the Montgomery family experienced, how that poverty connected to their extended family and their broader community, and how that poverty inscribed gendered tensions between father and son.

Chapter 5 turns the reader's attention to the ways in which Oregonians, and specifically the residents of the Brownsville area, both integrated and failed to integrate the Montgomery parricide and McKercher murder into their local history, much of which already revolved around violence and even genocide. Coinciding with the agricultural depression of the last years of the nineteenth century was the large-scale die-off of those who made up Oregon's so-called pioneer generation. These were Loyd's direct ancestors. They had arrived in the Pacific Northwest in the 1840s and 1850s, had warred against the region's Native Americans, had taken and then settled on the indigenous people's lands, and had developed a white civilization that further spread the evolving US empire across the continent. The deaths of members of this "heroic" generation, multiplying exponentially in the 1890s, caused something of a cultural crisis on top of the economic one concurrently searing the land. Celebrating their contributions and the violence that they had earlier perpetrated, while also grappling with the meaning of a parricide that struck one of those pioneer families, led to troubling silences and deceptive choices in the telling of local and regional history.

In part 3, I explore the many-sided story of the killing of Loyd Montgomery and the roughly two months leading up to his death. In chapter 6, I connect the most notable and symbolic material resources used in the boy's execution—the scaffolding and the hangman's noose—to the broader story of industrial change, environmental alteration, and expanding global capitalism. For many years, American farmers had pushed for such things while at the same time becoming ensnared by them. Thus, the industrial products of these developments—here, namely lumber and rope—now employed as gallows and noose to execute a farmer's son, symbolized the broader history of American agrarians during the 1890s.

In chapter 7, I provide a narrative account of the disposal of Loyd Montgomery. It follows the period from the moment when the boy's murder weapon fell silent to the moment when his heart did while he was dangling from a rope behind Linn County's jail. That stretch of time lasted a little less than seventy-three days. On the way, the chapter considers how the people of Linn County sought to mete out justice, reestablish authority, and save Loyd through multiple means, including through the efforts of men, women, and God.

# PART 1

## "AIDED BY BOYS UPON HORSEBACK, WHO CARRIED LANTERNS"

*Boyhood in Rural Oregon*

After the young Montgomery children discovered the butchery that had befallen their home, it took about ninety minutes for the unspeakable news to make its way by word of mouth the three miles to the offices of Albert Cavender, editor of the newspaper in Brownsville, the town closest to the tragedy that also possessed its own press. When the messenger relating the tragic story arrived, "he was so excited he could not tell an intelligent story." Cavender, who had founded the *Brownsville Times* in 1889, soon pieced together from the mutterings what would become the biggest story in his newspaper's short history. Setting out for the murder scene, which he longed to do, proved somewhat complicated. By then it was 6:00 p.m., more than an hour after sunset, with nightfall limiting visibility. Skies were especially dark that evening since the moon was but a sliver and partial cloudiness obscured what light might have shone down from the stars above. Further hindering travel was the country road connecting Brownsville to Sam Templeton's hop farm. Although abnormally dry conditions prevailed across western Oregon that autumn, a good dousing of rain had soaked the

Willamette Valley a week earlier, transforming earthen lanes into muddy quagmires, their more typical seasonal condition.[1]

Faced with poor roads and darkness but with a pressing need to make haste, Cavender reached out to a dependable and all too often historically forgotten source of local know-how for assistance: "boys," as he called them—clever country lads experienced in maneuvering about a landscape that they knew like the backs of their hands. On this evening, Cavender's youthful guides perched themselves on horseback and vigilantly carried lanterns to illuminate the journalist's way. That a seasoned newsman should reach out to boys to assist him in one of the most important journeys he would make as a rural reporter reveals the central role that children played in that society. And yet the identity of these particular Brownsville boys remains a mystery. They, like the vast majority of their ilk—nameless and faceless creatures from the past—have gone unheralded simply for being so youthful. "Rarely obvious historical actors," the historian Steven Mintz observes of bygone children such as these. "They leave fewer historical sources than adults, and their powerlessness makes them less visible than other social groups."[2]

Parricide demonstrates that even young children are not always powerless; it also violently disrupts traditional patterns that exclude children from the historical record, convulsing them and pushing their concerns to the surface. Part 1 of this study focuses on issues of childhood, since children make up so much of this story. At center stage is the murderer who was a mere eighteen years old, an age at which a male at that time was considered still not quite a man. Circling out from him were other youngsters. Loyd's younger siblings and a cousin were the first to discover the results of his terrifying act. Their cries and screams alerted others to the slaughter. They would provide essential testimony at the various inquests and the trial that followed. Other activities they participated in, such as the meting out of justice and their occasional trips to the county jail to visit their brother, would also make their way into official recordings for two or so months after the murders. There was also an entire cast of youthful background players, those beyond the Montgomery and Templeton families, including friends and acquaintances of Loyd who provided useful insight, and even problematic boys in other places and times who would pass onto and off of the stage, their deeds and lives recalled to illuminate, contextualize, and perhaps explain what their Oregon counterpart had done.

The central question in all of this was the same one that Cavender posed on 20 November 1895, when the coroner's jury concluded "that Loyd Montgomery is the guilty party." In shock, Cavender asked what many another had puzzled over for generations about children who kill: "Accused of murdering his own father and mother! How can it be?"[3] That query would burn on the minds of many, both near and far, over the weeks to come. As journalists like Cavender went about seeking an answer to that very question, they naturally focused a good portion of their reporting on children. They dredged up news and histories of Loyd for the purposes of gauging and explaining a crime that they considered to be, despite its having been committed by a youngster, or perhaps because of that, "the most hideous ... ever committed in the Pacific Northwest."[4] Furthermore, the youth behind the parricide sparked a debate that revealed multiple social concerns about children and youths, especially those who endured the hardships, real or imagined, of rural life. This discussion revolved in particular around issues of failed relations with parents, unpleasant personal habits and physical traits of both "normal" and "monstrous" youths, and the innate qualities and acquired deficiencies of children gone bad. A question hung in the background: what role did America's young people, however troubled they might be, play in the future of an agrarian republic that during the 1890s seemed to teeter on the brink of collapse?

This discussion lays bare much about life and childhood on American farms during the concluding decades of the nineteenth century. Chapters 2 and 3 explore the facts and fictions of Loyd's life and the lives of other young people like him in the time and place he lived. They search for the possible reasons for his actions. They examine the ways in which the community and society in which he lived reacted to him and his crime. More deeply, they investigate the era's larger social anxieties and ideals about the state of rural America and especially its boys—concerns and hopes that framed a community's and the larger society's need to know who Loyd was and what his deeds meant and perhaps what they portended for the future of their community and even civilization itself.

But I begin with chapter 1. It considers the idealized version of country and farm living widely disseminated at the very time when Loyd was born and reared. It also explores the hidden, deathly meanings and stories lurking beneath the landscape on which that idealized society formed and functioned. Farming and rural and village life had been the locus of US civilization from the time of the American Revolution, serving, among other things, as the imagined wellspring of the nation's republican ethos. But it was also a civilization made possible by dispossession, bloodletting, and avarice. After the Civil War, that civilization faced new and increasing challenges. The country's urban population was growing at twice the rate of that of the countryside, being fed especially by a stream of rural residents who gave up and moved to the city. Part and parcel of this was the economic shift away from agrarianism to modern industry. Although farm production expanded during these years, financial crises in 1873, 1883, and 1893 (some regard the entire era from 1873 to 1896 as one continuous depression), declining prices for harvested crops, and, in some parts of the United States, droughts, severe winters, and soil exhaustion all contributed to the failure of farmers and the weakening of rural America's clout.[5] All of this heightened a cultural emphasis on rural boys and youths, their upbringing, and their relationship with society, both in the here and now and in the future, given that young people were in fact the future, and the future seemed a precarious one at that. An appraisal of this cultural backdrop in chapter 1 provides contextualization for the real social concerns expressed about boys like Loyd generally and, more specifically, the tragic proportions of his deeds, which chapters 2 and 3 consider.

CHAPTER 1

# "The Hope and Life of the Nation"

*Boys and Families on the Republican Landscape*

**THE EVENTS EXPLORED IN THIS BOOK TOOK PLACE ON** a republican landscape that was by 1895, when Loyd Montgomery murdered his parents, under considerable stress. It was a landscape by then steeped in myth and history. It was also already soaked in blood.

Thomas Jefferson, who early theorized American republicanism, became the best-known purveyor of a vision of the landscape and its importance. His early nineteenth-century vision of a perfect American society called for small family farms that extended ever westward in a system whereby wealth was dispersed among them and not concentrated in the hands of a few. As such, the landscape was the guarantor of the future of American democracy. He saw cities, on the other hand, as the great menace. In his opinion, they imperiled morality and health, they led to mob mentality, and they increased joblessness and the dependency of the many.

At the center of the Jeffersonian landscape stood the farmer, a figure known as the yeoman. He owned his own land, independent from others. On it, albeit with the help of his family, he produced the lion's share of what was needed for the maintenance of his household. The yeoman and his family also had, in Jefferson's view, a special, divine connection. "Those who labor in the earth," he declared, "are the chosen people of God, if ever he had a chosen people, whose breasts he has made his peculiar deposit for

25

substantial and genuine virtue. . . . Corruption of morals in the mass of cultivators is a phænomenon of which no age nor nation has furnished an example." As for children—in addition to placing them as workers on the family farm, Jefferson envisioned that the republic's expansion would be through natural reproduction. He also masterminded the system whereby townships would each support schools that local children would attend for free. The basic education of America's offspring was a fundamental part of preserving and perpetuating the republic.[1]

The Donation Land Claim Act (DLCA) for Oregon was one of several early federal policies that sought to expand the republican landscape.[2] Much of the American West beyond the Mississippi Valley turned out not to be geographically or climatically suited for the small family farming that Jefferson had envisioned. On the other hand, western Oregon's gentle weather patterns, abundant water, low elevation, and fertile soils made it one of the places where a republican landscape might be achieved. When Congress enacted the DLCA in 1850, it secured the existing claims of the earliest white American settlers in the Pacific Northwest and lured more migrants to the region. In 1854, modifications to the law began to offer even American children (at least those orphaned during the westward migration) the opportunity to acquire land. By the DLCA's expiration at the end of 1855, 2.5 million acres of Oregon land and about 300,000 acres in Washington were officially and legally in the hands of American claimants.[3]

Jefferson's vision of the future of America and its families on the republican landscape was something of a rosy one. It both willfully and unwittingly ignored, concealed, and miscalculated reality. As it turns out, Jefferson's republic was one based in race, violence, and racial violence. Jefferson himself proclaimed the ideal farmer to be Anglo-Saxon.[4] He feared immigrants. He enslaved people of color and fathered children with one of them. He recommended that for the nation's future, emancipated Black persons be resettled in Africa. He did think that America's indigenous people would one day amalgamate with the white race, though amalgamation in itself was really just a way to clear them from the path of progress.[5] Issues of racial and immigrant exclusion, as well as the willful ignoring of the indigenous people's title to the land, all went into the DLCA's political calculus in transforming Oregon into a republican landscape.[6]

By design, the republican landscape would be the salvation of American democracy. The Jeffersonian plan of independent farmers scattered across the land would help disperse wealth across the population and thus create a sense of equality. As historians have also shown, the constant expansion of the republic would also help to ward off any developing class discontent and animus by constantly providing the lower strata of the American populace with more lands where they could start their lives anew. This redirected potential class violence outward onto other, racialized peoples who stood in the way of the expanding republican landscape—peoples such as Native Americans, whose home had been that land since time immemorial, and also those of other nations, such as Mexico, whose boundaries were inconvenient to the swelling United States. The process was nasty and bloody. While it often turned on extralegal actions and was habitually performed by Americans outrunning the jurisdiction of the federal government (all of which happened in Oregon), perhaps even more tragic was that the bloody process was just as often something that American law, legislation, and executive orders directed.[7]

Given the unending violence that American expansion entailed, back in 1985, when the historian Richard Slotkin looked at the totality of America's frontier history, he unsurprisingly dubbed the place "the fatal environment." A decade before, the historian Francis Jennings, who examined the nation's history from more of an indigenous perspective, described North America as a "widowed land," rather than a "virgin land." The latter term was one that European and Euro-American expansionists had long and purposefully utilized to shield themselves from the notion that they had stolen the land from its indigenous inhabitants.[8] Both these characterizations speak to what American republicanism and European colonial expansion (prior to being dressed up as the former) wreaked on the land. They are each applicable to the American settlement history of the Willamette Valley and to the long frontier heritage of its early white settlers prior to their arrival in Oregon. By 1895, when a boy murdered his parents on a small parcel of this landscape, this was a place that had been for decades a fatal environment and a widowed land.

At the time of Loyd's atrocity, the idealized republican civilization built on death, violence, and land grabs was imperiled. The nation's farmers who worked that land and who had long imbibed Jeffersonian ideals were now facing new and increasing troubles as the country catapulted ever more toward industry, globalization, and urban living and as it reached the limits of the continental spaces into which it could expand. In the opinion of some, such as President Theodore Roosevelt in 1910, the problems endangering farmers were "bad for the whole nation."[9]

Those desirous of saving rural America, and thus the nation, did not think so much at this time about the republican landscape's very real substrate of violence and death. Rather, they focused on the mythological society founded on it, with special emphasis given to its children and in particular its boys. Reformers became ever more romantic about the virtues, benefits, and importance of agrarian life, and they also offered advice on how to salvage these very qualities. This spirit of reform animated the Commission on Country Life that Roosevelt created in 1908. It conducted a national assessment of the challenges facing rural residents and their children, and it proposed solutions. It even held hearings in Oregon in which children were both directly and indirectly discussed as being among the priorities of rural reform.[10]

Slightly earlier, at a time when Loyd's parents reached adulthood and this boy experienced his earliest years of life, the most idealistically vocal and widely distributed advocate for rural life and reform in western Oregon was the *Willamette Farmer*. The mouthpiece of the Oregon Grange, this newspaper was variously published in Salem and Portland between 1869 and 1887 and carried agricultural news from throughout the Pacific Northwest, as well as relevant reports from elsewhere in the nation. It naturally had a special relationship with the Willamette Valley, where it was published.

The *Willamette Farmer*'s many articles, commentaries, and advice columns, such as the regularly appearing "Home Circle," "Young Folks' Column," and "For the Children" venerated farming life, rural families and children, and their underpinning of the nation. It constantly promoted a recipe for how these could, should, and would be maintained, despite or because of the many portents that loomed on the horizon. The idealized life of the countryside that it promoted ignored entirely the violent history of the land. Its cheerful depictions also hardly matched the realities of life one would find in the Willamette Valley and certainly not anything that Loyd truly experienced. It thus serves as a sort of monument to the myth of republicanism—to all that was seen and unseen within this political monolith, an homage to something that never truly existed in its idealized form. What that weekly espoused provided the improbable cultural backdrop against which Loyd's society imagined, viewed, and judged its boys.

In items ranging across the years that it appeared in print, the *Willamette Farmer* described farmers' children, both boys and girls, as "the hope and the life of a nation" since they, as opposed to their counterparts elsewhere, would grow up to be "intelligent, moral, patriotic." Moreover, and though it vehemently opposed rural youngsters leaving for the city (a trepidation about urbanization that reached back to Jefferson), the newspaper also on occasion explained that were it not for the "fresh blood" that farmers' children yearly infused into the city, such places "would soon degenerate."[11]

Although the publication included females in the above assessment, it emphasized country lads much more, given that they were males and that someday, as farmers, they would be the individuals about which that patriarchal society would revolve. Here the newspaper reverted to old republican tropes, such as commenting on the farmer's closeness to nature that had inculcated *him* with traits such as patience, perseverance, faith, confidence, hope, honesty, and integrity.[12] In stressing the future leaders of public and civil life, then, it was hardly surprising that farmers' boys were the focus, as they "are to be the men after a few more years have passed away."[13]

One example of the propensity to shine light on boys is another commentary that did place girls next to them as "the grandest product of the farms." But that editorial is actually entitled "Training the Farmer's Sons," and except for an introductory sentence mentioning girls, it in fact considered only boys: "In every avenue of life where thrift, capacity and energy are required, the man who pushes to the front is a son of a farmer." His intelligence, common sense, constitution, capacity for labor, noble purpose, and unfaltering courage—all traits superior in country as opposed to city boys—"were born to him on the farm; they were woven into his fiber by early years of toil; the warp and woof of his life were threads of gold."[14] As boys would inherit the farm, the logical conclusion is that it really was they, rather than their sisters, who formed the main strands of agrarian society.

While the *Willamette Farmer* underscored and romanticized rural boys and men, it did not forget women and girls. Their most valued responsibility, however, was the support of men and boys. The character of girls benefited from rural life to be sure, but it was the success of their brothers that would contribute most to their own "pride and joy." When girls became mothers, it was not just an expectation but their "duty" to ensure that their sons would become "manly men," meaning the central figures in and the executors of the republican system. Women, in the role of what scholars have termed the "republican mother," a concept emanating from an earlier era, would instruct boys in obedience and civil law. The *Willamette Farmer*'s emphasis on mothers and their role in the rearing of children also reflected the central message of child-rearing manuals that began swelling in number in the 1830s.[15]

The greatest social anxiety haunting late nineteenth-century rural America was the drift of its boys to the city (figure 1.1). On the one hand, this exodus robbed the countryside of its best and brightest. On the other, and contradicting other *Willamette Farmer* suggestions that country boys invigorated the city, many worried that those who headed there might become debauched by lurid enticements, further undermining the republic as a whole. "There again are a host of young men full of strength and courage," one column in the weekly warned, "who would have been happy, had they been content to cultivate the soil; but instead they enter the attracting whirlpool to be found in the midst of large cities, which soon swallows up their health, strength and character."[16]

Part of the answer for keeping boys on the farm, the *Willamette Farmer* advised, was found in transforming the rural home, a job especially for women. Thus, one editorial opined that while "girls will stay at home if home be the dullest place under the moon ... boys will not." Therefore, with the latter in mind, the home needed warmth, light, open windows, entertaining books, pictures hung on walls, musical instruments, and parlor games. It was also up to the mother to vitalize the home through her very being. Since it was "a mother's face [that] brightens a home like sunbeams or shadows it like a thunderstorm," an 1886 advisory declared, "the mother should be an optimist, should always see the silver lining to the dark cloud. When clouds of trouble over-shadow the little faces her face should be sun shining through."[17]

In fact, as many young women in that era fled the countryside for the city as did young men, something that the *Willamette Farmer*, in its intensely gendered focus on boys as the future of that civilization, passed over as a secondary matter.[18] Nevertheless, the newspaper's editors did occasionally comment on the lifelong misery that awaited the rural lass should she forsake the elevated life of the countryside for the "hideous circle of corruption in the midst of large cities." After arriving in the city and there "having met with nothing but deception," "loss of health," "hearts filled

Figure 1.1. A boy leaving the family farm. Rural boys fled from the American countryside for the city in droves in the late nineteenth century for reasons related to the drudgery of farming life, limited opportunities in the countryside, and the perception that agriculturalists faced a bleak future. As such, the loss of rural youth to the city was one of the major social worries of the time. This depiction of a youth bidding farewell to his parents made up the half-title page in a volume of Horatio Alger's eight-volume Luck and Pluck series. Source: Horatio Alger Jr., *Sink or Swim; or, Harry Raymond's Resolve* (Boston: Loring, 1870).

with bitterness," and the forfeiture of "any aptitude for labor," should they return to the countryside for "reunions and social gatherings, these young women are no longer the objects of attraction to the young men, whilst those who remained at home are sought after and contract honorable and happy marriages."[19] Such sentiment clearly framed young women as the companions to and helpmates of young rural men.

Other counsel that the *Willamette Farmer* offered parents for how to keep sons on the farm related to tempering their labor on it, warning that too much dreary work was the leading reason boys escaped to the city. "The daily routine of farm life," the editors admonished, "usually experienced by boys is . . . irksome and not at all calculated to attract a boy to agricultural pursuits." To temper this, the newspaper recommended that parents should provide their sons a stake in their farming operations, perhaps by granting them a piece of land to cultivate or some farm animals to care for and reap the profits from, whether by sale or entering them for prizes at the fair.[20]

As an example, the newspaper ran the likely apocryphal story, gleaned from Chicago's *Prairie Farmer*, that a "Mrs. Watson" related about her two sons, aged fourteen and sixteen. When the boys began the unsettling talk about leaving for town to find work as store clerks, their parents quickly decided to give them each an acre of land, a yearling calf, a colt, and their choice of a pig or lamb. The Watsons also turned over to their sons and their daughter the care for all the chickens and turkeys. The boys retained all the financial proceeds they earned, except for what they shared with their sister. The scheme did the trick, and a year later the youths were busily planning on expanding operations. They also started talking of attending agricultural college.[21]

On the other hand, just where to draw the line for what would be too much work for boys when laboring for themselves or toiling for their parents was never clear in the columns of the *Willamette Farmer*, indicating the difficulties the newspaper's editorial policy sometimes had when reconciling idealism with, well, idealism. The editors routinely glorified the farmer boy who labored ceaselessly. Thus, in 1873 it lauded twelve-year-old Bryant Lafollet of Marion County, where the newspaper rolled off the press. Entirely on his own, this lad cultivated sixty acres, plowing it twice, sowing it with oats, and harrowing and rolling it. He raised twenty-one hundred bushels, despite the smut diminishing his crop. Additionally, if that could be, "Bryant did chores and cultivated a garden, and did other work about the farm. He has gone to school regularly . . . and is said to be one of the best scholars in the district, as of course would be natural, for it takes a smart boy to make a good farmer."[22]

The reality was that boys did work hard on Oregon farms in the 1880s and 1890s. Loyd spent almost his entire life on farms. We do not have a full itemization of his labors; a more thorough record of exactly what it was like for him comes from the Joseph and Lovina Gragg family, who lived on a farm in Benton County, about twenty miles west-southwest of Brownsville. The three youngest sons in the family—Philo (born 1874), Vernon (born 1876), and Marcus (born 1878)—overlapped in age with Loyd (born 1877) and his brother Orville (born 1878).[23]

Surviving Gragg family correspondence from 1886 through 1891 mentions all manner of chores that the boys regularly performed. A partial list provided in just a few sporadic letters includes husking and shelling corn, cleaning stables, killing vermin, fetching water, plowing and harrowing, drilling for planting, sowing seed, killing hogs and beef cattle and preparing the meat, mending fences, leading animals to and from pastures and stables, capturing escaped cattle, feeding the livestock, chopping wood, tending chickens and building coops, screening grain, picking fruit, harvesting potatoes and wheat, pressing cider, taking produce to town for sale, patching flour sacks, burning straw off harvested fields, cleaning firearms, repairing the well from within it, grubbing tree stumps, mending farm implements, and tending the flower garden. The boys also attended school.[24] Clearly, the reality was that a boy's farm life was a laborious and monotonous one.

While the *Willamette Farmer* freely gave advice and held up examples (often contradictory) for farming parents about the amount of work boys should or should not do on the farm, in fact the management of the farm and thus the decisions about labor were in the purview of fathers. The newspaper did, however, also outline both in prose and poetry the more sentimental obligations a father had for raising the right sort of boy. These included setting an example for sons; participating in leisure activities with their boys; providing lads with friendship, intimacy, and good fellowship; and offering them true affection.[25]

The weight given to intimacy and affection as essential to the parent-child relationship was not simply rhetoric but reflected changing conceptions of children and childhood. Oddly, a good deal of this change emanated from the city, where families were arguably undergoing more intense rearrangements than in the countryside. Economic contributions of all members of the family had long been and remained essential to farming success, and rural children continued to play an indispensable role, tending to a host of chores, taking care of younger siblings, and lending helping hands to fathers and mothers, both of whom labored intensely.[26] In the urban middle-class setting, however, economic production left the home and became invested in shops, factories, and trading houses where fathers went away to work. As historians have long noted, this rearrangement in the relationship between family and production transformed children into an economic burden rather than a laboring asset and thus led to a declining birthrate among the urban middle class in the nineteenth century. As such, it also required a new foundation for the parent-child relationship; the glue binding the family became increasingly the adhesive of love and affection. Love, in its romantic form, simultaneously emerged as the basis of marriage itself. This new relationship between parents and children, and even the rationale for having children, led to the recognition of—or some would argue the "invention" of—children as beings with their own varied emotional, psychological, and physical needs; having specific stages of development; and having a malleable nature, thus able to be shaped. It gave them, in other words, a childhood.[27]

As mothers in the urban middle classes also lost their formerly essential role in the direct economic production for the maintenance of the family, their work now became more intensely focused on the upbringing of the children. The *Willamette Farmer*'s strong emphasis on motherly duties in terms of the welfare, moral uplift, and education of children reflected this bourgeois ethos. Not forgetting the many arduous duties that continued for farm women, the newspaper nevertheless now also assigned to them more sentimental responsibilities in cultivating their sons. The heightened emphasis on mothers and sons was the rural quest to create the next generation of republican farmers and to preserve them as the foundation of American society. This was all the more imperative because rural males and especially youths seemed so embattled at this time.

In its calculations the *Willamette Farmer* did factor in the importance of fatherly love and affection, and it emphasized that both parents are "the mightiest of all agencies to lead the young in paths of virtue," doing so through crafting an "atmosphere of love." But the newspaper especially promoted the significance of female love in the lives of rural boys. "Get hold of the boy's heart . . . love him; love him practically," one column plainly stated in 1884 to mothers and sisters. In doing so, "you may pilot him whither you will." A decade earlier, an item entitled simply "A Sister's Love" described the female sibling's heart as "a realm of pure and earthly affection, and happy should that brother be to whom she clings through the changing scenes of the blighting world." And yet another item, modestly entitled "Mother," explained that one's "mother is thy best earthly friend . . . thy mother will love and cherish thee while living, and if she survive thee, will weep for thee when dead, such tears as not but a mother knows how to weep." Other occasional items reflected on the boy returning his mother's love. The short article "In Love with His Mother," for example, alternately described a boy's love for his mother as second in importance only to the love of a husband for a woman but also as a love affair that no other in the "world . . . can surpass." Similarly, "Mother and Son," printed in 1877, claimed that "there is no tie in the world more beautiful than that which binds a mother and a son."[28]

Much of the *Willamette Farmer*'s emphasis on boys as the hope of the nation was in its prescription for ensuring the survival of the republican body politic and the agrarianism that was its beating heart. In all that they proposed, the newspapers' editors were aware of changing conceptions of childhood and the growing power of bourgeois culture in that transformative process. In a larger sense, all this advice to parents about how to approach the raising of their children—employing love, improving the home, offering instruction in civics, encouraging competition at fairs and thoughts of agricultural college, rationing workloads while providing responsibilities, and distributing land and livestock—was not just offered as a way to palliate major alterations under way in the United States or even the more specific limitations confronting rural society in the Willamette Valley. They were also the product of those alterations and limitations. Much of the focus in either case was preparing the boy for this new world and the challenges that its advent posed.

In terms of the Willamette Valley, by the 1870s available land for further expansion of the agrarian population had seemingly become in short supply. Part of this shortage, as the *Willamette Farmer* surmised, was due to the DLCA's generosity. It allowed American couples arriving in Oregon to claim a parcel up to a square mile in size. Locked-up lands meant limited growth and opportunity. The newspaper thus in the 1870s began admonishing large landowners to break up their holdings. "The best interest of every community is secured," the newspaper scolded in 1874, "when every member is thrifty and independent, and when all the land is occupied to the best advantage, which can only be when it is held in small farms and thoroughly worked and made productive." This would be a boon to society, the editorial reminded, as it would make possible a larger population, which could then support local institutions, such as churches and schoolhouses, as well as provide the "charm of social intercourse." But breaking up large estates also had an effect on men as men. "Ownership in the soil," it reminded in republican terms, "endows the man with independence and self-respect that encourages thrift and enterprise. The land-owner is self-reliant and a man among men."[29]

The *Willamette Farmer* clearly intended that at least some of those new farms were to go to the region's boys when it encouraged parents to give them plots and livestock to practice with, and then when fretting over the drift of boys to the city. Simultaneously, as chapter 3 explores, Oregon faced a considerable social and cultural crisis from its boys in the last third of the nineteenth century as opportunities for the state's urban and rural youth dried up and as the economic depression deepened. The *Willamette Farmer*'s advice to create more farms and its unending instructions to parents about how to raise their children properly was in part an answer to that deepening crisis.

More broadly across the United States, the post–Civil War era's transformation of the nation into an industrial and urban society, with new limitations imposed by stagnant continental boundaries, seemed to lead to the social disorder that Jefferson had worried about—violent labor upheaval, political corruption, and health and moral problems beyond what even Jefferson's vivid imagination could foresee. Historians who have examined the social-cultural-economic-political turmoil of the era, known as the Gilded Age in the American context, have spoken of a "search for order," the rise of "bourgeois paternalism," the "incorporation of America," the implementation of new regimes of "discipline and punishment," the formation of a "managerial class," and the evolution of "modern bureaucracy"— all forms and systems of controlling the growing social chaos and molding a once atomized society of small towns, dispersed settlements, an endless frontier, and independent shopkeepers and farmers into the modern, corporate body politic.³⁰ While on the one hand the *Willamette Farmer* sought to preserve a fading republican landscape and looked backward to a past social order for inspiration, in fact its advice to parents on how to shape, educate, and direct their children on the shifting and endangered terrain of agrarianism reflects the spread of Gilded Age discipline, paternalism, order, and control. The *Willamette Farmer* sought to marshal the forces transforming the republican countryside and its social relations in the name of stabilizing what was changing. Boys were at the quaking epicenter of this volatile landscape.

The romanticized rural boy and his family, idealized agrarian values, and the vaunted republican civilization that the *Willamette Farmer* promoted were depicted and disseminated elsewhere in that place and time. A prominent visual example is the *Illustrated Historical Atlas Map of Marion and Linn Counties, Oregon*, which the Edgar Williams Company of San Francisco published in 1878, the year after Loyd's birth. The first volume of its kind in Oregon, the Marion and Linn Counties atlas, like its many counterparts that appeared between 1861 and 1889 in other American counties densely populated with freehold farmers, gave brief overviews of the progress of the counties, as well as their assorted towns and villages.³¹ The Oregon version also offered a complete list of Linn and Marion Counties' original Donation Land Claim settlers and pinpointed their claims' locations. The atlas was likewise current: it enumerated present-day (as well as past) state and county officers; provided the most up-to-date population statistics available; offered beautifully rendered and colorized maps, including town plats, present-day farm boundaries with owners' names, the position of existing homes, orchards, and cultivated fields; as well as the less-movable features of the landscape, such as the courses of streams and rivers and other significant topographical features. Setting aside the obvious profit motive, the publisher instead gushed that "it has been our sincere wish to publish a work in which [locals] might feel a just pride in showing... the Willamette Valley." He also wrote of the atlas's value to posterity.³²

Civil engineer Edgar Williams arrived in Linn and Marion Counties sometime before 4 January 1878 to promote the atlas project. Among prominent locals, he circulated examples of Thompson & West's 1876 *Historical Atlas Map of Santa Clara County, California*, to which he had contributed. Close to one hundred of the Linn and Marion County residents who viewed the volume then signed on to a newspaper endorsement of the Oregon project. All the signatories were men.[33] To be profitable, the *Historical Atlas* demanded subscriptions. They cost fifteen dollars a piece, a significant amount of money at that time. Nearly sixty of the notables whose names appeared in the initial promotion became subscribers. For their patronage, they, with some seven hundred others, received a listing in the "Patrons' Business Section." It included each subscriber's name, place of birth, occupation, location of residence, and when they arrived (or were born) in Oregon and in either Marion or Linn County. For considerably more money, one might purchase space for a biography or a lithograph of home, farm, and business. Illustration sizes ranged from less than a quarter page up to a full page (17.5 by 14.5 inches).[34]

Once Williams determined that his proposed atlas would be profitable, he moved swiftly. In April two civil engineers working with him commenced drafting the maps using county surveyor records, and they concluded their work in early May.[35] By the middle of that month, the illustrators began sketching. One of the two artists Williams employed was Linn County resident Junius Whiting, a thirty-three-year-old Albany-based landscape painter and engineer. Responsible for most of the views, Whiting completed his efforts in September. Albany's *State Rights Democrat* declared on the thirteenth of that month that his renderings were "perfect work."[36]

In early June, Williams began collecting local histories and biographies, and the *State Rights Democrat* encouraged residents to provide information. Likewise, the newspaper's editor stoked interest in the lithographs, gushing that "there is nothing so conducive to the cultivation of good taste and sentiments as fine pictures, and we trust that our people will embrace the opportunity to get fine lithographs of their houses."[37] A total of 59 illustrations would ultimately adorn the atlas's 104 pages. Nearly 80 percent of them were of farms. Reinforcing the republican nature of that enterprise is that all but one of the farms depicted carries the name of a male owner. Likewise, the 49 biographies, all of them dedicated to men, included wives and children as if they were as much the property of the men as were the lands on which they resided. The finished atlas was ready for distribution by the end of 1878.[38]

The historical geographer Michael P. Conzen has explained that county atlases such as Williams's compilation purveyed "personalized symbols of pioneer pride in agrarian progress and individual achievement, local roots, civic accomplishment, and a sense of personal participation in the epic of

American westward colonization."³⁹ Certainly a publication such as the *Historical Atlas* would necessarily include only pleasing images of farms. But they are all the more remarkable when placed next to the editorial entitled "Country Homes" that the *Willamette Farmer* offered on the very same day that the Albany newspaper had declared Whiting's depictions of Marion and Linn County scenes "perfect." The *Willamette Farmer* piece decried "slovenly farmhouses, with wood-piles, cow-yards, and pig pens at the door" as a lead cause in "why young people don't like to stay on the farm, but long for town life."⁴⁰

Thus, the lithographs are sanitized republican pictorials, showing neat farmsteads with perfect fence lines; productive gardens, orchards, and crops; well-manicured barns and pastures; plump and healthy livestock; and lovingly tended rural homes. They are also all peopled, usually with what appear to be varied members of families. Men and occasionally youths are at work. In some instances, children run about and even chase dogs. Because these are exterior views, motherly figures had to be positioned outdoors, but in ways that still promoted their domestic ideal. They are therefore framed in doorways to the homes, stand on porches and front-yard paths, or even tend flower gardens. In a couple of instances, competitors clad in Victorian attire engage in spirited croquet matches, while pastoral scenes stretch out behind them. As such, the atlas depicts an idealized rural republican landscape: men engaged in agrarian labors, women as symbols of rural home life, and children, like farm animals, placed about them.

Collectively, the atlases also tell the story of that rural republican landscape's colonial advance across North America. Few atlases appeared in the nonrepublican, plantation-dominated South, given the lack of the required density of freehold farmers there to make the venture profitable.⁴¹ The earliest exemplars of the atlas generally appeared first in the Northeast and Midwest and only chronologically later in the subsequently settled West Coast region.⁴² A larger part of America's colonial advance across the continent meant of course removing those who were already there. But when viewing the bucolic lithographs that adorn these atlases, one is left to imagine for oneself the ghosts of these victims to republicanism that lurk beneath the surface. One also has to imagine the very real problems endured by the families depicted.

One illustration from the Oregon volume is a half-page lithograph of the farm and residence of James Finlayson in Linn County, an image that

Figure 1.2. Farm and residence of James Finlayson, 1878. The romanticized version of rural life in the nineteenth-century Willamette Valley as depicted here belies the suffering, death, murder, and killing that were also part of the story of the American colonization of Oregon. Even the home and farm of Finlayson had its own dark secrets to tell. Source: *Illustrated Historical Atlas Map of Marion and Linn Counties, Oregon* (San Francisco: Edgar Williams, 1878).

is of central importance to chapter 3 and one that soon developed its own more proximate and fearsome ghosts (figure 1.2). Finlayson was an occasional correspondent for the *Willamette Farmer*. He was born in 1820 in Scotland, where he married his wife, Ann. In 1841, the couple and the children they had at that time immigrated together to the United States and then, in 1849, to Oregon. Finlayson's land claim in the northern Willamette Valley's Clackamas County received Donation Land Claim recognition in 1853. He and his family moved to Linn County in 1857. Ann died there in 1863, and Finlayson then married Janet Dalgleish, who also had been born in Scotland. Janet is likely the female figure opening the gate in the half-page lithograph, with James the figure approaching from the right. Finlayson's grandson Charles, who was ten when the sketch was rendered, is no doubt the boy standing behind Janet in the front yard. Charles came to live with his grandparents in 1873 after his father, Colon, died from tuberculosis. Charles's mother had succumbed to the same disease two years earlier.[43]

In addition to lending his voice to the *Willamette Farmer,* Finlayson was active in agrarian politics. For example, on 8 December 1873, a cool, drizzly Saturday, he took a lead role in a farmers' organizational meeting held at the county courthouse in Albany. Area farmers had been hit hard by the worldwide financial crisis of that year. Their "movement" in Linn County was designed, according to the local press, "to disenthrall them from the vassalage of those soulless corporations and grasping monopolies who have heretofore pocketed the fruits of their labors and grown rich upon the profits from their hard-worked soil." Finlayson chaired the credentials committee and delivered a "stirring speech to his brother farmers," encouraging them to create a cooperative warehouse for their produce before the next harvest. Described as the "Bobby Burns of Linn" (after all, Finlayson came from Scotland), he then read aloud an original poem that concluded the meeting and received "a hearty cheer." It is worth quoting in full:

Now farmers all, arise in might,
    To crush those soulless traders down!
Unite—come forth—demand your rights!
    Your work with glory be crowned.

You are oppressed on every side
    By those infernal moneyed men;
They take your wheat for less than cost,
    And crush you to the earth again.

If you stand back and don't unite,
    Our battlements will surely fall.
Now rally round the farmers' flag—
    Unite! Show front, both one and all.

Sturdy yeomanry, come forth
    With banners flying in the breeze;
Protect your rights at any cost,
    With railroad, rivers, traders, seas.

We have an enemy to fight,
    Who is so powerful, we're told.

> They soon will crush the farmers down
>     Because they're armed with swords of gold.
>
> Our success now with you depends
>     Upon the action you may take.
> Show to the world that you are men,
>     And for protection wide awake.
>
> Let anxious traders mock and sneer,
>     As long ago, in Noah's day.
> Let's build our ark and straight and steer—
>     The flood will wash them all away.
>
> The farmers, then, will rise above
>     Those circumventionists so bold;
> The profits then will come to you,
>     And line your purse well with gold.
>
> If every farmer does his part,
>     Those sharpers soon will disappear.
> They soon will get a Judah's place—
>     I think before another year.[44]

Finlayson's verse outlines the challenges that farmers across America were already facing by the early 1870s. Chapter 4 of this volume explores the reality of these challenges in greater detail. Here, suffice it to say that when considered together, the contents of Finlayson's 1873 poem and the illustration of his home and property in the 1878 *Historical Atlas* afford conflicting visions of farming life in the late nineteenth-century Willamette Valley: the textual rhetoric of the former belies the visual semiotics of the latter. But appearing alongside the *Willamette Farmer*'s articles, commentaries, and advice columns that admired and touted farming, country living, and rosy-cheeked rural children was also the very real news of agricultural instability, slovenly farms, rural death and despair, and the imperiled farmer's son. Each of these latter themes of tragedy, or of less-than-hoped-for living conditions, appears in period assessments of the life of Loyd Montgomery and in the expression of social anxieties about him. These are examined in greater detail in the next two chapters.

The republican landscape of western Oregon as depicted in the *Willamette Farmer* and especially the *Historical Atlas* is certainly a captivating one, at least for the members of posterity to whom Edgar Williams intended his volume to appeal. These romantic representations of a peaceful, bucolic setting peopled with happy families is a memory that has long animated more popular versions of the region's history. Certainly there is much in those particular memories to admire and take as a source of pride. But like any sort of memory, there is so much that is silenced and hidden—that which is shameful, less admirable, and as soon forgotten. Silences and hidden meanings, forgetting and sequestering—these are all things that commit violence on history itself. They make up much of the story of a boy and his murders. That they composed the real landscape on which that boy lived, killed, and died is no mere coincidence.

CHAPTER 2

# "A Child, Sick with Scarlet Fever"

*The Traumas and Violence of Rural Childhood*

**MOST OF WHAT WE KNOW ABOUT LOYD MONTGOMERY** comes to us from the period after his crime, when locals strained to make sense not just of his seemingly senseless act but also of a youth who made no sense at all. In the wake of the triple murder, one news editor admonished locals to "refrain from" making "statements relative to his temper, recklessness, discontent, impudence, etc.," until all the facts were at hand. People being people, they largely ignored such advice, freely expressing views that another journalist described as "all unfavorable to the accused, who is represented to be a violent character and given to ungovernable temper."[1] Clearly referencing Loyd's past, such sentiments were based on the memory of the murderer's earlier life, now refracted through the prism of parricide. Anyone using these sources has to be aware of that. But the range of negative opinions, their sheer volume, and the varied sources from which they emanate do suggest that Loyd had significant behavioral problems from an early age.

There were a few individuals at the time, however, who suggested that there might be more to the lad than what public opinion held. Of course, such observations were proposed at considerable peril to those who proffered them. For example, the *San Francisco Examiner*, a newspaper owned by the sensationalist William Randolph Hearst and which became much hated in Linn County because of its more favorable reports and editorials on Loyd, published a supposed confession given by the lad some two months after his crime. In it the purportedly real Loyd sensitively reflected on his life, claiming that it had somewhat more dimension to it than what otherwise circulated in the press. "I may have been considered a bad boy by some of my neighbors," the fictionalized Loyd voiced submissively, "as every person has his enemies, and those are the ones that always are ready to tell of the bad deeds; but never do they relate the good ones, no matter how many. I know as well as every other young man that some time through life I have done things I should not have done, and often our bad traits are noticed while our good ones go unnoticed."[2]

Another example, much closer to the time of the crime than the *Examiner*'s questionable confession and much closer to the source, appeared in Portland's *Oregonian*. That newspaper's editor regularly sent reporters to Albany. One of its journalists visited Loyd after his trial and came away with the disarming conclusion that "to all appearances he is nothing more or less than an average son of a farmer, where life has been spent in constant rustic surroundings, with little educational advantages."[3]

If we take at face value one of Loyd's repeated claims that he could find no real reason for what made him do what he had done, then it *is* possible to imagine that for the eighteen years prior to the moment of his murderous rampage he was neither more nor less than an average farmer's son of that era. The *Oregonian* editor—at least initially in the affair (his views would later change)—suggested that very conclusion when broadly explaining that "it is not unusual for farmers' boys, whose homes represent the pinching economies of life to the exclusion of most of its pleasures, to feel and nurse a grievance at fate and its supposed arbiters, their plodding, hard-worked parents. Happily, this grievance seldom takes a more violent form than that of 'running away.'" In turning his sights on Loyd specifically, though, the writer added that youthful resentments do "sometimes . . . take on a homicidal feature," as the Montgomery case "clearly proved."[4]

This journalist, as well as a few other writers, mostly from afar, understood that children have different sides to them, both good and bad. They also sagely recognized that children can and do respond quite differently to challenging events and experiences, with murder only one potential outcome. They even alluded to the effects of poverty on farmers' boys. In our times, psychologists, criminologists, and child-development specialists have linked childhood poverty, especially lasting destitution, to the increased likelihood that those who suffer it are more prone to committing violent offenses.[5] The Montgomery family did endure considerable poverty. Their privation played a role in the parricide, a topic that chapter 4 explores in greater detail.

I offer this chapter, however, in response to another finding of current-day psychologists, criminologists, and child specialists about the effects of early experiences on development and behavior. Namely, they have concluded that trauma in childhood is linked to increased anger, aggression, and anxiety; difficulty in attaching to, or empathizing with, others; and even self-destruction and murder. Researchers have examined a variety of such traumas in childhood, including direct experience of or simply exposure to severe illness, disease, and difficult medical procedures; the death of loved ones; bodily blows, beatings, and abuse; bad accidents and violence or simply witnessing or hearing of them; and other sorts of upsetting and frightening events.[6]

Chapter 3 ponders the issue of child abuse in Loyd's biography. It was something that period commentators did reflect on, though most also rejected it as an explanation for his actions. A San Francisco newspaper, thinking even more broadly, commented that there might have been "some cause for [Loyd's] abnormal desire for blood" that traced to "the lad's environment."[7] Issues related to Loyd's environment, such as violence and trauma, entirely escaped the imagination of the period observers closest to him as the possible cause for how he behaved and what he did. Rather, like the San Francisco editor, people more distant from Loyd tended to be the ones who considered factors such as his upbringing, a topic discussed in more detail in chapter 7.

In reality, affliction, tragedy, and violence inscribed childhood in late nineteenth-century rural Oregon.[8] It is possible that the commonness of that trauma blinded adults there to the possible effects that it had on their children (let alone themselves). Their myopia might also have been due to the idealized version of farming life on the republican landscape that danced in their heads. And finally, it really did not seem to matter in the case of Loyd, where the imperative was balancing the scales of justice.

It is impossible to psychoanalyze Loyd from afar, let alone determine how his life experiences affected his actions on 19 November 1895. It is also impossible to know all the trauma that he may have endured, simply because so little of his early life actually made it into any sort of record. This chapter's twofold purposes, then, are merely suggestive. First, the chapter explores the many and varied afflictions, tragedies, and violent occurrences of late nineteenth-century rural Oregon childhood, especially as related to boys, and, when documentation exists, specifically in the case of Loyd. The goal here is to show just how traumatic childhood was at that time and in the place where Loyd was born and raised and where he ultimately committed his own heinous acts of violence. In pursuing that goal, this chapter also draws attention to how different the reality was for rural children and their families as compared to the romanticized version of the agrarian ideal.

Loyal Bryson Montgomery, known as Loyd, was born on 26 August 1877, on a farm near Brownsville, in the vicinity of where he would later kill his parents. By the time of the 1880 federal census, when he was three years old, there were roughly 365 children in Linn County of the same age (192 of them were males). Loyd was born into a rural society of relative youth. In 1880, 46 percent of the 12,686 people who lived in Linn County were seventeen years old or younger. The youthfulness of that population was partly due to the recent Euro-American settlement there and partly due to the incredible fecundity of that population.

Loyd was the firstborn in his family. In time, four siblings joined him: Orville Ernest (born 1878), Eva E. (born 1881), Robert C. (born 1883), and John Clarence (born 1886). Their parents, John B. Montgomery (born 1851) and Elizabeth Ann Couey (born 1856), were also each born near Brownsville and were among the first generation born on Oregon soil to parents who had migrated on the overland trails. They married in a quiet ceremony held at the home of friends in Crawfordsville on 15 November 1876, nine months and ten days prior to Loyd's birth. For all the years of Loyd's life, except when his family briefly took up residence in Brownsville, which had a population of only 580 in 1890, the Montgomerys resided on farms in the area.[9]

Farming households tended to have more residents than other households at this time. Even so, when complete, John and Elizabeth's family's size was somewhat larger than typically found in the Willamette Valley and elsewhere in the country. In 1890, when the Montgomerys' numbers reached a total of seven in one domicile, the average size of a Linn County family whose members were living together was slightly less than five.[10] Wealthier farmers and parents older than the Montgomerys, on the other hand, tended to have larger households, often with nonrelated members, such as hired laborers, residing therein.[11] John and Elizabeth were relatively poor. Their co-resident family size by 1890 reflected the numbers found in wealthier farming households. This suggests, given their reduced circumstances, that they experienced additional stress when it came to resources, something that likely contributed to pressures on their interpersonal relationships.

Disease and prenatal complications rendered birth, infancy, and childhood precarious affairs at this time and in this place; medical treatment was limited, germ theory was only nascent, and the only vaccine available was for smallpox.[12] In the winter of 1882, as scarlet fever raged through different sections of the Pacific Northwest, the illness visited the Montgomery home. On 22 December a local newspaper cryptically related that "John Montgomery has a child, sick with scarlet fever." One suffering from this bacteria-borne infection endures high fevers, vomiting, difficulty breathing, intensely sore and swollen throat and limbs, and uncomfortable and peeling skin. The infection can spread to various parts of the body, such as the heart, kidneys, liver, and even bones. The experience is an especially agonizing one, whether one lives or dies. But this Montgomery offspring was among the lucky; a week after the initial report on the disease striking a youngster, the very same newspaper explained that the child infected was improving and "the prospects are good for its recovery."[13]

Which Montgomery child suffered here went unreported. By late 1882, Loyd, Orville, and Eva had all been born. Scarlet fever is more common in children between the ages of five and fifteen. In 1879 the average age of youngsters who succumbed to it in the Willamette Valley was just under seven. Loyd was the eldest of the Montgomery children and was five years old by December 1882, thus making him the likely victim.[14] Regardless, all three of the Montgomery children escaped death from scarlet fever during its 1882 call on their home. This was newsworthy. Just a couple of years earlier, scarlet fever was the single greatest harvester of life for those under twenty-one in western Oregon. But other equally feared scourges also took a heavy toll, including diphtheria, typhoid, cholera, a host of unspecified brain infections, and the related ailments of consumption, tuberculosis, and scrofula. In 1879, maladies such as these accounted for almost half (223 of 480) of the deaths of children under five in the entire state of Oregon.[15]

There were no reported deaths among Oregon children in 1879 from smallpox, likely due to the availability of the vaccine for it. The disease did, however, occasionally make its appearance.[16] In November 1888, there was a newspaper report of one case of smallpox near Brownsville. It took the life of a man who had recently returned from visiting his afflicted son in Portland. The same newspaper used the occasion to promote the vaccine, noting that a "fresh" supply was available from the town's physicians, Isaac Starr and Orlando Reese.[17] In fact, this news suggested that people could procure the vaccine at a doctor's office and administer it themselves. This seems to have happened at the beginning of 1889 in, for example, the Joseph and Lovina Gragg family, who lived in neighboring Benton County. Both Gragg brothers, Philo and Vernon, ages fourteen and twelve at the time, received vaccines in December 1888 from an unknown source. Philo wrote to an older brother on 7 January of the new year that "there are not any more of us got sore arms as yet." But two days later, he reported of his littlest brother that "Ma vaccinated Marcus this evening."[18]

Diphtheria, also a bacterial illness, was as common and as dreaded as scarlet fever. During the winter of 1877, a few months before Loyd's birth, James Finlayson reported that diphtheria had hit Linn County particularly hard: "many of the young have fallen by this fatal disease."[19] Little more than a year earlier, in November 1875, Joseph and Lovina Gragg lost three of their young children to the disease: eight-year-old Mary on the fourth, three-year-old George on the thirteenth, and six-year-old Cordelia on the fourteenth.[20]

The impact of the loss of such little ones on family and survivors is of course unfathomable. One glimpses the depth of mourning in the Robertson family of Marion County; over a two-week period in November 1880 the family lost two of its children to the combined ravages of diphtheria and scarlet fever—three-year-old Elmer and five-year-old Nancy. Integrated into their single death announcement was the especially doleful elegy that their fifteen-year-old sister composed in memory of her young siblings:

Over the river they beckon to me,
    Loved ones who've crossed to the further side;
The gleam of their snowy robes I see,
    But their voices are drowned in the rushing tide.

There's one with ringlets of sunny gold,
    And eyes, the reflection of heaven's own blue;

He crossed in the twilight, grey and cold,
    And the pale mist hid him from mortal view,

We saw not the angels that met him there;
    The gates of the city we could not see;
Over the river, over the river.
    My brother stands waiting to welcome me.

Over the river the boatmen pale
    Carried another—the household pet;
Her brown curls waved in the gentle gale,
    Darling Nannie! I see her yet.

She crossed on her bosom her dimpled hands,
    And fearlessly entered the phantom bark;
We watched it glide from the silver sands,
    And all of our sunshine grew strangely dark.

We know she is safe on the further side,
    Where all the ransomed and angels be;
Over the river, the mystic river
    My childhood's idol is waiting for me.[21]

Although the Montgomery children certainly suffered from illnesses in the early years of their lives, they avoided the tragic death in infancy and early childhood that regularly called on the homes of many Willamette Valley families, sometimes with a vengeance. On the other hand, 32 percent of males and 28 percent of females who died in the Willamette Valley in 1879 and who were younger than twenty, died at birth or during their first year of life. Additionally, almost 53 percent of females and 61 percent of males younger than twenty who died that year did so during their first four years of life.[22] Should western Oregon children make it through their first few years of life, then their chances of survival to adulthood improved considerably.

In addition to death from disease, children succumbed to congenital afflictions and other medical conditions. For example, also in 1879, a nineteen-year-old and a two-day-old, both males, were the two children that year who died from epilepsy or fits in the Willamette Valley. The numbers belie the pervasiveness of the suffering. One can find many references to epilepsy in local newspapers, whether accounts of the afflicted or remedies that miraculously cured it. Dr. S. A. Richmond & Company's "Smaritan Nervine" was such an elixir. Widely advertised, it carried any number of testimonials taken nationwide from satisfied epileptic victims or their parents. Henry Knee of Vervilla, Tennessee, for example, wrote that the medicine "cured our child of fits after given up to die by our physician, it having over 100 in 24 hours." Miss Orlena Marshall of Granby, Missouri, on the other hand, spoke for herself, stating that the potion "cured me of epilepsy of nine years' standing."[23]

We do know that Loyd suffered seizures, which might have been epilepsy. What brought this condition to light was a startling episode that occurred during his incarceration. In his jail cell on the evening of 28 November 1895, Loyd suddenly commenced kicking, screaming, and beating himself in the face. He then fell convulsing to the floor. The sheriff, with the help of an inmate, had been struggling for an hour to subdue Loyd when a passerby, who heard the commotion, investigated and was instructed to send for a deputy sheriff, who brought restraints. When he arrived, the three bound Loyd's arms and shackled his feet and then sent for two physicians. The doctors first administered morphine and then later chloral to completely pacify Loyd. But in a subsequently calmer state during the same attack, Loyd conversed, argued, and shadowboxed with imagined persons, and at another time he whistled for a dog and shouted instructions to his father while apparently thinking himself to be engaged in hunting. After fully regaining his senses days later, Loyd claimed to have had no recollection of the episode or awareness that any time had passed since immediately before the onset of his delirium.[24]

Many people in the community thought this was just one of Loyd's many notorious pranks. Others surmised that this might be a ploy to assist him in claiming an insanity defense; Loyd's lawyers would base their defense on the boy's mental condition. At least three physicians observed or examined Loyd at the time of his jailhouse seizure or in the days that followed. They each testified in the trial specifically as to how Loyd's fits might relate to his mental condition during the commission of the crime for which he stood accused. In the end, they all agreed that what afflicted Loyd did not affect his mind at the time of the murders, but they also differed in their opinions over the exact nature of the convulsions or even if they were medically real. An especially skeptical James Wallace, who began practicing in Albany in 1884 and also witnessed Loyd's convulsion in jail, thought that the youth feigned his attacks. He also argued that the symptoms the youth exhibited did not comport with epilepsy. Isaac Starr and another doctor, Matthew Ellis, on the other hand, concurred that Loyd suffered a "transient mania." They opined that it could have followed an epileptic seizure, but they also believed that Loyd would have regained complete lucidity afterward.[25]

Ellis, like Wallace, had arrived in Albany in 1884 and was likewise on hand during Loyd's jail-cell spell. Starr, an Oregon native and a Brownsville physician since the late 1870s, invoked Edward Payson Hurd's translation of Jean-Martin Charcot's *Clinical Lectures on Certain Diseases of the Nervous System* (1888) to support his diagnosis, which also included the view that a lengthy epileptic seizure could weaken the sufferer's mind. Charcot is considered the father of neurology. He had enormous influence in the late nineteenth century (and beyond) on the study of various neuroses, nerve problems, and, beginning in the 1880s, epilepsy. Starr did not witness the jail-cell episode, but given that he had practiced in Brownsville for years, he actually knew something more than the other experts about the boy's medical history. Just about a week before the murders, Starr was called to the Montgomery home when Loyd suffered a similar convulsion. On the witness stand, Starr testified that this earlier episode was likely due to overeating. He explained that he had found Loyd's stomach, bowels, and liver all inflamed, apparently as a result of the boy gorging himself. Loyd's seizure in the jailhouse on 28 November also occurred after he had eaten a reportedly rather sizable meal served for Thanksgiving. A condition known as "eating epilepsy" does affect some individuals. Possibly Loyd suffered from this disorder, though his spell in jail appears somewhat more elaborate than those medically observed in other times.[26]

On the other hand, evidence exists that for some time Loyd had been experiencing spells that left him, according to some observers, mentally debilitated. Over several years, three of Loyd's longtime friends observed some of his episodes and stated that he "appeared to be simple minded and [he] acted as though he did not know what he was doing. And at other times he would complain of his head and would look wild and he would soon get in the condition that he would not appear to know anything for hours at a time." The three also claimed that these spells—during some of which he seemed to become especially enraged—had only increased in frequency during the last year of his life.[27] Such observations, when placed side by side with the findings of at least some physicians, do suggest that Loyd may well have suffered some neurological disorder.

Accidents, as compared to illness and disease, claimed the lives of fewer youngsters in 1879 in western Oregon. But of course accidents were a regular cause of death and even more regularly a part of life. Correspondence among members of the Gragg family mentions numerous occasions between 1882 and 1890 when dangers and accidents confronted Philo, Vernon, and Marcus, as well as their friends and acquaintances. In February 1882 an older brother, Herman, admonished Philo, who was but seven, to take care playing with his little ax so as not to cut his feet. In March 1887 Vernon, then ten, was making a chair with broomsticks and cut his hand badly enough that it required him "to rest a while." In October 1888 Philo, then not quite fourteen, was helping his father harrow the fields, each driving his own team. Something spooked Philo's horses, causing them to bolt and nearly collide with the elder Gragg's team. Luckily, the only damage was to the farm machinery, but the episode so frightened Philo's father that he relieved the boy of that chore. In January 1890 Philo and Vernon, aged fifteen and fourteen by then, both received black eyes but for different reasons. Philo took a hard fall while ice-skating and suffered a severe gash near his left eye, while Vernon received his bruise when he accidentally knocked his head against that of his younger brother.[28] As far as reports of accidents involving others in their district, in 1890 a neighbor boy to the Graggs broke his leg while playing on a pile of hay in a barn.[29]

Rural Oregon was a dangerous place for children. In 1879, boys and girls in the state were as likely to succumb to accidental deaths as they were to die from disease, though there were differences in the sorts of accidents to which they were prone, in part due to variations in how society approached the rearing of boys versus girls. Girls more typically stayed closer to home and with their mothers and suffered domestic mishaps, such as burns and falls. Boys, on the other hand, roamed the countryside more freely. In doing so, they often came in contact with its numerous and varied water features. Boys not only swam in rivers and streams, but millraces and ponds as well lured many to play on the logs and rafts that bobbed within. Boating and fishing, at times associated with pleasure, at others with the labor that boys or their fathers performed, also tempted them.³⁰ As a consequence, boys were twice as likely to die from drowning as were girls, and in 1879 drowning was the second-ranked cause of death among boys, sickness being the first.

Drowning so stalked boys, especially during the summer swimming season, that as early as 1872 the *Willamette Farmer* provided "Rules for Bathing," a list of ten items. It appeared in the same issue containing a report about two local drownings, an article placed just opposite a third especially sad story of two brothers' watery deaths, this one likely manufactured for didactic purposes. In it, one nine-year-old went bathing in a river but got in too deep and began to sink. His older brother went in after him, but his lack of strength and skill only led to the two being drawn under. As the pair surfaced "for the last time, they saw a third brother, the youngest . . . running down the bank for the purpose of trying to save them. Then it was that the nine-year-old acted the part of a hero. Struggling as he was with death, he gathered all his strength and cried to his brother on shore 'Don't come in or father will lose all his boys at once!'" The youngest did as instructed. The other two were found sometime later downstream "clasped in each other's arms."³¹

Although all such episodes are tragic, two stories, because of their different circumstances, demonstrate the commonness of Willamette Valley youths' contact with water and the perils it presented. One concerns seventeen-year-old Robert Yost of eastern Linn County, who, on Sunday, 2 August 1891, while bathing in the upper Santiam River, decided to wade across. When he found the water too deep and attempted to return, he lost his footing and was drawn under. A ten-year-old witness, also a boy, ran home and alerted his own father, who, after a short search, recovered Yost's lifeless remains.³² The other tale comes from the town of Sheridan, on the other side of the Willamette Valley, in early June 1876. Some teenaged boys who had played a game of baseball in town were heading home in a wagon and attempting to cross the South Yamhill River at Garrison's Ford, the way they had come in the morning. During the day, however, the river had become swollen. When the lads attempted to recross, the torrent swamped their wagon. Floundering horses led to confusion as the wagon swung into the current and sank. "Some [of the youths] could swim and some could not," the local newspaper reported, "but those who could helped the others, thereby saving all but one, a young man 18 years of age, named M. G. Getchell." One of the horses also drowned.³³

Certainly Loyd swam and played in streams and ponds. The Calapooia River was but a stone's throw from his home in 1895. Drownings of boys did occur there. In July 1887, for example, Elmer Shanks, who was the same age as Loyd—the two likely knew each other—was boating on the Calapooia just downstream from Crawfordsville with some other unnamed boys. Their craft capsized, and "despite the efforts of his companions [Elmer] drowned." Indicating how this loss impacted his community, Elmer's Sunday school teachers memorialized their departed pupil in the newspaper. Meanwhile, Brownsville residents raised fifty-six dollars for Elmer's surviving mother, who had recently lost her husband to cancer. "It is not difficult to reach the hearts and pockets of the people of Brownsville," a newspaper explained, "when circumstances demand it."[34]

As these descriptions indicate, death by drowning was typically a violent affair—boys struggled for their lives against powerful currents, sank, resurfaced, flailed about, and sank again as any rescue efforts failed. Sometimes their bodies went unrecovered for days. Their survivors—their friends, playmates, and schoolmates—were obviously shaken by such loss. A vast variety of other sorts of violence constituted part of the daily routine for farm children. A brief enumeration of these from the Willamette Valley includes children being crushed, mangled, lacerated by, and thrown from wagons and carriages; suffering pocketknife injuries; cutting knees and amputating fingers and toes while chopping wood or playing with axes; being thrown from, dragged by, and kicked by horses, sometimes to death or having bones broken or losing eyes in the process; being set upon by vicious cows and sows and being attacked by bears; burning to death or suffering severe injuries while playing with gunpowder; falling from haylofts and trees or into wells; being crushed by trees; and being overcome by fumes while digging wells.[35]

Perhaps more disturbing is that children might have their lives threatened or even taken by other youngsters, whether accidental or otherwise. In December 1889, eleven-year-old Marcus Gragg wrote to his mother, who was then away, about three local boys, all cousins to each other and ranging between nine and ten years of age, who got into a scuffle that escalated to frightening proportions. One of them became especially angered and "took out his knife and was going to stab" his kin. Marcus further reported, however, that "some of the big boys" were present, and they intervened to prevent a catastrophe.[36]

Deadly tragedies involving young person–on–young person violence did occur. Just one example comes from a Linn County hopyard where various laborers had converged in September 1894. There a fourteen-year-old boy was cutting down a small tree when a girl whose age was not recorded objected to what he was doing and attempted to intervene. The quarrel escalated and the boy picked up a stick and threw it at her, hitting her in the side of the head. The blow instantly killed her.[37]

More common were accidental deaths from gunfire. While none of the boys and youths aged twenty and younger who were enumerated in the 1880 mortality schedule died due to gunshot wounds, two young men, each aged twenty-one, in fact did. But as in the case of rivers, creeks, millraces, and lakes, guns, which even very young lads possessed, were a common part of life, and just as commonly newspapers carried stories of deaths and injuries from inadvertent gunshots, misfirings, and hunting accidents. One example from 1885 involved two fourteen-year-old friends in Benton County who were playing with a revolver. One of the lads unintentionally shot the other in the side of the head, the bullet entering below his ear. The injured boy cheated death, however, with 143 fragments of bone discharging with pus from the wound over the next three weeks. His doctor expected him to recover fully.[38]

Other youths were not so "lucky." In 1872 nine-year-old Willie Noble of Lane County was climbing a fence when his gun accidentally fired. The bullet entered his head and killed him instantly. His helpless mother watched the unfolding tragedy from the family's nearby home.[39] Accidental death from guns also touched the lives of the Gragg family, namely in an 1887 hunting accident involving two young men from their neighborhood. They were pursuing deer together in the Coast Range when Wade Malone, who was nineteen, mistook his twenty-four-year-old companion, Jeremiah Clark, for game and shot him through the chest. The victim lingered a few days. Bettie Gragg, who related the story in family correspondence, explained that Clark "endured much suffering" while "W. Malone is almost crazy with grief over the accident as the two boys were firm friends and to think that he was the cause of the death of his friend is almost more than he can endure." The tragedy affected more than just those directly involved. "The sad affair," one newspaper reported, "has cast a pall of gloom over the whole community, where the deceased was well and favorably known."[40]

Guns were widely available in rural America. They served as important tools, for example, in hunting and in protecting livestock and crops from wild animals. As the above cases show, even young boys possessed them. In some places in North America in the 1890s, prowess with a gun was even becoming a mark of a youth's masculinity. It is hardly surprising that such weapons were the most commonly used in instances of patricide in that time, with sharp-edged instruments used only slightly more often in matricides. In more recent times in America, males who kill their parents most typically resort to guns to commit their acts, and they are more likely to do so when killing their fathers as compared to their mothers.[41]

Children, and especially boys, also witnessed and participated in the violence of slaughtering farm animals or other creatures killing animals. Such was routine for the boys of the Gragg family in the 1880s. Their correspondence relates coyotes killing the family's lambs in the meadow, a dog suspected of doing the same to some goats, and a weasel that carried away one of their chickens.[42] The subject of hog slaughtering occupied many lines of their letters in 1889 and 1891. The boys were especially proud when either they or hired hands successfully avoided making the pigs squeal when dispatching them with a bullet to the head. Occasionally, however, more than one shot was needed to fell the suffering creature. And then there was the actual preparation of the meat and lard for later use, something that the boys participated in and described in vivid detail. This included using a horse to drag the hog carcass to the scalding box, which was used to loosen the hair on the animal's body; setting aside the intestines for sausage casings; rendering lard and even the entire pig's head by boiling them; getting grease all over themselves and the floor; and feeding what was unwanted to voracious chickens. That the entire affair was a particularly messy and unpleasant one is attested to in a letter that their sister Bettie wrote to their mother, Lovina, who was in a Portland hospital for some unmentioned reason during the hog-slaughtering season of 1889. "Ma you got out of hog killing in fine shape this year," Bettie chided. Lovina agreed, responding from the infirmary, "I got out of hog killing pretty slick this year." But she quickly added that she would have "rather been well and at home to helped [sic] with the butchering than cooped up here in the Hospital."[43]

The Gragg boys also engaged in the killing and torturing of other animals and vermin. Such acts included dispatching birds with slingshots, squirrels and gophers with rifles, fish with clubs, and mice and rats with traps. They also once tied a string to the hind leg of a captured gopher and then "had lots of fun seeing" one of their dogs "pick it up and shake it." They also at one time struggled to open up a hole in a tree to expose a skunk, which another of their dogs then went after. "You ought to have seen Tip shake it," Philo gleefully wrote to his older brother. Mice were an especially persistent problem in the Gragg farmhouse. Philo once lost part of his spelling book to nighttime gnawing. Another time he nonchalantly wrote to his mother, who was away at the time, that "the mice are getting pretty thick in our house, so I think that we will have a mouse killing as soon as we get through with hog killing." The Graggs' occasional method for dealing with the ubiquitous mice sounds somewhat unorthodox. One time, "Bettie got the mice drunk and they kicked around like everything," Marcus explained in 1889, adding, however, that "I dont [sic] hear them gnawing tonight."[44]

A boy's life in late nineteenth-century rural Oregon was filled with all manner of violence and trauma. Because of the limited information we have on Loyd's childhood, we do not know much about his specific relationship to the above sorts of violent activities and misadventures. He did at one time threaten "to beat [the] head off" of a young man in his neighborhood whom he believed had shot his dog.[45] And of course he did commit a triple murder, which is at the extreme end of the spectrum. We also know that he suffered seizures for some years, and he also likely suffered from a terrible and painful disease when only five. He also lived on farms where animals were slaughtered, and he operated farm machinery, chopped wood, worked in harvesting, and hunted with rifles. Beyond these more verifiable instances, we know that all manner of frightening threshing accidents, violent kicks from horses, shotguns misfiring, people thrown from buckboards, farming mishaps, horse tramplings, crushings by timber, laden wagons rolling over bodies, and collapsing bridges all either maimed their victims or took their lives in and about the very neighborhood in which Loyd lived during the 1880s and 1890s.[46] He was undoubtedly aware of these accidents, not to mention the deaths of extended family members. He may have very well witnessed some.

Trauma such as what Loyd experienced, witnessed, heard of, or otherwise engaged in may help to shed light on his "violent character," "ungovernable temper," and "grievance at fate and its supposed arbiters . . . [his] hard-worked parents." Locals who knew Loyd and community-based journalists who investigated him, however, hesitated to connect the dots. But these sources did directly describe his behavioral problems. They proposed that he did not know the difference between right and wrong, that his mind was affected, that he regularly had "gloomy spells," and that he was either a "maniac or an idiot." Another suggested that his unusual fits of anger as a child naturally led to later bursts of more violent passions. And yet another source proposed that his "devilish proficiency in crime" was something he acquired at an early age.[47]

Loyd survived early childhood. In doing so, he was like most other boys—they succeeded in navigating the ever-present diseases, illnesses, and accidents that claimed the lives or at least the limbs of so many of their cohort. The survivors, as they aged into older children, were expected to fit into family, community, and larger society by adhering to parental guidance, attending school, and performing more and more demanding work and additional chores. Parents, community, and society all viewed these as the process by which boys became men who in turn could, would, and should support their own families and contribute in meaningful ways to the civil functioning of their communities and the larger society. As the *Willamette Farmer* simply phrased it, "American boys are expected to become manly men."[48]

At the same time, physical disfigurements brought about by childhood trauma, not to mention chronic afflictions, followed many of these lads through their youth—years when a whole array of other dangers, ranging from naughty mischief to outright criminal temptation, confronted them on their pathway to adulthood. Regardless of the constant stream of overwrought hyperbole that poured forth from the printing presses of the *Willamette Farmer* concerning the region's boys, the newspaper did on occasion strike a more realistic tone when reporting on them. In one such example, the editor commented on the hazards that threatened the boy who typically is "away all day" from home. "How much time there is at noon and after school for Satan to find mischief for that boy's idle hands! How many evil schemes can be patched up in a few moments!" With mothers and fathers otherwise occupied with business and housework, "the little boy . . . is getting wound up in some wicked older boy's scheme. . . . It is a wonder, then, so many boys wind up in an institution?"[49] In another and closely related piece, the *Farmer* rhetorically asked, "How much cheaper it would be to have every boy properly educated, trained and disciplined so that he would be a blessing, instead of a curse to the world. He is sure to become one or the other."[50]

That many boys, Loyd numbering just one among them, did not then successfully maneuver through the social hazards and temptations that lay before them on route to manhood only added emphasis to the fears of the *Willamette Farmer*, the voice of rural Oregon in the late nineteenth century. The next chapter turns its attention to such matters.

CHAPTER 3

# "Spare the Rod and Spoil the Child"

*The Bad-Boy Problem and the Montgomery Parricide*

ON 26 AUGUST 1887, THE DAY OF LOYD MONTGOMERY'S tenth birthday, the *Willamette Farmer*'s editors brought the curtains down on the weekly's nearly twenty-year run. Having "devoted . . . the prime of life's physical and mental activities to working for the farmers of the Pacific Northwest," the publishers confessed that they had grown weak with "age and gray hairs."[1] As such, the passing of this most vocal advocate for a romanticized agrarian life in the region symbolized the civilization that it had so steadfastly promoted.

Coincidentally, in the same year that the *Willamette Farmer* departed from Oregon's landscape, Loyd Montgomery's newsworthy persona appeared on it. In 1887, illness again visited the Montgomery family, but this time it came calling on John and Elizabeth. In early December, newspapers reported that they both suffered from an attack of fever, which lingered through the early part of the month. During their malaise, Loyd reportedly "got hold of a 50-cent piece, and went to Brownsville . . . and offered to bet it with the boys of the town that his father would die before morning."[2]

Some eight years later, on Sunday evening, 1 December 1895, and less than two weeks subsequent to the parricide, the Reverend Bengal Joy Kelly of the United Evangelical Church in Albany, in the midst of a fierce religious revival in town (see chapter 7), took to the pulpit before a large and anxious

61

audience to speak on "why Loyd Montgomery killed his parents." Kelly, like both Loyd and John, was Oregon born, descended from an esteemed pioneer family, and grew up on a farm. Like John, he was father to several children. Kelly's sermon recalled the ghastly 1887 incident to illustrate the youth's "irreverence for his parents." "The principal reason" for Loyd murdering his parents, Kelly concluded, "was obtained from Proverbs: 'Spare the rod and spoil the child.'" He then instructed his audience, if in fact its members needed such tutoring with the recent unnerving events still weighing on their minds, that "children must be trained in the way they should go to come out all right."[3]

Kelly's terse recounting and summation reveals much. First, the minister clearly viewed Loyd as a child, though the lad was on the cusp of manhood. Second, in noting Loyd's "irreverence" and in detailing his wicked actions, Kelly echoed a good deal of the reporting after the murders; in seeking insight into the mind of Loyd, it focused on his innate disposition, his indifferent relationship to obedience and dutifulness, and his wayward undertakings. Third, in referencing Loyd's interactions with other boys, while not putting to rest the idea that they might have taken him up on his morbid wager, Kelly acknowledged the existence of a society of boys and that it had unsavory elements. Finally, in invoking Proverbs 13:24, Kelly, without realizing it, laid blame for Loyd's actions on his own parents, a notion that locally became the topic of an especially heated debate. All these themes, each of which voiced anxiety about boys and, in varying degrees, rural life itself, appear in the fierce reaction against Loyd.

DUTY, OBEDIENCE, AND RESPECT

On 20 November 1895, the afternoon following the murders, Albert Cavender's special issue of the *Brownsville Times* rolled off the press. When locals picked it up, they found not only a gruesome description of their three butchered neighbors but also summaries of and even direct quotations from the testimony of several witnesses whom the coroner's jury had interviewed that very day. Among them were the statements of five children and youths, including Loyd, who was yet days away from his first confession to the crime. Naturally, the youngsters peppered their accounts of what they heard, what they did, and where they were at the time of the murders with descriptions of childish things, such as returning home from school, chasing a squirrel up a tree, throwing rocks, and tending to chores.

Loyd also explained that on the day before the murders, he had gone hunting, returning home the next afternoon. Hunting was a common pastime for boys in nineteenth-century rural America. Despite their many chores, they generally had more free time than their fathers to follow this pursuit, done both for sport and to supplement food stores. In the Willamette Valley, it was traditional for youths to retreat into the foothills of the nearby mountains to hunt deer and bear during the autumn months.[4] That Loyd had been doing such a thing in November would not have surprised those perusing Cavender's report.

Also rather mundane were the doings of Loyd's sixteen-year-old brother, Orville; he "was plowing" in the fields at the time of the murderous events. Typically, farm boys during this era commenced heavier farm labor, such as plowing, around fourteen years of age, when they were physically strong enough to manage it.[5] That Orville had been thus engaged, preparing already for the next planting, was something of the everyday at that time of year.

In and of themselves, then, neither of these two laconic recapitulations of boys' activities are especially noteworthy. They provided, however, the foundations of a sort of prodigal son parable that simultaneously elicited public opinion and framed public perceptions of Loyd. That is, on the evening of 25 November, while in his Albany jail cell, "unable to endure the weight of the terrible crimes upon his mind," Loyd finally broke down. Weeping profusely, he admitted to the killings. In his new version of events, he acknowledged that on the day when he had left to go hunting, he had given no notice to his parents, instead simply deserting home and responsibilities without taking leave. Upon his return Tuesday afternoon, his father got after him not simply for abandoning his parents without word but because he had neglected his duties in doing so. Boys' chores—chopping wood, fetching water, pulling weeds, helping their mothers with laundry and ironing (which typically fell on Mondays and Tuesdays, the very days Loyd went missing), cleaning barns, collecting eggs, tending farm animals, and, for older boys, heavier labor in the fields—were central to the successful functioning of the farm.

Although Loyd might have felt he was a man, or nearly so, his parents and his society viewed him as shirking his duties. His transgression was a serious affront not only to his family but to the fundamental ordering of rural society. The gravity of the former is evidenced in John's response to his wayward son when he reappeared: "Father asked me where I had been," Loyd said. "I told him I had been hunting. Then he slapped me in the face and told me to go and cut some wood." The fact that Loyd's disobedience was an offense against the larger community is apparent in that Daniel McKercher felt entitled to express his opinion on the matter. He "sided in with father while we were quarreling," Loyd explained.[6]

Loyd's confession to the murders reinforced the conclusion, whether formative or already hardened in the neighborhood, that "the boy was extravagant for a plain farmer's son, and did not seem anxious to help his parents to any extent."[7] Juxtaposed against this was Loyd's brother Orville, who was more like the ideal farmer's son whom the *Willamette Farmer* had lauded for years. Locals could not help but make the comparison between the two lads. "Neighbors," a news item announced, "declare that [Loyd] was always different from his younger brother, who is well spoke of, that Loyd was not liked as well, and was always causing more trouble."[8]

There was more to it than Loyd's unfavorable comparison to his brother. It was his entire nature. James McFeron, the county sheriff and a relation of the Montgomery family, summed it up so: "Lloyd [sic] was unruly and bad-tempered from childhood, and gave his parents a great deal of trouble. . . . When quite a youngster, and it was found necessary to punish him for some of his meanness, he would never admit his wrong-doing" (figure 3.1).[9]

Other such opinions freely circulated in the press after the murders. "I can say," a "Brownsville Citizen" confidently penned in a letter to the editor, "there is not one person in 10 miles of the place of the tragedy but believed Montgomery did all of the killing, simply for pure cussedness. He has no reputation for truthfulness where he lived." Furthermore, "Lloyd [sic] Montgomery had," this writer continued, "made threats against his father repeatedly, the first thing that was said by nine-tenths of the people in this neighborhood, immediately after the murder, was that Lloyd [sic] was the guilty party, and, in fact, he was asked by some of his relatives, when he notified them of the killing, 'Lloyd [sic], did you do it?'" In the view of so many in the community, Loyd was simply by nature "wild," "reckless," a "violent character," and "a very cheerful liar," and he had an "ungovernable temper." Even Loyd (reportedly) admitted in an interview proximate to his arrest that "he had a violent temper, and was easily angered."[10]

Figure 3.1. James Andrew McFeron (1859–1940). As sheriff of Linn County in 1895, McFeron arrested Loyd after the boy committed the murders. McFeron had known Loyd throughout the boy's entire life and was married to the murdered John Montgomery's first cousin, Elizabeth McHargue. Source: *Weekly Herald-Disseminator* (Albany, OR), 6 February 1896, 3.

Forthcoming commentary, some of it likely apocryphal, that Loyd had been "at variance with his parents" spoke directly to the theme of irreverence. An unnamed couple from the Montgomerys' neighborhood emerged with details of a conversation—"tending to show the unnatural animosity of young Montgomery toward his parents"—that they allegedly conducted with Loyd when he stopped by their house during his hunting trip. When the couple asked him whose rifle he was carrying, Loyd purportedly shot back, "'It belongs to that darned ___ ___ ___ father of mine.'" The woman attempted to shame Loyd for speaking "that way of as good a father as you have." Loyd's alleged "heartless answer" was, "You don't know him, or my mother, either, or you would not say so."[11]

There had long existed in Western culture two opposing interpretations about nature versus nurture when it came to children's characters. One of these viewed children as innately wicked and in need of breaking. The other saw them as innocent malleable bundles of innocuous energies in need of shaping. The hegemony of one view over the other depended on historical timing. By the 1890s in the United States, the latter opinion had largely prevailed.[12] The many *Willamette Farmer* columns advising parents on how to raise their boys all gently attest to this view dominating in the region by then, at least among the official purveyors of culture. As early as 1875, for example, the *Farmer* ran a piece entitled "Rough Boys." In it, a woman desperately sought counsel on what she could possibly do with her ten-year-old son. Within just a matter of days, he had "drowned seventeen kittens, tied pans to the tails of nine dogs, washed his father's new silk hat against the nap and blown up his sister's pet canary with a firecracker." The response was that his boyish pranks merely indicated "life, activity, energy and force," which proper guidance could turn in an appropriate direction. Should that happen, the lad might even be shaped into a vivacious minister whose preaching would certainly avoid putting his congregation to sleep.[13]

This editor likely spent less time at home with children than did this poor woman. But despite his counsel, the vestiges of the perspective that children simply had depraved natures remained at a more vernacular level, as is clearly demonstrated in the aforementioned conclusions proffered about Loyd. Some who held such opinions even reached out to the science of the day to reinforce the view of his innate evilness. The field of neurology, which then included psychology, was newly emerging at this very time. One of its theories, albeit strongly debated, held that atavism explained the asocial adult. Likewise, bad behaviors in childhood portended criminality later in life. Thus came the view that Loyd's murderous acts were "the sudden awakening of hereditary criminal instincts within him."[14] Criminology studies of both late twentieth-century and nineteenth-century parricides have found that a significant number of perpetrators of the crime had a history of sociopathic tendencies.[15]

And so it was that Loyd's other miscreant activities teleologically led to murder. There was of course the story of him gambling on the life of his ill father. Other reports focused on a more recent episode, when he had forged his uncle's signature to several monetary notes, converted them to cash, and had then run away from home, his father soon tracking him down and then making restitution for the stolen money.[16] Relatedly, among the earliest of theories proposed for why Loyd committed the murders was simple "cupidity"—he killed his parents in an attempt to rob them of money they had freshly obtained for their hop harvest. Samuel Templeton abetted this story. He related that, when he returned home some hours after the murders, he discovered that the drawer in the bureau in which he kept his harvest payment had been pried open and looted. Loyd "knew where the hop checks were kept," Templeton assuredly announced, in the process ignoring the myriad other neighbors who had milled about the crime scene in the interim.[17] That locals framed one of their interpretations of Loyd's reason for killing his parents around his real and supposed past episodes of betting and stealing money and theorized about the murders in connection with the recent harvest's infusion of cash into local hands is hardly surprising. This took place during a depression when money, or the lack thereof, was on everyone's mind.

The belief also circulated that Loyd was neither more nor less than any other farmer boy. This view must have unnerved other farmers. Over the weeks following Loyd's arrest, commentators from afar reached yet more deeply into the countryside, offering the defense that "he is the product of his environment," the "untutored simplicity of a country boy."[18] Such a defense in a sense indicted the rural civilization that had indeed produced Loyd: "the pinching economies of [farm] life to the exclusion of most of its pleasures" had supposedly made the murderer what he was.[19]

The negative effects of rural life on boys had long been a concern to those who fretted about farming society and its future. In the case of Loyd, such anxiety spread beyond holding the general nature of farming life accountable for his actions. That is, it would even lay the blame squarely on the parents' doorstep, as Reverend Kelly's December 1895 sermon suggested. The fabricated voice of Loyd that the *San Francisco Examiner* published as his confession expressed such sentiments when it declared that "ofttimes the evil ways of children should be placed at the feet of their parents."[20] Even the governor of Oregon, William Paine Lord, acknowledged this view when he explained that some who wrote asking him to pardon the youth did so by claiming that Loyd was no more than "the outcome of bad environment." Although admitting that he had "no proof of it," Governor Lord nevertheless accepted this, stating that "it is probably true . . . that Montgomery is ignorant, was bred under bad surroundings, has had no moral training, and is devoid of a proper sense of duty to his parents and society."[21]

The local press repeatedly rallied to the defense of Loyd's parents as "nice people and respected by all." It generally placed the blame for Loyd's misdeeds on his very own innate character. And yet, the weight of the widely acknowledged view that parents held responsibility for shaping their sons into the proper sort of citizen occasionally erupted from the pages of the local press when assessing Loyd, though if only for didactic purposes. An Albany editor, for example, did consider the debate over nature versus nurture in the case of Loyd without coming to the usual firm, local conclusion in favor of the former on the matter. "It is not easy to assign the actual blame for this awful crime," the editor admitted in this rare instance, "and many who attempt it fail." At the most, this journalist could only offer that the case "suggests the necessity of boys starting right, with something higher ahead of them than their present happiness, and of parents getting closer in love and sentiment to their children."[22]

SPARING THE ROD

Loyd's confession on 25 November hardly surprised locals. Those long acquainted with him immediately believed in his guilt, much like the coroner's jury that Loyd had only days before sought to fool. During that emotional confession, Loyd passingly stated that his father had "always abused me." Initially ignoring this bit of information, the journalist to whom Loyd was speaking only later returned to it in his interview. "How had your father abused you[?]" the reporter queried. "Had he flogged you?" "No," came the youth's response, "but I had worked hard all my life, and he always treated me mean and abused me."[23] Given the circumstances in which Loyd found himself, his limited knowledge of the workings of the world, and the details of the nature of the abuse that he endured, it is unlikely that he offered this revelation as a defense for his actions.

A news editor in Lakeview, Oregon, east of the Cascade Range and near the state line with California, thought differently:

> The fact that the father became angered at the boy's conduct and slapped him in the face in the presence of a neighbor, leads us to conclude that possibly he had been in the habit of cuffing the boy about from childhood, the same as some two-legged brutes will kick and cuff a dumb animal that can offer no resentment [sic]. Who can say that, possibly, the father is not responsible for this whole affair? Not from any inherited tendency of the son, but from the fact that this brutish, frenzied depravity bordering upon insanity had been drilled into the boy by the treatment of a reckless and an unwise parent.[24]

Loyd's passing reference to "abuse" became a flashpoint of public debate, as it did relate to the conditions of his upbringing and, more specifically, his parents' treatment of him and therefore their responsibility for the whole mess. In our contemporary era, criminology and psychology have pointed to physical abuse experienced in childhood as an underlying condition in parricide. One study found that 90 percent of parricides that are perpetrated by juveniles are committed by youths who have suffered severe abuse.[25] But exactly what *abuse* means depends on the one suffering it and how larger society defines it. Corporal punishment did occur in the Montgomery family. Whether it was "severe" or even what that means is difficult to gauge.

The historian David Peterson del Mar has explained that the men of Oregon's early American migrant population regularly used force against their wives. Parents of that generation enjoyed even more freedom when physically disciplining their children. Peterson del Mar has attributed the prevalence of these physical punishments not only to traditional male authority and parental prerogatives but also to the culture of individualism that was part of American migrant society in the West.[26] Domestic violence against wives and the abuse of children in this era and in this place might even be seen as yet another type of violence endemic to the republican system. Patriarchal as it was, it necessarily contained strong imbalances in power among its members, something that some scholars have linked to domestic violence. Some have even related the violence that westering Americans perpetrated on indigenous people to violence they committed in their homes.[27]

Parents continued to employ physical discipline, sometimes quite harsh, in the raising of their children into the late nineteenth century, though it was becoming increasingly questioned, even by rural reformers.[28] As early as 1875, for example, the *Willamette Farmer* reprinted an item from the *Phrenological Journal*, to which a father had written for advice. He had tried everything, it seems, even the use of corporal punishment, but nothing seemed to work in the case of his fifteen-year-old "troublesome boy." The journal's editor, after looking over the evidence, faulted the parents and their methods as "largely responsible for his waywardness. Their unwise whippings did no good. Instead of governing by love, they doubtless attempted to do it by severity and by fear, and failed."[29]

A few years later, the same newspaper offered its own injunction against whipping. Calling such treatment barbarous, it charged that "many children are of such quality that a blow makes them cowardly, or reckless, or deceitful, or permanently in temper. Whipping makes children hate their parents. Whipping makes them lie. Whipping makes home unpleasant, makes boys run away, makes girls seek happiness anywhere and anyhow."[30]

That this advisory appeared amid a several-week discussion of coercive methods in the raising of boys speaks to the fact that the issue was certainly up for debate. In this long-running deliberation, the farmer J. B. Knapp started the ball rolling, writing to the newspaper about his relationship with his own son. He described a multitude of instances of the superiority of reason for correcting his son when he had done wrong. But Knapp's approach to parenting did not go unchallenged. After receiving pushback from advocates of a harsher approach, the otherwise gentle father did have to admit that more forcible methods might very well be warranted, especially for the "boy or youth that persists in wrong doing from malice or pure cussedness."[31]

Even the *Willamette Farmer*'s editors at times contradicted their advice about not whipping children. An 1875 piece entitled "Training Up a Boy" recommended, in the case of a boy who does not admit guilt for a bad deed, that one should "take down the rod and tell him that you will thrash him to death if he doesn't 'own up.'"[32] Such approval for the use of the rod as a tool in parenting reverberated two decades later in Kelly's sermon about Loyd. Clearly, in the 1890s corporal punishment as a method of parenting had hardly vanished from the landscape.

Loyd did explain that his father's slap is what set him on his rampage. Whether that strike was part of a larger pattern of physical violence in the Montgomery household is challenging to confirm. Loyd claimed that his father abused him but supposedly also said that the abuse he endured was not actually of the physical variety, even though Sheriff McFeron also spoke of instances of corporal punishment in the Montgomery family's past. On the other hand, there is evidence of domestic violence in Elizabeth Montgomery's biography. In 1859, when she was only three, her parents, Mary (Griffith) and John Couey, separated in a highly publicized case. The Oregon legislature twice considered it before granting Mary's petition for divorce. In bringing suit against her husband, Mary presented evidence of John's neglect and abandonment and described an occasion when he repeatedly struck one of his infant children in the mouth. Testifying to the dysfunctional nature of Mary and John's relationship, and thus the familial atmosphere Elizabeth experienced as a young child, the couple remarried within months of the bitter divorce. By 1870, however, John Couey was dead and Mary was now wedded to another. Elizabeth and her two siblings were then living with their maternal grandparents near Brownsville. It appears that Elizabeth continued to reside with them until the time of her marriage in 1876.[33] Elizabeth's brother William, as an aside, married Clara Montgomery, sister to Elizabeth's husband, John.

We know that domestic abuse and violence can run in families. But any public discussion of physical discipline in the Montgomery family related to John's ineffective management of Loyd. It is unlikely, given the evidence and regardless of her own childhood trauma, that Elizabeth physically abused her own children. Loyd would even wistfully explain from his jail cell that "my poor mother had always been kind and good to me, and I thought the world of her. I was never so happy as when I had my fiddle playing her a tune, it always pleased her so." On the other hand, it may be that the strong sentiment attached to the idealized mother-son bond sheltered Elizabeth from any suspicion of guilt and may have been behind those words that Loyd supposedly uttered. People could, however unforgivable it was, imagine a father-son relationship culminating in the way it did in the Montgomery case but not in the case of a mother and her boy. "Everybody understands how it would have been possible for you to kill your father . . . in a fit of rage," a reporter who interviewed Loyd at once declared, "but it seems incredible that you could have brutally murdered your mother." And thus, the press would credit the emotional burden of that very act with forcing Loyd's confession. "In the solitude of his cell . . . over and over again the voice that [had] sung lullabies to him in infanthood he must have heard screaming, pleading, and imploring for mercy. The phantom of those pleading faces, the recollection of those terror-stricken voices, continually before his mind could nauseate his guilty soul and cause him to seek relief by sharing his terrible secret with the world. It is no wonder that he confessed."[34] And yet oddly, save in rare instances, newspapers throughout the more than two months of reporting on the Montgomery affair were all but silent on the topic of Elizabeth and her life. Only on a couple occasions in the hundreds of pages of reporting did they actually use her first name.

FROM BOY CULTURE TO BOY PROBLEM

The Reverend Kelly's sermon about Loyd's 1887 gamble with his father's life placed the youth in the company of other boys of the Brownsville area and squarely within some of the unpleasant doings that boys were known to engage in. For those who lived on farms, the nature of that life, their ever-toiling parents, and the conditions that led children frequently to labor on their own all meant that they often went relatively unsupervised. For boys in particular, when away from home in the countryside or in small towns, whether by themselves or with comrades, they often played games and sought adventure. When unchaperoned, it was also a simple matter for them to defy whatever rules and guidance their parents laid down. In boy culture, then, they might also participate in more mischievous and asocial activities, including fighting, torturing other boys and animals, using profanity, playing with guns, vandalizing, and menacing their country teachers.[35] Where the more innocent features of boy culture ended and the more wayward elements began was not exactly clear. Rural advice columns routinely cautioned parents that their sons' activities away from home and especially in the company that they kept could lead them down a road too far.[36]

The following are just a few varied examples culled from the many that come from western Oregon during the era in which rural and small-town boys engaged in repellent exploits. Some "rude boys" in Albany in March 1891, for example, "gathered on the street and made a vigorous attack" on a local Chinese man who was driving his wagon. They pelted him violently with snowballs, hit him in the head, and drove away his team. Some years earlier near Salem, "a couple of young rascals" discovered another, younger boy bathing in a stream. Apparently "out of pure deviltry," they destroyed his clothing and then choked and threatened to drown him. In April 1890, several boys in Albany were strongly suspected of throwing rocks that barely missed the heads of passersby. In January of the same year and in the same place, police apprehended four bad boys "in the habit of stealing . . . around the city." A few months later near Salem, a pair of twelve- and thirteen-year-old boys found themselves apprehended after burning eight barns for the fun of it, "being anxious to see the excitement." In the small town of Dallas in January 1877, groups of boys regularly frightened women in their homes when their husbands were away. A rural Marion County youth in 1895 described his pals as nothing more than "a band of hoodlums." They enjoyed luring smaller boys into their culture of "profanity, vulgarity and slang." And then, one Saturday evening in 1878, an unspecified number of sons of the "most prominent farmers" in one corner of the Willamette Valley got intoxicated and behaved like "untutored savages." A more deadly instance of boys gone wild was the story from Riddle in 1892, when a fifteen-year-old youth, who secretly armed himself with an open pocketknife, taunted a seventeen-year-old into a fight after school, stabbing him several times and causing his death.[37]

The ubiquitous schoolhouse bully also plagued teachers in towns and countryside alike. Rumors spread through Albany in 1895, for example, that "big muscular bullies" planned to "run the teacher and the whole school." The plan fizzled when "a live energetic teacher put in an appearance ... and 'wiped the floor' with the bully."[38] But other examples demonstrate that not all teachers, some of whom were women, had the ability to confront problematic boys with force. Bettie Gragg, who taught school in the rural district of Alpine in 1887, felt that all her students minded her well save for one. When she asked the annoying creature to fetch a pail of water, he refused. "He just deliberately told me," she described in a letter to her brother, who was also a teacher, "he would not do it and said if I wanted any water to go and get it, that it was the teachers [sic] place." Bettie asked her brother for advice on what he would do, admitting, "Oh how I wished I was strong enough to give him a good whipping and make him do it[.] But I just shamed him and asked another boy to go and get it and he did so without parlyeing [sic] any about it."[39]

In Loyd's case, we have only bits and pieces about how he intersected with boy culture. On the more mundane end of the spectrum, he pitched rocks at squirrels and had a keen interest in pet dogs, lamenting those he had lost and desiring to trade for new ones.[40] He also went hunting with other youths, including many times over the years with Egbert and Ernest Martin, who were three and five years older than he.[41] Less innocently, one boy he knew, fifteen-year-old Clyde Philliber, who was also a cousin to Loyd through marriage, declared before Loyd owned up to his crime that "Loy" was likely the one who did it and that he "was a tough lad."[42] Two other young men from Crawfordsville who also knew Loyd characterized him somewhat differently. "He had always been like most boys," they said, "good hearted and generous," though they also added that he "had a quick temper and was headstrong."[43] Of course Loyd had also forged checks, stolen

a    b

money, run away from home, and threatened to beat another young man's head off.[44]

Boys' use of profanity was a cultural concern at that time. Some thought it offered a window into a youth's soul and conceivably his future. That the issue came up with regard to Loyd is hardly surprising. On the one hand, the Montgomerys' neighbors, who supposedly encountered Loyd on the day before the murders, quoted him as referring to his father as "that darned ___ ___ ___ father of mine." And yet, one journalist who interviewed him in jail explained that he "is not profane judging from his conversation yesterday, and does not use much slang." Another report similarly asserted that "he either does not know any slang or refrains from using it, and if he uses profane language, he carefully avoids it in the presence of a reporter."[45] Given the circumstances of the crime with which he was charged and the fact that he was behind bars, it might also be that Loyd purposely tempered his speech at these times.

We also know that Loyd had gone to school and purportedly did have difficulties there. One teacher explained that when Loyd attended her Brownsville lessons between 1891 and 1893, he had "gloomy spells." A male instructor, who did not divulge precisely when the events he alleged took place, did eagerly recall that "on the third day" of Loyd's attendance at his

Figure 3.2. John Fox (a), Marshall Fox (b), and William "Harry" Pool (c). Ages twenty to twenty-four, these three friends and acquaintances of Loyd Montgomery were only slightly older than Loyd at the time of their arrest for burglarizing a store in Crawfordsville. They were incarcerated in the Linn County Jail at the same time Loyd was there. According to the *State Rights Democrat* of 7 February 1896, they said that Loyd "had always been like most boys, was good hearted and generous, but had a quick temper and was headstrong." Courtesy of the Oregon State Archives, Salem.

c

school, something happened to cause him to give Loyd "a good whipping and he quit school at once."[46] The exact nature of Loyd's troubles is not clear. He may have had behavioral problems, as other evidence strongly suggests, or perhaps a learning disability that led some of his teachers to believe he was recalcitrant. Both the above teachers explained that he had difficulty absorbing his lessons and speculated that he might have had some cognitive issues.[47]

Loyd's boyish pranks and even some of his felonious associates followed him into his jail cell. On 24 December 1895, just days after Loyd's trial, twenty-four-year-old John Fox, his twenty-year-old brother Marshall, and their twenty-year-old friend William "Harry" Pool broke into the general store in Crawfordsville, near their homes, and carried off a considerable amount of merchandise (figures 3.2a, 3.2b, and 3.2c). Local constables quickly tracked them down and placed the three under arrest. The Fox brothers also admitted to having stolen from others in the area at other times. They also had known Loyd his entire life.[48] They, along with Pool, were soon reunited with Loyd in the Linn County Jail.

A few days after the accused burglars landed there, a report came that Loyd was "much pleased with their company." On New Year's Eve, he and Harry Pool, in the adjoining cell, "blackened their faces with charcoal, and with some red blankets from their beds, decked themselves out as Indians and began dancing in aboriginal fashion. The Fox boys beat a stick on the steel bars for a drum, while the condemned murderer and his companion yelled and danced until a crowd was attracted by the din, and the sheriff was forced to quiet the hilarity." By then Loyd had been sentenced to execution by hanging, leading Sheriff McFeron to conclude that his actions were for the "purpose of relieving his mind as much as possible from distressing thoughts of the horrible murder."[49]

Boys, youths, and young men such as Loyd, Pool, and the Fox brothers, and especially their mischievous culture that could lead to serious wrongdoing, drove both rural and urban society to despair and action in the late nineteenth century. By 1884, reformers had labeled the conditions in Oregon a full-blown "bad boy problem." They began searching for solutions to it outside the family, an institution they saw as clearly failing to contain and to reform youths' worst behaviors and activities.[50]

Efforts directed at child welfare began in the state as early as 1866, when reformers founded the Oregon Children's Aid Society in Salem; they opened a home there two years later for twenty-five children. By the 1880s, the problems that the state's children were confronting and the types of mischief they engaged in had only grown. Advocates for a state-operated reform school became more vocal in the 1870s, and reformers in Portland took the lead, creating the Boys and Girls Aid Society of Oregon in 1872. The pervasiveness of the problems for the state's youth by then was partly related to the growing population generally, which resulted in increased numbers of children in danger. But the response to the problems also had to do with the shifting view that increasingly conceived of children as distinctly different from adults, with specific stages of development, and also the belief that they could be shaped into productive members of society when the appropriate forms of guidance and discipline were applied—as long as it was not too late. Related was the growing concern that youths who committed serious crimes ended up incarcerated with the very worst criminals in state prisons, where their bad ways, it was believed, would only harden them into confirmed recidivists.[51] Between 1890 and 1893, in fact, 138 youths aged fourteen to twenty were imprisoned in the Oregon State Penitentiary; 18 of them were between fourteen and sixteen. The vast majority of their crimes were forms of either larceny or burglary. Such offenses, as opposed to rape and murder committed by those with whom they mixed in prison, made them potentially salvageable and suggested a reason for doing so.[52] A "home" of their own where this could take place, albeit one run by the state, seemed a quasi-domestic alternative to the prison.

After years of reformist advocacy, in 1889 the state legislature authorized the construction of the Oregon State Reform School, but for boys only (figure 3.3). Cost overruns, as well as the fact that the legislature convened only biennially, prevented the allocation of sufficient funds needed to complete the facility until November 1891. It was a multistory building with a basement, stood on a knoll facing west, had a stream running along its base, and looked out over 377 acres of Willamette Valley farmland a few miles south of Salem, the state capital.

Those identified for detention there were between eight and sixteen years of age. They had to have "committed a crime or been charged with having done so ... and in like manner any incorrigible or vicious boy, whose parents or guardians surrender him for that purpose, also any boy neglected by his parents or having none and in danger of growing up to lead a vicious life" could be housed there. The boys had to work to support the institution, including laboring on the school's farm, which provided for themselves and for extra income for the institution. During the 1896–97 biennium, the boys produced 1,050 bushels of wheat, 3,204 bushels of potatoes, and 192 tons of hay, as well as quantities of vegetables, fruit, dairy products, poultry, and livestock.[53] The prescription of such labor was part of the reform process. That it was agriculturally based makes sense, given the needs of the institution. But it is also apparent that the old agrarian ideal was at work here: laboring in the earth had long been believed to make men virtuous.

Corporal punishment was banned, save in "extreme cases, where everything else has failed." If deemed necessary, the punishment had to be administered under the watchful eye of the institution's superintendent. When it was employed, it was to be a "strap upon the open hand" and "aimed to be remedial, not retributive." In fact, complaints had already been registered by 1894; an investigation in reaction to them demonstrated that the rule had been routinely ignored, to the detriment of the boys.[54]

The Oregon State Reform School was a modern invention. It was implemented on the understanding that boys were distinct from men and thus needed their own place where they could be separated from the harshness of the prison walls and molded. It was also modern in that, at least officially, it attempted to avoid inflicting pain on the body. It opted instead for what

The Original Main Building.

Figure 3.3. Oregon State Reform School. Opened in 1891 on Willamette Valley farmland to deal with the growing bad-boy problem, the original Oregon State Reform School building was designed to house forty residents, ages eight to sixteen. Within a year, however, its population, drawn from across the state, was almost double that, indicating the enormous challenges that the state's boys, their families, and the larger populace experienced at that time. Source: Oregon, *Second Biennial Report of the Oregon State Reform School at Salem, Oregon, 1895* (Salem, OR: Frank C. Baker, 1894).

were understood to be gentler methods of control and redirection, including having boys labor in farm work, receive school lessons, perform military drills, train in a variety of vocations, and participate in religious services—all to transform them into "independent, useful citizens."[55]

Oregon's reform school was also modern in that it was a new state instrument marshaled to discipline boys who (at least according to perception) were inflicting increased chaos and disorder on their society. The family—both urban and farming—had failed to control its boys. The problem was so acute by 1890 that the state had to step in. And step in it did. Originally designed to hold forty inmates, within a year of its opening the institution already housed almost double that figure, forcing boys to sleep two to a bed (which raised moral alarm).[56] The youths came from all corners of the state, and by the end of the decade only Multnomah County, where the state's largest city, Portland, is located, was contributing more boys to the institution than Marion and Linn Counties, which ranked second and third, respectively.[57]

It is clear from the institution's registers that some of the boys were indeed exceptionally challenging and that their parents and local communities were desperate. But one also gets the sense that many parents and courts simply wanted to dump these children there; that the reform school opened just when the depression of the 1890s set in seems hardly an accident. As that depression deepened, the number of boys at the school, whether bad or good, increased markedly. American settler society had earlier removed the indigenous people from the land to build upon it a republican landscape. Now, part of what imperiled that idealized republican landscape was its own progeny. And like methods of old, this new problem was also banished and confined to its own sort of penal reservation. This was also the era of industrial boarding schools for Native American children and of the Dawes Act, designed to force the idealized agrarian lifestyle onto tribal people (as well as take more land from them).[58]

Among the earliest arrivals at the reform school were in fact boys from Linn County. Lawrence Compton, whose father was an impoverished farmhand in the county, was merely ten years old when his parents committed him for incorrigibility in 1892. He remained three years. Also arriving in 1892 was thirteen-year-old Albert Rounds, from Brownsville. His mother, a single parent, was unable to deal with his bad behaviors. Relatives in Albany took him in for a while, but when he stole a watch their patience gave out and they sent him to the reform school.[59]

Another case, also from 1892, was that of fifteen-year-old William Claud McHargue, a second cousin to Loyd. Only months older than Loyd, William was also born on a farm outside of Brownsville and was one of several siblings. In 1887, his father, James McHargue Jr., born the same year as his first cousin John Montgomery, gave up the life of a farmer and joined the many other rural residents who were moving to town, in this case to Albany. There James obtained employment at the woolen mills but later moved on to eastern Oregon, where he operated a hotel. After the McHargue family's arrival in Albany, William admitted that he had "done what other bad boys do." Reform school commitment papers describe him as incorrigible, turbulent, disobedient, and a habitual truant who was "becoming vicious and depraved and immoral by using vulgar and profane language." It was thus no wonder that his "parents are unable to control" him. He finally landed at the institution for the crime of larceny. McHargue's first stay there lasted a little more than a year. A few months after leaving, he returned for another stint, was discharged again, and within a few months was back for another stretch. He escaped on 24 August 1897 and the next year landed in the state penitentiary after an arrest for forgery. Before his arrest, a posse of men had hunted him down in Eugene, where they found him armed and hiding in a barn. When the Albany press got hold of the story, it naturally made much of McHargue's recidivist history, stating among other things that, although just twenty-two, "he is of a wild, reckless and ungovernable disposition. . . . He is one of a gang of tough youngsters in Albany who styled themselves the 'sewer gang,' committing all sorts of depredations in true western border type."[60]

It is a wonder that Loyd did not end up in the reform school, given all the reported annoyances he had caused his parents and others in his neighborhood prior to his murderous rampage. Among the most egregious recalled and recalled again was when he forged a note in his uncle's name for five dollars and then attempted to run off to eastern Oregon. His father caught up with him, brought him home, and paid the debt. Granted, this happened only weeks prior to the murders and thus Loyd was beyond the age of sixteen—the upper limit for boys taken into the reform school. (State officials were at the time considering raising that limit to nineteen. Some of the institution's wards, such as William McHargue, in fact did mark birthdays beyond their sixteenth during their time in and out of the school.)

It might be that John Montgomery took his fatherly duties seriously and thus sought to discipline Loyd himself, rather than foisting him onto the state (the youth might have gone to prison in this instance). But there seem to have been other reasons for John to try keeping Loyd down on the farm: he desperately needed Loyd's labor to keep his failing family afloat during the depression.[61]

Examples such as Albert Rounds and William McHargue, who came from farms and villages and ended up in larger cities, led some reformers and even a few farmers themselves to conclude that the bad-boy problem was born in the countryside and then moved to town. In December 1908 the Country Life Commission held hearings with farmers and reformers in Portland. In one meeting, William Schulmerich, a dairy farmer, made the claim "that the undesirable farm boys were the ones to flock to the city, where they worked for a wage barely sufficient . . . and spent their spare time in saloons and theaters. He said the farm was well rid of such people." While a "storm of protest from the audience" awaited Schulmerich, he was likely not alone in his sentiments.[62] One early and long-influential theory about rising rates of homicide in rural areas in the late nineteenth century argued the position somewhat differently. In this view it was in fact the better elements who had migrated to cities, leaving the "least desirable" in place, where they contributed to the higher rates of crime and murder in the countryside.[63] Clearly, no one knew for sure what was happening, but that it was happening in the countryside could not be denied.

Given the aforementioned examples of boys gone bad, some of whom had directly touched Loyd's life or at least trod the same landscape he did, it is clear that the bad-boy problem was present in rural Linn County by the 1890s. In this context, that the specific crimes of Loyd Montgomery, the Fox brothers, and Harry Pool related to each other and to other offenses from the local to the national level did not go unnoticed. Lumping their different yet roughly concurrent felonies together, one editor referred to them collectively as an "outbreak of crime" in the community.[64] During the period when Loyd and the Crawfordsville burglars made headlines, a resident of Brownsville, taking aim at some sympathetic remarks that a Portland journalist had made about Loyd, retorted expansively that such comments only encourage crime. "It is getting to be unsafe for a person to travel for fear of being shot," he continued. "Not long since a murder was committed near Sweet Home, in this county, and the fact is, there seemed to be no one concerned in it and the murderer is at large. It is unsafe for a person to leave his store, or property, for fear of some one breaking or carrying it off. Crime is getting to be common and the punishment is not severe enough."[65]

And then came the unsettling story in January 1896 of a family on Beaver Creek in Benton County, the next county to the west of Linn, who had a son with a "savage disposition." The boy had recently read accounts of Loyd's crime, it was asserted, and had spouted opinions that Loyd had done the right thing in killing his parents and their visitor, Daniel McKercher. One evening, during a moment of family strife, "the youth jumped up from the dinner table, seized a Winchester rifle and threatened to kill the whole family. 'I will make another Lloyd [sic] Montgomery affair,' he shouted with such emphasis that a stranger who happened to be at the house at the time smelled danger and left." Within days, the story had spread to Linn County.[66]

Bad boys such as these, some with national infamy, were legion by the time Loyd Montgomery committed his heinous act. Their names and crimes appeared in the press to amplify assessments of Loyd. In one example, an Albany news editor, after stating that "the terrible crime just committed in this county, the horrible atrocity of which is laid at the door of a mere youth... calls attention to the prevalence of criminal instincts in the youth of our land," went on to detail the career of Jesse Pomeroy, the boy-murderer of Boston. In the early 1870s, beginning when he was merely fourteen, Pomeroy sadistically tortured a string of young children and murdered two. Hardly skipping a beat, the Albany editor then offered up for comparison San Francisco's Theodore Durrant, whose twenty-three "years scarcely carry him over the line between youth and manhood." Just months before Loyd lit up the headlines, Durrant had murdered two young women in rapid succession in the Golden Gate City and endured a trial that was a national sensation.[67]

But the earliest comparison the press made between Loyd and another boy-murderer came from much closer to home. In fact, it came from Linn County and from a mere dozen years before. That story returns us to the James Finlayson family from chapter 1.[68]

It began on Saturday, 3 November 1883, which dawned rather gloomy and cold in Linn County, as autumn days there often do. A heavy frost had settled in overnight, and an unbroken cloud layer persisted through the day.[69] Despite the icy, glum conditions, farming activities naturally moved forward as usual. On Finlayson's farm, James and his now sixteen-year-old grandson Charles, who had lived with his grandparents for the last ten years, worked together fixing a fence and tending other chores. Meanwhile, James's wife, Janet, who was sixty-one and actually the step-grandmother to Charles, was tending household duties, including preparing to bake bread. Some weeks prior, James had arranged to travel that day to Brownsville for a two-night trip on business. Before he headed off at 12:45 p.m., he instructed Charles to tend to the plowing. Instead, having a headache and not feeling well, the boy retreated indoors, lounging about the sitting room. Soon from the kitchen came a remonstration from his grandmother, who reminded him of his duties and accused him of laziness.

Charles later explained that he had frequently quarreled with the old woman and that she often "abused" him; others declared he always had an ungovernable temper and even resorted to violence at school when experiencing disagreements with classmates. On this particular Saturday afternoon, his grandmother's nagging set him off on a reckless course. When he marched into the kitchen and made some "impudent remark," Janet struck the youth on the head with a piece of wood, though apparently only lightly. When she turned around to feed the stick into the woodstove, Charles took hold of a nearby ax used for splitting kindling and struck her on the left temple, leaving a three-inch gash that opened up the skull to the brain. Stunned, but astonishingly not dead, Janet staggered to her bedroom, also located on the home's main level. There she collapsed on the floor. Charles followed her and, with a knife that he had grabbed from the kitchen table, repeatedly stabbed her on the head, shoulder, and upper back. Still not dead, at least according to the youth's testimony, she asked for a glass of water while plaintively whispering, "Good-bye Charlie; say good bye to all my friends."[70] She then expired.

Charles hurriedly pulled the blankets from the bed and covered her body as the blood was pooling from her wounds. He dropped the murder weapon and retreated upstairs to his room, where he changed his bloodied clothing and then rifled through the drawers in his grandfather's desk, finding within it $26.50. He exited the house, locked the doors, threw away the key, saddled a horse, and lit out for Albany. There he nervously entered the merchandise store of Montieth & Seitenbach, where he purchased an overcoat and new shoes, leaving his blood-spattered boots behind. The next day, Charles sold his horse and saddle for $37.50 in the small town of Jefferson, not far from Albany, and walked to the village of Turner in Marion County, where he caught the train the next morning, Monday, for Portland. There, in the central part of the city at Fourth and Pine Street, he had the nerve to join a crowd gathered to take in a demonstration of a balloon ascension. He then caught another train for eastern Oregon.[71]

Meanwhile, at about 12:15 p.m. on Monday, with the weather still quite cold but the sun now managing to poke through broken clouds, James returned home from Brownsville to discover his farm disquietingly quiet and the doors to the house locked tight. With the help of a neighbor, a Mr. Wren, Finlayson climbed through an unlatched window on the second floor of the structure. Descending the staircase, he let Wren in through the kitchen, where the two found washed dishes sitting on the table, a dishrag in the pan, and an unbaked, unraised batch of bread dough. Finlayson entered his and his wife's bedroom, where he immediately spotted the bedclothes piled on the floor. Fearing "something terrible," he called for Wren, urging him to "come here quick there has been death here." Pulling back the blankets, Finlayson exclaimed, "My God, my wife is dead." The two traced a trail of gruesome evidence, including a bloodied doorknob, back up the stairs to Charles's room. Neighbors were alerted, and quickly the frightful news spread to Albany. A reporter for the town's *State Rights Democrat* newspaper soon arrived at the Finlayson home, where some twenty to thirty people had gathered. "The sight was too horrible for most to witness," the journalist wrote, "and many turned from the scene with a sickened heart." Of course, given the condition of the property and that Charles was nowhere to be found, suspicion immediately fell upon him. Still days before his arrest, when he had not yet had a chance to speak for himself, the news reporter who first arrived at the scene described Janet as having "been a mother to him. She was kindness itself. Never a harsh word came from her, no matter how impudent he might be."[72]

Both the Linn County government and a relation of the murdered woman each put up separate $125 rewards for the apprehension of Charles, just as the manhunt ensued. Authorities arrested the boy in eastern Oregon about a week later. In the new year he was found guilty of murder in the first degree. But some days later, the judge ordered a new trial when Charles's counsel produced an affidavit, signed by James Finlayson himself, that prior to the trial a man who served on the jury had boldly stated "that the boy ought not have a trial, but that he ought to be taken out of jail and hung." On 11 April 1884, before the second trial, a version of that jury member's wishes came true: sixteen-year-old Charles committed suicide by hanging himself in the jail privy.[73] Already by February 1884 James had given up his farm and moved away to Forest Grove, in the northern end of the Willamette Valley. He married a third time, this last wife still living when he died in 1890 in Philomath, which was then his home.[74]

The *Willamette Farmer*'s most noticeable consideration of the Finlayson murder was an editorial that utilized it for didactic purposes. The piece appeared in print on 30 November 1883 and was predictably entitled "Another Lesson to Boys." For years, the newspaper had railed against the perceived threats that "trashy" and "perverted" Victorian dime (and nickel) novels posed to the minds and characters of youths. In fact, the supposed effect of lurid fiction on youthful minds was a national mania at that time. In the newspaper's view, "dime stories tell of things that never did happen ... but young men ... read these wild, exciting incidents, where is blood, murder, suicide and robbery, and believe them, till their minds get perfectly bewildered. ... Then at some time the foolish boys will imagine themselves ... in some situation where they can be a hero too, and then they will follow the example shown in the last yellow covered novel." In 1876, calling attention to the recent Jesse Pomeroy affair in Boston, during which his alleged addiction to violent novels became a sensation, the *Willamette Farmer* explained that the Boston murderer had "confessed to have read sixty dime novels; in view of which fact the wonder is that he did so little killing." And then in November 1883 the editors of the newspaper received word from "a reliable source" that "young Finlayson ... was a constant reader of the Police Gazette and all such foul and wicked publications, where not only is the reading bad, but there are pictures calculated to excite the basest of thoughts."[75]

On 23 November 1895, three days after Loyd's arrest, a Portland newspaper explained to readers that his case was reminiscent of the Finlayson hatchet job of a few years back.[76] Journalists in Linn County chose to draw comparisons between Loyd and the more distantly situated Durrant and Pomeroy. They did not mention Charles Finlayson. It is impossible to know with certainty what accounts for this omission. Regardless, residents of this section of the Willamette Valley clearly understood Loyd within the context of the bad-boy problem that reached from the national level down into the American countryside and even into their own communities and, dare they admit it, their very own homes. Within this context, Loyd was the worst of the bad boys, not just because he slaughtered his very own mother and father but because he did it on the farm, the long-hallowed wellspring of the nation.

FROM BOY TO MAN

When a newspaper recalled the case of young Finlayson in November 1895, it added that "young Finlayson, like young Montgomery, was large and overgrown for his age. He was nearly six feet high, when only 14 years old."[77] This was patently false. Descriptions of Charles put out to guide the "manhunt" for him in 1883 explained that the boy was five feet, seven inches tall, and he weighed about 130 pounds.[78] With that said, a reporter who interviewed Charles after his arrest described him "as a tall, muscular, raw-boned boy, and except for a very youthful face, appears 18 or 19 years old."[79] There was reason for embellishing Finlayson's size, given that he was a mere sixteen years old and thus technically a boy.

There was likewise an intense interest in Loyd's body. Some more generous reports described him as being, "although only 18 years old[,] ... as large as a full-grown man, and his magnificent physique might well be the envy of a trained athlete."[80] Admiring accounts such as these came much later in Loyd's saga; earlier ones described him in menacing terms: "He is a stout, heavy-set-fellow, weighing 180 pounds, of swarthy complexion, an[d] looks older than 18"; "He is a large over-grown boy of 18 years, and weighs between 180 and 190 pounds"; and, "Though eighteen years of age he is full grown, and very weather beaten, being a large, raw-boned young man. . . . He is a dull looking boy, but with inclinations of a strong will power."[81]

Over the years, the *Willamette Farmer* occasionally published height and weight charts for boys and men. One in 1887 entitled "The Life of Men" described that at twenty-five years of age, a man will have acquired his maximum height, which ranged between five and a half and six feet tall. At a medium height, a man's weight should be about 140 pounds. By all accounts, at eighteen Loyd had exceeded these dimensions, standing already six feet tall and weighing between 170 and 190 pounds.[82]

That he was a man in physical stature was significant in that, given his age as well as other aspects of his life, Loyd was neither legally nor culturally a man in the context of rural America generally and Oregon law specifically. In the view of the reform school's officials, he fell precisely between seventeen and nineteen, the gray area in which he was neither a boy nor quite a man. In Oregon, a male did not gain the civil and legal rights of manhood until he was twenty-one. In farming society, manhood came from other, social factors, some of which Loyd met but most of which he did not. One step toward manhood was leaving school, which Loyd appears to have done. By 1895, the state of Oregon was requiring parents to send their eight- to fourteen-year-old children to school for at least twelve weeks during the year. Public schools in Albany by the 1890s were operating nine months out of the year, while elsewhere in Linn County, on average, schools operated for about six and a half months. In fact, while the law required it, parents did not universally send their children to school throughout the county, though John and Elizabeth Montgomery did, at least when their children were younger.[83] Evidence for Loyd suggests that he attended school as late as 1893, when he was about sixteen. By the fall of 1895, his younger brother Orville, who was then sixteen, may have left school, too—he was out plowing in the fields while his younger siblings were attending their lessons on the day their parents died. It might be, however, given that young people could come and go from school even during the ages when they were required to attend, that both Loyd and Orville still did or would have attended school in the 1895–96 school year. After all, some boys in their neighborhood as old as twenty did attend local schools at the time.[84]

Related to leaving school was that manhood also meant entering into the workforce. Loyd certainly did labor but did so within the context of his family's economy. For reasons discussed in greater detail in chapter 4, young farming men in the Willamette Valley were remaining on their parents' farms for longer periods of time as the nineteenth century progressed. Some farming fathers even expressed the view that their sons should remain and work for them until twenty-one, when they became men by law.[85] On the other hand, young people spending more years in parents' homes, something that generally occurred as part of the nineteenth-century transformation of the family, could also result in increased strains between parent and child.[86]

The heavy labor that Loyd and Orville performed in the fields, as well as the fact that they were equal partners with their father in the sharecropping activities for Samuel Templeton, was actually something that culturally bestowed manhood on them, but this was of course attenuated by the fact that they were not yet truly independent of their father. Boys' work, on the other hand, routinely centered on the house and barnyard and included tasks like chopping wood, feeding animals, milking cows, collecting eggs, and perhaps helping their mothers with the laundry.[87] Loyd did labor in the fields plowing and harvesting, but he also performed the work and chores of a boy. In addition to still residing and working for and with his farming family, not to mention being subject to the discipline of his father, Loyd also acted in ways that clearly show him enmeshed in rural boy culture rather than in the culture of men.

In practically all elements of his life—his residence, his work, his behaviors, and his legal age—Loyd was a boy. This fact naturally hung in the background to questions about his dreadful crime. That Reverend Kelly alternately referred to Loyd as a boy and as a child in his December 1895 sermon no doubt added to social anxieties. The tradition in America was that children as young as seven could be convicted of murder if it was demonstrated that they had criminal intent, as would be the case for an adult.[88] By the end of the nineteenth century, thanks to the child-welfare movement and alterations in the meaning of childhood, the age of responsibility had generally risen to roughly eighteen.[89] Although its officials advocated for changes to the law, the Oregon State Reform School still would not officially take in offenders who were older than sixteen, suggesting that authorities felt that was the cutoff age for both responsibility and the potential for being saved. And yet, although Loyd stood at eighteen years, his age and thus his culpability were taken into consideration by some in the legal system. Sheriff McFeron, when soliciting a confession from Loyd, had explained that "it might be better for him on account of his age to tell the whole truth about the murder, and that he might be dealt with more leniently in court if he did so."[90]

Given questions such as these, plus many of the facts of his life that demonstrated Loyd's boyishness, it was all the more imperative to describe his body as that of a man. And yet, news reports, witness accounts, editorials, and the like applied a range of terms to him, including "man" and "young man" but also "youth," "boy," and "child." From this muddle of inconsistency two patterns emerge. First, opinion in favor of Loyd's manhood was generally voiced when explaining and speculating on his murders of men—his father and Daniel McKercher. At times such as these the press, drawing on the opinions of those who knew the family, focused on Loyd's extraordinary size and physical strength. Second, and on the other hand, when the press reflected on the issue of matricide, it consistently infantilized Loyd: when asked about his mother, he broke down and cried; he was unable to provide "reason" for why he killed her; his mother's screams as he slew her were from a voice that had "sung lullabies to him in infanthood"; and he had once nursed at the breast and prattled at the knee of the woman he had murdered.[91]

The two portrayals of Loyd worked in unison. As a cold-blooded murderer of a mother—the one person most culturally revered at that time in the emotional life of the farm boy—Loyd became nothing more than an animal and thus unsalvageable as a human. But as an able-bodied man in relation to other men, he became an adult fully culpable for his actions under the Oregon legal system. Mingling these two views, one witness summed it up this way: "The mere truth is that he is a dangerous human brute, a mad dog in form of a man, whose removal from the world ought to excite no more interest than that of his four-footed prototype."[92]

To many observers, not to mention those who suffered directly from it, the bad-boy problem had settled in over small-town and rural Oregon with the vengeance of parricide during the last two decades of the nineteenth century. The simultaneous and constant cultural refrain about the idealized republican landscape, as well as the proper and expected role of boys in it, only increased the volume of the perceived, if not entirely real, bad-boy problem. Linn County boys like Charles Finlayson and Loyd Montgomery exemplified the worst of the bad boys and the complete subversion of the rural ideal. Both boys would be violently snuffed from that society—Charles through his own hands, Loyd through execution, and both through strangulation. In the latter case, the reporting by the press over the weeks leading up to that inevitable event, the actions taken by the court in convicting him, and the pageantry surrounding his confessions, his trial, and his hanging combined in intricate ways to restore the appropriate relationship between parents and children, authority and obedience, men and boys—all things that bad boys and parricide had otherwise shattered. They also worked to transform Loyd from a bad boy into a salvaged man but only moments before his unavoidable death—something perhaps more needed for the society he offended than for his own salvation.

That story is taken up in chapter 7. But first this volume turns to another matter that contributes to our understanding of his parricide and the society in which it occurred: the stories of agricultural decline and the cultural crises caused by the concomitant demise of the state's founding fathers and mothers.

# PART 2

## "ONE BY ONE THEY ARE DROPPING LIKE THE AUTUMN LEAVES"

*Agricultural Decline, Dying Pioneers, and Parricide*

When, on the day following the Montgomery and McKercher murders, Albert Cavender of the *Brownsville Times* printed the first news story to appear anywhere on the tragedy, he began his account with an appropriately melancholic description of the crime scene:

> Situated upon the Crawfordsville road, 3 miles east of Brownsville, is the hop farm of Sam'l Templeton . . . at present covered with poles and dead hop vines, the remnants of this year's crop. At some distance from the main road, shaded by [an] immense maple, and other large trees, is the dwelling house occupied at the time by John Montgomery, his wife, and five children. This house, which is of unpretentious style, unpainted and plainly finished, one and a half story in height, blackened by exposure to the elements, being devoid of paint . . . is an ordinary square structure [that] stands east and west[,] the front or properly speaking, side, facing the south; the building is surrounded by a rough picket fence.[1]

Downcast for obvious reasons, Cavender's somber eloquence also captured the reality of the poverty that the John and Elizabeth Montgomery family had long endured. And although their destitution also went largely unspoken in subsequent news coverage, their penury hung palpably in the background of the affair. The Montgomery parricide and the McKercher murder, the subsequent investigations, and the trial and execution of Loyd Montgomery, after all, transpired during the deepest part of an economic depression that racked not just Oregon but the nation and even the larger Western world. It was, truth be told, part of a broader late nineteenth-century decline for American farmers such as the Montgomerys. It was a decline that had commenced some two decades before that family's final downfall, and it had stalked John Montgomery throughout his adulthood. In very real ways, on 19 November 1895 that depression, which had already taken so much and had wrecked so many lives, claimed those of John and Elizabeth and their friend and neighbor Daniel McKercher. On 31 January 1896 it also took the life of Loyd. Indelibly marked by these events, the survivors, their families, and the community were left to pick up the pieces.

Within a couple of days of the Montgomery-McKercher murders, other newspapers both near and far also began to report on the appalling events and the stunning revelations that came in their aftermath. One of the newspapers that produced some of the most exhaustive investigations and offered some of the most penetrating editorials on the affair was the *Oregonian* in Portland. Three days after the Linn County murders, a reporter from that publication interviewed that city's very own Charles Templeton about the Montgomerys. Templeton, a respected dentist, was nephew to Samuel Templeton and an older cousin to Clyde Templeton, the latter being the lad who had accompanied the Montgomery children to their home from school minutes after the tragedy occurred. Portland's Charles Templeton, like John, had been born near Brownsville. There he had spent his early years and had known John well as a boy. After local schooling, however, Charles's parents sent him to Albany for further education. Like many of the sons of farmers during that era, Charles took advantage of the opportunities that city life afforded; he soon headed to Portland and there opened a successful dental practice.[2]

As Charles recounted bits and pieces of his relation's life for the *Oregonian* reporter, he made a casual comment regarding John, about "his people being pioneers." Although information about the larger local network of the Montgomery kin occasionally appeared in varied reports over the several weeks of the affair, only this once was the term "pioneer" used to describe people in the circle of the parricide. But like the Montgomerys' poverty, this element of their lives and their past also hung in the background throughout the affair. In fact, both John and Elizabeth were the children and grandchildren of Oregon "pioneers"—and some of the most revered ones at that. John's birth in 1851 and Elizabeth's in 1856 placed them among the earliest of those born on Oregon soil to parents who, sometimes with their own parents, had trod the overland trails into the West in the 1840s and 1850s. Those Oregon migrants had been responsible for founding many of the Pacific Northwest's small industries and farms. They had also created early institutions of self-government before any empire had clear control over Oregon. And in time they helped wrest that disputed control from Great Britain and the indigenous people, the latter having lived on and shaped the land for millennia.

Members of the pioneer generation were also fast dying off in the last quarter of the nineteenth century, something that contributed to the already uncertain tenor of the era. Hugh Brown, for example, died in 1888. He had been a cofounder of the town of Brownsville, which carried his name. He was also John Montgomery's grandfather, an immigrant of 1846, an original American settler of Linn County, proprietor of the first mercantile in that region of the Willamette Valley, and a one-time member of the Oregon territorial and state legislatures. The introduction to his obituary that occupied an entire column on the front page of more than one local newspaper captured the reflective mood swelling in the state about the passing of its various founders. "Another one of Oregon's pioneers has gone," the tribute solemnly commenced. And then it continued, "One by one they are dropping off like the autumn leaves, and in a few years more nothing will be left of them, but their names and history of their daring deeds, and noble acts of heroism, in crossing the plains, beset on all sides by dangers, such as no other set of people ever faced, with all that was near and dear to them—to come to this coast and establish a home for themselves and build up a great empire."[3]

The veneration of dying pioneers such as the Montgomerys' forebears coincided with the romanticizing of rural and agrarian life and the anxiety about, as well as the reality of, the forbidding fate of farmers during the depression of that period. The concurrence of these phenomena and events reinforced each other. They also provided not just the context in which the Montgomery parricide occurred but the emotional resources that family, friends, and community drew on when making sense of it, when integrating the distressing events into their understanding of the workings of their world, and when subsequently transforming the story of this pioneer family's downfall into social memory and historical amnesia.

Part 2 of this study examines these matters. Chapter 4 explores the economics of Loyd's triple murder, investigating the relationship between agricultural decline that began as early as 1873, the economic and political fate of many of the personages involved directly in the case or who moved about its periphery, and the very events that transpired at the Templeton-Montgomery home on 19 November 1895. Chapter 5 considers both the broad and explicit meanings and connections between the Montgomery parricide and the death of Oregon's pioneer generation, something that reached its apex in the 1890s, and the creation of both silences and social memory about violence, death, and the Montgomery parricide.

CHAPTER 4

# "The Pinching Economies of Life"

*The Agrarian Crisis and the Murder of Parents*

IN THE YEARS IMMEDIATELY FOLLOWING THEIR INITIAL occupation of Linn County, American farmers there produced little more than at the subsistence level. For example, in 1850, less than four years after arriving on the upper Calapooia River, Hugh Brown's family cultivated a mere 50 acres of land out of the 640 acres they owned. That was actually among the highest number of cultivated acres of farms in the area that year. The Browns, who then numbered eight, produced a "meager" one hundred bushels of wheat for the year. Two years later, resident Thomas Kendall, who lived farther down the Calapooia, wrote to friends back in Indiana about the continued limitations to farming in Linn County, lamenting that "few of our farmers are yet prepared to cultivate the earth in such a way as to ensure the highest results." Instead, he wrote, "our emigrants often hurry in a crop after they arrive, with as little preparation as possible, in order to bread them the following year; others attempt nothing more than to raise a sufficiency for their own use."[1]

But it was also about the time when Kendall penned his description of the lackluster state of affairs that area farmers began producing for wider markets. At first they did so for an increased demand in California and then, in the 1860s, for the growing gold-rush populations in the interior Pacific Northwest. These, in turn, called forth the building of two territorial roads in the Willamette Valley, county-built infrastructure, and the expansion of steamboat travel to the upper Willamette River.[2]

Most of the valley's produce funneled northward through Portland since the Willamette River flowed to that emerging city and then into the Columbia River and out to the Pacific. In 1868, merchants there shipped Oregon-produced wheat for the first time directly to London. Those entrepreneurs likewise acted as intermediaries between Willamette Valley farmers and the growing mining districts in Idaho and western Montana in the 1860s and 1870s, since the best route to the interior was through Portland and then up the Columbia River on steamboats and later by rail.

In 1870 the Oregon and California (O&C), a land-grant railroad, began construction southward from Portland. It reached Albany on 8 December. On that "ponderous day in the history of Albany," the editor of the local *State Rights Democrat* wrote of the event, "the last rail connects us by iron bands with the Metropolis of our State." Ben Holladay, the railway's principal organizer, arrived at 12:30 p.m. on a decorated train carrying some three hundred passengers and dignitaries from Portland, Salem (the state capital), and other towns along the route. Local and county officials, area residents, national banners, and the Albany Brass Band greeted them. Portland's Abigail Scott Duniway, the region's leading suffragist, was on the train as well; she performed the ceremony marking the locomotive's inaugural arrival at the county seat.[3]

Construction extended the O&C another one hundred miles southward by the fall of 1872. The panic of 1873, followed by other shakeups, prevented its completion into California until 1887. By then it had become part of the Southern Pacific Railroad. A separate narrow-gauge line, the Oregonian Railway Company, which bypassed Albany altogether, connected towns on the eastern side of the Willamette Valley directly to Portland in 1880. It reached Brownsville on 28 December of that year.[4] That line became such a competitor with the O&C that the Southern Pacific acquired it, too, and then expanded it into a standard gauge, completing that effort by 1890. Well before then, however, and back in 1883, the Northern Pacific Railway, the first transcontinental railroad that connected the Pacific Northwest to the eastern part of the United States, reached Portland and then terminated in Tacoma.

In time, farmers came to rue what they thought were the railroad's monopolistic rates, but they advocated for the iron horse all along; it allowed for the expansion of their operations. In 1870, Willamette Valley farmers harvested more than 2 million bushels of wheat, with some 20 percent of that coming from Linn County. A decade later, and after direct connections to the East, production climbed to 5,365,117 bushels in the Willamette, with 911,411 of it harvested in Linn County.[5]

Wheat remained the single most important crop in western Oregon through the end of the nineteenth century. Nevertheless, farming families produced a variety for the market, with oats and wool also significant, but fruit, garden produce, potatoes, and dairy likewise significant. In 1879, the farm of Robert and Eveline Montgomery, Loyd's grandparents, produced 816 bushels of wheat, as well as 12 tons of hay, 180 pounds of butter, 500 eggs, 416 bushels of oats, 30 bushels of potatoes, and 50 cords of wood. In that year, in addition to Robert, who was the only one in the family listed as "farmer" in the census, the others in the Montgomery household were his wife Eveline ("keeping house"), a nineteen-year-old daughter ("at home"), a fifteen-year-old son ("at home"), an eleven-year-old son ("at school"), and three other younger children (one of whom was an infant). Save for the infant, all these people, even without recognition from the census, worked for the success of the family. Tasks such as making butter, caring for chickens, and tending gardens were typically wives' and very young children's contributions to farmers' commercial success.[6]

Through the last quarter of the nineteenth century, however, the overall Oregon economy, and across the United States more generally, increasingly shifted to other industries than agriculture. The center of the population also shifted to cities. Oregon's urban population (cities with more than 8,000 residents) grew 224 percent between 1880 and 1890, while rural areas and smaller towns lagged at 63 percent. From 1890 to 1910, the percentage of Oregon's rural population declined from 73 percent to 54 percent of the state's total. Much of the urban growth was concentrated in Portland, which multiplied almost 4.5 times from 1890 to 1910, when its population reached 207,214.[7] The rise of urban commerce and improved transportation allowed for other industries, such as logging, fishing, and mining, to surge in the Pacific Northwest during these years. This meant that the value of agriculture—while it might have increased in absolute terms—declined as a portion of the overall economy. Between 1880 and 1890, Oregon's farms declined from one-half of the state's assessed wealth to only 27 percent. The year 1890 marked the first time when, for the nation as a whole, the total value of manufactured goods eclipsed that of agricultural commodities.[8]

While the agricultural portion of the region's economy contracted and the clout of urban areas grew, still the number of farmers did increase and they continued to expand production.[9] A rising urban and industrial population, better transportation, and growing national and international markets demanded it. At the same time, factory-made consumer goods invaded the countryside, widely available thanks to expanding means of shipping, small-town merchandisers, and mail-order catalogs. Many of the goods rural residents consumed and the crops and livestock they raised clearly show their ties to national and international systems of trade. Advertisements in the *Willamette Farmer* hawked consumer goods and farming equipment and tools from Australia, New Zealand, Ireland, the Ottoman Empire, France, London, San Francisco, Iowa, and Chicago. These ads likewise promoted crops—wheat, oats, hops—and fruit trees that were not indigenous species. Livestock included Essex and Berkshire swine; Cotswold, Leicester, and French and Spanish merino sheep; Jersey cattle; Clydesdale horses; and Italian bees.[10]

Local newspapers encouraged the purchase of these and other goods when advocating for the construction of better homes and farmsteads. News columns and advertisements promoted books, pictures, windows that opened, improved stoves and ovens, dishes and cookery, ready-made clothing, the latest gardens and a variety of flowers, and the newest sorts of farm machinery and gadgets. Even when offering advice to parents for making farm life more interesting to boys and instilling in them a work ethic, the *Willamette Farmer* promoted consumerism and the credit system. For example, it recommended that parents take their boys along on visits to village stores and let them pick out new suits of clothing. Should the cost amount to more than whatever money the boy had, the newspaper instructed parents to provide the lad additional work to earn what he needed to pay them back.[11]

An indication of ever-increasing ties to store-bought goods, the market network, and even the debts these incurred as a result comes from the lives and relations of the Montgomery family. John Montgomery's grandfather Hugh Brown and his mother's cousin James Blakely opened the first mercantile in what became the town of Brownsville in 1850. It was also one of the earliest such establishments south of Oregon City. Blakely's son-in-law, George Cooley, took over in the 1860s, operating the store for years before passing it on to his own son.[12] When Robert Montgomery, John's father, passed away at the end of 1880, he owed Cooley's store $227.60, and even more to other local merchants, for a wide variety of goods, including farm implements, hardware, tools, clothing, hats, shoes and boots, handkerchiefs, cigars and tobacco, a remarkable assortment of fabric and notions, flowers, food, sugar, and spices. It is likewise evident that he had also traded farm produce like bacon and lard and especially the work of his wife and children in the form of butter and eggs to area merchants in partial payment for what he purchased on credit. As far as Robert's estate is concerned, in addition to his considerable acreage and farm tools, animals, and produce on hand, his personal property at his death included an organ, a parlor stove, six beds, bookends and two looking glasses, several chairs, forty-five yards of carpet, a clock, a cooking stove and fixtures, kitchen furniture and dishes, tables, and a brass kettle.[13] Robert's willing, perhaps necessary, participation in the expanding market economy is also evident in that in the early 1870s he lent his name to a testimonial run in a series of newspaper advertisements for firms that promoted flaxseed as a new seasonal cover crop.[14]

Adam Smith, the father of capitalism, had predicted a century before all the above took place that the sorts of trade items and commercial networks listed here would behave as a sort of invisible hand. That is, they would all quietly and mysteriously lead to the lessening of the burdens of life and work and to improvements in the standard of living. And so it was, at least in some ways, in the Willamette Valley. But these trade items and commercial networks also enmeshed agricultural families more deeply in an expanding global market system over which they exercised no control. "Enthusiastically or reluctantly," the rural historian David B. Danbom has written of late nineteenth-century commercial farmers such as the Montgomerys, they "were increasingly vulnerable to forces beyond their control. In particular, they struggled with the three Ms—markets, middlemen, and money."[15] These invisible hands vigorously and viciously pushed and pulled them from 1873 forward. The worst drubbing came in 1893, when the fiercest depression up to that time shook the land. In that year, the nation's railroads went bankrupt, having expanded beyond the demand for them, and Britain ended the coinage of silver in India, which resulted in the closing of innumerable mines in the American West. By 1890 the US government had imposed exceptionally high tariffs to protect domestic manufacturing. This not only increased the costs of foreign imports for farmers but made it more difficult for them to sell their produce in those foreign markets.[16]

A stark visual summary of agriculture's downward spiral through this era appeared in the *Southern Mercury* in 1893 (figure 4.1). The Dallas, Texas, publication's article, entitled "The Farmer and Demonetization," offers two illustrations of the same farmer, one in 1873 prior to the recession that began that year and the other in 1893, at the beginning of the darker depression that shadowed that decade. The sketches frame a table that enumerates the yearly decline in prices for cotton, corn, and wheat on the Chicago market, as well as the plummeting value of silver. From a high of $1.47 a bushel for wheat in 1872, a crop that was the most important to Oregon farmers of those listed in the *Southern Mercury*'s table, prices had tumbled to less than half that twenty-one years later. A once well-fed, prosperous farmer who had a lovely home and farm with productive fields, industrious field hands, and healthy children and farm stock had been rendered a gaunt figure with a rundown property. His hired hands had disappeared, along with most of the flesh of a visibly starving nag. Noticeably absent, too, are the farmer's children, who had probably since left for the city (where his wife was in either of the two views is anyone's guess). Failing to keep up with mortgage or tax payments, moreover, the farmer's property was now up for public auction.

The situation for Oregon farmers was similarly bleak. In the last quarter of the century, the highest price Oregon wheat attained was $1.11 per bushel (1877) and the lowest was $0.43 (1894).[17] This collapse was part of what led Willamette Valley farmers to dedicate fewer acres to wheat. In 1880, Linn County farmers cultivated 75,810 acres of the crop. In 1890 this figure had dropped to 55,374 acres (though the yield had actually increased). The acreage had risen again, to 71,871 in 1900, but then plummeted to only 25,188 in 1910.[18] Another reason for the reduced production in the Willamette Valley was growing competition from the newly opened farming region along the Columbia River in eastern Oregon and in the Palouse of eastern Washington, where climate and soil conditions for wheat were superior to those in western Oregon.

As wheat declined, farmers searched for replacements. One was hops. In Linn County, the Templeton family was instrumental in introducing and nurturing that industry. Their involvement was partly due to their growing relationship to the Pacific Northwest's "Hop King," Ezra Meeker (1830–1928) of the Puyallup Valley in Washington. Although some hop growing had existed in the region prior to the Civil War, the industry really took off in the postwar period, especially when local brewers had difficulty procuring

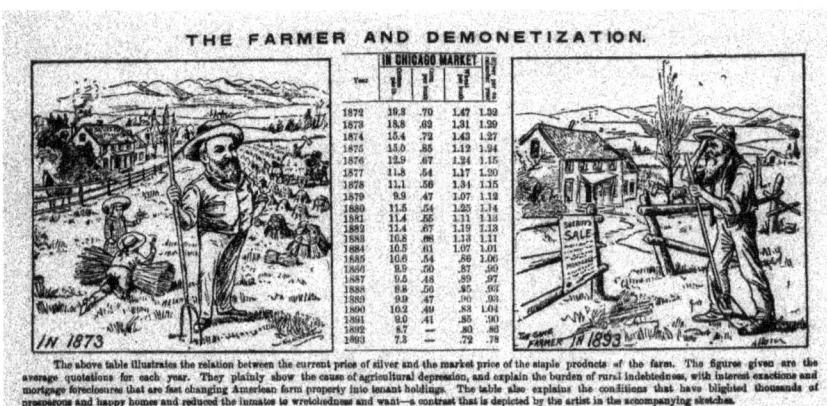

Figure 4.1. The American farmer in 1873 and in 1893. The graphic, which pictures a robust and successful farmer in 1873 and his diminished body and farm twenty years later, captured a certain reality about the general trend for agriculturalists across the nation and in Oregon's Willamette Valley during the last quarter of the nineteenth century. Source: *Southern Mercury* (Dallas, TX), 19 October 1893.

product from eastern and European suppliers. In 1870, Oregon and Washington Territory produced almost sixteen thousand pounds of hops.[19]

Through his energy, drive, and commercial acumen, Meeker, migrant to the Pacific Northwest in 1852, became the central figure in the region's hop industry, in which he was a grower, a promoter, and an agent. William A. Templeton (brother of Samuel) met Meeker's daughter Ella while on a trip to Puget Sound with his brothers sometime in the early 1870s. The two married in June 1872, and soon thereafter, possibly as early as 1874, the Templeton brothers acquired their first roots from Meeker and began cultivating hops on their father's farm along the upper Calapooia River. William and his son Fred, meanwhile, both worked as Meeker's agents in the Willamette Valley.[20]

Although brothers Samuel, John, and James Templeton received a patent for a hop-drying machine that they invented in 1877, the latter two brothers were prepared to give up on the crop just two years later.[21] But Samuel urged otherwise. "The boys have got their hops roots pruned and are going to set the balance of the ground around the Edge of the field," their father wrote to another son that year, and "they would have give it up but Samy Insisted on it and I Dont [sic] know but it was well enough for they have gone through all the expence [sic] and the prospect is better for the Next Crop[.]"[22]

In 1879, the very year when they nearly gave up on hops, the Templeton brothers planted 8 acres. They harvested some 9,025 pounds.[23] The number of acres of farmland devoted to hops in Linn County in 1879 was only 30 and in the Willamette Valley, 302.[24] Thus the Templetons, due to Samuel's efforts, were among the pioneers in that industry. Combined, the various Templeton families produced 23,500 pounds of hops in 1885, which was 15 percent of the county's entire harvest from 32 farms. In 1895, they harvested 54,200 pounds of hops. By then, the number of farms in Linn County producing hops had risen to 103. Combined, they produced 706,581 pounds.[25]

Samuel was also instrumental in securing the Templetons' early labor force. According to family sources, he traveled to the Warm Springs Reservation, east of the Cascades, and approached the leader, Sky tus, with an offer to employ his people. In fact, indigenous people from throughout the western portions of the Pacific Northwest and British Columbia supplied much of the early labor in the region's hop fields (figure 4.2). As early as 1881, Linn County newspapers described the arrival of the Warm Springs people at the Templetons' farms at the beginning of the harvest.[26]

The Templetons had also employed Chinese laborers by the mid-1880s. Because of anti-Chinese sentiment, which was especially strong in Linn County, the family also received disapproval for doing so. When the prices for hops dropped precipitously in 1885, Samuel and his brothers brought in Chinese workers, whom they paid at a lower scale. A critic complained that this wage would "hereafter . . . shut off white labor." Nevertheless, the Templetons persisted and the next year brought in sixty-eight Chinese from Albany to work their fields, which was most of that city's Chinese population at the time. By 1888, however, they seem to have reverted to employing principally "Indian pickers," though a news story noted that the remainder of the Brownsville-area farmers that season "intend to have whites."[27]

The changing economics of the 1890s did appear to alter the complexion of the labor force in Linn County's hopyards, at least for a while. Although it is not clear who the Templetons specifically employed in 1890, the local press explained that in Linn County as a whole neither Chinese nor Indians were present; instead, white pickers gathered the harvest. As the economy deteriorated, the needs of white pickers, who were now willing to work for lower wages, pushed or attempted to push racial minorities out of the hop fields, sometimes through the use of violence. In 1893, for example, white pickers endeavored to drive the Chinese from the fields in Marion County,

Figure 4.2. Hop harvesting in the early Pacific Northwest. Indigenous people from throughout the Pacific Northwest, including British Columbia, supplied much of the labor for Oregon and Washington's early hop industry. The Templeton family employed people from Oregon's Warm Springs Reservation at least as early as 1881. In this illustration, people of the Yakama Reservation in central Washington Territory are shown harvesting hops on the Carpenter farm in 1887. Source: *West Shore* 13, no. 10 (October 1887).

while the hopyards near Lebanon in Linn County employed no Native Americans because "there are too many white people who are anxious to work who need it more than the Indians do." In all of Linn County that year, reportedly no Chinese were employed, and even the few Chinese growers who were there utilized white pickers. Around 1902, when Samuel died, the Templetons leased some of their hopyards to Suey Gee, a Chinese immigrant.[28]

Despite the depression, hop production expanded in the Willamette Valley. In 1900, the total acreage devoted to the crop stood at 14,772.[29] And yet, the 1890s depression had an effect, and on more than racial tensions. Early in the decade, the hop harvest along the Calapooia River was credited with putting much-needed money into circulation; in 1890, hops sold at a price of between $0.325 and $0.36 per pound locally, bringing in $8,755.22 for four Brownsville-area hop farms alone. In October 1893, well after economic depression had enveloped the nation, the merchants in Brownsville breathed a huge sigh of relief when the sale of hops in the vicinity injected "many thousand dollars" into the local economy, leading business to pick up. So hopeful was the mayor of North Brownsville, he even gushed that hop raising was "becoming one of the principal productive elements of the truly pushing and lively town of Brownsville."[30]

Within the year, however, the bottom had fallen out of the hop market. A number of Brownsville-area growers advertised that, "owing to the exceedingly low price of hops," they would be unable to hire pickers because profits seemed unlikely. Instead, they opened their fields to anyone who wanted a job without the promise of wages; the only incentive was that after expenses were paid, whatever returns might be realized from the sale of the harvest would be shared between the owners and the pickers.[31]

The hope that hops had instilled in 1893 was likely a factor motivating John Montgomery in 1894, just before the devastating nose-dive in prices, to seek out Samuel Templeton, the brother to two of his sisters' husbands, to take over sharecropping his thirty-acre hop field. John probably had experience picking hops, since he was landless and was related to the Templetons. Moreover, he would have benefited, if one cares to call it that, from the pressure that white pickers applied on employers to rid the fields of Chinese and Native American workers as the depression of the 1890s advanced. The Montgomery children no doubt had also participated in harvesting. As early as the 1880s, records indicate that schoolchildren from Brownsville lent a hand in local hop picking, which kept them from attending lessons for the few weeks of the September harvest season.[32] We do know with certainty that Loyd picked hops in the fall of 1894.

The portentous decline in the price of hops that year, of which Samuel, given his position in that industry, was no doubt well aware, might have been motivation for him to rent his hopyard to John and his two eldest sons. In addition to providing Samuel with a quarter interest in the harvest at no work to himself, the deal also freed Samuel to hire out as a laborer on nearby farms, thus helping to further secure his own finances while the Montgomerys maintained his farm, which suffered a decline in the value of its produce.[33]

The leasing of Samuel's historic hopyard to John Montgomery had fateful consequences for the struggling farmer. The less-than-favorable financial situation for hops that began in 1894 continued into the next year, when the harvest sold for only seven cents a pound, down from twenty-two to thirty-three cents a pound as recently as 1892, and seventeen cents in 1893. At the end of the 1895 harvest season, a Brownsville grower balanced the varied costs involved in raising and picking hops and, given the current market climate, concluded that it was "a losing business." The added problem for hop growers, unlike for those who might be able to withhold their wheat from the market until prices rose, was that hops quickly lose their potency and thus their value in storage. In 1895, the hop empire of the Templetons' in-law, Ezra Meeker, began teetering under the weight of debt. It collapsed entirely in 1896, taking with it Meeker's once spectacular fortune.[34]

The 1890s depression was especially brutal for farmers in the Willamette Valley during this transition away from wheat and search for other agricultural possibilities. As the price for all crops declined, so too did the value of farms. Between 1892 and 1895, the value of Linn County's taxable real estate shrank by $34,149 (22 percent) at the same time that delinquent taxes had increased from roughly $29,000 to more than $57,400 (a 47 percent increase in the year 1895).[35] For Oregon as a whole, the actual value of all farms declined from more than $11 million in 1891 to just under $4.5 million in 1894.[36] Delinquent tax lists and announcements of sheriff sales routinely appeared in newspapers. A. J. Rader, an observer visiting "old friends" in Linn County in August 1893, wrote to an Albany newspaper that among many of the "once well to do, we find . . . the sure indications that all is not well, and it takes but little inquiry to elicit the fact that the farm does not pay expenses; that from year to year, the bills of expenses are larger and larger and the income smaller and smaller. Rigid economy is required in many instances now, where, only a few years ago, plenty reigned and prosperity was seen on every hand."[37]

The depression of the 1890s was more than the crash of prices, glutted markets, the decline in farm values, and rising rates of unpaid taxes. It also meant a limit to the amount of cash in circulation and the tightening of credit. Across the Pacific Northwest banks failed.[38] Just one example of this and its snowball effect in Albany commenced on 14 January 1893—during the initial days of the worldwide crisis. On that day, the Linn County sheriff ordered the closure, for insolvency, of T. L. Wallace & Company, touted as "The Largest Clothing Dealers in the Valley." This was only days after the store had widely advertised a huge sale at reduced prices. The sheriff's order came in part from the demands of Albany's Linn County National Bank, attaching the merchandiser for $7,000. Other attachments against the store also came forward, but the debt owed to the bank was by far the greatest of these.[39]

The failure of T. L. Wallace undermined the Linn County National Bank itself. It had been established in the spring of 1890; its major shareholder was James L. Cowan, who was also serving as the Albany mayor when the bank opened. Other notable shareholders were William S. Ladd, a prominent politician, businessman, and banker in Portland, and George Chamberlain. Chamberlain, a Democrat, had earlier served in the state legislature from Linn County, had also acted as district attorney, and then in the early 1890s became the state's first attorney general. After the turn of the century, he would be elected Oregon's governor and later a US senator.[40] Chamberlain was also well acquainted with the Montgomery family. When Loyd's grandfather, Robert, passed away at the end of 1880, the court appointed Chamberlain as the guardian *ad litem* for the five minor children of Robert while the disposition of some of the property was in question. Chamberlain also provided information to the press about the Montgomerys in the wake of the parricide.[41]

Back in the late spring of 1893, rumors had spread about the Linn County National Bank's solvency. That, and the worsening economy, led depositors to withdraw heavily on 22 June. A local newspaper, which always painted a cheerier picture about the economy than reality warranted, stopped short of calling this a run on the bank, which it surely was: the next morning, officials placed an alarming notice on the doors. Referring to the "stringency of the money market," the placard explained that the institution would suspend payments and, rather hopefully, "depositors would be paid dollar for dollar." The bank reportedly held about $350,000 in assets, including $170,000 in depositors' accounts and $29,000 in funds from other banks. Linn County itself had $34,000 of its tax funds deposited there. On the other hand, the bank held only about $11,000 in cash reserves. Besides the failure of businesses that owed the bank money, the bank manager reportedly had absconded with $12,000 in May.[42]

As early as 3 July bank officials promised to make payments to depositors soon; a few days later, the institution went into receivership. As of September, depositors still had no access to their funds when newspapers printed new rumors of an imminent payment coming in early October. It also did

Figure 4.3. Red Crown Roller Mill, Albany, Oregon. Many Linn County wheat farmers stored their unprocessed grain at Red Crown and awaited higher prices before authorizing its milling. Financial improprieties by the mill owners, which resulted in a huge loss for area farmers, led to talk of a lynching in Albany in the spring of 1895, during the deepest depths of the era's depression. Courtesy of the Albany Regional Museum, Albany, Oregon.

not materialize, and by November depositors, including the county itself, had become desperate, to put it mildly, as one news source did. In fact, it was not until 27 December when the bank began to pay 35 percent on deposits. Other payments trickled out every few months well into 1895.[43]

Bank failures were perhaps the worst, since they affected such a large swath of the population and brought commerce to a standstill. But other failures affected Linn County farmers more specifically. An example is the Red Crown Roller Mill in Albany, which succumbed in March 1895 (figure 4.3). Area farmers had stored large amounts of wheat there, much like they would their money in a bank, authorizing the mill to grind it into flour when they needed to convert their harvest to cash. The inability of the mill to pay its own debts, however, resulted in officials grinding wheat and selling flour, unbeknown to the farmers, and then using the proceeds to pay their bills, both business and personal. A later examination of the books revealed that at the end of May 1893, a shortage of thirty-five thousand bushels of wheat already existed. Company officials juggled what they had on hand and what continued to arrive for close to two more years, at which point they simply could do so no longer. When the mill should have had up to thirty thousand bushels on hand, farmers found that its bins were empty and their wheat had vanished.44

Both the manager of the mill, J. R. Stockman, and the president, John Isom, went on trial for malfeasance later in the year. The former was convicted and sentenced to a year in the state prison. In the latter's trial, to the consternation of many, the jury could not come to an agreement. This hung jury apparently ended Isom's problems with the law. That was shortly prior to Isom serving on a panel of men who on 31 January 1896, minutes before Loyd's execution, visited the youth in jail and read his death warrant to him.45 Isom's cousin, Thomas "Crock" Isom, a farmer who lived about a quarter mile from the Montgomery-Templeton home and hopyard, heard the shots Loyd fired there on 19 November 1895. He was also one of the first on the scene in the aftermath of the murders. He served as a witness in the case. Also, as it so happened, on Crock's farm on the day of the tragedy Samuel Templeton was earning extra money by plowing fields and sowing a winter crop.46

With the failure of the Red Crown Mill, farmers were left holding the empty bag. Frustrated and angry, they met in Albany on Saturday, 8 April 1895. "It looked for several hours," one newspaper reported, "like a couple of county conventions. Large knots [of farmers] were seen everywhere." Someone had even displayed a caricature of events and their results. In the depiction, farmers carried their wheat to the Red Crown Mill "with their pockets out, while Messrs. Stockman, Isom and Lyon [another mill official] were observed in rich attire, one with a crown on his head, and money bags in hand." Although they conducted themselves in an orderly fashion, some farmers called for a lynching.47

Little wonder that farmers such as these and their families would participate in varied agrarian protest movements of the era, beginning with the Patrons of Husbandry (popularly known as the Grange) in the 1870s, continuing with the Farmers' Alliance in the 1880s, and culminating with the Populists in the 1890s. Manifestations of each of these appeared in the Willamette Valley. Each time, Linn County farmers were among the most active leaders and participants anywhere in Oregon.

The earliest agrarian organizing in Linn County came on 22 June 1871, when a group of farmers met at Shedds Station (later simply Shedd), located on the O&C line south of Albany. They formed the Linn County Farmers Union. The union was less involved in politics than it was in the construction of a warehouse where farmers could store their wheat and await the highest market price paid in the county.[48] Within a year, however, truly activist farmers' clubs had formed in the Willamette Valley, protesting middlemen and transportation rates on the Columbia and Willamette Rivers and calling for the construction of more cooperative warehouses. From a general meeting of such clubs that took place in April 1873, the Grange movement emerged in Oregon, some half dozen years after the Patrons of Husbandry had first appeared in the eastern part of the United States. The number of Granges quickly swelled. By July of that year, ten had formed in Linn County—half the total in Oregon—with the Brownsville Grange, the nineteenth formed in Oregon, among the most recent. A year later, the Brownsville Grange had more than sixty members, both male and female. In 1876, a newspaper article described it as "one of the most earnest and harmonious families in our State." Its "sisters" and "brothers" held regular meetings, which included socializing over community-sponsored meals.[49]

The Oregon State Grange formally organized on 24 September 1873 in Salem. Although the call for the meeting had gone out to the existing Granges in August, the gathering actually took place within days of the stock market's collapse and the failure of the Northern Pacific Railway, which took with it the Jay Cooke investment bank. This began a depression that lasted several years. Two of the three uppermost officials chosen to lead the Oregon State Grange, the overseer and the secretary, came from Linn County.[50] While it remained nonpartisan in principle, the Oregon Grange was in fact political. It called for federal appropriations for river improvements, a cooperative system of trade, buying and selling in bulk, the adoption of the credit system, the establishment of Grange stores, lobbying efforts to reduce shipping rates, and the patronizing of "home mechanics in preference to foreign."[51]

Soon, area Granges built a number of cooperative warehouses, gristmills, and stores throughout the Willamette Valley, with examples of each of these in Linn County. They also created a short-lived steamboat service on the Willamette River. All the cooperative measures had pretty much foundered by the end of the decade, however.[52] Likewise, Grange membership rose and fell over the years, increasing dramatically at times of renewed economic decline. Nevertheless, the organization persisted, participating in politics with calls for tax restructuring, state regulation of railway rates, direct election of US senators, and direct election of the president.[53]

Economic downturn in the mid-1880s also invigorated the Farmers' Alliance. Northern and southern branches formed in those regions of the nation in the 1870s. As early as 1887 they had a presence in Oregon but did not fully formally organize in the state until 1890 and 1891, when a stream of lecturers arrived from the plains states.[54] When Farmers' Alliance representatives appeared, historian Margaret Kolb Holden has written, they discovered that Oregon farmers "shared many of the same concerns and needs as agrarians in the South and Midwest. High taxes, onerous freight rates, a lack of circulating money, usurious lending rates, and declining prices contributed to the precarious position of Oregon farmers. Four years before the depression of 1893, Oregonians felt the pressure of economic decline." In some ways building on the Grange, in other ways departing from it, Holden explains, the Farmers' Alliance "energized Oregon farmers towards political insurgency."[55]

The following spring, mounting dissatisfaction with both the Republican and Democratic Parties' seeming unresponsiveness to farmers' deepening distress led the Farmers' Alliance, along with other progressive reformers, to found a branch of the People's or Populist Party in Oregon. It espoused many of the interests of the Grange, including reducing freight rates and curbing the power of the railroads, federal funding for improving river transportation, and tax reform. It was also virulently anti-Chinese, instead promoting "native" labor.[56]

The Grange, the Farmers' Alliance, and the People's Party in Oregon were forward-looking when they embraced markets and modern means of transportation and, notably, advocated for government intervention to achieve such goals. The last of these measures in particular, but the others in some ways, too, were decidedly contrary to the ideals and myths of the republican landscape, which advocated self-sufficient farming to ensure the population's independence and to disperse power across the countryside. On the other hand, these farmers' organizations were backward-looking in the sense that they most wanted to preserve the agrarian way of life and small-property holding.[57] Their racial views and exclusionary programs also marked them as heirs of American republicanism.

Given that agriculture was the mainstay of Linn County, it is not surprising that the county had become one of the hotbeds of Populist appeal and activity in Oregon by 1892. Linn County had long been a bastion of the Democratic Party, in part due to the area's agrarian economy. Moreover, many of its residents, like other ruralites in the state, came directly from or had ancestral roots in the South and the Middle Border; they remained sympathetic to that region of the country and many of its social causes. A manifestation of their presence and influence was enshrined in Oregon's constitution back in 1859. In approving the constitution, Oregonians voted 7,727 to 2,645 to reject slavery but 8,640 to 1,081 to approve a clause to exclude free Black persons from the state. During the constitutional convention, delegates also discussed the possibility of excluding Chinese, Hawaiian, and even indigenous people. In time, the legislature adopted a variety of fines and punishments levied against Black people who did continue to reside in Oregon or who attempted to enter it, but these were rarely enforced. Likewise, other early laws against African Americans and other racial minorities included levying poll taxes, barring intermarriage, and proscribing the ownership of land.[58]

The Montgomerys had strong southern roots. Robert Montgomery had been born in Missouri in 1827. His father, John, and mother, Ellen, who also came to Linn County, had been born in Kentucky and Tennessee. Robert's uncle William, whom Robert and his parents lived next to in Missouri at the time of Robert's birth, enslaved people there. Robert's sister Sarah married James McHargue in Missouri. The two also settled on the upper Calapooia River in 1847. James McHargue's brother William, who was already also a friend of Robert's in Missouri, came to Linn County a few years later. Before doing so, he sold the people he had enslaved (a forty-five-year-old man, a nineteen-year-old woman, a twelve-year-old girl, and a three-month-old boy in 1850) in 1853 for a "high and quick sale."[59] Robert's wife, Eveline Brown, had been born in Tennessee, as were both her parents. Hugh Brown, Eveline's father, served in Oregon's legislatures as a staunch Democrat; he also worked in Brownsville-area politics in 1856 to outmaneuver both local Know Nothings and "Black Republicans." And Elizabeth (Couey) Montgomery's father originally hailed from Georgia. He had received a Donation Land Claim Act grant, though in Lane County.[60]

While the Democratic Party had historically garnered significant support in Linn County, many of the farmers who counted themselves members had become disillusioned with it by the 1890s and joined the new People's Party in large numbers. There were other strong local manifestations of this sentiment. In 1893, John Dean, a longtime editor in Oregon, founded the *Oregon Populist* newspaper in Albany. Another Populist newspaper, the *Oregon Silver Imprint*, also appeared at this time in that city, as did the *People's Press*, a socialist mouthpiece.[61]

The historian Margaret Kolb Holden has declared that 1892 was the high-water mark for the Populist movement in the state. In that year, the Populist Party candidate for US president, James B. Weaver, came within 149 votes of carrying the state, which Republican Benjamin Harrison managed to do with a plurality. The Democrat and incumbent Grover Cleveland trailed distantly. That Weaver captured a majority of votes in Linn County is evidence of Populist strength there. Cleveland had won Linn County in 1888, though by a slim margin.[62] The economic situation must have been perilous in order to draw so many voters in Linn County away from the old Democratic standard.

In fact, Populist popularity did not seem likely to abate in Linn County anytime soon. In addition to the newspaper *Oregon Populist* appearing in Albany in 1893, reformers that summer held a two-day rally in Brownsville. It provided the impetus for the creation of the Linn County People's Party. One of the principal speakers was the Oregon Populist Party chairman from Oregon City, William S. U'Ren. An advocate for a variety of progressive reforms, including most notably the single tax, U'Ren spoke at the gathering on his favorite cause—the initiative and referendum, which he saw as a tool for realizing the single tax. Those gathered at the rally pledged to carry Linn County in the state and local elections scheduled for the next spring.[63] Within days of the rally, a news correspondent from Crawfordsville wrote effusively of the silver issue.[64] A few months later, on 9 March 1894, Linn's Populists held their first county-level nominating convention. Some 144 delegates gathered in Albany. North Brownsville, South Brownsville, Crawfordsville, and nearby Brush Creek precincts sent a total of eighteen representatives.[65]

The spring election that year proved especially exciting in Linn County. Candidates from the three major parties fanned out across the county between mid-May and early June, canvassing for their causes. On Election Day, 6 June, significantly more voters turned out to cast ballots than at any time in the past, both locally and in the state. Portland's *Oregonian* explained of the Populist showing in Linn County that it was "stronger than expected." In fact, for a time it appeared that the Populists would capture one of the county's seats in the lower chamber of the state legislature, but the Democratic and Prohibition candidates drew votes away in the final tally. As a result of the split across the races, Republicans enjoyed major victories both in Linn and across much of Oregon. The total Populist vote cast that June in Linn County amounted to approximately fifteen hundred, while the Democratic vote stood at fourteen hundred and the Prohibitionists at one hundred, but the Republicans captured eighteen hundred. In a number of precincts, the Populists did well, even outpolling the combined Republican and Democratic vote in a few cases. In Brownsville and Crawfordsville, however, they did less well. Even the local candidate for county treasurer, Jode Pearl, who would serve on the first coroner's jury in the Montgomery murder case just a year later, lost the two Brownsville precincts and the one Crawfordsville precinct by considerable margins.[66]

Given Linn County's past voting record, it was a major surprise that the 1894 election flipped its entire state legislative delegation—two representatives and two senators—Republican. One of the representatives was William Templeton, from Brownsville, husband to Ella Meeker, in-law to two of John Montgomery's sisters, and brother to Samuel. The Templetons, unlike the Browns and Montgomerys, had long been Republicans.[67] The sensation of Linn County sending Republicans to Salem in 1894 is indicated by the party affiliations of those it had elected over the course of the twelve previous legislative cycles (one of them a special session), which dated back to 1872. Of the fifty-eight representatives elected over those years, fifty were Democrats and only two were Republicans. The others were independents. Of the thirty-one state senators elected, twenty-eight had been Democrats, two were Republicans, and one was an independent.[68]

The Linn County Populists elected their first representative to Salem in 1896, in the same year when more Populists (thirteen) went to the Oregon House chamber than at any time. But that was the same year when Oregon Populists, like their national counterparts, factionalized over fusion with the Democrats. Linn County did go that year for William Jennings Bryan, though the state did not, and the splintering had a devastating effect. The last Linn County Populist convention occurred in 1900, the same year in which the county sent its last Populist legislator to Salem.[69]

Like so many others in his family, John Montgomery, Loyd's father, had been a member of the Democratic Party. In 1886, he was unanimously elected as "teller" (a vote counter) for the party's primary held in Brownsville. I did not find evidence that he moved into the Populist Party. It may be, however, that the "pinching economies of life" that some newspapers at first surmised had led Loyd to "nurse a grievance" against his "plodding, hard-worked parents" did push John in that direction, as it had so many of the area farmers.[70] But it is clear that financial constraints made it impossible for him at the time to pay his poll tax in the early 1890s. Thus, during these years, he was unable to directly participate in elections.

What we do know about John is that hard times drove him to the doorstep of Samuel Templeton in 1894.[71] He had struggled for years as a farmer, despite the advantages he might have otherwise enjoyed as a result of his family connections; in the wake of the Montgomery parricide a newspaper described the Templeton family as "people of the best standing in this community, of acknowledged moral worth, and financially well-to-do."[72] A nephew of Samuel explained at the same time that John "did not seem able to make much of a success" of farming, "never getting more than a living out of it. He moved from one farm to another."[73] According to land records, in fact, John appears never to have actually owned real property in Linn County, something confirmed in local and federal agricultural censuses for 1880, 1885, and 1895.

In addition to marking their poverty, the above details hint specifically at what might have been perceived at the time as John's impaired manliness, something that played a profound role in the ultimate outcome of his and his wife's lives. The glorification of the republican farmer that so pervaded official agrarian rhetoric during that time trumpeted a manhood based on a man's ability to support and provide for his family.[74] For male farmers, the ownership of real property was obviously key. But John never owned land. Additionally, and after his murder, his relation and the sheriff of Linn County, James McFeron, described John as "an excellent man, who did everything in his power to provide well for his family."[75] That McFeron felt compelled to make such a statement, however supportive of John it was, indicates that questions in fact did exist about his ability to do just that. In fact, already by 1895 he was unable to put bread on his family's table. Instead, John borrowed on credit from Daniel McKercher, proprietor of the old Finley gristmill.[76]

Not being a landowner, John instead rented farms or worked as a hired hand or sharecropped, all of which placed him on the lowest rungs of the agricultural status ladder. In 1879, two years following the birth of Loyd, John might have worked as a hired laborer on the farm of his own father, Robert, who did pay $250 in wages and board to hired labor for twenty-seven weeks that year.[77] From 1880 to 1900, farmers on roughly one-fourth of the farms in Linn County either rented for cash or sharecropped. The rate of renting in Linn County was consistently higher than in the Willamette Valley as a whole, which ranged from 17 percent to 21 percent of farms. And although the figures fluctuated, in fact in the 1890s the figure in Linn County rose from 23 percent to 26 percent of farms being rented.[78]

John's inability to secure land was likely due in part to his limitations as a farmer and lack of business acumen. It was obviously also due to the enormous economic problems that all farmers confronted during that era. It was also partly a result of larger structural issues related to landownership in the Willamette Valley that dated to Oregon's founding. The historian Cynthia Culver Prescott has explained in her study of the region's men and women that second-generation males born in the 1850s, like John, found it difficult to obtain land because their fathers had claimed the best of it through the generosity of the DLCA and were reluctant to relinquish control of it to their sons.[79] Such reticence of fathers to transfer land to sons had happened elsewhere and at other times in American history, typically with the intention of the former of maintaining authority over the latter. In those places, such actions on the part of fathers increased intergenerational tensions.[80] Issues related to inheritance, in fact, were a prime cause of parricide in nineteenth-century America.[81]

John was the eldest of the eleven children born to Robert and Eveline. When Robert died on 31 December 1880, he had no will. His probate records do not indicate that John received any land from the estate. Perhaps Robert, while living, had provided John an inheritance or payout when John married and set out on his own some years before. Eveline and her five minor children at the time of Robert's passing, on the other hand, held on to most of the estate.[82]

Also awkward for John was that when he rented the hopyard from Samuel, he did so in a way that increased his own dependence on two of his minor male children—Loyd and Orville. Each of these boys, like their father, received a one-quarter interest in the crop. Samuel received the other quarter, which was the rent owed to him. Part of the deal, furthermore, was that Elizabeth, in addition to caring for her own family, contributed her labor by keeping house for Samuel.[83]

John's dependence on his two sons reversed the situation in the Willamette Valley for many a second-generation farmer like him. More commonly they remained reliant on their own fathers, delaying marriage and living at home, where they worked as landless laborers until receiving their inheritance or until they had saved enough capital to venture out on their own. Alternatively, they joined the exodus to the city or migrated over the Cascades to the more open regions of the arid or semiarid interior portion of the Pacific Northwest.[84] Many of John's cousins and brothers did just that. John, however, stuck it out, for whatever reasons. In doing so, he came to own no land that he might use to leverage control over his sons. That he had been further reduced to sharing equally in the proceeds from sharecropping with his minor sons by 1894 only further undercut his fatherly authority, independence, and consequent ability to direct his boys. His dependence on his sons also appears to have led him to do whatever he could to keep at home a willful boy who apparently suffered emotional problems. That, of course, was only one of John's fateful decisions, though a decision that free will had little to do with.

Tax records for the 1890s plot John's decline. In 1890, his only wealth was nine horses, valued at $500. His only assessment that year was a poll tax, which went unpaid. In 1893, John held $20 in "merchandise and implements," $65 in "household furniture, carriages, watches, jewelry, etc.," two horses, one cow, and three pigs. Tax appraisers valued his estate at $145. He paid $1 in taxes. In 1894, John's personal property had declined to $115 in value, and his $1 poll tax again went unpaid. In the year of his death, John's estate had dwindled to $55, and he was listed as owning no farm animals.[85]

John's downward spiral is placed in greater relief when compared to how his mother and his two Templeton sisters fared through these otherwise lean years. Eveline Montgomery saw her estate decline in value by about $2,000 between 1892 and 1895, but in the latter year she still held 268 acres of land, valued at $2,570, and farm animals and personal property valued at $310. The estate of John's sister Sarah and her husband, Albert Templeton, dropped from $6,270 in 1893 to $5,010 in 1895, but in that latter year they still held 439 acres, valued at $4,590. John's sister Orpha and her husband,

Robert Templeton, actually saw their estate increase in value. From $5,768 in 1892, it grew to $6,920 in 1895. In the latter year, Robert's property included 40 acres valued at $800, farm implements valued at $30, personal property valued at $40, and $120 in farm animals. He held another $4,250 in accounts and notes. Orpha, in her own name, owned an additional 180 acres of land plus two lots in the town of North Brownsville, all valued at $1,680.[86] The 1927 publication *History of the Willamette Valley, Oregon*, described Robert, who yet lived, as "a man of many sterling qualities.... He has at all times commanded the confidence and respect of his fellowmen and is regarded as one of the solid and substantial citizens of Linn county."[87] Granted, Robert likely paid for the *History of the Willamette Valley* to carry his biography, the writer of which resorted to a cache of ready-made expressions to glorify the volume's patrons. But that Robert, whatever his qualities actually were, could afford luxuries such as this, was another indication of how he was set apart from men like his brother-in-law John. Truly, the Templetons' reputations and success cast a long shadow over others in that region of the Willamette Valley, something that likely only dimmed John's view of his own prospects.

Perhaps also challenging for John was that the lands on which his mother and sisters lived in 1895 were contiguous to or near that on which he resided. The proximity to these relations no doubt provided Elizabeth additional emotional support and resources to draw on during the dark years of 1894 and 1895, as she did on the day of her death, when her female in-laws helped her in the garden. For John, the proximity of a successful mother and the even more successful marriages of his sisters must have weighed heavily.

Furthermore, when John and Elizabeth fell on the beneficence of their relations, they actually did so on the least successful of the Templetons. In 1895, Samuel held ninety-four acres valued at $970, and the remainder of his estate carried a tax-assessed value of $130.[88] Samuel remained single, and while he had been principally responsible for promoting the Templeton family's association with the hop industry, during much of his life he was committed instead to prospecting, usually unsuccessfully. While his mining expedition up the Calapooia canyon with his brothers Albert and Robert and their in-law John Montgomery in 1890 manifested newsworthy hopefulness, in actuality his prospecting activities across the West and Alaska, according to a niece, resulted in Sam "mostly coming home broke."[89]

The relatively little time that Samuel invested in farming as compared to his usually fruitless mining expeditions, and possibly his choice not to marry and have children, contributed to the relatively lower value of his farm and home, when compared to what his brothers and their families had. His house of "unpretentious style, unpainted and plainly finished, one and a half story in height, blackened by exposure to the elements, being devoid of paint," contrasted sharply with the homes of the other Templeton brothers and their families, such as that of James Templeton, pictured in the 1878 *Illustrated Historical Atlas* (figure 4.4).[90] James was one of the Templeton boys who had patented the hop dryer.

Much was collapsing in on John and Elizabeth Montgomery in the 1890s. The political party they had long supported was foundering. John was unable to pay his poll tax on occasion, rendering him unable even to participate in elections from time to time. In addition to facing a depression of enormous dimensions that raged across the countryside, the Montgomerys' personal wealth had diminished to an all-time low. And yet also surrounding them were family members whose fortunes and prosperity were impressive, some even gaining wealth during the worst of the depression years. Some of these relations had also enjoyed elevation into significant political office while representing a party long opposed to the one John had supported. John and Elizabeth, furthermore, had become dependent on the beneficence of that extended family, albeit on one of the least successful among them, for a home blackened by the elements and an income undermined by declining crop prices. John had hardly lived up to the republican farmer ideal—the yeoman who succeeded in his endeavors, who became an independent agrarian on his own property and on his own merits, and who properly supported his own dependents. In fact, John was himself dependent on a shirttail relative for a roof over his family's head, on a nearby businessman for food on his family's table, and on two of his minor sons to do much of the labor to pay his rent and support his family.

Moreover, by all reports, one of those sons was a lad who had problems; had suffered and witnessed trauma and violence and illness and seizures; had experienced crushing poverty, gloomy spells, and struggles in school; had stolen and run away; had moved from farm to farm but continued to labor intensely wherever his family took him; had gambled on and threatened his parents' lives; and had been expected to live up to illusory expectations that even his father had been unable to fulfill. No doubt

FARM & RESIDENCE OF JAMES R. TEMPLETON, 2 MILES EAST OF HALSEY, LINN COUNTY, OREGON.

Figure 4.4. James Templeton's home and farm, 1878. Captured in this Junius Whiting lithograph from 1878, the house and farm pictured here depict the wealth and status of most of the Templeton brothers and contrast sharply with the home and farm of the less successful Samuel Templeton, where John and Elizabeth (Couey) Montgomery lived and met their end at the hands of their son on 19 November 1895. Source: *Illustrated Historical Atlas Map of Marion and Linn Counties, Oregon* (San Francisco: Edgar Williams, 1878).

he also saw only more want, darkness, and unyielding challenge when and if he looked into his future.

On 18 and 19 November 1895 all came undone for John and Elizabeth when the pinching economies of their lives directly contributed to their tragic demise. Loyd simply left the one day to go hunting without notice and without permission. Perhaps he no longer felt the need to ask his parents, given all the above. When he reappeared on the afternoon of the nineteenth, he first asked his female relatives assembled at this home for something to eat, which they provided, though it was not the regular mealtime. Afterward, he began mixing with the men coming and going in the front yard. Besides his father, the first of these was Edgar Gilkey, the hop buyer who delivered the crushing news about the rock-bottom prices for that year's harvest. As Gilkey departed, Daniel McKercher rode up; he hoped that John might pay part of his debt for the flour that he had been supplying that impoverished family. Loyd even later recounted that he had heard McKercher ask his father "how he was fixed for money; that he would like to get a few dollars father owed him." In fact, the debt McKercher carried for the Montgomerys, and no doubt some others in the vicinity, is likely what had led the miller earlier that very day to borrow twenty-two dollars from the Brownsville bank to cover some of his own mounting obligations.[91]

It seems probable at that very moment that John's past failures, his mounting bills and deepening poverty, his dimming hopes, and his inability to control his eighteen-year-old son, on whom he also depended for a living, brought him to the breaking point. With the prodigal youth nearby, John snapped. "Father commenced getting after me for going away from home and neglecting my work," Loyd explained in his first confession to the crime. Only exacerbating matters, McKercher, who likely felt some authority in the situation, given that he was a man and Loyd yet a boy and also that he had been at least partly responsible for feeding the Montgomery family, "sided in with father while we were quarreling."[92] Perhaps the backing that John felt from McKercher led him to go one step beyond what he otherwise might have, this time pressing both manly and fatherly prerogatives that he really no longer maintained. That is, just a few days later, Sheriff James McFeron, who had known the Montgomerys for years, asserted that for some time John had not used physical force when correcting Loyd for his various misdeeds. In fact, McFeron made the remarkable statement, referring to corporeal matters, that "Mr. Montgomery was afraid of the boy, who was much the better man of the two physically." But on 19 November, likely emboldened in the presence of another man who sided with him—or perhaps embarrassed by his misfortune and his uncontrollable son in the face of a debt collector and neighbor—John lashed out.[93]

"Then he slapped me in the face," Loyd explained, "and told me to go and cut some wood."[94] Loyd was not exactly a boy anymore, for reasons previously outlined. The comments that McFeron made about Loyd's physicality put meat on such a conclusion and suggest Loyd's sense of his own manhood. It may therefore be that Loyd thought his own emerging manhood was threatened, not just by his father's blow but by his father ordering him about as though he were a boy and doing so in front of another man of the community.

The criminologist Phillip Chong Ho Shon has analyzed more than two hundred parricides that took place in the United States between 1851 and 1899, gathering information from news items about them in the *New York Times* and the *Chicago Tribune*. Shon determined that fully one-third of these parricides grew from "arguments of a trivial nature" between parents and their murderous children. Among these trivial disagreements were assaults on male children's "sense of masculinity, honor, and face." Another "trivial" matter concerned money.[95]

Matters related to money were central to the problems the Montgomery family faced. So, too, was the issue of manliness. The *New York Times* in fact did report on the Montgomery murder. It merely noted that Loyd "was not on the best of terms with his father, and that the motive for the murder was revenge."[96] This item mentions neither an assault on Loyd's masculinity nor matters of finance, but that terse description might have landed this parricide in a category that Shon would have assessed as trivial in nature. By now it should be clear that the causes of the quarrel between Loyd and John that boiled over into murder in the late afternoon of 19 November 1895 were neither "trivial" nor "frivolous," another term Shon has employed.[97] Rather, it was the scalding climax to developments in that family, the local community, and broader agrarian society that had been simmering from at least the early 1870s onward.

Whatever they might have been in Loyd's mind, his father's actions were something that he said "made me so angry that I did not know what I was doing." In this moment of uncontrolled passion, "I went into the house and got father's rifle."[98] Although he clearly intended to kill his father, Loyd would also kill two others. Criminologists explain that "assaults carry a momentum of their own, enticing the aggressor into" yet more killing.[99] As such, the collateral murders of a local businessman and a mother who just happened to be on the scene are likely best explained in this way. With that said, McKercher's interference in Montgomery family matters may have also contributed to Loyd's deadly course.

The depression of the 1890s ended for John and Elizabeth Montgomery at roughly 4:15 p.m. on 19 November 1895 at the hands of their own son and at the end of John's own rifle. Perhaps because their personal estate had declined so, there was nothing left to probate in the wake of their demise—no record of such exists. John and Elizabeth of course left five children and many other immediate and extended family members who carried on. For some, their amount of time on this earth, scorched by economic ruin, was longer than for others. The depression for the remainder of the community and the nation finally abated in about 1897, but by then many of the dreams of American farmers turned Populists had collapsed.

At the precise moment when the rural economy had started to turn downward in 1873, and then over the next two and even more decades as the uncertain future advanced, another phenomenon of immense proportions marched across the Oregon landscape: the death of its original, American pioneer settlers—the parents and grandparents of people like John, Elizabeth, and Loyd, the generation that had brought so much hope with it as its members themselves had marched toward the Oregon Country in the 1840s and 1850s. As the pioneers dropped in larger and larger numbers like the autumn leaves, their past hardships, experiences, and fortitude took on a deeper cultural resonance for those who carried on in that era of privation, desperation, and nostalgia.

Among the events of the pioneer past that especially infatuated survivors were, of all things, episodes of violence and killing. Certainly the eroding economy as much as the bad-boy problem contributed to the downfall of John and Elizabeth Montgomery. That all this happened in a culture preoccupied with death and killing and the celebration of such gruesome matters seems hardly surprising.

CHAPTER 5

# "His People Being Pioneers"

*Parricide in an Age of Death and an Era That Celebrated Killing*

**AT 9:30 ON THE MORNING OF 20 JUNE 1895, ALMOST FIVE** months to the day before the Montgomery-McKercher murders, the eight-year-old Linn County Pioneer Association (LCPA) convened in Brownsville for the second day of its annual reunion. The membership of the organization was drawn from migrants who had arrived in Oregon prior to 1 January 1855 and who still resided in Linn County. The events that morning included the yearly roll call of those who had passed away since the previous year's gathering. The three-person Committee on Death read a tribute as part of the occasion:

> Pioneers of Linn County we have been Permitted to meet again and receive Happy Greeting. But amidst our glad Hand Shakes and cordial greetings there is a sadness and Heartache when we recall so many familiar Faces whom we were wont to see in our annual reunions. Who Have answered the Roll Call of the Death Angel and Have gone to their Eternal Home. Death has made sad Inroads Among our Sturdy Pioneers. Many who were with us the Past two and one year ago will meet with us no more on Earth. We are fast Passing Away. A few more years and the last Pioneer Shall have gone to his final reward.

At the homage's conclusion, the committee submitted the names of a dozen recently departed.[1]

Although the cause and mood of the annual reunion of the pioneers was celebratory and forever cheerful, the yearly roll call of an ever-increasing number of the dead always provided a moment of solemnity. After all, an event that sought to bring together and applaud an older and inexorably aging generation necessarily had to contend with the demise of yet more and more of the very people being reunited and feted. The survivors, moreover, were always reminded (if need be) by the grimly named Committee on Death itself, that their number would soon be up as well. "A few more years and the last Pioneer Shall have gone to his final reward" was a constant refrain during the otherwise happy festivities.

Through the last third of the nineteenth century, many Americans were busily engaged in what the historian Drew Gilpin Faust has called the "work of death." The work that she described emanated from the massive and gruesome human toll that was the Civil War. It included a fixation on mortality, alterations in the meaning of death, crises of belief, the shattering of intellectual life, the development of the notion that death could be a patriotic endeavor, the recovery and identification of those missing in action, and enormous memorializing efforts that, at least initially, focused on simply remembering those who had fallen.[2]

Where other parts of the nation in the last years of the nineteenth century fixated on death that was the memory of civil war, in Oregon, which had been somewhat removed from the bloody battlefields of that national epic, a different atmosphere of death settled thickly over the landscape.[3] The expiration of the venerated pioneers generated the ether, but other events intensified the air of decay. One was the demise of a hallowed rural way of life, believed to have stretched back to the nation's founding and that the pioneers had triumphally brought with them to early Oregon. The other was the last sputtering gasps of the agrarians' political hopes in the flailing People's Party. These and what they meant for this civilization contributed to the fixation on the pioneers and the meaning of their momentous passing—embellishing, memorializing, and romanticizing their persons and their past deeds.

Some of the Oregon pioneers' past deeds most venerated and most applauded in memorializing efforts were heroic martyrdom at the hands of "Indians" and their own brutal removal and killing of indigenous people.

As substitutes for participating in the Civil War, the region's "Indian wars," both the large-scale endeavors and the more personal acts of violence, provided a means to share in the myth and reality of building and expanding the nation-state, each of which, Faust has argued, came out of the death that was the Civil War.

Recalled and cheered, commemorated and honored, transformed and sanitized, violence, dying, and slaughter suffused the atmosphere in which Loyd Montgomery committed his own murders—murders not just of his parents but of two people who were the children and grandchildren of some of the most respected pioneer families of Oregon. This chapter investigates the culture of death, violence, and killing in turn-of-the-century Oregon, explores how it aligned with, in the most curious of ways, the Montgomery parricide, and examines how locals silenced and remembered that parricide alongside other murderous, even genocidal aspects of their collective past.

Official organizations dedicated to the pioneers in Oregon commenced their existence in October 1873, thus coinciding with the financial panic that triggered depression across North America and Europe. At that moment, a group of still comparatively youthful pioneers met at a place called Champoeg, in the northern Willamette Valley. The choice of this site was especially symbolic. It was there in the early 1840s, before the region had become part of any formal empire, that the first nonindigenous Oregonians—the earliest American arrivals, some mountain men among them, as well as men retired from the Hudson's Bay Company—created self-government. For years, Oregonians pridefully recalled it as "the first American civil government west of the Rocky Mountains."[4]

When pioneers convened at Champoeg in 1873, they formally organized the Oregon Pioneer Association (OPA) (figure 5.1). Its initial membership numbered 145. At its commencement, the OPA opened its ranks to people who had settled in the Oregon Territory prior to January 1853 (when the US government separated a new Washington Territory from Oregon). As more and more stalwarts passed away and its ranks thinned, the OPA changed the criteria for "pioneers." It first extended the cutoff date for inclusion to those who had arrived by 1855 (the same year the Donation Land Claim Act concluded), and then later still, to 1859 (the year when Oregon transitioned to statehood). By definition, a membership thus constrained ensured that the organization itself would in time wither and perish. But before that day, the

Figure 5.1. Oregon Pioneer Association, 1887. Oregon "pioneers" founded many memorial organizations in the last quarter of the nineteenth century. The largest was the Oregon Pioneer Association, a statewide group that originated in 1873. It held annual parades and gatherings for years, until diminishing numbers of qualified members led their survivors to form successor organizations—Sons of the Oregon Pioneers and Daughters of the Oregon Pioneers—in the early twentieth century. Courtesy of the Oregon Historical Society Research Library, Portland. Negative number 35248.

OPA established an annual reunion that within a couple of years would always meet in Portland in mid-June. The event became more elaborate over time, with parades, banquets, dances, and speeches being added here and there. The OPA published its proceedings, addresses, recollections, biographies, and histories in its *Transactions*, thus creating an important record of pioneer memory and early Oregon history.[5]

By the 1890s, the OPA's longtime secretary, George H. Himes (whose own family traveled the overland trails in 1853 to Puget Sound), was furnishing Portland's *Oregonian* newspaper with an annual list of Oregon pioneers who had passed. Himes even tracked the lives and deaths of those who had moved on to other territories and states after having helped found Oregon.

By the end of 1895, Himes estimated that only about two thousand such pioneers still lived. When the list for 1896 reported the passing of several hundred more, the *Oregonian* stated frankly that "with each successive year, the little band of pioneers grows smaller, and soon will be recorded 'Finis.'"[6]

Other groups and organizations with the goals of recording Oregon's early history and commemorating its dying pioneers also appeared in the 1890s. The Oregon Historical Society (OHS) incorporated in 1898, with Himes as one of its most active early supporters and curators.[7] The Oregon Native Sons and the related Oregon Native Daughters formed in 1899. Less exclusionary than the OPA, the groups opened their memberships to those who did not necessarily have pioneer heritage, so long as they had an interest in Oregon's pioneer history. However, they still had to have been born in Oregon and, importantly, had to be white.[8]

Both the Native Sons and Daughters eventually had a number of chapters, or "cabins" as they rustically termed them, throughout the state. Members studied Oregon history, collected various relics from the past, laid plans for special pioneer exhibitions, and invited old-timers to their gatherings to share stories of pioneer days (figure 5.2).[9] All cabins bore the names of significant Oregon pioneers. On 9 June 1899 interested Brownsville men instituted a local cabin of the Native Sons that they christened in honor of James Blakely, one of the two cofounders of Brownsville and a man related to Loyd Montgomery. The first president of the Blakely cabin was Albert Templeton, Loyd's uncle. The list of the cabin's original officials read like a virtual who's who of officers and members—past, present, and soon to be—of the LCPA. It also included many who were or had been deeply involved in Linn County politics and were from different political parties.[10] Despite some stark partisan differences among its members, they nevertheless worked in fraternal communion since their shared cause was celebrating the local, pioneer past. Besides, the Native Sons expressly forbade political and religious discussions in meetings due to their divisive nature.[11]

Working in concert with both the OPA and the OHS, the Native Sons early on created the office of "Grand Librarian," whose holder had the responsibility of collecting "any and all materials . . . showing the difficulties, the labors and the triumphs of the pioneers in founding our great state, and [documenting] who these heroes and heroines were."[12] The Native Sons, composed of men who had access to more financial resources than the women of their sister organization, also published its own glossy journal,

Figure 5.2. Native Daughters of Oregon. Various pioneer and Oregon historical organizations formed in the 1890s with the goal of celebrating the state's founding fathers and mothers while also staking a claim to inclusion within, as well as the advancement of, the American nation. Racially exclusive, they nevertheless were interested in collecting the myths and place-names associated with the indigenous people. Their symbols, however, drew from the state's white pioneering past. For example, both the Native Daughters and the Native Sons termed their local chapters "cabins" and named them in honor of notable pioneers. Here the Marguerite Tuff's Cabin is shown with the float they created for a parade. Courtesy of the Oregon Historical Society Research Library, Portland. Folder 416-A.

the *Oregon Native Son and Historical Magazine*. In addition to organizational news, it featured legends, poems, geographical names, histories, short stories, photographs, and biographies—all related to early Oregon history. Although the Native Sons' and Native Daughters' racial barriers to membership excluded Native Americans, both organizations nevertheless sought to record Indian place-names and preserve Indian traditions and lore.[13]

The heroic themes about Oregon's first (American) settlers and the seemingly contradictory leitmotifs of happier bygone times versus hardships and privations perpetually colored these varied memorialization efforts. By focusing on pioneers having overcome adversities—such as the ordeal of the crossing of the plains, the constant worry about Indian attack, homesickness, illness, disaster, and even death itself—the OPA and the Native Sons and Native Daughters attributed to the pioneers a host of virtues such as vigor, intelligence, courage, morality, and perseverance. In their view, pioneers bequeathed those traits to Oregon, providing the state and its people the characteristics needed to overcome the complexities of the modern era. A focus on hardship, more and more apparent in, for example, the annual addresses at the OPA's reunion beginning in 1888, also provided lessons by way of comparison to the difficulties Oregonians were increasingly facing as the 1890s approached and then advanced. The theme of happier days in the past likewise provided a direct contrast to and even criticism of the contemporary era.[14] Moreover, that theme, as well as whiteness, shaped the interpretations and content of the state's official record from early on.

The OPA, OHS, and Native Sons and Native Daughters were statewide organizations. Among the most successful local groups of these sorts was the LCPA. On 30 July 1887 nine men, all well known and connected in the area, met in Crawfordsville and laid the groundwork for the organization. One was James Scott. Though not exactly a pioneer—he had come to Linn County in the 1870s—he had an interest in the local history. As a businessman who operated a store in town, he was also supportive of community activities. Eight years after participating in this foundational gathering, Scott served as a witness at Loyd Montgomery's trial; he testified that Loyd had stopped at his store on the day of the murders, on his way back from hunting. He also claimed that Loyd had inquired if Scott knew whether or not Samuel Templeton had received payment for his hops. Since it is clear that Loyd did not commit murder in search of money, it is likely that Scott's testimony was not exactly truthful. Still, slightly earlier that same year, when Loyd had forged his own uncle's name on a check for five dollars, the youth had written out the note to Scott's son. The shopkeeper no doubt remembered that event well when he took the witness stand against Loyd in December 1895. More grimly, on 31 January 1896, Linn County officials chose Scott, one of a dozen electors, to witness Loyd's execution. How Scott felt about his trial testimony at that precise moment is impossible to know.[15]

Back in 1887, when Scott had met with other Crawfordsville men to plan happier events, he helped arrange for a picnic and reunion of Linn County pioneers to take place in town on the first three days of September. Included among those who made their way to this very first reunion were sixty-eight locals who had arrived in Oregon prior to 1855. On the first day of the 1887 affair, they primarily transacted the business involved in founding a new organization. Given that it was western Oregon, rain deluged them on the second and third days. Dampened but not dispirited—they were stalwart pioneers after all—members retreated indoors, one day into the schoolhouse and then the next into the Presbyterian church. Much of the third day was given over to swapping tales from the past.[16]

It was also on the third day when one of the most celebrated among the locals made her way to Crawfordsville. Fifty-year-old Eliza (Spalding) Warren, resident of Brownsville, was the daughter of the famed early Oregon Country missionaries Henry and Eliza (Hart) Spalding, companions to Marcus and Narcissa (Prentiss) Whitman. At the time of the so-called Whitman massacre in 1847, the young Eliza, who otherwise lived with her parents at the Lapwai Mission some 120 miles away, was with the Whitmans at their Waiilatpu Mission, where she attended school.[17] At ten years of age, she became witness to and participant in the terrifying events that took the lives of the Whitmans, as well as the vile treatment of the Cayuse people prior to and after that event.[18]

After the demise of the Whitmans, the Spaldings, on the invitation of Hugh Brown, settled on the Calapooia, arriving in 1848.[19] They took up land between Brown and his nephew James Blakely, who, according to local lore, adjusted their claims, moving them apart to make room for the Spaldings. The missionary couple and their children would live there for some years. The elder Eliza died in 1851 and, with her burial, the community established Brownsville Cemetery (see map P.5). Henry was later able to return to Lapwai, by then in Idaho Territory, where he resumed his work among the Nez Perce people. When he died and was buried there, Eliza's remains were exhumed in Brownsville and reinterred next to her husband. The younger Eliza, who had been born at Lapwai in 1837, met her husband, Andrew Warren, in Brownsville, and the two lived there off and on for some years, the latter dying in 1886. Eliza's younger sister, Amelia, married a son of Hugh and Clarissa Brown, thus making her Eveline (Brown) Montgomery's sister in-law, aunt to John Montgomery, and great aunt to Loyd.

Since membership in the LCPA was limited to "immigrants" who arrived prior to the first day of January 1855, Eliza was not, strictly speaking, eligible for inclusion, as she was not an immigrant. But so revered was she in Oregon history that upon reaching the Crawfordsville reunion, she was accepted as a member by acclamation, "an honor highly merited from the fact," a journalist in attendance recorded, "that she was the first white child born west of the Rocky mountains."[20]

Unlike the Native Sons and Native Daughters, the LCPA did not have a racial restriction on membership. However, the emphasis at the LCPA's organizational meeting on Eliza (Spalding) Warren's whiteness is indicative of the racialized nature of the association and how early residents (and later ones as well) framed the history of Oregon. Given the exclusionary residential regulations inscribed into Oregon territorial and state laws, however, and the LCPA membership being limited to immigrants who arrived prior to 1855, this surely restricted, if not entirely proscribed, nonwhite participation in the original body.

The so-called Whitman massacre shook the white-American constructed Pacific Northwest to its foundations in 1847. Marcus's and Narcissa's deaths were effusively bemoaned and then deliberately misconstrued into a story of martyrdom for the cause of white, American, and Christian civilization in the Far West. As such, the massacre became one of the foundational stories of Oregon and its pioneers.[21] The entire affair was especially gruesome and its gory details remained part of the widely disseminated accounts. An inaccurate pictorial of those events appeared in 1870 in an early Oregon Country history written by the highly regarded Frances Fuller Victor (figure 5.3).[22]

For her role in the Whitman affair, young Eliza became known as the "girl heroine of the Whitman Massacre." During that event, some Cayuse Indians took her and others from the mission, and the young Eliza then (according to tradition) served as an interpreter. She had grown up learning the language of the Nez Perce, a neighboring tribe among whose members her parents worked.[23] As such, Eliza's story provided the Pacific Northwest and especially the people of Linn County with their own captivity narrative. During this very era, as the writer Molly K. Varley explains, political and social reformers concerned about America's future in light of urbanization and immigration recovered captivity narratives of old and used them to promote a national identity, celebrate rural living, and relieve the conscience

Figure 5.3. The Killing of Marcus and Narcissa Whitman. The so-called Whitman massacre became one of the foundational stories of the white people of early Oregon. A later resident of Brownsville, Eliza Spalding Warren (1837–1919), was witness to that event. She was related to Loyd Montgomery through marriage, and she became an honored member of the Linn County Pioneer Association. At its annual reunion in 1894, she even regaled attendees with her recollections of the affair. The image here, which is part of the iconography of early Oregon, appeared in Frances Fuller Victor's *The River of the West: Life and Adventure in the Rocky Mountains and Oregon* (Hartford, CT: Columbian Book Company, 1870). It does not portray events accurately but rather suggests that the Whitmans were innocents, something that helped frame them as martyrs for early Oregon.

of some Americans regarding their treatment of the nation's indigenous peoples.[24] Eliza's story, which she continued to tell, performed such work locally and regionally. But gore was a favored part of her tale.

In 1894, Eliza served as a featured speaker at the LCPA reunion held in Brownsville and focused on the Whitman "massacre."[25] A record of what she actually said there has not come to light, but it is likely that Warren provided the grisly details that her audience hankered to hear. She was an eyewitness, after all, and freely recorded many such particulars in her later memoir. These included: "Dr. Whitman lay on the floor his head cut open, gasping his last breath, and near him, the oldest Sager boy, aged 18, was lying in a huddled heap, his throat cut from ear to ear, not yet dead. . . . Mrs. Whitman was shot again and beat over the face and head with a war club." Warren also recounted various other details of others killed there—shootings, disembowelments, a victim "groaning and begging to be put out of his misery."[26]

In addition to the Spaldings, another family that settled on the Calapooia and had a connection to the Whitmans' downfall was the Osborns. Josiah and Margaret (Findley) Osborn had come west in 1845 and spent that winter at the Whitman Mission. In the spring of 1846, they continued on to the Willamette Valley and settled on the upper Calapooia. In 1847, Marcus Whitman journeyed there specifically to request that the Osborns return to Waiilatpu, as he needed Josiah's help in constructing two mills. On the day of the Cayuse attack, 29 November, the Osborns and their three children, all ill with the measles (they had just lost one additional child to the disease), sought refuge under the building's floorboards. Undetected, they escaped in a harrowing flight later that night.

In 1850, Josiah Osborn provided testimony in a controversial Oregon territorial government trial for five Cayuse men captured and charged with the "murder" of the Whitmans. The five men were found guilty and publicly executed. Back in the spring of 1848, Osborn had written the first known printed description of the awful events (at least the bloody fates of the white victims) at the Whitman Mission. It included macabre details, such as Marcus's "head was badly mangled and his throat cut"; "Indians fired several balls into Mrs. Whitman, and kicked her bleeding body into the mud"; and "the screams of women and children—the groans of the dying." Osborn's letter appeared in the widely distributed magazine *Littell's Living Age* in October 1848, within a year of the events it described.[27]

By the time Josiah Osborn wrote his article, the Osborns had returned safely to the Calapooia, where they told and retold their gory story over the years, making it part of the local lore. As late as the 1930s and 1940s, their stories of unfettered violence against the Whitmans still circulated in Linn County. Leslie Haskins, a local resident and photographer working for the New Deal's Writers' Project of the Works Progress Administration, collected several of them at that time while interviewing longtime residents. Those stories closely followed elements of Osborn's 1848 account and the official reports that had appeared over the years in publications, suggesting the long-lasting influence these tales had had locally and elsewhere in Oregon.[28] Oddly, or perhaps not, this all happened during the same moment when some Oregonians fretted over the imagined influence that the violent and sensational content of dime novels and trashy Victorian tales had on the region's youth, including perhaps even inciting them to parricide, as discussed in chapter 3. But no one seems to have raised a concern about the effects that the regular transmission of stories such as Osborn's and Warren's, including in some cases during events of celebration, might have had on Oregon's children.

Unlike Eliza (Spalding) Warren, Margaret and Josiah Osborn did not survive to see the founding of the LCPA in 1887. At that first reunion, which Warren attended, members of the new organization appointed a constitution and bylaws committee, consisting of three prominent locals, including James Blakely. The committee took up the task of drafting the institution's documents and reporting back the next year. Members set the next reunion for June 1888, again in Crawfordsville. Save for a very few early exceptions in terms of both place and date, the annual meeting and reunion would subsequently take place in June and in the town of Brownsville.[29]

"The object of the Association," as set out in its original constitution, "shall be to collect from living witnesses such facts relating to the Pioneers and History of the settlement of Linn County as the Association may deem worthy of preservation, and to promote social intercourse among its members."[30] As with the OPA, the LCPA took this charge seriously. As early as 1890, for example, a request appeared in newspapers asking LCPA members to write down stories of early days as quickly as possible. The president of the local association, who issued the appeal, fretted over the fact that "soon none of us will be here to relate them" and they would be of such "great importance in the future . . . furnishing our children with a true history of the experience of our ancestors."[31]

The second goal of the LCPA—the promotion of social intercourse—emerged early on as the organization's most sustained activity. The association's principal work became the planning of the annual reunion. Its various parades, songs and musical productions, visits by politicians and dignitaries, prayers, baseball games, foot and bicycle races, picnics and other varied events and attractions, which ranged from taffy pulls and tugs-of-war to horse-powered merry-go-rounds, to hot-air balloon assents and parachute jumps, came to occupy three to four days. Some of the attractions were racially charged, violent, and so named, such as the carnival game in which contestants threw balls at baby-doll-like figures of African Americans. Victors won oranges, candy, or cigars for each one they struck out. A good portion of the reunion was of course given over to speeches and addresses about the pioneers of the county specifically and of Oregon more generally. Beginning in 1888, reunion organizers set aside time for the aging pioneers to publicly recollect the very early days and to reminisce about incidents that occurred while they crossed the plains during the 1840s and 1850s.[32] Given that this was the biggest social and entertainment event in the county at that time, save perhaps for the county fair, and also that Brownsville (or someplace close by) always hosted, no doubt Loyd Montgomery and his family regularly attended.

As with the OPA, the nature of the LCPA's membership led it regularly to reflect on the death of the very people for whom and by whom the organization was founded. The 1890 reunion appears to be the first for which officers appointed a special committee "to draft suitable Resolutions in Memory of our departed." This is also the first year in which the association's minutes recorded the names of those who did not answer the annual roll call—one of these was Sarah, wife of James Blakely. The 1890 report ended with the committee's trust that the departed had ended up in "a happier land."[33]

Likewise, the local *Brownsville Times* dependably reported each year on the reunion and the fact that the old-timers were fast disappearing. In 1901, for example, it explained that "death has been, and is still busy, in their ranks, thinning [the pioneers] perceptibly."[34] In 1910, it lamented that during the annual roll call "quite a number did not respond when their names were called. This recalled the fact that the honored state builders are rapidly passing to their eternal reward."[35] A few years earlier, the newspaper printed the "Pioneer's Song," which a reunion attendee had composed and which was sung to the mournful tune of "Auld Lang Syne." It concluded with this sorrowfully hopeful verse:

> We're getting old and feeble now,
>    Our lives are nearly passed;
> To some of us old Pioneers
>    This gathering is our last.
> We hope to meet old Pioneers
>    All safely on that shore —
> Yes, every one of our loved band,
>    To live forever more.[36]

Between 1900 and 1907, the minutes of the LCPA recorded the names of 315 local pioneers who had died during that time.³⁷

One of the most lauded to pass during the relatively early years of the LCPA was the Montgomerys' relation James Blakely. He died on 29 January 1913 at the age of more than one hundred. With his wife, Sarah, his uncle and aunt Hugh and Clarissa Brown, and his cousin Eveline Brown, James had crossed the plains to Oregon in 1846 in a wagon train that he captained.³⁸

James and Sarah Blakely were founding members of the LCPA. After her passing in 1888, James continued to attend, help organize, and participate in the event many times over the years. At the age of ninety-eight, his frail body prevented his leading the Parade of Pioneers as grand marshal on horseback, due to concerns of potential mishap. But at ninety-nine, safely protected within a vehicle, he was able to command the automobile section of the procession. Blakely was even known on occasion to make the long journey to Portland for the OPA's annual reunion.³⁹ An indication of Blakely's significance to the entire state came only days after his death when the Oregon House of Representatives unanimously adopted a resolution in his honor.⁴⁰

In the early years of the new century, newspapers throughout Oregon carried stories about Blakely's longevity specifically and his pioneer life generally. When he turned one hundred in October 1912, even the *Oregonian* in Portland (a Republican newspaper, and Blakely was an avowed Democrat) described the occasion and the birthday celebration in Brownsville. In addition to remarking on some of the accomplishments of this "honored pioneer," the article told of the family gathered at the event. Those assembled there included eight of Blakely's nine surviving children (he had fathered ten), eleven grandchildren (he claimed eighty-nine), thirteen great-grandchildren, and two great-great-grandchildren.⁴¹

Part of the memorialization of Blakely in life and in death of course had to do with his advanced age. When he passed away, he was touted as the "oldest pioneer" in Oregon. He also had a life that was well worth recalling, at least to a large number of Oregonians at that time. He had cofounded Brownsville, he had been a successful businessman in that town, and he had at one time served in the Oregon legislature.⁴²

But there was more to his local fame than these accomplishments: Blakely was also celebrated in particular for having served as the captain of one of two Linn County volunteer regiments that had participated in southern Oregon's vicious Rogue River Indian War of 1855–56. This information—and even occasionally the tidbit that he had earlier served in the Seminole War—typically appeared front and center in news reports about him over the years, indicating its import to Oregonians. Another Calapooia settler, Jonathan Keeney, organized the other Linn County volunteer regiment. Dozens of Brownsville-area and Linn County men fought in that war, including Loyd Montgomery's grandfather Robert and the then very young Samuel Templeton. The two had both served under Blakely. Earlier, in the Cayuse War, the campaign that followed directly from the killing of the Whitmans, Blakely and his uncle Hugh Brown (great-grandfather to Loyd) had also volunteered.[43]

These so-called Indian wars, as well as other early incidents wherein American settlers in the Willamette Valley confronted indigenous people, are understood now (and on occasion in the nineteenth century by the more thoughtful) as having been in many cases wanton acts of cruelty and even murder, typically perpetrated by the Americans for the purpose of expropriating their victims' land. Some historians have even applied the terms "genocide" and "war of extermination" to the Rogue River event because of its outrageous brutality.[44] In the post–Civil War era and to people like the Linn County pioneers and their progeny, recollecting Indian wars helped them insert themselves into a militarized version of national belonging growing in America after the Civil War.[45]

Like other surviving pioneers, the volunteer veterans of the Pacific Northwest's Indian wars also organized; they founded the Indian War Veterans of the North Pacific Coast (IWV-NPC) on 22 September 1885 in Salem during the state fair.[46] Members of the IWV-NPC included James Blakely, along with a number of other Linn County men, such as Cyrus Walker. Touted as the male counterpart to Eliza (Spalding) Warren, Walker was known as the "first" white male child born in Oregon, having arrived in the world at the Whitman Mission in 1838. His parents were also companion missionaries to the Whitmans and Spaldings. Walker became a member of the LCPA and president of the OPA, and he long served as grand commander of the IWV-NPC.[47] This latter organization's goals included acquiring military pensions for the volunteers, as well as "correcting" some of the newly circulating histories that were beginning to paint them and their deeds in less than flattering terms. The historian Marc James Carpenter has explained that the veterans' substantial lobbying and promotional efforts had succeeded in achieving their goals by the early twentieth century. These included, in concert with other pioneer organizations, (re)writing an Oregon history that "glorified race war and excused or erased any war crimes by exalting those who had taken up arms against Native people."[48]

The IWV-NPC and other pioneer associations celebrated James Blakely, Robert Montgomery, Samuel Templeton, and the many other pioneer men for their very acts of killing people. Even the LCPA participated in such efforts. At the 1922 reunion, and with the assistance of the American Legion, the LCPA staged an elaborate recreation of the Battle of Big Meadows. The original event was a major and, arguably, the culminating engagement of the Rogue River Indian War. Blakely and the volunteers he commanded had participated in it on 28 May 1856 and then in some mopping-up activities in the days that followed. As those original events concluded, Blakely's lieutenant, Timothy Riggs, would later recall in a piece for the *Oregon Native Son* that Captain Blakely "sent an express to inform the citizens of Linn county that he would be at Brownsville . . . on the 4th of July, where we were met by our wives and children and friends, who had prepared a bountiful repast for us." Riggs was one of the founding officers of the LCPA in 1887. A decade later, as an Indian War veteran, he gave an address at the reunion.[49]

Having been feted in Brownsville back on 4 July 1856, the veterans (or at least their memory) were celebrated again sixty-six years later on 15 June 1922 with the Battle of Big Meadows reenactment. Some six thousand enthusiasts attended the faux affair, doing "honor to the pioneers of Linn county." Staged on a field at Washburn Park on the town's south side, it was arranged so that the audience could watch from their automobiles if desired. For the event, the American Legion procured "something like a hundred yelling redskin warriors," who were actually white men dressing the part. The legion also built a replica of the stockade that Blakely's men had erected in 1856. In 1922, the white men playing Indian set it on fire. A raucous event—some twenty-five hundred firearm rounds were shot—the whole excitement concluded with an enormous fireworks display provided by a Seattle firm. The last two known veterans of the war were also on hand. One was eighty-nine and the other, William "Jim" Sperry, was eighty-seven. Back in 1896, about a week subsequent to Loyd Montgomery's execution, Sperry had provided an address at a memorial service held for Daniel

McKercher. It was an elaborate affair that the *Oregonian* termed the "Last Chapter in [the] Montgomery Tragedy."⁵⁰

An advertisement that ran in an issue of the *Brownsville Times* coinciding with the 1922 reunion clearly evokes the patriotic, militarized, and nationally relevant meanings that it held for its sponsors, promoters, participants, and audience. The ad is simply entitled "The Pioneer." The Blain Clothing Company in Albany sponsored it. It begins with the definition of *pioneer* from Webster's dictionary—"An Advance Soldier"—and then explains that "we honor the Advance soldier—the MEN who fought the Indians and the hardships of the frontier days to save the Oregon country—MEN and {lest we forget} WOMEN who depended upon the rifle and the cunning of their hands to wrestle a living from a strange land."⁵¹

Oddly, it would seem at first glance that three days after an Albany newspaper first announced the LCPA's plans for reenacting a famous battle to eliminate indigenous people, another Albany newspaper carried a lengthy biography of Brownsville's "Aunt Eliza," the so-called and misremembered Last of the Calapooia Tribe. By 1922, the Kalapuya woman, commonly known as Lize, was believed to be about one hundred years old. Her age had long been pegged to reports that, of all people, James Blakely, "the authority on her age," had supposedly made back in 1846. Lize had therefore been a fixture in the Brownsville area from the earliest appearance of white settlers; her life would be framed by their memory, too. The 1922 article on Lize was one of many that the local and early historian of the LCPA, Everett Earle Stanard, penned for his regular column, "Old Stuff & New." Stanard was himself a descendant of a local pioneer family and had grown up in Brownsville. His grandfather, Alphonso Stanard, had served as a Linn County volunteer in the Rogue River Indian War and as president of the LCPA from 1891 to 1897 and again in 1905.⁵²

In his biographical article on Lize, Everett Stanard repeated many stereotypes about the local indigenous people. "The Calapooia Indians were a feeble and more or less cowardly people," the article at once stated, further explaining that Lize's "people were addicted to petty thievery, and when settlers would seize an Indian and flog him within an inch of the aborigine's life, the Indians all took it as a matter of course."⁵³ This follows closely a letter that Timothy Riggs had written on the history of the upper Calapooia area in 1901 and that was published in the *Oregon Historical Quarterly*: "The Indians in these early days were in the habit of stealing horses and cattle from the settlers and butchering them, and the settlers would trail them up and if able to catch them would flog them severely, but the Indians seemed to care about as much as a cur for such treatment and would laugh about it as if it was a huge joke."[54]

In his telling of Lize's story, Stanard also reversed the storied Pocahontas trope. Stretching far back into history to even before the life of its namesake and then reappearing at various times in American history, including elsewhere in the history of the early Pacific Northwest, the Pocahontas myth alleges that at various crucial moments in American history, indigenous women have intervened to save the lives of white men, thus allowing them to continue their ultimately triumphal colonial and national efforts. Sometimes, the white man and the indigenous woman then become romantically involved.[55] In Stanard's biography of Lize, it was the American settlers of the Calapooia and their descendants who intervened at various moments to assist *her*. This included taking her in and providing her a home for many years; town children kindly guiding her through the streets when she became blind; and, in time, even Linn County providing her a pension. Through such interventions on the part of white people, Lize was able to survive and outlive the rest of "her own people," who, according to Stanard, had "long since, one and all passed on to the Happy Hunting Grounds."[56]

On 19 August 1922, roughly two months after the Linn County pioneers raucously reenacted the Battle of Big Meadows in Brownsville's Washburn Park, "Indian Lize" peacefully passed away in bed at the Brownsville home of the John Moore family (descendants of Rogue River War veteran Jonathan Keeney). Unlike the June celebration of pioneers' exterminating the Indians, Lize was eulogized and her death mourned. These June and August events seem disconnected, perhaps even contradictory. In fact, they were of a piece. Long had American settlers worked to eliminate the indigenous people from the land, even taking up the cause through wars of genocide. At times, as we have seen, they also applauded such actions. The requiems for "Indian Lize," elegies that had begun to appear well before her death, centered on the view that she was the last of her kind.[57] An article about her death and planned funeral, for example, concluded with authority that, "with her passing, the last of her kin and clan has vanished. Her life-span saw her tribe in full strength, and in complete extinction."[58] Behind the words that spelled sorrow and regret lurked another reality and history: Lize's end was what Oregon's venerated pioneers, and even their children, had long worked toward, and then jubilantly reenacted in fireworks-illuminated affairs, stories told and retold in addresses at pioneer associations and in their captivity narratives, and the conquest even celebrated in advertisements for clothing stores. They also misreported Lize's death as the conclusion to the planned extinction process; other Kalapuyas continued to survive, most of them on the Grand Ronde Reservation in the Oregon Coast Range but others on reservations elsewhere across the Pacific Northwest.[59]

During her life, Lize had attended, whether in person or in spirit, the LCPA's reunions for many years. A news report from 1907, for instance, claimed that she had not missed a single reunion. That same source actually used the word "pioneer" in its reverential description of her, although it did place that word between quotation marks, setting her off from the true pioneers whom the association officially recognized. At the 1913 reunion, a Miss Leona Powell read the poem "Indian Lize" to the audience assembled; Everett Earle Stanard had composed it. One is left to imagine its contents.[60]

Additionally, other reports claimed that at various pioneer celebrations Lize would sing duets with Albert Templeton, Loyd Montgomery's uncle.[61] Perhaps the two did so in Chinook Jargon; Templeton was known to belt out songs in that language, which he reportedly learned from the Warm Springs people whom his family had long used as hop pickers.[62]

Of all the Brownsville-Crawfordsville area families, the Templetons demonstrated the most loyalty to and influence over the LCPA (figure 5.4). Although no Templeton from the immigrant generation appears to have attended the foundational meeting, the family would command the organization in years to come. Albert took the most active role. He served as vice president as early as 1889 and then from 1919 through 1926 as its president. He also oversaw the "Sons and Daughters" wing of the organization for many years, beginning in 1895. Five of his brothers and nephews also served as president, vice president, secretary, director, or as some other officer during the association's first thirty years. The Templetons also often appeared on the reunion's programs.[63]

Another well-known local pioneer family related to the Montgomerys who made their way into the records of the LCPA were the McHargues. James and his wife Sarah (sister to Robert Montgomery) had crossed the plains to Oregon in 1847. When James passed away in the autumn of 1897,

Figure 5.4. The Templeton Family. Among the earliest American settlers of the Brownsville area were the Templetons, who later supported the Linn County Pioneer Association. Elizabeth (Ramsey) Templeton, the matriarch, is seated in the front row, flanked by her sons (*left to right*) James, David, and Joseph. In the back row are her children (*left to right*) Samuel (at whose house Loyd committed the murders), Matilda, Robert (husband to Loyd's aunt Orpha Montgomery), William, and Albert (husband to Loyd's aunt Sarah Montgomery). Courtesy of the Oregon Historical Society Research Library, Portland. File number 1032.

the *Oregonian* in distant Portland carried notice of his death, remarking on his "pioneer" status. Indeed, he had led a life notable for its contributions to local and state history, having helped found the first flour mill and then later a woolen mill in Brownsville. He was included in the LCPA's list of pioneer deaths in 1898. About a month before the 1897 meeting of the association, Sarah had passed away. Her memorial in the LCPA minutes effusively praised her "virtuous and worthy character."[64]

The McHargue family had long been important along the Calapooia for reasons related to death. Back in 1852, when their oldest daughter passed away at age seven, James established McHargue Cemetery with her burial on the corner of his Donation Land Claim plot (figure 5.5; see map P.5).[65] Josiah and Margaret Osborn of Whitman Mission incident fame were buried there. Most of the Templeton family ended up there as well. So too did John and Elizabeth Montgomery, interred in a single grave. John's parents, Robert and Eveline, also found final resting places in McHargue Cemetery; a massive tombstone symbolizing their weight in the community calls attention to their pioneer background by commemorating the years 1846 and 1847 (inscribed on either side of its base), when the two arrived in Oregon.

The McHargues' connections to the Montgomery parricide did not end at those gravesides. One of James and Sarah McHargue's daughters married James McFeron, the Linn County sheriff; he arrested Loyd after his murderous acts. Another of the McHargue daughters married Joseph Hume, who met with Loyd on the day of his execution and was finally able to extract from the lad a complete confession, something others had frustratingly been unable to do and something that put to rest any lingering doubts as to the boy's guilt.[66]

These and a host of other pioneer relations of the Montgomerys were the very people for whom, as newspapers reported in the aftermath of the murders, "much empathy is expressed." They were, after all, "people of the best standing in this community, of acknowledged moral worth, and financially well-to-do."[67] They were also the sort of people of Oregon's pioneer generation who were effusively eulogized after their own deaths. For example, no less than the impressively entitled *History of the Pacific Northwest* stated of John Montgomery's grandfather Hugh Brown, a year after his 1888 passing, that "there is usually something distinctive and characteristic about one who leaves the impress of his name upon any region of locality. This we find to be the case with reference to [Hugh Brown]." The same piece went on to

Figure 5.5. McHargue Cemetery. The massive tombstone of Robert and Eveline (Brown) Montgomery in the foreground marks the final resting place of Loyd's paternal grandparents at McHargue Cemetery southeast of Brownsville. On this side of the monument is the inscription "Pioneer of 1846," in honor of Eveline. "Pioneer of 1847" is on the opposite side and honors Robert. Stones such as these served as monuments to local history as much as to the people atop whose graves they sat. The considerably more modest stone marking the single grave of the murdered John and Elizabeth (Couey) Montgomery is just visible to the right and in the background near the trees. Other tombstones pictured here are for various members of the equally revered Templeton family. Also interred here are Josiah and Margaret Osborn, who survived the so-called Whitman incident. Photograph by the author.

describe his wife, Clarissa, who yet survived, as "a noble and beautiful woman."[68] When John Montgomery's mother, Eveline (Brown) Montgomery, passed away in 1911, the *Brownsville Times* reported of her husband, who had died some thirty years before, that "his memory" was still "held in high esteem by all who knew him." Of Eveline herself, the newspaper maintained that "her life will remain as a constant testimony to the reality of the hope of immortality.... Her memory will be a constant invitation to her children and her friends to meet in the land of endless day."[69]

The roll call of the dead at the 1896 meeting of the LCPA, the group's first reunion held in the aftermath of the Montgomery parricide, did not include mention of John and Elizabeth Montgomery. Given the financial circumstances of the family, they likely did not belong to the organization (dues were twenty-five cents a year), although John and Elizabeth both would have qualified for membership in the Sons and Daughters branch, which their brother-in-law Albert Templeton presided over at the time of their murders. To be completely accurate, however, in these early years the association only included mention of the deaths of member pioneers; a few years later, it would include all Linn County pioneers who passed away in a given year, regardless of their affiliation with the association.

With this said, it is still noteworthy that the so-called Necrology report at the 1896 reunion was by far the most elaborate and reflective to date. "Death and the Grave are never satisfied," the report began. It then continued,

> They are ever crying give give; During the Past year they have taken from us seven (7) of our number, who shall Heed no more our Roll Call.... But are numbered with the Generations of the Dead. Viewed in a Proper light However, who would disterb [sic] their Peaceful Sleep; They Rest from the long and Sometimes tiresom[e] Journey of Life.... Fellow Pioneers, we who remain are no longer of the young but of the Old. Life's work is almost done; Let us not therefore live repiningly[sic][,] fretfully, or gloomily, but let us live cheerfully, gladly and Hopefully Expecting soon a reunion with All the Pure; the blessed and the Good, not only of our own association but of all the generations of the Past ages.[70]

It is impossible to know if the three-person committee who penned the tribute thought about the Montgomery murders when doing so, but it is worth noting that one of the committee members was James Templeton, brother-in-law to two of John Montgomery's sisters. Because of all this, one is led to imagine the possible ways in which the unfortunate decline and horrible demise of John, Elizabeth, and Loyd factored into this 1896 lamentation over dying pioneers and the hopefulness expressed that in the welcome slumber and restfulness of the grave one would be reunited with "All the Pure; the blessed and the Good, not only of our own association but of all the generations of the Past ages."

While the minutes for the LCPA's 1896 reunion in Brownsville do not indicate any obvious influence that the recent tragedy might have had on the atmosphere of the gathering that year, it is difficult to imagine that those who attended did not talk about it. After all, the crime had occurred just a few miles away and involved prominent locals. Immediate and distant family members still resided in Brownsville and surrounding environs. No doubt they or many others involved in the case attended the popular event. We actually know of some. James Blakely served on that year's arrangements committee. In addition to his membership on the "necrology" committee, James Templeton also delivered an address at the reunion.[71] The Reverend J. E. Snyder, who led a prayer on the scaffold moments before Loyd Montgomery's execution on 31 January of that year, provided an invocation.[72] Also giving a speech was the Reverend Robert Martin, the father of one of Loyd's lawyers as well as of two other youths who were longtime acquaintances of Loyd and were called as witnesses either before or during his trial.[73] It is hard to imagine that these and other people at the 1896 reunion did not gossip about those recent events.

These speculations about the 1896 reunion are better evidenced in other ways in which the infamous Montgomery murders have been remembered and recalled, as well as suppressed and forgotten in Linn County's pioneer history. This is especially intriguing given the ways in which other violent or murderous episodes associated with that history have been told, retold, illustrated, written about, recast, celebrated, reenacted, and illumined with patriotic firework displays.

However much the parricides affected the lives of the surviving members of the immediate and extended Montgomery family, when such people passed away over the next several years, no mention was made in their obituaries of what no doubt constituted the single most significant tragedy to impact their lives. The obituary of James Blakely is an example, though he was something of a distant relation. Considerably closer to the parricide were John Montgomery's sister Orpha, who had left the scene moments before the tragedy and was among the first to view its aftermath, and Samuel Templeton, the owner of the house where the murders took place and blood drenched the ground. Their obituaries also elided the event. Even the premature death of Clyde Templeton, which occurred in 1901 when he was but eighteen, brought forth recollections that forgot what was likely the most memorable episode in his short life: at age thirteen, he had been one of the first to discover the Montgomery-McKercher murders.[74]

Most notable are the silences in the obituary for Eveline (Brown) Montgomery, the mother of the murdered John and the grandmother of the murderer, Loyd. When she passed away in 1911, the *Brownsville Times* explained that she had given birth to eleven children; it provided the names of the nine who survived her and no mention was made of her son John or of the impact on her life of his murder or the crime that her grandson had committed. Rather, her obituary, which was especially long, no doubt due to her history and prominence in the community, instead commented at great length on her steadfast faith in the Lord, the glorious afterlife that awaited her, and the cherished memory she provided her many survivors.[75]

It is of course a convention of obituaries to focus on the positive aspects of people's lives rather than on the tragedies that befell them. And with regard to pioneer women, it was also the convention to focus on and applaud their inner qualities and characteristics, their motherhood, and their religious faith. This contrasted with the earthly accomplishments more typically brought up in the obituaries of pioneer men. But in fact the substance of many a pioneer obituary was to celebrate their subjects' lives by recalling, among other things, that they had overcome past adversities and hardships, many related to overland travel and early settlement.

Obituaries for men in that time and place typically recalled their heroic participation in some of the region's most violent episodes and in doing so placed them into the patriotic context of expanding the American nation. When Eveline's cousin James Blakely passed not even two years after she did, orbiting prominently through the tributes to his "remarkable galaxy of achievements" was his role in the murder of people. Of course his complicity was not couched in such verbiage, given that the people he had had a hand in killing were Oregon's indigenous people and his acts had taken place under cover of "war." In fact, whereas the local and regional stories of the depredations perpetrated by indigenous people literally wallowed in blood and guts, the tributes to the "Indian fighters" avoided the messier parts of war and genocide altogether. So James Blakely became a figure who quietly "assisted in organizing Company E, Oregon Volunteers, in March, 1856, and was elected captain. He organized his neighbors ... for a three months' war with the Rogue River Indians and returned home July 4 with the 'Declaration of Independence from Indian Troubles.'" Another newspaper thoroughly transformed the reality of that brutal event by stating simply that

Blakely had "secured peace from the Indians," who signed "an agreement not to molest the white settlers any more."[76]

There were rare occasions when memorials to pioneer women referenced past brutalities that were part of their lives, though these were also sanitized. When Eliza (Spalding) Warren passed away in 1919, news of her death traveled across the region; commemoratives uniformly recalled her role and her presence at the Whitmans' killings.[77] The occasion of her death even brought forth the aging Cyrus Walker, who, when he reflected on Warren's life and experiences, recalled his own at the Whitman Mission, discussed the "massacre," and also made another pitch for the Indian War veterans.[78] Moreover, after Warren's death in Idaho, where she was living at the time, her body was brought back to Brownsville for burial. Locals affixed a bronze plaque to her monumental gravestone. It forever and first and foremost memorializes her as the "Heroine of the Whitman Massacre."[79] For Warren, the violence she witnessed at age ten is something that defined her own death, perhaps more than it did her life. Even the *Brownsville Times* remarked at the time of her passing that her life was "very unusual" because of the episodes of violence that had marked it. The same newspaper, on the other hand, entirely expunged the Montgomery parricide from the obituaries of those who had been about as close to that event as Warren had been to the Whitman affair.[80]

And then there is the example of one of the most famous women and longtime fixtures of Brownsville who passed away during these years: Aunt Lize, the "Last of the Calapooia." Her life was, at the time of her death and even in the years just prior to its end, fair game for public scrutiny, comment, and unrestrained gossip. Whereas obituaries and memorials to white women avoided topics like penury, domestic violence, and other troubles even obliquely, those to Lize described her poverty, her falling on the beneficence of area residents and even the public coffers, her supposed mental weakness, her propensity to beg on the streets, the feeling that "she became something of a pest," and her alcoholic and wife-beating husbands. They even recalled homicide and prison sentences—namely, those of one of her husbands, who reportedly served time in the penitentiary for twice committing murder and who himself "was finally killed in a drunken brawl with a number of other . . . Indians." These comments also more directly racialized Lize by employing terms such as "redskin" and remarking on what was supposedly "innate in her Indian nature."[81]

And so, when the same *Brownsville Times*—the very newspaper whose owner and editor had been the first on the spot when Eveline (Brown) Montgomery's son and daughter-in-law were brutally slain by her grandson on 19 November 1895—stifled any references to those events in its lengthy memorial to her in 1911, it was suppressing the worst hardship of her life and the one that most affected the remainder of it. It was a silencing act every bit as precarious and racialized as the silencing of the harsher realities of affairs like the Rogue River Indian War, the guilt of the Whitmans, and the (apparent) extinction of the Kalapuyas. These stories were repurposed as prideful claims to national belonging with phrases evoking the "first" American civil government west of the Rockies, the "first" white female and male children born in that same region, and the Whitman incident as martyrdom in the service of the advancing nation and Christianity. They were stories that also militarized that national belonging: of Indian wars that, as if by providence, concluded on the Fourth of July, and of "pioneers" defined as "advance soldiers."

In sparing the memory of Eveline Montgomery from the real, unseemly sorts of things that in fact regularly took place in pioneer families, the *Brownsville Times* was only doing what the LCPA, the OPA, the IWV-NPS, and the Native Sons and Daughters, not to mention publications such as the *History of the Pacific Northwest*, the *Willamette Farmer*, Edgar Williams's *Illustrated Historical Atlas Map of Marion and Linn Counties, Oregon*, and in time Eliza (Spalding) Warren's memoirs had been doing and continued to do for years. Each wrote an incomplete history that legitimated an official story of the supposedly heroic killings committed in the name of an expanding republic. They also uncritically promoted the racially lopsided version of the violent pioneer story and silenced the less than pleasant realities of people's real lives and horrific actions. The murders that Loyd Montgomery committed—both he and they being products of the landscape and culture that were Oregon's foundations—threatened to reveal the truth to the lie, hence the need to suppress it.[82]

The earthly story of Eveline and specifically her relationship to the murders of her son and daughter-in-law and the execution of her grandson had actually been somewhat darker and considerably more complicated, as one might imagine. On 19 November 1895 she was one of the first to learn the news of the slaughter, and that news came from her own grandson's mouth.[83] It had also been only minutes before the murders that Eveline had actually concluded her own visit to her son and daughter-in-law. Had she extended her stay even briefly, her life might also have been lost. Of this she seemed well aware—she reportedly cautioned law officers after the arrest of her grandson to "be sure and have a strong guard over him, or he will be back and murder a lot more of them."[84] Long aware of Loyd's "character," as the newspapers put it, Eveline even "declared immediately" that her grandson committed the crime.[85] She also later appeared as a witness in her grandson's trial, testifying that during her visit just before the murders, Loyd had returned from his unaccounted for absence and "look[ed] guilty as if he did not want to meet his parents, as a child would look if it was ashamed of something."[86]

In the weeks after the murders and Loyd's incarceration, newspapers noted that none of Loyd's surviving family had visited him in jail, which the press also claimed was hardly surprising, given the "blackness of the crime."[87] But after Loyd was found guilty and sentenced to die for his offense, his grandmother relented. Eveline took Loyd's younger siblings with her and finally visited him in jail, remaining about an hour. We can only imagine what happened during that time. What we do know is that upon their departure, Loyd "broke down and wept bitterly when he bade them goodbye."[88]

In the 1950s, Eveline's granddaughter Bessie E. (Templeton) Leonard (daughter of Orpha and Robert Templeton and sister to Clyde) provided something of a fuller account of the effects that the Montgomery parricide had on Eveline's life. Leonard had accompanied her grandmother and her mother on their visit to her Montgomery relatives on that fateful day back in 1895. They had helped Elizabeth harvest cabbage for the making of sauerkraut, a task they further planned for the next day. In her account, Leonard first explained, in a sentiment similar to Eveline's 1911 obituary as well as to period pioneer memorials more generally, that she "marvel[ed] at the courage and fortitude of that precious Grandmother as she faced life without her helpmate and large family of small children." But after enumerating a short list of some of what Eveline had accomplished in her life in the absence of a husband who had passed away all too early, Leonard did not hesitate to describe the slaying of her uncle and aunt at the hands of her cousin and how this touched her grandmother's life, noting specifically that she took in and raised her surviving Montgomery grandchildren, one of whom had been named after her. Eveline's obituary in 1911 did not even mention that she became mother to her four surviving Montgomery grandchildren.[89]

Bessie Leonard's recollections in the 1950s also indicate that the triple murder, however much it was silenced in certain ways, was nevertheless long remembered in the Brownsville area. It might seem perverse to claim that it had also been celebrated, but in one sense of the word it had been, at least in the earliest days after the fact. Thurston Pierce Hackleman, a Linn County resident, wrote in his diary for the very day of the murders: "It is the most dreadful tragedy that this County has seen in many respects."[90] Press reports mirrored this sentiment. The local *Brownsville Times* the next day called it "one of the most horrible crimes that has blackened the criminal calendar of Linn [C]ounty for many years."[91] A newspaper in Albany called it "one of the most heinous offenses ever recorded in this country."[92] And Portland's *Oregonian* carried a letter to the editor from a Brownsville resident who characterized the crime as "the most hideous . . . ever committed in the Pacific Northwest."[93]

In utilizing superlatives—the *most* dreadful, the *most* horrible, the *most* heinous, the *most* hideous—to describe the Montgomery-McKercher murders and then attributing to them both local and regional historical significance, witnesses and bystanders elevated the event to celebrity status. This imparted to it a notoriety that came close, at least locally, to supplanting the infamy of the Whitman incident.

The erection of monuments over the graves of Eliza (Spalding) Warren ("Heroine of the Whitman Massacre"), Robert and Eveline Montgomery ("Pioneers of 1847 and 1846," respectively), and others of their vintage laid to rest in community cemeteries during these same years were likewise local and family efforts to celebrate the pioneer past. These mirrored larger state, regional, and national endeavors to erect shrines in honor of Oregon's founders during this same era. As such, they were also similar to Civil War monuments going up in other parts of the country.[94]

The Templeton family's indefatigable in-law Ezra Meeker, for example, began his national campaign at this time to mark the path of the fading Oregon Trail. To do so, he retraced the trail several times with ox-pulled wagons and an automobile made to look like a Conestoga. He lectured, met with officials (including President Theodore Roosevelt), raised funds, and placed any number of markers in just a few short years. In 1905, officials installed the bronze sculpture *Coming of the White Man* at Portland's Lewis and Clark Exposition. They also did the same with a bronze of Sacagawea, who had accompanied Lewis and Clark. The latter was less a tribute to Native Americans than a celebration of women's contributions to Oregon, and it was specifically commissioned to promote woman suffrage in the region. In 1919, the University of Oregon in Eugene installed on its grounds a bronze statue entitled *The Pioneer* and, in 1932, a bronze entitled *The Pioneer Mother*. The donor of the 1919 statue explained at its unveiling that "the pioneer represents all that is noblest and best in our history. The men and women who saved the west for this country were animated by the highest motives." In 1936, the federal government, thanks to the advocacy of residents in the Pacific Northwest, established what was then called the "Whitman National Monument" at Waiilatpu. Through these years, other bronze statues to pioneer women and men appeared across the Pacific Northwest.[95] Loyd Montgomery's grave in Albany, discussed in more detail in the epilogue, remains unmarked.

Some of these monuments have endured on the region's landscape, others have not. Similarly, some of the organizations and associations founded with the intention of commemorating Oregon's pioneers also passed into oblivion, while others underwent fundamental reformulation. Both the Native Sons and the Native Daughters of Oregon had folded by 1905. With the actual numbers of qualified OPA members sorely diminished, in 1901 the Sons and Daughters of Oregon Pioneers (SDOP) succeeded it. While the latter still exists, the *Transactions* of the OPA ceased publication in 1928.[96] In Linn County, the continued reduction in qualified members had made it difficult and at times impossible for the LCPA to conduct its business by 1921. As a result, in that year those who remained in the organization, led by its president, Albert Templeton, elected to change its name to the Linn County Pioneer Memorial Association (LCPMA).[97] Likewise, over the years in and near Linn County, the Montgomery parricide and McKercher murder still occasionally resurfaced, though as a sort of compartmentalized episode in the lore and history of Brownsville, a topic continued in the epilogue. The LCPMA still meets to this day. Every June it hosts the Annual Linn County Pioneer Picnic.

# PART 3

## "WE'RE GOING TO HANG HIM RIGHT HERE, ON THIS TREE"

### Killing Loyd Montgomery

Florence McKercher had been born near Brownsville in 1887. She was the daughter of John McKercher, who was the older brother to the slain Daniel. When Loyd murdered Florence's uncle, she was all of eight years old. Many years later and approaching ninety, she recounted for local historians what she had witnessed back in 1895. Time, perhaps age, and likely multiple tellings over the years had rearranged some events, altered a few details, and perhaps clouded memory. For example, Florence stated that after Loyd had finished shooting and while he was walking past a window to his home, he saw his mother stirring. So, "he took . . . an ax, and hit her in the head, and they said hairpins were driven right into her head."[1] No reports from the era vouch for this version. However, as we have seen, residents of the area in the immediate wake of Loyd's killings did readily recall another Linn County boy-murderer, Charley Finlayson, who had in fact taken a hatchet, though to his grandmother's skull, just a few years before Loyd shot his parents. Perhaps the two stories over the years had bled into one.

Florence also said that it was neighboring men in the immediate aftermath of her uncle's slaughter who delivered the heartbreaking news to her family at their farm, located not terribly far from Samuel Templeton's hopyard. What her father heard from these messengers of death, Florence recalled, "paralyzed him, he just couldn't move." But her mother pulled him together and the McKerchers set out for the murder scene. "When we got there," Florence explained, "they had a great big rope on a maple tree." Such a tree did in fact stand at that location. In his report the day after the Montgomery-McKercher murders, the *Brownsville Times*'s editor, Albert Cavender, described an "immense maple" that shaded the Montgomery home. Given that characterization, it was undoubtedly a bigleaf maple (*Acer macrophyllum*).[2] Indigenous to the region, it typically grows in riparian habitats such as along the Calapooia River, which still flows not far from where the Montgomery home stood. In exceptional cases, bigleaf maples may live up to three hundred years. They may grow as tall as one hundred feet, support a canopy that spreads a like distance, and have a trunk measuring eleven feet in diameter.

To such a maple tree that stood as sentinel above Samuel Templeton's home, men conducted John McKercher, at least in his daughter's recollections, on the late afternoon of 19 November 1895. With Loyd yet milling about the place, likely in a daze and feeling unbearably alone, and with his parents' and Daniel's warm bodies still lying only steps away, those men "said to my dad," Florence related, "'Now you say the word, we're going to hang him right here, on this tree.' But [my father] said, 'No, I won't do that, just let the law take its course.'"[3]

In addition to official reports proximate to those events that verify the existence of a large maple tree at the scene of the slaughter, others do mention "ugly rumors about a lynching" circulating through Brownsville.[4] So, this much of Florence's story may be an accurate depiction of those long-ago events. If so, then John's decision and counsel, like so much else in this story, form something of a link between past and future on the banks of the Calapooia—a complicated epoch of adjustment that is at the heart of this study. Tragically, lynch mobs were scarcely a thing of the past in America in 1895, and yet in western lore they connote a certain association with an older, frontier-style of justice, or injustice, as the case may be. But when John McKercher reached for "the law," eschewing an improvised hangman's noose wielded by "mob law and disorder," as a period newspaper actually referred to it, he also reached out to a system whereby rules, calm, discipline, and government prevailed over the extralegal actions and untamed passions of vigilantes and lynch mobs.[5] In a very real sense, then, John McKercher's actions symbolized the larger pattern of social and administrative change slowly sweeping over America as it inched toward the twentieth century. The late Richard Maxwell Brown, historian of western violence, described this pattern, one that replaced older forms of justice for newer ones in the West, as "the conservative, consolidating authority of modern capitalist forces" that "propelled... the incorporation of the whole of America during the late nineteenth century."[6] As other historians of lynching have explained in a slightly different way, it was the flexing of the muscle of industrial society in union with the power of government over an agrarian past.[7]

At first blush, tales of vigilantism and mob violence make for colorful, yet dark and painful reading. Stories of law, order, government, and discipline, on the other hand, ring dryly bureaucratic. Part 3 of this study, rooted as it is in the latter reality, proves that imperative far from accurate: John McKercher's decision to side with bureaucracy over passion allows for the telling of the considerably more complicated and thought-provoking story of Loyd's last two months of life and the juridical, economic, and cultural forces that animated his execution.

Two of the stories that McKercher's decision allows to be told about Loyd's end are stories of other hanging ropes and other hanging trees. Those compose chapter 6, where I explore, via the resources used to build the gallows on which Loyd's killing took place, the subtle and not so subtle processes by which farmers, small towns, and other populations in Linn County, the Willamette Valley, and elsewhere in America were increasingly drawn into nationalizing and globalizing marketplaces and systems of labor. Loyd's execution, made possible through resources that these marketplaces and systems of labor provided, symbolizes, in a sense, the very way in which those who put him to death were themselves increasingly ensnared by the forces of expanding capitalism that were well beyond their control and perhaps even their consciousness.

In chapter 7, I recount the last months of Loyd's life—from the time of his arrest to the moment of his execution. In following the happenings of those two months in a nearly day-by-day fashion, I demonstrate the way in which the ticking of the clock in an otherwise out-of-the-way, rural county seat synchronized with larger historical trends and developments occurring across America in the waning years of the nineteenth century.

CHAPTER 6

# "The Scaffold Is All Framed and Ready to Be Put in Place"

*Executing a Boy on an Altar of Global Capitalism*

**ON THE DAY THE OREGON STATE APPARATUS EXECUTED** Loyd Montgomery, it did so behind wooden barriers erected to prevent the affair from becoming the huge spectacle that public hangings typically were in those days. Oregon had adopted the law sealing off executions from curious eyes in 1879.[1] This was just one small part of the expansion of authority, discipline, administration, and government in that era, and these measures had as their purpose the controlling of social chaos. Subsequently, audiences at the state's executions were composed of a few assorted officials, members of the press, representatives of religious institutions, and others whom county sheriffs, who were in charge of such matters, invited to the event. Such limitations and precautions hardly warded off the hordes who continued to collect in the vicinity of death, namely in the public byways outside of the state-mandated cordons. For Loyd's hanging, reportedly hundreds of mostly men and boys took to the streets in hopes of getting any view of the event that they could or at least in hopes of being able to hear the rattle of a death that they longed to see.[2]

A debate concerning such matters followed Loyd's hanging. Should executions remain as the Oregon legislature intended when it adopted its

1879 law? Should they be further removed from the disorder of the streets to the quiet of the penitentiary? Or should they be opened up to those who, for whatever reason, wanted to witness someone being put to death? One argument heard on the streets for a more open, public viewing was that "the people paid for it and had a right to see it."[3] Much of what "the people" had invoked to justify the execution of Loyd over the course of the weeks until the deed was done was couched in terms of high-minded principles—the protection of respectable society, justice for the citizenry, the peace and safety of the human family, and the improvement of humankind. But it is also obvious that just as many "people," perhaps even more, reduced the whole affair, and the meaning of life that was at its heart, to a few dollars and cents. But why not? So much of what that society was based on, and what had practically bled it dry during the depression of the 1890s, was monetary exchanges for goods that regularly occurred (or not so regularly, as the case was during economic downturn) in the public marketplace.

What did those people who clamored to see their dollars and cents at work actually pay for? They likely did not realize that they had paid for the wooden barricades thrown up to keep them at bay. They also probably did not think so much about their money going into the lumber and rope used to do the very deed that they wanted to see done. Much, in fact, of the way capitalism and markets and the exchange of money worked in that rural society was unseen, unknown, and not understood—similar to what all went into Loyd's execution and, at least in principle, in keeping with Adam Smith's invisible hand. Much of the cost of all that also actually went unpaid by the people who claimed to pay for it. Rather, it was absorbed in the suffering of the less fortunate and dumped onto the natural environment. This chapter tells a bit of that larger story—how Loyd's body briefly dangled at the center of global commerce, his life and limbs connected by the invisible hands of dollars and cents stretching outward to the world and then back again, entwining them with all sorts of visible and invisible processes and peoples.

We start that story on the North Santiam River, which had formed the northern boundary of Linn County since that entity was demarcated in 1847. The river flows in a westerly direction out of the Cascade Range and is joined by the stream's south fork, just before their combined waters pour into the Willamette River. "Santiam" comes from the name of the band of Kalapuya people who had lived for millennia along the banks of the river that now bears the same appellation. They used the river valley as a corridor for traveling into the Cascades, where the neighboring Molalla people lived. There they spent a good portion of the summer and early fall hunting, fishing, and collecting a variety of materials from nature for food, clothing, tools, transportation, and home construction. The US government had largely removed the Kalapuya and Molalla peoples from the area in the 1850s, scattering survivors to the Warm Springs, Grand Ronde, and Klamath Reservations.[4]

In 1887, Canadian-born carpenter and sawmill operator John Shaw established the Santiam Lumbering Company on that river, some thirty-five miles northeast of Albany. Shaw had come to the area from Stayton, in Marion County, where he managed a mill. In founding his own lumber business on the North Santiam, he also founded the village of Mill City (see map P.4). By early 1890, his mill had become the largest on the river. One newspaper proclaimed it "an honor to the country." It produced lumber, lath, and shingles, as well as timbers for railroad construction. The company employed twenty mill hands and forty loggers, and a "building boom" was under way in the village, which soon reached a population of two hundred. Mill City and Santiam Lumbering developed a close relationship with Albany. In large part, the supplies that the loggers, mill hands, and their families needed came from the county seat. The firm also opened a lumberyard in Albany to market its products. It was located at the end of Jackson Street, above the Willamette River, and right on a railroad spur. In 1891, Santiam Lumbering supplied, at below market prices, the planks Albany needed for rebuilding some of its sidewalks. Newspapers in the larger town regularly devoted column space to gossip from the smaller community.[5]

By the beginning of 1890, the Mill City mill had attained a cutting capacity of fifty thousand board feet per day, and much of what it produced funneled through Albany, arriving daily by rail.[6] Although by this date the Pacific Northwest's more accessible forests along the lower Columbia River and around Puget Sound were feeding a demand for softwoods in California and elsewhere in the Pacific Basin, isolation and the limits of transportation confined the southern Willamette Valley's lumber production mostly to the local market. Nevertheless, the amount that had been harvested in Linn County by 1895 was impressive. "The demand for lumber is yet but local," an Albany newspaper explained at year's end, "but the mills of this county this year produced 20,000,000 feet."[7]

In fact, the transition to twentieth-century-scale operations began on the North Santiam in the 1890s. Already in 1893 investors from Michigan, whose vast forests were fast falling to the lumberman's ax, had arrived on the Santiam in search of new timberlands to buy up. About 1897, just as the depression was lifting, the steam-powered donkey arrived on the Santiam. With this machine, loggers could more easily and speedily pull felled trees from the forest. In 1898, Shaw sold his mill to the Curtis Lumbering Company, based in distant Chicago, the financial and marketing center for the Great Lakes lumbering region. By then railroad connections had made transporting Linn County lumber eastward to the country's population centers routine.[8]

As with other logging companies and mills of the era, Santiam Lumbering's production processes generated considerable waste. Part of it was in human life and limb: every sort of accidental injury, from cuts and bruises received in milling mishaps to crushed skulls and bodies from falling trees, occurred along the North Santiam.[9] Part of the waste was also the resource itself. Santiam Lumbering desired Douglas fir (*Pseudotsuga menziesii*) for lumber and western redcedar (*Thuja plicata*) for shingles. Given the abundance of the resource—forests that had never seen industrial-level harvesting—one could be choosy, selecting only older trees with the straightest of grains. The technology available also placed limits on the size of the usable trees. Nevertheless, trees that Santiam Lumbering's loggers felled were sizable. In 1891, the company marketed "timbers of any size or length, to 85 feet." A delivery for that same year was made up of "whoppers"—pieces of lumber seventy feet long by sixteen inches square.[10]

Trees that were not the right dimension or were unwanted species, such as western hemlock (*Tsuga heterophylla*), red alder (*Alnus rubra*), and bigleaf maple, were ignored. But to get to the favored specimens and bring them out, the undesirable trees were either cut down or, if left standing, smashed and mangled when loggers felled what they wanted. Moreover, loggers at this time typically began cutting a tree some ways up the trunk. As such, large stumps, unwanted branches, and shattered and discarded trees and wood were left behind. As accumulated waste dried during the warm summer months, fire danger increased considerably. It had become a major headache across the Pacific Northwest by the turn of the twentieth century. One such fire that burned in the summer of 1893 began on Santiam Lumbering's cutover lands. One report claimed that the conflagration destroyed fifteen hundred dollars' worth of the firm's own property and "much valuable timber."[11]

But there was yet other environmental alteration. With trees gone from mountainous slopes that receive 60 to 120 inches of precipitation a year, erosion increased. Major landslides and flooding occurred near Mill City and elsewhere on the North Santiam several times in the 1890s, in the process destroying some of the company's own equipment and portions of its sawmill.[12] Log drives blocked streamflow and changed streambeds and riverbanks. And yet more of nature's handiwork succumbed to and was consumed by the construction and operation of logging railroads. By 1892, Santiam Lumbering's own track had already stretched to a mile above Mill City. With the extension of railroads came the transformation of more forests into industrial worksites. Early in the 1892 season, for example, the firm's "improvements" included "a new flume, pump and saw dust elevators, building an additional 1800 feet of railroad to carry the track to their newly constructed dam across Ford creek, where they now take logs, and have otherwise re-arranged and extended their log chutes up the mountain sl[o]pes."[13] Other dams, like the one at Ford Creek, were already impeding fish migration in the North Santiam drainage by 1890.[14]

Whatever environmental concern that existed at this time focused more on the effects of milling rather than on the consequences of harvesting. In the 1870s, Oregon and Washington both adopted legislation that prohibited mills from dumping their sawdust into streams. The worry here was less "environmental" as we understand it today and more that the practice seriously harmed salmon runs, imperiling another of the region's major industries. John Shaw ignored such laws, regularly dumping sawdust into the North Santiam. In 1892, Oregon sued him and won. An Albany newspaper decried the state's victory, stating that it "put to a great disadvantage" the firm that provided jobs for eighty hands. By year's end, however, the Oregon Fisheries Commission happily was reporting that since the news of the Shaw decision had spread, "there have been no complaints on account of sawmill men putting sawdust in the streams," a boon to "maintaining the supply of trout and other food fishes in many of the streams."[15]

Like Linn County farmers and other area businesses during the 1890s depression, Santiam Lumbering and its employees suffered. Between 1892 and 1896, the value of the mill declined 50 percent. Between 1891 and 1894, sales declined from $7,613 to $1,198. At the same time, laborers lost 80 percent of their wages.[16] In September 1895, an Albany newspaper reported, in somewhat veiled terms, that the company's local lumberyard, "though not rushed . . . has an established business that keeps moving."[17] The mill and the lumberyard survived, if barely.

During the depression of the 1890s, Santiam Lumbering's most notable sale at its Albany lumberyard, if not in the dollars that it brought in then at least in its intended purpose, occurred in January 1896, while Loyd Montgomery sat in the county jail blocks away. The business sold $7.32 worth of lumber to Linn County to be used in the construction of the scaffolding for the boy's hanging and for the enclosure to block its view from the prying eyes of the public.[18]

That wood had undoubtedly come from a Douglas fir that had been growing in the lush forests of the Cascade Range above the North Santiam since long before Loyd's grandparents had journeyed to Oregon on the overland trail. Loggers, grateful for the work during the depression, felled that tree and limbed it. Likely, human muscle and gravity had skidded that log down the mountainside. Or maybe a team of oxen had dragged it to a flume or a nearby stream that then carried it down and dumped it into a holding pond. There, other laborers fished it out and loaded it onto a railcar, sending it on its way to Mill City. The log likely lay there to dry for some time; while living, a Douglas fir holds a significant volume of water.[19] Once the log had cured, sawyers at the mill first made the rough cuts and then sent those pieces through the planer. When the process was complete, Santiam Lumbering shipped the finished product to Albany by rail. All along the way, from forest to lumberyard, the efforts and resources expended on that lumber contributed to the significant social and environmental alterations occurring in Oregon's Cascades.

The lumber sold to Linn County was stacked in the Albany lumberyard when, in January 1896, the county hired carpenters Isaac Conn and John McChesney, who were brothers-in-law to each other and business partners, to fashion Loyd's deathtrap and build the enclosure to surround it. They received twenty-three dollars for their efforts. Conn was fifty-four at the time and had resided in Linn County since 1861. His family had long had its hand in varied local businesses, and Isaac had been for many years one of the few builders in Albany. McChesney was twelve years Conn's junior. He had only recently arrived in town, coming from Tacoma in 1888. He had learned carpentry years before. He married Isaac's younger sister in November 1891.[20]

A miniature functioning model of the gallows that they built circulated in Albany—Sheriff McFeron displayed it to Loyd at his request on the morning of his execution.[21] It is likely that Conn and McChesney worked from that model, since neither apparently had experience in constructing such contraptions. The last legal execution in Albany had taken place in 1877, and the builder of that scaffold is unknown. But the two men had substantial experience as craftsmen. A period source stated of McChesney, "He has a correct appreciation of the substantial and lasting, as well as artistic and pleasing, and with almost no exceptions his work has been satisfactory in all of its details."[22]

The two carpenters undoubtedly picked out the wood themselves. They constructed Loyd's gallows right at Santiam Lumbering's lumberyard, completing it on Tuesday, 28 January. It was about fourteen feet square, with the platform some eight feet above the ground and the crossarm eight feet long. The next day they transported it to the county jail, ten blocks away, and there commenced work on the enclosure. A ghastly news item related that "while the nails were rattling," Loyd, in his nearby jail cell, "was singing and fiddling 'Home Sweet Home.'" The selection of music, given that the boy had murdered his mother and father at their home, stretches credulity. But it seems to have been a favorite tune of his or at least in the morose imaginings of the press. At another point during the construction of the scaffold, the condemned boy also reportedly noticed some young men through a jail window and asked of them, "What are you doing out there boys[?] Why don't you go round and help build the scaffold[?]"[23]

From that scaffold, Sheriff McFeron and his deputies suspended the hangman's rope. The story of that rope is more challenging to unravel than is assembling the facts of the gallows. Few references were made to it in the press. The most specific comes from an Albany newspaper that reported on 30 January that the "sea grass rope" for the hanging "has been received." It had the "regulation ¾ inch" diameter. In the same issue, we also learn that McFeron and Deputy Quincy Propst tied the noose's knot.[24]

The phrase that the rope "has been received" implies that McFeron likely ordered it from afar rather than having casually picked it up at the local mercantile. His duties as sheriff included overseeing, planning, organizing, and carrying out all aspects of the execution. Since this was the only hanging that he ever presided over, he must have spent considerable time studying up on all matters related to such an affair, rope included. By the late nineteenth century there was quite a science to hanging, and a botched execution was to be avoided at all costs. It is unlikely that the rope that McFeron chose was truly made from seagrass. On one occasion, a newspaper described it as "hemp." When "seagrass" appeared in reports (a total of three times), it seems to have been more a general reference rather than an exact description of the material used to make the rope.[25]

To be sure, there was a seagrass rope industry in North America at this time. The purpose for the rope it produced, at least by the 1880s and 1890s, however, was not for cordage. The center of that industry was along the Great Lakes and St. Lawrence River. There, what was actually hay from marsh grasses but popularly called "seagrass" was harvested, dried, twisted into rope, and then shipped chiefly to mattress factories, where, once unraveled, it was used for a cushy stuffing. Seagrass produced in such fashion also supplied insulation for ice houses, water mains, and even streetcars.[26]

During these years, the term *seagrass* was occasionally used interchangeably with *henequen* (which comes from the agave plant and is typically called sisal) but sometimes also used to describe rope made from ramie (a nettle) and hemp (from the genus *Cannabis*), none of which is a seagrass.[27] Also during the era, the press readily employed the term *seagrass*, as it did in Loyd's case, when referring to ropes used in hangings—whether done through legal execution, lynching, or suicide. It is unlikely that all the deaths reported in these instances actually occurred at the end of genuine seagrass rope. In fact, in some of these cases, given descriptions of where the specific rope came from and how it performed (or failed) under the weight of its victim, the cord was likely sisal.[28] Finally, by the mid-1890s, fibers utilized in American cordage manufacture came principally from common hemp, sisal, and manila hemp.[29]

For hanging rope, on the other hand, manila hemp was a preferred material by the second half of the nineteenth century. The famous English executioner William Marwood, who perfected the science of hanging in that same period and who was widely consulted because of that, used manila hemp in his executions.[30] The Philadelphia cordage producer Weaver, Fitler & Company supplied some hanging ropes during this era. Through much of the nineteenth century that firm used different hemps and specifically manila hemp in its cordage products, with the latter entirely replacing the former by the turn of the century.[31] And, too, there was that one reference to Loyd's rope as "hemp."[32]

In his preparatory study of the art and science of hanging, Sheriff McFeron, given the gravity of the task before him and his inexperience with it, likely consulted and read widely. Having done so, he would have learned that manila hemp was a favorite among executioners. Given his own, earlier farming background and the fact that agriculture dominated in the county, McFeron also would have been familiar with varied ropes and twines made from manila hemp, employed by farmers in western Oregon. He would also have known who produced the vast majority, if not all, of it: the Portland Cordage Company.

Entrepreneurs founded that rope factory in Portland in 1887, the same year John Shaw established Santiam Lumbering. One of the cordage company's founders was William S. Ladd, who had been a major shareholder in Albany's Linn County National Bank, which went under in 1893. The Portland Cordage plant and its warehouse sat on two blocks in the city's industrial area north of the central business district and west of the Willamette River. In 1892, the Tubbs Cordage Company in San Francisco, largest ropemaker on the West Coast, bought the Portland works but for years continued to operate it under its original name and with separate management.[33]

In the 1890s, Portland Cordage exclusively used sisal, imported from Mexico, and manila hemp in its products. Sisal fiber had many agricultural applications. For example, the Portland firm used it to produce a twine specifically for the support of hop vines.[34] Very likely the Montgomerys used this firm's product on Samuel Templeton's hop farm, given the manufacturer's near stranglehold on the Oregon rope and twine market. Portland Cordage also made manila twine (much stronger than sisal), rope and twine of manila and sisal combinations, and pure manila-hemp rope for more industrial applications. It also produced manila cordage in the same size as the rope used in Loyd's hanging.[35]

Just as manila hemp is no seagrass, neither is it hemp. It comes from a tree-like plant (*Musa textilis*) that closely resembles the banana tree; the two actually share the same genus. It first became popular in the Western maritime industry in the early nineteenth century due to its superior qualities. It remains strong when wet and resists shrinkage as well as rot, even without having to be treated with tar, as other sorts of marine ropes then were. This made manila lines lighter.[36] Portland, like San Francisco, had a ready market for such a product: it was a seaport with significant ship traffic. It also faced the Pacific, across which, some fifty-nine hundred miles away, lay the only source for manila hemp: the Philippine Islands. There the fiber is known as abaca.

Abaca use began early in the history of the islands, the people there having used the fiber for years in many applications, including clothing. The industrial trade in abaca took off in the nineteenth century. In 1818, the islands exported 41 tons of it; in 1900 they exported 89,348 tons. The expanding maritime and industrial empires of Great Britain and the United States consumed 70–90 percent of those exports. That demand made abaca one of the two most important industries (along with sugar) in the islands by the 1890s.[37]

To be profitable and to meet demand, abaca needed to be grown on extensive plantations, the development of which, like the transformation of the temperate forests of the Pacific Northwest into industrial sources of timber, had both far-reaching environmental and social consequences. Although cultivation methods for abaca vary depending on terrain, soil, and precipitation, typically tropical forests were entirely cleared to make room for it. The average yield per acre across the islands by the end of the nineteenth century was about 335 pounds. This means that perhaps 600 square miles would have been cleared of forest to supply the 67,864 tons of manila hemp exported in 1890.[38]

Plantation agriculture led to the emergence of a Filipino grower elite.[39] The workers, of course, were the humbler people. Their lives changed dramatically as their land was transformed into expansive farms, their homes into plantation villages, and their bodies into laborers on abaca estates. The development of plantation agriculture in the Philippines soon denied peasants access to areas previously used as commons for grazing and timber. The monoculture of abaca and other plantation crops such as sugar and rice contributed to local food shortages and starvation. Shifts in population and increased trade with the larger world brought more diseases to the islands' people and livestock.[40] The labor on the abaca plantations included clearing forests, preparing the fields, planting and tending the trees, harvesting by hand with a machete-like knife, stripping the fibers from the gathered stems, drying them, baling them, and then loading the product onto ships for distant markets. According to a 1905 Portland Cordage publication, "All labor is performed with crude implements by native Filipinos. The process is slow and care must be exercised. . . . Two natives can prepare about 25 pounds of dressed fiber per day."[41]

Portland Cordage began receiving manila hemp from the Philippines in 1888. Managers of the company soon personally visited the islands. In June 1895, the company received a cargo of 2,300 bales transported on the Oregon Railroad and Navigation Company's steamer *Chittagong*.[42] Those bales had a combined weight of around 316 tons.[43] Given average yields for the time, it would have taken nearly three square miles of the Philippines' former forests to produce it. According to Portland Cordage's figures on the industriousness of Filipino workers, it would have taken 277 "natives" half a year to dress those fibers.

This abaca shipment seems to be the only one that Portland Cordage received in 1895. Given the proximity of this cargo's arrival to the events in Albany the next January, if this factory supplied the rope for Loyd's hanging, and it likely did, then it might also be that the manila hemp, which was also likely the fiber composing the rope that killed the boy, arrived in Oregon on the *Chittagong*. This was a steamship that burned coal, another major industrial resource taken in large quantities from the earth during these years. Its mining, processing, and burning had its own significant consequences for all living things—for those where it was consumed, for those who dug it from the earth, and for nature, from which it was taken and to which it was then returned as noxious gases, ash, and slag.[44] The manila hemp that arrived in Portland on a coal-burning vessel had been produced by the intensive efforts of Filipino workers and for the profit of a wealthy few. The former had done their work on land that had once been tropical forests and that had once supported a simpler life. In Portland, stevedores unloaded it at wharves that stretched along the Willamette's west bank. Horse-drawn wagons likely transported it the few blocks to Portland Cordage. There the nimble fingers of laborers, many of them children younger than Loyd, tended various spindle, stranding, and traveling machines, fashioning the abaca into rope.[45] A coal-burning steam engine pulled the freight car that transported that rope to Albany, where it had arrived by 30 January 1896. McFeron and Propst tied it into a noose and suspended it from Conn and McChesney's scaffold.

Manila hemp was a favored material for the hangman's rope at the time Loyd met his end. The industrial demand for that fiber had transformed the social and environmental landscape of the Philippines by the end of the nineteenth century. That process would only accelerate, as would those islands' tragic relationship with the United States, when the expanding American empire gobbled them up in 1898. That was just two years after

Loyd's execution. In the new century, Portland Cordage announced the opening of a one-million-dollar factory-warehouse complex near the city of Manila.[46]

At the very same time, on the opposite side of the Pacific, on the slopes of the Cascade Range, which forms the eastern edge of Oregon's Willamette Valley, a similar sort of process was at work. Lumbermen like John Shaw were creating industrial work zones out of the forests—forests that supported all manner of flora and fauna and that had earlier and lightly sustained indigenous people for millennia. The Oregon businessmen were also constructing mills and building towns where workers and their families labored and lived, suffered injury and met their death, valued their paychecks and then, during depressions, agonized over the very value of those paychecks. Lumbermen like Shaw then sold these mills, their resources, their blighted landscapes, and their mangled workers to expanding capitalists who lived in distant imperial cities. That process also accelerated remarkably just a couple of years after Loyd's death.

Not to be forgotten in all this, American settlers like the Montgomery and Templeton families had also been busily altering social and environmental landscapes in the Willamette Valley since the 1840s. They forced, and often violently so, indigenous peoples from the land. They exterminated menacing wildlife such as wolves and grizzlies. They rerouted streams and drained the countless marshes of the valley floor. Their hogs rooted out meadows of camas (*Camassia quamash*) and gobbled up acorns of the Oregon white oak (*Quercus garryana*) that the Kalapuya people had nurtured for years for their own sustenance. They pulled fallen trees and stumps from rivers to clear the way for steamboats and log drives. They then dammed other streams to power gristmills and woolen mills. They brought in cattle and chickens, which replaced native white-tail deer and flocks of wildfowl that had once blackened the skies. They divided the land into private parcels and grew upon them vast fields of wheat and hops.[47] They encouraged and participated in expanding markets of trade that soon stretched across the nation and around the world, importing foreign and domestic manufactured goods and products for their farms and homes. They likewise shipped their own produce to markets back East and to hungry people overseas. But they also learned that those markets back East and overseas did not always hunger, leading to incredible suffering on their own farms and within the walls of their own rural homes.

On one of these suffering farms in the late afternoon of 19 November 1895, a sixteen-year-old boy was quietly engaged in the virtuous work of the republic—toiling in the soil, plowing fields, and doing what he could to help alleviate the suffering of his family. Meanwhile, his slightly older brother was performing the less-spoken-about sorts of work that had also gone into fashioning the republican landscape, work that transformed his family's suffering farm and home (neither of which was really theirs) into a scene of unspeakable horror.

As *Pioneering Death* has argued thus far, what *merely* appears to have been an intensely personal, family story of parental failure and a boy who harbored darkness, anger, and passion was in fact a story that can be neither fully explained nor entirely comprehended by what *merely* went on within the walls of a weather-beaten house or even within the bounds of a rotting picket fence. The stoic decision to let the lawful wheels of justice turn, a decision made by an aggrieved John McKercher while he stood under an immense maple tree and in the midst of a furious lynch mob, reveals this to be true. That decision tied a boy's life and especially his death to a more complex story whose elements drew from a plot, setting, characters, theme, and conflicts connected to places far beyond a small hopyard situated on the banks of the Calapooia. It was a story of an ever-expanding state apparatus and a story of global trade networks, items—lumber and hemp—that the state apparatus then fashioned into the contraption of death on which that boy would stand. And he stood there, however momentarily, as the fulcrum of the processes and resources that were transforming his world and the world beyond his. People invited to watch his death and those who could only imagine it from beyond the barriers that sealed it from their eyes claimed to have "paid for it." It is unlikely that they ever knew exactly what all they did and did not pay for.

There is yet another story of the killing of Loyd Montgomery to be told. It is the intensely local and personal story that unfolded between the time when a lynch mob swung a rope under a bigleaf maple to the time when the boy finally swung from a manila-hemp cord suspended from a Douglas fir scaffold. It is a story, or really multiple stories, that involve the local citizenry, a small community, a family, and, most of all, a boy. They are the subject of chapter 7.

CHAPTER 7

# "At 14½ Minutes His Heart Ceased to Beat"

*A Boy's Life from 4:30 p.m., 19 November 1895, to 7:26 a.m., 31 January 1896*

**IT WAS ABOUT 4:30 P.M. ON 19 NOVEMBER WHEN A YOUNG** and anxious Robert Montgomery entered his humble home. There he immediately discovered Daniel McKercher's body. Not yet noticing his mother's remains in the dining room or those of his father at the corner of the property, Robert turned quickly. Screaming about a dead man in the doorway, he raced back to the picket fence, where the other children, along with Loyd, had by then gathered. Crying, Loyd jumped onto McKercher's horse that was yet tied there and set off to alert family and neighbors. Meanwhile, Robert ran to find his sixteen-year-old brother, Orville, who was out plowing.[1]

On McKercher's steed, Loyd first headed to the home of his aunt and uncle, Orpha and Robert Templeton. There he found the former, who herself had only recently departed the Montgomery home. He bade her to "come quick; pa and ma and another man is killed." Then off he flew to the farm of his grandmother, Eveline Montgomery. She had also not long before left Loyd's home. "Making a good deal of noise," the boy exclaimed, "'Grandma, come quick, pa and ma and Daniel McKercher are shot and killed.'" This information about the bodies and their identities became something of a problem for Loyd in days to come, given that he claimed to know nothing about the shootings and had not seen any of the bodies in the presence of the other children. That and his notoriety in the neighborhood would cause suspicions immediately to fall upon him. But before then, and as Loyd raced through the countryside to alert family, he also chanced upon others. The first was the Brownsville physician, Joel Henry, whom Loyd encouraged "to hurry to the house." Henry would be the first adult on the crime scene. Loyd also came upon a hired laborer and two farmers who worked or lived in the vicinity. He informed each about the identities of those murdered and urged them all to make their way quickly to the Montgomery-Templeton farm.[2]

Within minutes, people descended on the murder scene. More than one hundred did so through the cool and grim night hours, picking their way among the bodies to get a good look at the horrors for themselves. Arriving around 1:00 a.m. were Sheriff James McFeron and one of his deputies, James Wilson. The two had traveled the twenty-five or so miles from Albany. McFeron had resided in Linn County since he was fifteen, having come with his parents from Missouri in 1874. They took up farming near Brownsville, where McFeron became acquainted with the Montgomery family and married John's cousin, Elizabeth McHargue, in 1882. This made McFeron an uncle to the bad boy William McHargue. It also made him related to Loyd. McFeron viewed his obligations in part as a member of the family, something that complicated his official responsibilities: when he went beyond his duties as a sheriff in attempting to extract a confession from Loyd, something for which the court later chastised him, McFeron explained that he had done so because the murders had taken place "in the family . . . and that I wanted to know the truth about the matter." In 1885, McFeron and his wife joined the exodus of farmers from the countryside and moved to Albany. There he worked as a drayman until elected city marshal in 1893. In 1894, he ran for the office of county sheriff. As he was a Republican, he benefited from the Democratic-Populist split that year and won, only the second Republican to have done so in twenty-five years.[3]

Those who first congregated at the Montgomery home learned of the events through the grapevine, which kept humming for days. "The people are all talking about the Montgomery murder," a newspaper remarked. Mixed as it likely was with misinformation, gossip, and speculation (much like news reports), this talk immediately altered daily routines for adults and children. For example, on the very morning after the murders, well before printed stories circulated, the nearby Linn County School No. 28, known locally as the Warren School, saw a considerable decline in attendance. On the nineteenth only one student of the twenty-two enrolled was absent. The next morning, only twelve showed up, and the teacher wrote into her records, "Murder of Mr. & Mrs. Montgomery and Mr. D. M. McKercher Nov. 19, 1895."[4]

The Warren School was so named as it sat on land once belonging to Andrew and Eliza (Spalding) Warren. The Montgomery and Templeton children, living as they did just west of the district line, attended school in Brownsville, but they knew students at Warren. One of them was Loyd's chum Marshall Fox, who was a student there earlier in 1895. Also attending Warren were several children from the Evans family. Their father, Edmond, served as foreman of the coroner's jury that gathered information on 20 November. One of the people he interviewed, Fred McCormack, was another Warren pupil. From his home's front porch, Fred had heard the shots and the screams that emanated from the Montgomery farm on the afternoon of the nineteenth.[5]

Of course it was also later on the nineteenth, well past sunset, when Albert Cavender of the *Brownsville Times* reached the murder scene, escorted there by boys carrying lanterns. It is also likely that these boys used their lanterns to throw light on the horrors that the journalist would later vividly detail. We really do not know, but whether in the name of news or to satisfy a macabre turn of mind, these boys undoubtedly saw for themselves the effects of a culture of killing that lurked beneath a placid agrarian landscape and also resided within the hearth and home of that landscape's pioneer families.

When the boys left the scene is unknown. Cavender, however, was again on hand the next morning when, at about 9:00 a.m., the Linn County coroner, Dr. Robert A. Jayne, arrived. Jayne, who was eight years younger than the deceased John Montgomery, had come to Oregon only recently, in 1891, but he had already built a successful medical practice in Shedd, another nearby village. He had succeeded to the Linn County coroner position in April 1894, by then having experienced his own share of family tragedy, despite being only thirty-six. His wife of less than two years suddenly took ill and died in August 1893, leaving Jayne with a two-month-old infant to care for. By November 1895, Jayne, as a private citizen, a physician, and a coroner of some twenty months, had seen his share of unsettling deaths, accidental killings, and even murder. But what he encountered at the Montgomery home must have been especially unsettling.[6]

Within an hour of Jayne's arrival, and with the assistance of Joel Henry, who likely remained at the scene through the night, Jayne empaneled a coroner's jury of five onlookers. Henry was forty-four, had originated in Kentucky, and had practiced in Brownsville since 1885. Locally trusted, the voters of Linn County had even sent him as their representative to the lower house of the state assembly in 1891. Those he and Jayne selected for the jury were Edmond Evans, John Arthurs, Martin Fruit, Jode Pearl, and W. J. Windes. Since women were excluded from much of official life at this time, these jurors were all men. They were well known in the area, trusted, engaged in politics, and active in the community. They commenced their investigations of the murder scene at 10:00 a.m.; the bodies remained in the same positions where they had fallen.[7]

Upon concluding an examination of the carnage, the jury's foreman, Edmond Evans, reconvened his panel indoors, it seems, in Brownsville. There they conducted interviews with varied witnesses, Loyd being the last. He "gazed with apathy upon the crowd of curious people," one observer claimed, "and appeared indifferent or unconscious of his terrible position." He buckled, however. When Sheriff McFeron suggested that he remain silent, "he burst into tears." Loyd then told a story that claimed his innocence, basically that he had seen nothing. Regardless, the jury found "good reason to believe that Loyd Montgomery is the guilty party."[8]

McFeron immediately arrested Loyd, who spent that night in the Brownsville jail. Reportedly he slept comfortably and soundly and awoke the next morning with a hearty appetite. This was also the day of his parents' funeral.[9] Deputy Wilson ushered Loyd, who was wearing overalls, a dark shirt, and a duck coat, onto the morning train and whisked him away to the county seat. It was likely Loyd's first time on a train. It was definitely his first visit to Albany (map 7.1).[10]

At the time, Albany had a population of roughly 3,100. In 1890, most of its residents were white. The others were Chinese, African American, and Japanese, with a head count of 109, 6, and 1 respectively. Of the entire population, including those who had originated in Asia, a total of 400 were foreign born.[11] They shared, albeit unequally, in a bustling community of commerce, manufacturing, and services that was situated on the

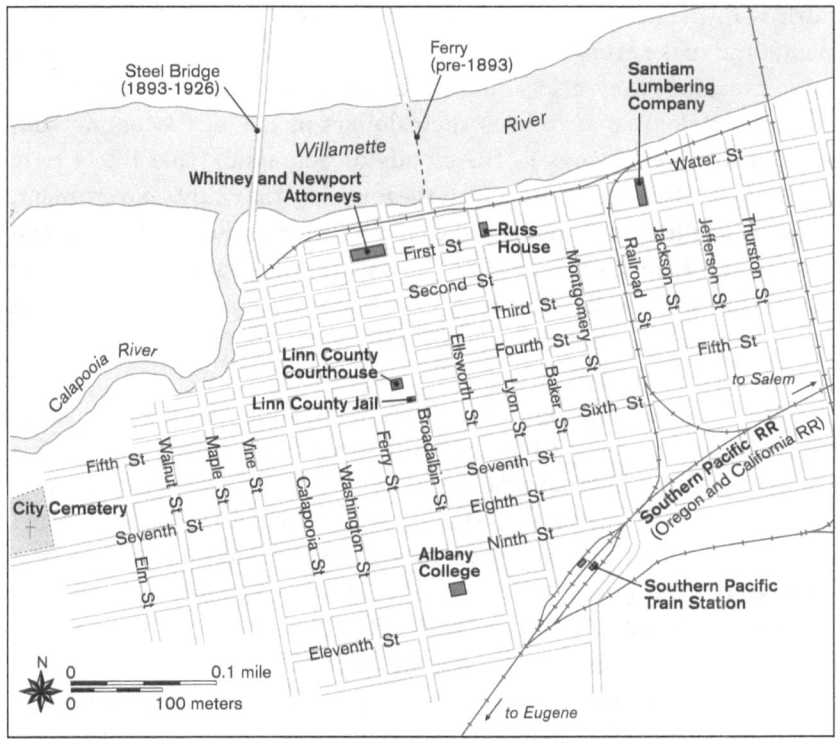

Map 7.1. Albany, Oregon, in 1896. Albany was the seat of Linn County, where Loyd ended up in jail, went on trial, and was executed. The map shows various locations and landmarks that played a role in Loyd's last days—the jail and courthouse, the offices of his lawyers, the lumberyard where his scaffold was built, and the cemetery where the county placed his remains after his family refused to have anything to do with them.

Willamette River just below where the Calapooia flows into it. In addition to the county's offices, Albany had many retail outlets, banks, hotels, factories (including those turning out flour, lumber, iron, sashes and doors, and wool, as well as a furniture and a wire-mattress works, a cigar manufacturer, a brewery, a soda company, and a tannery), a variety of churches and benevolent societies, a philharmonic, a number of newspapers, and a college, as well as the homes of some of the wealthiest people in the county.[12]

Albany had suffered terribly during the depression. Its newspapers regularly resorted to pep talks at the time, urging locals to "brace up," "do battle with the fiend of depression," get involved in the "forward movement," and make every "effort until your limbs ache and the cell of your lungs crackle." They also admonished residents to resist purchasing through catalogs so as to keep their dollars in the local economy and pointed to silver linings in the clouds of depression that likely only boosters could imagine.[13] In reality, the town saw the county government, whose offices it hosted, lose significant public funds during the financial crisis, and Albany also experienced business closures and shakeups of its stores, banks, and mills. The depression had started early in Albany and stayed late. In 1890, it was the fourth-largest city in the state; by 1900, it had dropped to ninth.[14]

In the spring of 1895, however, the county was able to muster the funds for a remodel of its aging jail in Albany (figure 7.1). The stream of criminals who passed through its doors later that year led Sheriff McFeron to remark that the improvements had come in the "nick of time."[15] The jail was located on the northwest corner of Fifth and Broadalbin Streets on a block of land occupied only by its own structure and the towering county courthouse.

The simplified Renaissance revival–style jailhouse had been constructed in 1871 of some two hundred thousand bricks. It had two stories, stood twenty-seven feet high, and had a rectangular footprint that measured thirty-two by forty feet. Before its remodel, the jail had five ironclad cells, and it had already been supplied with electric lighting. For the 1895 renovation, the county contracted with Albany Iron Works. Locals proclaimed Albany's lockup "one of the safest jails on the coast" upon its completion in June. The building now contained seven steel-barred cells on its ground floor, which was poured cement. (The sheriff had personal accommodations on the second floor.) Six of the cells were arranged in two rows of three. One of these was a "dark cell," which probably meant solitary confinement. Although a surviving description of the remodel is not specific on the matter, it did state that "the sanitary arrangement is complete." Albany began developing a sewer system in 1890; it drained directly into the Willamette River. Around all of the cells was a steel cage. A corridor between the rows of cells and inside the cage allowed the inmates to leave their cubicles during the daytime and yet remain secure. Another corridor separated the grated cell block from the walls of the building so that nothing could easily be passed through the windows, nor could inmates carve through the relatively soft brick and make an escape, which actually had

Figure 7.1. Linn County Jail. The remodeling of the Linn County Jail (*left*), originally built in 1871, was completed in early June 1895, less than six months before the sheriff lodged Loyd Montgomery there. The enclosure for his execution was constructed between the jail and the rear of the courthouse. This view is from Fifth and Broadalbin Streets and looks to the northwest. Courtesy of the Albany Regional Museum, Albany, Oregon.

happened in the 1880s. A separate cell, near the jail entrance, was set aside for female inmates.[16]

Deputy Wilson locked Loyd in the southeasternmost cell.[17] The nearby cell for women was occupied at the time by another notorious early-Oregon murderer: Emma Hannah. On 26 September, Hannah, a married farm woman with children who lived near the hamlet of Jordan (to the northeast of Albany; see map P.4), donned men's clothing, including a hat, spectacles, and a fake mustache that had but a touch of gray added to it. Impersonating a book sales rep, she made her way the mile or so from her farm to town to call on Lottie Hiatt, a divorced woman whom she suspected of having an affair with her husband. When Hiatt opened the door, the pretend peddler produced a pistol and fired several rounds. One hit Hiatt in the back of her head, splitting her skull and forcing a piece of bone through her brain. Hiatt's aged and enfeebled mother, whose home it happened to be, was there, too. She had enough strength and gumption to whack Hannah on the side of the head with a stick of firewood; the blow dislodged her glasses and mustache and knocked her hat to the ground. Hatless, Hannah fled homeward. As Sheriff McFeron investigated the case, witnesses told him that they had heard Hannah threaten Hiatt's life. The sheriff also found the footprints of the same woman's shoe at both Hiatt's and Hannah's homes, as well as a bloodied coat and revolver at the latter's domicile. He also discovered that Hannah's face carried a bruise, presumably where the chunk of firewood had landed, and he matched the hat she had left at the scene of the crime to the head of her son. Incredibly, Hiatt briefly regained consciousness and also identified the perpetrator. She lingered for nine days before expiring. Hannah was then charged with murder.[18]

On the day Loyd arrived at the jail and encountered Hannah there, the court appointed him counsel, which consisted of three lawyers: John Whitney, N. Monroe Newport, and Barney Martin. Whitney had arrived in Albany in 1867 after a circuitous route that began in Defiance, Ohio, where he had been born in 1840, and took him to law school in New York, and then ran briefly through California, Nevada, Idaho, and Portland. As a Democrat in Linn County, he succeeded to a number of elected positions over the years, including county judge, district attorney, and even state representative. As such, he was highly respected and became known locally simply as "the Judge," even after his political career ended and he worked in private practice. In 1878, Whitney paid a sizable amount for one of the lengthiest biographies to appear in the *Illustrated Historical Atlas Map of Marion and Linn Counties*.[19]

Newport was the legal partner to Whitney. Their offices were located four blocks directly north of the courthouse. Newport had been born in 1864, and he came to Oregon in 1880, receiving his law degree from Willamette University in Salem in 1892. Shortly thereafter he began practicing in Albany. Newport was a Republican and in later years would engage in elective politics.[20]

Martin, the youngest of Loyd's three lawyers by one year, had lived with his family in Brownsville in the late 1860s, moved away, then returned for good in 1882. He and two younger brothers, Ernest (born 1872) and Egbert (born 1874), became acquainted with Loyd early on. They often hunted together, and the two younger Martins overlapped with him in school. Barney earned his legal credentials in 1892. At the time of the Montgomery-McKercher murders, he was living and practicing in Brownsville. He appeared with Loyd at the coroner's inquest held there on 20 November. In later years, Martin helped found the Sons and Daughters branch of the Linn County Pioneer Association. He served as its first vice president and later as its secretary. Martin was a Democrat.[21]

By the time Loyd arrived in Albany, rumors were spreading widely about the reasons for his actions, with everyone assuming his guilt. These ranged from his supposed desire to steal his parents' money, to revenge for a fancied wrong, to moral defect, and to simply being an ingrate. Although his defense team must have admonished Loyd to keep his mouth shut, the boy in fact could not, likely due to his youth and to the horrors that weighed on his mind. Over the first days of his incarceration, he spoke to a plethora of journalists. He told them the same story that he had put to the coroner's jury. The reporters typically found him "in a very distressed state of mind," as one could imagine. "I was heartbroken and discouraged," he readily admitted. Deeply agitated, he wept often and profusely. During the nights, when news reporters were absent, he lay awake trying to engage desperately sleepy inmates in conversation.[22]

On the evening of Monday, 25 November, when a reporter visited him yet again, Loyd broke down under the "weight of the terrible crimes upon his mind, and . . . made a full confession, admitting that he killed all three of them."[23] Well capturing Loyd's anguish, another reporter imagined that "in the solitude of his cell he must have over and over again seen his father fall under the deadly bullet; over and over again the voice that sung lullabies to him in infanthood he must have heard screaming, pleading and imploring for mercy. The phantom of those pleading faces, the recollection of those terror-stricken voices, continually before his mind could but nauseate his guilty soul and cause him to seek relief by sharing his terrible secret with the world. It is no wonder that he confessed."[24] Shattered, Loyd described in emotional detail the horrific events of the nineteenth. In contrast to the rumors about his murderous motives, he only stated, "I don't know what made me do it. I just began shooting, and kept on until I shot them all."[25]

Earlier in the day of his confession, the Linn County court selected the grand jury to consider Loyd's case. During its deliberations over the next day or so, Loyd met with it and repeated his admission. The jury also examined seventeen other witnesses, including Loyd's brothers Orville and Robert; his aunt Orpha and uncle Robert Templeton and their son Clyde; Samuel Templeton; and the Warren School student and neighbor boy, Fred McCormack.[26]

Between the time when the jury initially met and when it delivered its determinations two days later, the court heard the sensational case of Emma Hannah. Her trial began on 25 November and concluded on the morning of the twenty-seventh. That jury found her guilty of murder in the second degree.[27] Roughly five hours later, at 6:30 in the evening, Sheriff McFeron escorted Loyd to the courthouse. "He was crying as he came up the aisle, and when ordered by the court to stand up as the indictments were read . . . he stood trembling and crying with his handkerchief to his eyes." The jury delivered three indictments, each for murder in the first degree. The court set his trial for 1:00 p.m. on Tuesday, 17 December, and gave defense attorney Whitney till the morning of 30 November to enter a plea.[28]

The grand jury had indicted Loyd on three counts of murder. The coroner's jury determined that the evidence pointed to Loyd. People who knew the Montgomerys were certain that the boy had done it. On top of all that, Loyd had confessed. This all suggested that the three weeks separating his indictment from his trial would be a period of simply waiting for the inevitable verdict of guilty. It was anything but that.

The day after his indictment was Thanksgiving. About 10:00 a.m., Sheriff McFeron visited Loyd in his cell, and the boy told him a different version of the events of 19 November. In this one, he laid the blame for his parents' death on Daniel McKercher. "He fired twice," Loyd explained, saying, "I rushed into the dining room and yelled to mother. 'McKercher has shot father and will kill us now.' I rushed back around the house. While doing so McKercher shot mother in the dining room. As I reached the front door he was there and fired at me, but missed me and I grabbed the gun, jerked it from him and shot him dead." McFeron did not believe him. No one did. This was only the start to the day.[29]

At about seven o'clock that evening, after eating a considerable meal, Loyd suffered one of his seizures. At that time and over the course of the next few days, three physicians observed him, including Dr. Elijah Irvine, who had worked several years at the Oregon State Insane Asylum. They debated what the seizures might indicate about Loyd's mental state or whether the episode was anything more than feigned.[30] Emma Hannah, whose cell was near Loyd's, did not buy any of it. She reportedly "made all manner of fun of him for being such a baby," whereas she claimed that in her case, she would "face the music." She did so four days later; the court set it to the tune of life imprisonment.[31]

Loyd's episode widely irritated those who learned of it. He had not entered a plea before his seizure, and rumors circulated that his counsel had put the bug of an insanity defense in his ear shortly after his indictment and the day before his wild antics. Some believed that this led him to act how he did. And then, only minutes before his attack began, Loyd allegedly asked another inmate, older and wiser, about what might happen to him if he was determined to be insane. His confidant responded that he would likely not be convicted.[32]

Loyd recovered enough from his fit to appear with Whitney in court at 9:00 a.m. on Saturday, 30 November, to enter a plea, or three in this case. Observers thought he looked sane, though his face bore scratches from the Thursday night kerfuffle; other newspapers reported that it was not until the following day when he completely recovered from his spell. Loyd's plea was "not guilty" to each of the charges, and Whitney then told reporters that "he was more firmly convinced than ever that the prisoner was not mentally accountable for the crime." Within a few days, defense attorneys Whitney and Newport had gathered statements from nine persons about Loyd's past seizures and troubled mind and moods.[33]

Some sources explained that Loyd then "settled down to a quiet life" while awaiting his trial.[34] Others told a different story—that his family neither visited nor wrote to him. Loyd did talk with his lawyers, news reporters, curiosity seekers who filtered in and out of the jail, and of course the sheriff and the deputies. But his only constant companion through these "wretched days and sleepless nights," one report dramatically described, was his own "haunting . . . thoughts" of the crime to which he had confessed.[35] He professed to Sheriff McFeron on 13 December, "I expect to be hanged, and I guess I deserve it. I would rather be hanged and have it ended than go to the penitentiary." The day before his trial, he began "to exhibit signs of uneasiness."[36]

The day of his trial, 17 December, rainy skies and cool temperatures prevailed over western Oregon. At 1:00 p.m., McFeron conducted Loyd, now for at least a third time, the short distance from the jail to the courthouse (see map 7.1).[37] The Federalist-style structure was a dark and imposing edifice, likely the greatest brick building Loyd had seen in his life. It certainly was the grandest. Large and prominent, it was visible from several vantage points throughout the surrounding countryside. Its size, color, and architecture imparted the weighty seriousness of the work that went on within its walls. To a country lad like Loyd, who now appeared to have no friend in the world, the building undoubtedly appeared foreboding.

The courthouse arose from the ashes of its more modest wooden predecessor between 1862 and 1865 at a cost of $25,000 (figure 7.2).[38] The principal contractor had been Perry Watson, an early Oregon immigrant, an original Donation Land Claim holder, and a successful farmer and brickmaker whose own stylish home and property in Marion County later adorned a half page of the *Illustrated Historical Atlas Map of Marion and Linn Counties*.[39] His Albany courthouse had two levels and measured ninety-six feet deep and fifty-three feet wide. It stood fifty-two feet at the roof's top, at the center of which an octagonal cupola rose another thirty-eight feet skyward. Atop it sat a tin dome. The sides and rear of the building had ornamented, half-relief pillars in between which stood a dozen massive windows.

McFeron likely ushered Loyd, who was that day wearing a light woolen shirt, a dark-colored coat, and overalls, through the courthouse's back door.[40] Those who came to observe the proceedings instead entered through the main doorway facing north to Fourth Street. It was arched and located under the high portico that extended across the building's façade, which itself was supported by four thirty-six-foot columns. Visitors immediately stepped into a vestibule. The courthouse's central corridor, fourteen feet high and wide and lined with various offices, stretched before them. Courtroom-goers, however, ascended a semicircular grand staircase, built by the carpenter John Kirkpatrick, a celebrated veteran of the Rogue River Indian War, directly up and into the "great Court hall."[41] The ceiling there was nineteen and a half feet high and festooned with elaborate cornices, together with chandelier-wreath moldings. Enormous windows surrounding the courtroom provided ample daylight. Spectators climbed seven feet up into the gallery, which continued to sweep upward in four tiers. They seated themselves on high-backed wooden benches.

When Loyd arrived, the gallery "was crowded by those wishing to witness the trial and see what manner of man it could be who would shoot down his own father and mother." The use of the term "man" here is significant, given Loyd's youth. When the affair began in November, the press

Figure 7.2. Linn County Courthouse. The front view here is from Fourth Street looking toward the south-southeast. A corner of the Linn County Jail can be seen just to the left of the courthouse. It was on this side of the jail where carpenters installed Loyd's gallows. His trial took place on the upper floor of the courthouse. Courtesy of the Albany Regional Museum, Albany, Oregon.

plainly referred to him as "a boy"; several news outlets pegged his years at a mere sixteen.[42] Soon enough, however, news reports aged him, embellished his size, and hardened his appearance. On 23 November one described him as "a large over-grown boy of 18 years, and weighs between 180 and 190 pounds."[43] A few days later, he became a "stout, heavy set fellow with dark complexion and swarthy countenance and looks older than 18."[44] The next day, another reported that "though eighteen years of age he is full grown, and very weather beaten, being a large, raw-boned young man."[45] After two more days had passed, Loyd became "a hard-looking fellow. He is only 19 years old, weighs about 170 pounds, and stands nearly six feet in height.... He is as strong and active as a lion. He has coarse, dark, hard, small eyes and coarse features. There is nothing prepossessing whatever about him."[46]

Over those same days, the press simultaneously made Loyd out to be a bad boy who had caused his parents' constant heartache. His widely reported bouts of weeping and sobbing became associated with his childishness and his crime against those very parents, in particular his "mother who gave him life, [whose] breast . . . nursed him, at whose knee he prattled the first [d]ays of childhood."⁴⁷ The murderous mother Emma Hannah even poked fun at Loyd for being such a "baby." And, yet, whenever compared to his father, he was transformed into a man, with Sheriff McFeron stating within days of Loyd's arrest, for example, that "Mr. Montgomery was afraid of the boy, who was much the better man of the two physically."⁴⁸ It was necessary for the state to place a man rather than a mere boy on trial for a crime that could lead directly to the gallows.

Although the aforementioned news item described crowds who wished to see the trial of a "man" who killed his parents, the state did not try Loyd for those slayings. Rather, it prosecuted him only for the murder of Daniel McKercher (figure 7.3). Reasons why are nowhere to be found in surviving documents. However, given the entirety of the events and the social and cultural atmosphere at the time, the prosecution likely reasoned that the case with reference to McKercher was less fraught with emotion and less muddied by potentially problematic stories of family dynamics. The state might also have wished to spare the remnants of a once-proud and respected Oregon pioneer family from further scrutiny, perhaps shielding it from dark and embarrassing secrets coming to light.⁴⁹

McKercher was thirty-four years old at the time of his murder. He, his older brother John, and their parents were relative newcomers to Oregon, having migrated from Canada in about 1887. The family took up a farm southeast of Brownsville. Shortly thereafter, in 1889, Daniel and John purchased the old Finley gristmill on the Calapooia. Daniel operated it, and with considerable generosity; for example, he extended substantial credit to John Montgomery during the depression so that he could feed his impoverished family. As such, McKercher became a well-regarded business owner and a respected humanitarian in the district. He was also prominent in community institutions. He had been a district deputy of the International Order of Oddfellows in Albany and a master workman in the Ancient Order of United Workmen (AOUW) in Brownsville. At the time of his death, he was serving as treasurer of the latter organization. While John McKercher married, Daniel remained single and devoted to his elderly parents. Within days of his murder, a newspaper described his mother as "almost insane with grief because of the death of her son, the prop and mainstay of her old age." The AOUW provided Daniel's parents $2,000 after his death, and it was under that organization's auspices that McKercher's funeral took place

Figure 7.3. Daniel McKercher and his trusted dog. Daniel (*far right*) is pictured here with other, unidentified members of his family, though the older gentleman is likely his father, Duncan, and the woman, his sister-in-law. Daniel's black-and-white shepherd accompanied him to the Montgomery home on the afternoon of 19 November 1895. The dog survived the shooting and took up vigil next to his master's body for hours. Those who came to the crime scene were unable to coax him away. Courtesy of the Linn County Historical Museum, Brownsville, Oregon.

on 22 November.[50] Daniel was all things that Loyd was not, and he was a considerably less complicated victim on which to mount a prosecution than John and Elizabeth Montgomery. Thus, when Sheriff McFeron conducted Loyd into Linn County's grand courtroom in the early afternoon of 17 December, the crowds there would actually see a "man" go on trial for cold-bloodedly slaying a respected businessman who was generous in spirit, enmeshed in the community, and steadfastly loyal to his mother and father.

Separating courtroom crowds from the courtroom's bar, where the legal proceedings took place, was floor space. The bar sat one foot above the floor level and was cordoned off with a balustrade. It contained substantial tables around which the varied legal teams assembled. Loyd's three lawyers were all present. The prosecution team was James McCain and Napoleon Humphrey. Both men were migrants to Oregon. McCain was born in 1844 in Indiana and moved west when only seven. Admitted to the state bar in 1868, he was elected the state's attorney for Oregon's Third Judicial District in 1892. He did not reside in Linn County; the Third Judicial District extended over five counties. Humphrey, the deputy district attorney, on the other hand, was an Albany resident and highly respected. He had previously served as a state senator—one of the few Republicans to have ever been elected in Linn County. Humphrey had been born in Iowa in 1840. He fought for the Union and was wounded during the Civil War. He migrated to Oregon in 1866.[51]

Above the tables around which all these men and Loyd assembled was the clerk's desk and, above that, the judge's bench. On 17 December, George Burnett occupied it. Burnett was a native of Oregon, having been born in 1853 on the Donation Land Claim of his parents, who had migrated to Oregon in 1846. Burnett was wholly educated in Oregon. Shortly after his 1875 admission to the bar, voters elected him district attorney for the Third Judicial District. He won election to the district's circuit court judgeship in 1892 and did so repeatedly until 1910, when he joined the Oregon Supreme Court as an associate justice. He later served as its chief justice.[52]

Burnett's first order of business on 17 December was to preside over filling the jurors' bench, which sat on the side of the bar and faced inward. There were actually two such benches—one on either side. One was for grand jurors and the other for trial jurors. Given that women in Oregon had not yet achieved suffrage, the jury would necessarily be composed of men. Given that Loyd was eighteen and that the legal age for voting and thus sitting on a jury was twenty-one, the jury would not be composed of his peers. As might be clear by now, just about all things involving formal justice in this story were "manly" in nature. The sheriff and his deputies were men. The county coroner and his jury of five were all men. The seven members of the grand jury were men. Loyd's three lawyers were men, as were the two attorneys representing the state. The judge was a man. Twenty-one of the twenty-four witnesses called during the trial were male, with sixteen of those being adults. The courthouse and the jail had been built by men.

Although the press had elevated Loyd from boy to man before his trial began, the court returned him to boyhood just before the proceedings against him began. The judge, the prosecution, and even the defense created a jury of twelve men who collectively looked a good deal like Loyd's slaughtered father. The jurors were Feicke Ackerman, Jonathan W. Burkhart, Adniram D. Craft, John H. Caldwell, William E. Githens, William A.

Gleason, Thomas N. Humphreys, William J. Obermeyer, James H. Richardson, Edwin C. Roberts, Frank Trites, and Elias Truax.[53]

These men were of course all white, like John Montgomery, and, like him, five had been born in Oregon to pioneer parents. The other seven had arrived in Oregon by, on average, 1871. They ranged in age from twenty-nine to seventy-three, but half of the jurors were in their forties and the average age of the entire body was forty-three. John Montgomery was forty-four at the time of his death. Of the twenty-three men whom lawyers excused from duty, only five were in their forties. All but one of the twelve jurors were married, and each married man had at least one child (some of them had as many as seven).[54]

Like John Montgomery, eleven of the jurors were farmers (the other was a miller). On the other hand, eleven of the twenty-three men dismissed from jury service had nonagricultural occupations—beer worker, laborer in a chair factory, two merchants, grocer, teamster, bank cashier, insurance broker, wage earner, postmaster, and real estate agent.

The average wealth of the jurors was $1,553, which was substantially more than that of John Montgomery, though one juror was worth a mere $80. But these twelve jurors were much closer to John's financial position than those excused from duty, whose average wealth was $3,565.[55] The best information available, albeit coming from the year 1900, indicates that five of the jurors who were farmers had mortgages on their farms, two rented farmland, and one was a farm laborer on his parents' rented farm. For twelve farmers excused from jury service, at least six had no mortgage.

The prosecution challenged eighteen prospective jurors. The defense objected to only five. The latter's complacency might have been because the defense attorneys realized that their client did not have much of a case. It might also be that they had little sympathy for their client. One cannot, of course, dismiss the considerable pressure exerted on the entire court, defense included, to find Loyd guilty of the most egregious of crimes, which in their minds he had no doubt committed. One news editor seeking quick justice back in November actually decried the "clever shyster" who might set "up a technical or emotional defense, to . . . defeat the ends of justice."[56]

The jury that Loyd faced, in any case, looked much like his father. Collectively, it was a white, less well-to-do farmer who was a father, who had lived in Oregon for years, and who was forty-three years old. In one sense, a reincarnated John Montgomery had returned from the grave to sit in judgment of his son, who was yet a boy. It was a small way in which the all-male justice system of an imperiled agrarian society could restore a piece of its waning authority.

And then there was the actual judge. Although never a father himself, forty-two-year-old George Burnett's experiences suggest that he did not suffer errant boys gladly. How much he believed it in 1896 is not clear, but in later years Burnett was quite vocal about bad boys and the significant problems of keeping them out of "mischief." On one occasion when he voiced such an opinion, Burnett pridefully recalled a story of how he had handled naughty boys when he had worked as a teacher in a small Willamette Valley town back in 1874. By the time of his arrival there, "the big boys had already put the last two teachers out by throwing them through the window, and the school directors wanted someone who could subdue the big boys and control the school." Burnett realized almost immediately that something was "brewing, so I kept my eyes open." Then he described the climactic event involving a particularly odious big boy. Burnett called on him in class and found that he "couldn't spell the simplest word." After Burnett ordered the lad to take his seat, he could tell by the actions of other students that the big boy was making faces at him. "I turned suddenly and caught him in the act. I walked back to his desk and quick as a flash I reached out and caught him by the collar and, holding him up, I cuffed his head till it seemed it would snap off. Changing hands[,] I cuffed the other side of his head. I kept this up till he had stopped trying to fight back and . . . commenced blubbering and howling. . . . I never had the least trouble after that and the students seemed anxious to please me and to learn." Burnett attributed his strength and physical presence in this instance, moreover, to farm work he had performed years before.[57] Burnett carried these weighty, meaningful memories, as well as the muscles that he had gained from his farm labors, as he ascended the judge's bench that towered over Loyd Montgomery.

The trial commenced immediately following the jury selection. McCain made the opening argument for the state. Whitney followed for the defense. The latter conceded that the state would likely prove its case but declared that his client committed the act without premeditation and that he was not mentally responsible. The prosecution then called eleven witnesses before Burnett recessed the proceedings until 9:00 the next morning. When the prosecution resumed, it called six new witnesses and recalled several from the afternoon before. In all, twelve men, four youths (Fred McCormack, Orville Montgomery, Robert Montgomery, and Clyde Templeton), and one woman (Orpha Templeton) appeared on behalf of the prosecution. The witnesses spoke mainly about what they had seen or heard on the day of the murders, issues related to hop income in the home, where bodies were positioned, what Loyd had done proximate to the time of the discovery of the bodies, what Loyd had said to members of the grand jury, and matters related to certain rights of the accused.[58]

According to an Albany journalist, through it all Loyd "exhibited no indications of insanity and watched the proceedings of the trial seemingly with studied indifference." What Loyd might have actually felt is of course impossible to know, though "indifference" seems doubtful; the same journalist also asserted that "when his little brothers were testifying as to the condition in which they found their murdered parents, he showed signs of weakening and almost broke into tears."[59]

The defense then proceeded, also on the trial's second day. Whitney called eight witnesses—four men (including three physicians), two youths, and two women. One of the youths was Orville, who had appeared for the prosecution the day before. The women were a former teacher and Loyd's grandmother. Whitney's witnesses spoke of Loyd's state of mind before and on the day of the murders and also about his health and seizures. Their combined testimony lasted about three hours.[60] Loyd did not take the stand. Following the defense, Humphrey provided the first part of the state's concluding statement. Newport and Whitney followed for the defense. McCain then wrapped up with the prosecution's conclusion. Judge Burnett provided something of a lengthy instruction to the jury.[61]

It was around 4:40 p.m. when the jury retired. Rather than sequestering in the jury room, its members instead headed out to dine at the Russ House, five blocks away (see map 7.1). Whether the jurors walked or took transportation is not recorded, but that establishment did operate a coach service. Whatever their means, it must have been a somber procession in any case; it was a rainy and cool day. Any spectators who stood outside the courthouse or lined the streets must have gazed expectantly at the men as they made their way through town. The Russ House dated to the 1870s. It was one of the most prominent hotels, boardinghouses, and restaurants in Albany. It was also among the earliest buildings there to be electrified. Given that it also hosted weddings and dinner parties, the establishment likely had a private dining room where the jurors could sup while they mulled the grisly evidence and decided Loyd's fate. While doing so, they ran up a bill of $13.50, which meant for that time and place that they ate well and at the county's expense. While there, they apparently had no questions for the judge. By the fifth ballot, they had agreed on murder in the first degree.[62]

Five of the jurors also happened to be fresh off the Hannah trial. She had stewed for some time about her now deceased nemesis. She had gone to considerable lengths to disguise herself and to journey to the home of her victim and there shoot her. Loyd, on the other hand, experienced a brief moment of rage before quickly killing his three victims. Comparing those cases, it might seem preposterous that the juries could come to such different conclusions: second-degree murder in the former case and first-degree murder in the latter. But the juridical result in Loyd's case makes sense. Even though he was technically tried only for the murder of McKercher, in fact he was really also convicted for the murders of his parents. Everyone clearly understood this. During his trial, Judge Burnett freely admitted testimony over the objections of the defense about "the killing of Mr. and Mrs. Montgomery, the defendant being on trial only for killing Daniel McKercher." And, at the time of his execution, a newspaper reported, incorrectly as to fact but true in spirit, that "parricide is the crime for which [Loyd] was hanged to-day."[63] Clearly at play in the minds of everyone, including the jurors, was what this study has laid out about the challenges facing agrarian society at that time, the role and expectations of boys in that society, the real problems that boys faced, the idealized relationship between fathers and sons, the prerogatives of fathers in their relationships with their children, the real and imagined struggles of farmers, and the emotions attached to the idea of a child killing his parents, especially his mother.

With all this filling their heads and a fine repast their bellies, the jurors made their decision. They had returned to the courthouse by 6:30 p.m. and handed their verdict to Judge Burnett. Upon its reading, "the prisoner," a journalist observed, "appeared unmoved." Burnett scheduled sentencing for 11:30 the next morning.[64] At that appointed time, McFeron and one of his deputies returned Loyd to the courthouse yet again. There the youth appeared alongside Whitney, who moved for a new trial, which Burnett denied. As Loyd stood before the court, Burnett pronounced that Loyd "be taken hence and confined in the county jail until the day fixed for your execution [31 January 1896]; that you be then taken from the jail and there suffer the punishment of death by being hanged by the neck until you are dead, and may God have mercy on your soul." Witnesses claimed that the boy "turned pale" and that "the look of despair plainly written upon his face, as he sat down, was the only evidence of the tempest within."[65]

The day that Burnett sentenced Loyd marked exactly a month since the youth had committed his crime. During that month, men had performed the labor of official justice largely to the exclusion of women. Only three women had been called as witnesses in the trial. Occasionally, the press had invoked the memory of Loyd's mother to emphasize the outrageous proportions of her son's deeds or to infantilize him. A newspaper during this time also reported briefly on Daniel McKercher's inconsolable mother, apparently to further sentimentalize the case. Also making it into the news was Emma Hannah, herself a mother, who taunted Loyd from her jail cell.

As the curtain came down on men, it opened the stage for more women to appear. The first was Eveline Montgomery. Immediately after her grandson's sentencing, she finally visited him in jail. She brought his four siblings along with her. What transpired there has been lost to time; a newspaper reported only that "they remained with him an hour or more, but to them he said no more about the murder than he had already confessed. He broke down and wept bitterly when he bade them goodbye. He asked his brother to send his violin to him," which he did. Loyd's siblings occasionally returned to see him during the next few weeks, with each reunion turning emotional.[66] Eveline never returned, though she undoubtedly facilitated the visits of her grandchildren, of whom she now had charge.

Women inserted themselves more directly into what remained of Loyd's life over the next few weeks. They sometimes did so in ways that historians have referred to as political motherhood. In the late nineteenth century, women took the authority that society had bestowed on them as mothers and used it to gain direct influence in the public sphere, a place from which they had been largely excluded. Claiming moral superiority as mothers in charge of uplift and education in their homes, women argued that they had a duty to transform broader society, especially when it came to issues involving youngsters. One such effort, beginning in the 1870s, was the campaign for the prevention of cruelty to children. Its proximate causes included mounting concern about urban and industrial conditions, in particular how poverty and unemployment seemed to lead to child neglect and even abuse in the growing city. More generally, it was part of middle-class women's concerns as women. "Every time child welfare movements have arisen, every time there have been concerns with the sufferings of children and demands for greater social responsibility for children," the historian Linda Gordon has told us, "feminism has been influential."[67]

In the case of Loyd Montgomery, "overly sympathetic women" soon "deluged" the Oregon governor, William Paine Lord, "with letters . . . begging him to interfere and save the life" of this mere boy. Amid this epistolary inundation, Lord gasped that the letters he received maintained that Loyd's crime was "the outcome of bad environment, for which the defendant is not responsible." In sharing this, Lord intimated that the correspondents expressed concern specifically over Loyd's home life—namely when he conjectured that Loyd may have been "bred under bad surroundings" and "had no moral training." Such conjecture, if not in name, at least in spirit pointed to the failings of Loyd's mother.[68]

Women outside of Linn County constituted the greatest force that offered the lad comfort and that called for the commutation of his death sentence. One such woman wrote to Loyd at Christmas, hoping to offer consolation. "I am the mother of three boys," she remarked, "one about your age, and my soul yearns over you and I would do by you as I would want some one to do for my boy were he in your place." Sympathetically, she added that "there must have been great provocation" to cause him to do as he did.[69] In another instance, a California woman who wrote to the Oregon governor claimed that she knew for certain that if Loyd were hanged, she herself would die instantly.[70] Some women took up Loyd's cause in political meetings. In early January, Jennie Pritchard, an official in the Oregon State Woman Suffrage Association who lived in Portland, addressed an organizational meeting on the subject of Loyd, "who, she said, ought not be hanged, but imprisoned, under conditions wherein he might develop the hidden spark of good with which God has endowed all mankind."[71]

The male-controlled press typically referred to these women's efforts as "sentimental gush" and disparaged those who offered it.[72] That term is all the more telling when one considers how often newspapers used the word *reason*, or some variation of it, when describing how the male-operated justice system had functioned in the case of Loyd. As such, news editors questioned the mental condition of the women who tried to insinuate themselves in the affair; when men took up the cause against Loyd's hanging, the press questioned their manhood. "If there is any common sense left in

Oregon," barked the editor of the *Oregonian*, "this sentimental conspiracy of hysterical women and womanish men to obtain commutation of the death sentence of Lloyd [sic] Montgomery ought to be checked."[73] That editor was Harvey W. Scott, younger brother to the famed suffragist Abigail Scott Duniway, who for years worked on behalf of women's rights throughout the Pacific Northwest. Harvey steadfastly opposed his sister's efforts.

One Albany news editor drew parallels to the actions of women who sought mercy in the remarkable Theodore Durrant double-murder case in San Francisco the year before, referring to his defenders as "weak minded women" who "shower flowers and attention upon such murderers."[74] Of the California woman who implored the governor to halt Loyd's execution, claiming it would kill her, one editor (once again, Scott) disposed of her as an "aggravated case of 'born fool and high fever.'" The poor woman also became a target of letters to the editor. One from Crawfordsville referred to her as "that woman" and stated that had she "been a neighbor and had seen that father, mother and kind friend lying cold in death ... had heard the wail of friends and children, and had spent as many sleepless nervous hours as we neighbors have, she would have kept her paper and pencil for a better purpose than petitioning the governor to let such a villain live."[75] But "regardless of the tears of women," one Albany news editor wrote specifically in response to the Californian, "if any one ought to be hung, it is Loyd Montgomery."[76]

It appeared to some through early January that the torrent of tears pouring forth from "hysterical women and womanish men" would indeed wash away the advancements that patriarchal justice and reason had established in Loyd's formal trial. Thankfully, other manly men might yet be called up to hold back the rising tide: "Neither the governor nor the supreme bench," Harvey Scott's *Oregonian* assured its readers, "is governed by weak sentimentalism."[77] Sounding perhaps more hopeful than reality might recommend, news editors helped shore up the governor's manhood against the waves of feminine sentimentality crashing upon him. "There is small danger that efforts in [Loyd's] behalf will be successful," Scott confidently stated, "as Governor Lord is not the man to yield to them."[78] And in the instance of the woman who knew she would die if Loyd were executed, an editor pointed out that her appeal by its very nature should have "a bracing effect ... if the governor needs to be strengthened in his purpose to let the law take its course in this case."[79]

In fact, these female-directed efforts did not succeed, and when Loyd's life ended, no one actually reported on what became of the California woman who so bound her fate to his. An Albany "lady," on the other hand, purportedly did go insane.[80] Men, working within official channels, also failed to alter the course of events. On several occasions over the couple of weeks or so after his sentencing, Loyd expressed a wish to die and asked that no effort be made to seek a new trial.[81] This stymied his attorneys, but as the day of his reckoning bore down upon him, Loyd buckled. On 15 January he asked Whitney and Newport to make an appeal.[82] By then it was rather late in the game, and although the lawyers were able to put together a one-hundred-page bill of exceptions and sent it to the proper officials on 21 January (receiving a deadline extension in the process), they had not enough time to perfect their appeal. Newport appeared before the Oregon Supreme Court on 28 January and failed to get a stay of execution. He then reached out to the governor, also unsuccessfully. And with that, Loyd's counselors felt they had "done their whole duty" and would simply "wait for the law to carry out its sentence."[83]

Just as the Linn County–based press and the locals who wrote to its editors protested women's interference, they also grumbled about the actions that Loyd's lawyers took on behalf of "this young monster, who killed his own father and mother." For so many, the facts were obvious, as was the need for the penalty of death. Moreover, there was the unnecessary expense of it all, especially during an economic crisis. For example, one Brownsville resident, who signed a letter to the editor merely as "Taxpayer," protested the public monies that would be paid out for more trials and delays. A self-proclaimed Albany "Witness" was incensed, believing (wrongly so) that Loyd's appointed counsellors were stretching things out in order to line their own pockets.[84]

Linn County journalists and residents also objected when newspapers from afar, especially those in California but also on occasion the *Oregonian* in Portland, provided a more sympathetic portrait of Loyd.[85] Editorially, the *Oregonian* held a hard line against Loyd. It also derided calls for leniency emanating from California, stating, for example, that "this sort of thing is to be expected ... where a low moral standard inherited from mining camps has degenerated still farther in an atmosphere of hysterical sensationalism and morbid and depraved public taste."[86] The *Oregonian* editor likely intended here to draw attention to the popularly understood differences between California and Oregon settlement: while the former had been settled by uncontrollable young men, not unlike Loyd, the latter had been a family affair.

But the Portland editor, Harvey Scott, was not always able to control the pen of his own reporters. One of those was wielded by George Piper. He became a favorite of Loyd, with the youth once stating that Piper had been the first to have "given me a square deal." This was, of course, to the consternation of Albany newspapers, whose reporters the youth soon refused to talk to and who condemned Piper's pieces. Beginning at the end of December and stretching into early January, Piper interviewed Loyd on several occasions, producing a series of articles that struck a more kindhearted tone.[87] Just as the Californian who claimed she would die if Loyd was executed became known in some quarters as "that woman," one of Piper's particularly annoying interviews became known in Albany as "that interview."[88]

For one, Piper offered a physical description of Loyd that differed from those that portrayed him as a hardened criminal. "Although only 18 years old," the reporter penned, "he is as large as a full-grown man, and his magnificent physique might well be the envy of a trained athlete. He might easily be called a handsome young fellow, with his dark eyes and hair, and well-shaped head. He has an expressive face, too, and seems to be naturally quite intelligent."[89]

A couple of days later, Piper wrote that "young, strong, well-grown, with the untutored simplicity of a country boy, uneducated and undisciplined—the thought forces itself even upon the most practical that, such as he is, he is the product of his environment, and, because of the slighted or thwarted possibilities of his life, an object of pity."[90] At another point, Piper explained that his conversations with Loyd "would incline any person to sympathize somewhat with him."[91] Some days later Piper went way too far when claiming that a good many in Linn County had changed their feelings about Loyd, writing that "it is generally believed that his execution could be postponed if any effort were made in this direction."[92]

Outraged, a "Citizen of Brownsville" wrote a stinging rebuttal. It roundly condemned Piper, stating that it "is getting to be unsafe for a person to travel for fear of being shot" and that prose like Piper's encouraged such conditions. As for the contention that a changed feeling existed, this writer put forth the opinion that "Montgomery has no sympathizers.... Every one has deserted him, and he should be deserted. Any one who would commit such a crime should not be allowed to breathe the same air that respectable people do for a moment. The general prayer here is that the sentence will be carried out, and the execution take place on the day fixed. This is the sentiment of all the people in this community."[93]

While all this hubbub swirled, there was of course the very real boy at the center of the storm. His most visible moments of despair occurred when his siblings visited. Otherwise, he appeared sanguine in his cell, pretty much accepting, perhaps even embracing, his fate. "I am ready to die," he told Piper on 28 December, "and the sooner the better. . . . Everybody thinks I killed my parents, and, even if I were free, I would suffer more than death by knowing that everybody thought I ought to hang. . . . What's the use?"[94] A couple of days later, in speaking with Sheriff McFeron, Loyd even stated matter-of-factly that he would even "spring the trap himself, if allowed to do so."[95] And another time his questions and musings perfectly startled Deputy Quincy Propst. Loyd asked him, "Does a man's mouth open when he is hanged?" When Propst responded, "I guess it does," Loyd replied, "Well, if mine does, I want you to throw a biscuit in it."[96]

The reality was, at least for a time, that Loyd's stay in jail appeared to agree with him. At the very least, he made the most of it. When he asked his brother on 19 December to send him his violin, he explained to the sheriff, "I want to have as a good a time as I can while I stay with you."[97] Some thought that his "more cheerful" and "brighter" disposition since his trial had something to do with him coming to believe as true the lies he told of McKercher killing his mother and father.[98] Sheriff McFeron felt that his "antics are the outcome of forced hilarity, to relieve his mind from thoughts of his awful crime."[99] Whatever the reason, Loyd regularly played his fiddle and just as often his harmonica, often leading his fellow inmates in song. He happily greeted and freely engaged in conversations with visitors. He read occasionally. He ate heartily. At one point he "smoked a cigar . . . with evident relish." And he slept like a log, reportedly undisturbed by bad dreams.[100] He also played pranks with cellmates, in particular his old friends the burglarizing Fox brothers and Harry Pool, who joined Loyd in jail in late December and remained there till after the 31 January execution date.

Loyd's reported carefree demeanor annoyed locals. What rankled them more was his repeated insistence that McKercher had committed the heinous deed and that he had killed the miller only in self-defense. Particularly maddening was that Piper gave voice to this claptrap in considerable news-column space. In those reports, Loyd seems to taunt those who opposed him. He made statements that called into question the integrity of locals, declaring, for example, that "several witnesses told some horrible lies" during the trial. More infuriating was his impugning the esteemed McKercher with proclamations like "my shot that killed McKercher sent him straight to hell . . . and nothing can stop me from going to God after I'm hanged." Most egregious of all was when this mere boy attacked McKercher's manhood. "I knocked the rifle up above my head," Loyd claimed of his imagined tussle with his adversary, "and, as it went off, grabbed McKercher by the throat with my left hand. If they will take McKercher's body up they'll find the marks my nails made in his neck. I noticed them after I killed him. I took the gun away from McKercher and shot him dead. He was an infant in my grasp, I was so much stronger."[101]

Three days later, a Brownsville resident's angry response in a letter to the *Oregonian* occupied two-thirds of a column in that newspaper. Its contents and descriptions suggested that the writer had actually examined the crime scene, and a significant portion of it was given over to defending McKercher's character and manhood. "There was no man in this community who stood higher than McKercher," the missive maintained. One of the letter's ten paragraphs held forth in this way:

> As to the terrible lies Lloyd [sic] speaks of having been told on the witness stand, there was none. This is simply a dodge of his to create more sympathy. As to the nail prints in McKercher's neck, there was none. There was a small hole immediately under his chin, probably an inch deep. Again, Montgomery could not have seen any prints in McKercher's neck, had there been any. McKercher lay on his face, and no one could possibly have seen his neck. Lloyd [sic] says McKercher was as an infant in his hands. This is not true. McKercher weighed 150 pounds, and could have held his own with Montgomery.[102]

So much ire did Piper's and other problematic stories like his raise (even leading McKercher's father, Duncan McKercher, to take pen to paper in defense of his son) that it caused the *Oregonian* quickly to make a statement supporting McKercher and scorning Loyd: "The attempt to smirch the memory of McKercher in order to help Lloyd [sic] Montgomery to escape his deserved fate on the gallows is thoroughly disreputable.... His memory should be respected and his good name defended by all decent citizens. Attack upon his character should be left to the tongue which soon will be stilled by justice."[103]

Extracting the truth from Loyd, in fact, preoccupied the people of Linn County and beyond more than perhaps anything else through the last weeks of his life. Their reasons for doing so varied, and they used multiple methods. Loyd's denials were troubling, and the more he embellished them, the more they seemed to some to become the truth. I. W. Rivers, arrested for stealing in Albany, spent time in jail with Loyd and spoke with him "a great deal" (figure 7.4). Unable to "draw from him one word that would indicate his guilt," Rivers admitted, "I began to believe the poor unfortunate boy was innocent." The *Oregonian* reporter Piper similarly stated that while Loyd's "story about McKercher killing his parents is generally discredited . . . there are a good many who are inclined to believe it." The San Francisco press also explained that Loyd's composure after his trial "created considerable doubt in the minds of many people" about his guilt.[104] It may be that some who had nagging misgivings sought his confession in order to assuage their consciences, given the severity of the punishment that the boy faced.

Journalists like Piper and those who wrote for San Francisco's newspapers, however sympathetically they approached Loyd, in fact did believe that he had committed the murders. They just differed from Linn County residents in their opinions as to why Loyd did what he did and what his responsibility truly was. The steady stream of journalists into the jailhouse was actually motivated in part to get Loyd's confession to a crime that they knew he committed. The boy constantly frustrated them, however. Not to be thwarted, in one case a newspaper simply whipped up a confession, though flavoring it with some facts that anyone who had been reading newspapers over the previous couple of months would have recognized. Not surprisingly, at least to residents in Linn County, the newspaper that did this, the notorious *Examiner*, was published in San Francisco, which they considered a center of half-baked notions. In doing its deed, the *Examiner* also claimed an exclusive: supposedly Loyd wrote his confession in his jail cell on the morning of his execution and addressed it directly to the newspaper's editor. It also included an illustration to add proof to the pudding.[105]

Figure 7.4. I. W. Rivers. Newspapers reported that Rivers, who was in the Linn County Jail for stealing at the time Loyd was there, had considerable influence over the boy. They attributed to him Loyd's reluctance to admit the truth of what he had done; he instead stuck to his lie that Daniel McKercher had murdered his parents. It seems, rather, that Loyd had more of an influence on Rivers. The older inmate later wrote a lengthy letter to a newspaper editor in which he described how the Salvation Army's work with Loyd and the pathos of Loyd's last days in jail led him to conversion. Courtesy of the Oregon State Archives, Salem.

Although Loyd would indeed confess at the very last minute and would write a farewell note, the *Examiner*'s piece was neither his actual confession nor his note, and much indicates it to be a forgery. Among the evidence, of course, are the real confession and note. Second, the published prose and its organization are clearly from the hand of an experienced writer, which Loyd was not. Third, it was signed "Lloyd," when plainly the name the lad went by was "Loyd." News editors in Albany, however, saw through it for other reasons—namely the accompanying illustration. The *State Rights Democrat* pointed out that it depicted Loyd—as did an *Examiner* illustration the day before that showed him speaking to his lawyer—as sitting "in the same horrid 14th century cell with its stone wall and small window, with a candle on his stand" (figure 7.5). "In view of the fact that the Albany jail is lighted by electricity and Montgomery's cell was an open steel latticed," the Albany newspaper stated, "the picture is a farce. . . . Sensation and not reliability is the order of the metropolitan press."[106] The *Examiner* certainly did employ all manner of sensation in its reporting on all sorts of issues over the years. It did so in part to outsell its equally dramatic rival, the *Chronicle*. But Albany and other Oregon newspapers were not innocent of employing such tactics. For any of these newspapers, getting Loyd's confession—real or otherwise—could mean big money.

Figure 7.5. Two views of Loyd Montgomery in his jail cell during his final hours. Source: *San Francisco Examiner*, 1 February 1896 and 2 February 1896.

LLOYD MONTGOMERY AND HIS LAWYER TALKING OVER THE SITUATION.
(Sketched in the cell of the boy murderer at Albany a few days ago for "The Examiner.")

Another profit seeker, albeit one who leavened the lump with charity, employed an entirely different approach in hopes of extricating the truth from Loyd. By the late 1880s, Thomas Edison's fantastical phonographic invention had made its way to Oregon, and itinerant entertainers typically exhibited it for a price. Not only did such gadgets play recordings for amazed audiences, but even more thrilling was that some could also make live recordings on the spot. In the fall of 1895, one such individual, whose name variously appeared in press reports as D. E. Jenkins or Judkin and sometimes just as "Mr. J," arrived in Linn County after a successful tour in Washington State. In early December he arrived in the village of Oakville, located between Albany and Brownsville, in possession of a "good assortment of records," including orchestral and band music as well as something simply referred to as "comic." "Everyone should hear this wonderful instrument," declared one witness, as "it is one of the greatest and most wonderful inventions of the age."[107]

Mr. J's equipment could also record. He visited Loyd shortly after his sentencing, promising the boy that if he confessed into the phonograph, half the proceeds from its exhibition would go to his brothers and sister. Mr. J's "piece of enterprise" did briefly tempt Loyd. In the end, however, "the phonograph man failed to secure Montgomery's confession." The visit was not entirely a disappointment: Mr. J was able to capture Loyd playing, reportedly on a flute, once again the tune of "Home, Sweet Home." Mr. J. subsequently exhibited the recording while "doing the valley." Unknown is whether he donated any money to the surviving members of the Montgomery family.[108]

While some sought Loyd's confession in the service of mammon, far more did so in the service of God. There were ten ministers or evangelists who can be identified by name who had a direct relationship with Loyd's story over the course of December and January. Most were what we in later times would describe as "evangelicals." Though the term existed then, it was used somewhat differently from how it is today. For the 1890s, it might be best to call them "revivalist-oriented Protestants." They focused less on tradition or the importance of the church as an institution and more on the need for an individual to get right with God, to be "born again." Loyd provided an ideal opportunity for them to showcase for the newspapers the kinds of spiritual transformations they hoped to spark across the nation.[109] They included the Reverends Bengal Kelly of Albany's United Evangelical church; Riley Little of Albany's United Presbyterian church; Charles McKee of Albany's Baptist church; John Shulse of the Methodist Episcopal church in the town of Shedd; Daniel Poling of Albany's Congregational church; J. E. Snyder of Brownsville's First Presbyterian church; Carpus Sperry of Brownsville's Baptist church; and Frank Dickson, a traveling evangelist, as well as the evangelist husband-and-wife team of Mr. and Mrs. W. L. Thompson, who operated the nondenominational Adelphi Mission on Albany's First Street.

While the press did not provide the names of any of the Salvation Army missionaries who came to visit Loyd, that organization played an especially significant role at the end of his short life and in his early death. In addition to emphasizing the need for individual salvation, the Salvation Army emphasized personal holiness and sought to perfect society through perfecting the individual. If it could root out sin in someone like Loyd, it could then do so in communities and eventually the world.

During that two-month period, newspapers also mentioned unnamed ministers—who may have been among the above or might have been others—as well as a number of both identifiable and unidentifiable lay individuals who either spoke to, wrote to, or prayed with Loyd over matters of his salvation. The goings-on at the jail from December through January might even be seen as something of an ongoing revival, which also had an effect on several other denizens of that place and spread outward into the community.

Religion was at the heart of American settlement in Linn County. The earliest arrivals immediately began holding services in their homes. As quickly as they could, they built churches and established Sunday schools and religious-affiliated institutions of learning. Among the settlers were also individuals sent by their churches to Oregon or appointed by them as missionaries after their arrival in the area. Examples in Linn County include Henry and Eliza Spalding from the Lapwai Mission, who arrived in Brownsville in 1848; the Reverend Wilson Blain, who settled just south of Brownsville and gathered the first United Presbyterian congregation in Oregon, in 1850; the Methodist circuit rider John McKinney, who took a Donation Land Claim near Brownsville and founded the first Methodist congregation there; and the Reverend Thomas Kendall, who migrated to Oregon in 1845 and founded the very first Presbyterian congregation in Linn County, at Oakville, just after his arrival.[110]

In 1867, Presbyterians founded a college in Albany. By 1875, they were also operating an academy in Brownsville, and in that same year the town had six Protestant churches for a population that might have reached six hundred. Brownsville's embarrassment of religious riches became a point of interest to an observer in 1879. He noted that "all tastes may be suited" in Brownsville for "getting into the kingdom of heaven" and that the variety of churches there "appear[s] to agree on the main thing, but differ in the non-essential details."[111] In 1890, across the entire county of barely more than sixteen thousand inhabitants, there were seventy-one religious organizations, forty-five church buildings, and twenty-one religious halls.[112]

The Templetons and the Montgomerys, although they had different political affiliations, were longtime Presbyterians and joined together in building that church in Brownsville. The parents of Elizabeth (Couey) Montgomery, however, had married in the Methodist Episcopal church in Eugene.[113]

The historian Ferenc Morton Szasz has written of the American West at the end of the nineteenth century that "evangelical Christianity did not shape the 'religious character' of the region. In fact, in many places it found itself a decided minority." This was not the case in Linn County, where revivalist-oriented Protestant denominations so dominated that practically the only route into heaven seemed to trace directly through their churches. The 1890 census reveals that 3,325 of the 3,495 members of churches in Linn County that year were Protestant. The other 170 were Catholic. No other faiths were represented.[114]

Although Linn County had fewer religious adherents than the national average in 1890 (21.5 percent versus 34.4 percent), this likely had to do with the nature of the Protestant denominations in Linn County, which demanded a person's expression of salvation in order to become a full member.[115] But regardless of the numbers, religion was in fact a serious part of life there. Moreover, area newspapers, in addition to reporting on local church news, also regularly included content on regional and national religious developments. To list but a very, very few so as to demonstrate their range, they included lengthy defenses of the literal interpretation of the Bible, consideration of the faith of the Chinese, and expansive coverage of the national assembly of the Presbyterian Church when it met in Albany in June 1894.[116]

Linn County was actually a center for revivalism in the 1890s, when revivalism was beginning to surge across the nation.[117] Rapid change due to technological innovation, the growth of cities, and scientific developments; the expansion of the American empire; growing political, race, and labor strife; the matter of immigration; issues of morality such as urban prostitution, the consumption of alcohol, the market in obscene literature, the dangers that lurked for children; advances made in religious liberalism and ideas about evolution; and of course the crushing depression of the era—all these and more contributed to the emergence of a highly individualized form of ecstatic religious fervor in America.[118]

And in the 1890s that fervor began to stir in startling fashion in Linn County, where agrarianism was under siege; where the economy was bottoming out; where the founding generation was heading off to its final reward; where the Populist movement, which itself acted as a form of fundamentalist revivalism, was momentarily ascendant; where race and immigrant labor issues provoked regular concern; and where an awareness of the growing power of the urban, the industrial, and the global was sinking in.[119] Many revivals occurred in Linn County just in the first half of 1895. Both the Methodist Episcopal and the First Presbyterian congregations in Brownsville held revivals in January. In February, the Congregational church in Albany held three weeks of revival gatherings while at the same time, but over only ten days, the Methodist Episcopal church in the town of Tangent did the same. In April, the Methodist Episcopal church in Lebanon held several revival meetings with a variety of ministers "from abroad" participating. The next month, a week's worth of revival meetings hit at Albany's Evangelical church. The following month, June, the city's Methodist Episcopal church conducted a full week of its own meetings. Evangelists from out of town, including from as far away as Georgia, participated. Itinerant revivalists were also active in the county during this period. These travelers included both male and female revival leaders, who held separate meetings in communities along the North Santiam River and in the towns of Halsey and Sodaville in February. In March, the target was the village of Gates. An itinerant female Baptist minister led an independent revival in Albany in May. And a camp-meeting revival took place near Lebanon in June.[120] (Various of the towns mentioned here are identified on map P.4.)

The grandest event of all that year in Albany occurred in the autumn. It lasted three weeks, starting in mid-November and concluding on 5 December. The Portland evangelists Earl Holdridge and Frank Dickson, who were already in the midst of a revivalist swing through several small

Oregon towns, led the affair, but other out-of-town preachers joined them. They had the cooperation of Albany churches, the YMCA, women's clubs, and a host of local ministers. Even thirty-four male and female proprietors of local businesses signed a pledge to close shop early every day through the duration of the revival. One of the most spectacular actions was a huge prayer meeting conducted by male ministers and female adherents simultaneously in fifteen different locales scattered across town. Other varied prayer groups and services occurred. Evenings offered lectures and sermons on topics ranging from the relationship between secret societies and churches, to the wonders of the conversion of a well-known Polish rabbi, to the "Second Coming of Christ." Some were so popular that those desirous of enjoying the rewards that they offered had to be turned away.[121]

Of course, it was while these fires of religious fervor burned that Loyd murdered three people, was lodged in the county jail in Albany, and endured the first dramatic days of his incarceration. Loyd also became part of the religious conflagration. Twice during the revival's concluding week, including on its very last evening, the Reverend Kelly of Albany's United Evangelical church mounted the rostrum and held forth on the reasons why Loyd killed his parents, reasons that he found in the Old Testament. In a matter of days, the evangelist Frank Dickson, who had been largely responsible for organizing the Albany events, visited Loyd in his jail cell and then later sent him a letter "urging the murderer to turn his thoughts to his maker and to pray for forgiveness." Loyd's father's cousin, who was also the wife of the county sheriff, also assumed a role in Loyd's path to redemption: she provided him with a Bible.[122]

At the end of December, when the *Oregonian* reporter George Piper met Loyd for the first time, their conversation turned to matters of the afterlife, at the former's prompting. Piper wondered if Loyd thought much about eternal punishment after death. "'Oh,'" Loyd replied, "carefully choosing his words, 'the Bible says that there is punishment in store in the next world for those who commit crime in this.'" When the journalist pressed him on his fate more specifically, Loyd responded, in keeping with the story of the killing that he was now spinning, "'I am innocent of any serious crime. I never murdered any one, and I killed McKercher because he killed my parents. I won't suffer for causing his death. I don't know anything about the next world, but I don't fear it in the least. If I had killed my parents, though, I should.'"[123]

And so remained his stone-like heart, unmoved by the torrent of ministers and others who visited and flooded him with letters over the next few weeks, begging him to confess and save himself. Repeatedly to them and others he claimed knowledge that God had forgiven whatever sins he had, but killing his parents was not among them.[124] He also had the nerve to give spiritual advice to others, including to his siblings, urging them to join the church. Two of those in fact did: they united with the First Presbyterian church in Brownsville. One did so, along with forty-nine other converts, during a revival that its minister, J. E. Snyder, conducted just after Loyd's execution.[125] It was also, however, about the time when Loyd's old friends the Foxes and Pool joined him in jail and when he took possession of his fiddle that he seems to have set aside his Bible, which he had previously studied "industriously."[126]

The ministers' repeated failures with Loyd only led them to try, with the patience of Job, ever harder. Much was at stake: if they could convert a parricide, anyone was a possible convert. They even varied their tactics, but the boy-murderer continued to vex. In early January, Loyd told a reporter that "one preacher spent an hour with me the other day and insisted upon me saying that I killed my parents. He said I would not get to Heaven unless I made such a confession." Annoyingly turning the minister's theological prescription back onto its advocate, "I told him," Loyd cleverly explained, that "I would be telling a lie if I did so, and that I did not mean to die with a lie on my lips." Loyd responded less well to the more firebrand-like ministering of the fiercest revivalists, as suggested here. He rather preferred those with a lighter touch, though their preaching fizzled, too. Of "another minister who visits me," Loyd also explained in the same interview, "I can say honestly that he gives me a lot of comfort. He tells me to ask forgiveness for my sins, and that I will reach God. He don't talk like a wild man and insist upon me confessing to a crime I never committed."[127]

On the other hand, the Salvation Army, which did preach a real and fiery hell, seems to have had an effect on Loyd—at least a newspaper declared that he "has become much interested" in them.[128] That might have been more due to the dazzling diversion that the Salvation Army provided for one who was otherwise stuck in a dull jail cell. The Salvation Army had burst onto the American religious scene in the late 1870s, making the transatlantic pilgrimage from England, and it rapidly spread to major and minor cities through the 1880s. Its tactics of singing, instrument playing, uniform wearing, street parading, and public preaching caught the attention and ire of just about everyone from the patrons of mainstream churches, who denounced them, to rowdy street gangs, who attacked them. But since the targets of the Salvation Army's missionary zeal were primarily the denizens and the debauched of working-class neighborhoods, red-light districts, and city slums, good street theater made good sense—the livelier and more colorful, the better.

The Oregon press regularly carried sensational items on the Salvationists in the 1870s, and the organization seems to have advanced on the state in the middle of the next decade, when it took the streets of Portland by storm. Naturally, the Salvation Army also ran into resistance in the region. By the early 1890s, however, as it became more accepted or at least tolerated around the United States, it also began making inroads elsewhere in Oregon, including in Linn County. That place was not exactly analogous to an urban ghetto, but it was ripe for reformation, and it did have an earthier side, as evidence presented throughout this book clearly indicates. In Linn County, the Salvationists seem first to have occupied the small town of Scio, about eighteen miles from Albany, in about 1890. They met with immediate success. One resident reported that the Salvation Army "captured the town" with thirty conversions, half of them gamblers. "No where in the U.S.," another view of the village described, "is the Salvation army treated so well as in Scio."[129]

Although by September 1894 the Salvationists had "laid siege to Corvallis and Eugene" and planned its "attack" on Albany, it seems that the invasion of the latter locale did not commence until about 1 January 1896.[130] When the Salvation Army started its advance, it did so with a bang, and other street evangelists joined the ruckus. "If any one says Albany is quiet," a newspaper editor admonished, "ask them to visit First street from 7:30 to 8 o'clock at night when the Salvation Army, God's Regular Army and the Adelphi Mission are all holding forth at once."[131]

Given that the Salvationists sought to reach the most downtrodden, the county jail seemed a logical field of operations. That the unrepentant caged there were a captive audience naturally improved the odds for a victory. Not only was Loyd incarcerated there, but so too was a phalanx of other recidivists, including the Fox brothers, Harry Pool, and I. W. Rivers. Additionally, and at roughly the same time, the jail sheltered the inmates David Black, who had burglarized the Russ House; and the male-female duo of A. S. McKenzie and Ella Holcomb, who had been arrested for lewd cohabitation (they occupied separate cells in the jail). Emma Hannah, however, had been sent to the penitentiary in Salem on 1 December 1895, well before the battle had begun. In time, the Salvationists conquered all the aforementioned sinners, some actually avowing that it was the Salvation Army's efforts with Loyd and the effects of his last fear-provoking days that led to their deliverance. All of this evangelizing seemed to have some effect on Loyd: he spoke with reporters on matters relating to sin, punishment, eternal damnation, forgiveness, hell, and future reward—all of which he seemed to know a good deal about. He also claimed conversion by the Salvationists, and yet, he still refused to surrender a confession to any of the group's officers.[132]

By the evening of Tuesday, 28 January, less than three days before his scheduled execution, Loyd "lost much of his bravado," a journalist reported. And in that moment, "he created quite an uproar in the jail. He had a prolonged and violent fit of weeping and declared he did not believe he could live until Friday [his appointed date with the hereafter]. He said he could see his father and mother, and they were pleading with the officers not to hang him." Loyd also desperately begged to see his brothers and sister once more. The sheriff arranged for them to come to him while also deciding to place two guards with him "to prevent any attempt at suicide." At least one of those was A. B. Kellogg, to whom the county paid two dollars for his services.[133]

Eva and Orville visited Loyd the next day, for the last time. According to the inmate Rivers, who interceded to have Loyd's cell door opened so that the youth could embrace his siblings, the visit "was most heartrending."[134] Also that morning, the Thompsons of the Adelphi Mission "prayed and sang with him and went out leaving him in . . . a serious mood."[135] That evening, members of the Salvation Army met with Loyd again, but with them he continued to stick to the story that McKercher had killed his parents. He also reportedly played "The Devil among the Tailors" on his violin to keep up his courage.[136]

By now, carpenters Conn and McChesney had moved the scaffold from the Santiam Lumbering Company's yard into place outside the jail and were busily constructing the enclosure (see map 7.1). Sheriff McFeron was likewise occupied, sending out printed invitations for the execution—about fifty of them—to sheriffs of other counties, reporters, ministers, politicians, and other select citizens. Among the recipients was John McKercher. As the invited and the uninvited descended in droves on Albany, McFeron's wife packed up the children and sought refuge with friends out of town.[137]

Thursday, 30 January, was the last full day of Loyd's life. It dawned clear and relatively warm for wintertime. In the morning, McFeron purchased a black suit for the boy—a thirty-eight-inch jacket and trousers measuring thirty-two by thirty-three. He also procured a white shirt and collar. Where McFeron bought these is unclear, but that he did so at a local vendor is evident from the reports.[138] For part of the rest of the day, McFeron and some of his deputies practiced with a deadfall on the gallows to make sure all settings and adjustments were in order. As these goings-on dominated that day's activities in and about the jail, Loyd took pen to paper and wrote a final farewell to his siblings. Demonstrating the effect that all things religious had had on him during his time behind bars, the letter spoke only of such matters. He congratulated his sister on joining the church in Brownsville, and he encouraged his brothers to do likewise. He warned them away from the wrong path. He spoke of his impending journey across "that dark river." He assured them that he was "ready to go meet our father and mother in heaven," where, in turn, he would wait for them to follow.[139] News reporters got hold of the missive. The ironies contained within it did not escape them. The editor of the distant *Republican Weekly* in Fresno, California, for example, wrote, "His victims had no time to prepare for death, and hence they may have gone to another place than the abode of the blest. This, however, may be considered fortunate, as an embarrassing rencontre will thus be avoided. It really would be discomfiting for Saint Lloyd [sic] should he casually turn his eyes while twanging a harp and discover that his left-hand or right-hand neighbor was an individual whom he had expedited to saintship by the shotgun route."[140]

Little else noteworthy occurred until evening, when the sheriff threw open the jail's doors to legitimate visitors as well as to the morbidly curious. McFeron allowed them unfettered access to the central corridor separating the two rows of cells. Several hundred streamed through, a reporter claimed. Among them were boys, and on several occasions Loyd beseeched them to take up the Christian path. There were also callers and neighbors from Brownsville, such as Dr. Isaac Starr. Another physician who visited was Albany's J. L. Hill. He interviewed Loyd in hopes of getting useful material for a study he was writing on heredity. The conversation, unfortunately, "failed to reveal much." Naturally, the religious were also out in full force.

The Reverends Snyder from Brownsville, Shulse from Shedd, and Little from Albany, as well as the Salvation Army, came to pray and plead with Loyd one last time. An untold number of "Christian ladies," as inmate Rivers described the scene, "thronged the coridor [sic] of the jail on their bended knees, praying, pleading with him amid songs of joy to yield the truth and confess all to God and man." But the boy, whose "cheeks were of a deathly pale as he broke out in a convulsive sobbing which revealed that the truth was yet within," still refused to reveal it.[141]

At about midnight, Loyd asked yet again for pen, paper, and envelopes. He wrote two more letters to family in Brownsville. Their contents are unknown; the "watchers out of respect to his feelings in writing a last message to the remnant of his broken family," an observer described, "remained perfectly quiet." When Loyd completed his task, he "broke the silence with the remarkable statement: 'It is hard for a fellow to seal an envelope with a 'chaw' of tobacco in his mouth.'" Shocked by such a sober statement and nonchalant action from and by a youth who faced imminent execution, those gathered composed themselves by asking Loyd if he might play his violin once more. He did, and yet again the tune of "Home, Sweet Home" flowed from his instrument.[142]

There are three versions of what happened next. One claims, given the late hour, that Loyd grew increasingly sleepy while fiddling away and eventually fell to slumber in his chair, and then a fellow inmate woke him and directed him to his bunk. Another account explains that it was McFeron, noticing Loyd's drowsiness, who asked him at about 1:00 a.m. if he might like a nap. Loyd then fell sound asleep. A third maintained that Loyd had persisted in his "boyish pranks," waiting, for example, till the other prisoners had fallen asleep and "then scare[d] them, laughing in mock mimicry at the effect."[143]

He did sleep, however, and at around 4:00 a.m. McFeron, with difficulty, awakened him for the final preparations. The sheriff informed Loyd that the execution would go forward in three hours. Loyd requested to see the model of the scaffold. McFeron produced it and instructed him on how it operated. McFeron answered a few questions the boy had about what would happen and who would be there. Then the Reverends Shulse, Snyder, and Little descended once more in a last concerted attempt to pry a confession from Loyd's sealed lips and heart. The youth withstood the onslaught yet again.[144]

Loyd then turned to conversing with Marshall Fox, his cellmate. Presently, Joseph Hume arrived. Hume lived near Brownsville and was married to Catherine McHargue. She was a sister to McFeron's wife and also a first cousin to Loyd's father.[145] On the one hand, Hume came to Albany as a representative of the family. On the other, he officially did so as one of the duly chosen twelve electors of Linn County whom law required to witness the execution.[146] Hume was not a minister, but he placed a hand on Loyd's shoulder and "told the boy impressively that he was in no condition to meet his God without making a complete confession of the crime, and not dying with a lie on his lips." According to reports, Hume then "prayed as few men ever pray." Such a description is difficult to imagine, given how many had prayed with Loyd over the previous two months. Regardless, and as we have seen, such prayer had never succeeded in getting Loyd to bare his soul, though it had undoubtedly struck terror into it. Hume had one more weapon in his arsenal. He was a father and a farmer. He was also about the same age as the slain John Montgomery, and he had known the Montgomery family for some years. And so, in meeting with Loyd in these last few minutes of the youth's life, "he treated him very kindly," an Albany newspaper reported, and then "talked to him like a father would to a *naughty boy*."[147] Where pure evangelism had failed, the addition of a fatherly touch succeeded. Perhaps that was something Loyd had needed all along.

And Loyd finally (re)confessed to all three murders. "I did it," he wrote, and there followed a simple statement: "I am guilty. O God! Have mercy on me. Take me as I am, a poor sinner. I am sorry for what I have done. God, do have mercy on my poor soul; for my sake do, and forgive all my sins, each and every one of them, and forgive those who sin against me. Oh, God, help the precious souls to see the way of life for my sake. Do help them and guide them through this life."[148] Reverend Snyder from Brownsville, who was as omnipresent as God throughout the community effort to save Loyd, or at least to secure his confession, joined the lad and Hume in the jail cell. The three prayed together, and Loyd "was very contrite, and wept bitterly."[149]

With his soul unburdened, Loyd put on his new suit, of which "he was much pleased."[150] It was about 7:00 a.m. now, and Sheriff McFeron conducted the condemned boy into the corridor of the jail. There, the twelve electors read his death warrant. Among their number were several men from Crawfordsville and Brownsville. Besides Hume, one was related to Loyd. The others had known the Montgomery family for many years.[151] "Don't feel bad[,] boys," Loyd supposedly stated. "I deserve to die. I hope you will forgive me and not feel too bad."[152]

McFeron then led the boy; three of his deputies; the Reverends Snyder, Shulse, and Little; and the twelve electors up the stairs of the jail, through the sheriff's private accommodations, and directly from there out onto the platform and scaffold that Conn and McChesney had constructed. About fifty men were assembled inside the sixteen-foot-high, forty-by-forty-foot enclosure. Among them was John McKercher, whose hat bore a band of black crepe. Hundreds of other men and boys eager to witness an execution gathered on the street and sidewalk beyond the wooden fencing. Unable to get the view they hoped for, they had to "satisfy their desire by peeping through the cracks" of the wooden barrier.[153]

It was then daybreak. Sunrise was coming at 7:33, but early morning rays of the sun already gilded the eastern sky. Loyd faced northward, with the north side of the jail to his back. He viewed those in the enclosure below him, the glowing sky to the east, and the rope that dangled above him. "Well, friends," Loyd spoke for the first time, "I am sorry for what I have done, and I hope you will all forgive me, and I hope the Lord will be with you, and I ask God to have mercy on me as a poor sinner, and I ask you to pray for me."[154]

Reverend Snyder stepped forward and offered a prayer, "one rarely to be heard, for it was full of pathos, bringing tears to the eyes of even the stern-visaged Sheriff." In part, Snyder used the "tragic sight" to further the ends of revivalism, calling on the Lord to move those assembled there, through the example of the "sad scene" before them, to go forward and "bring more souls unto the Lord Jesus Christ." He also took the opportunity to remind the omniscient Lord that the "citizens of this commonwealth" in putting another to death were not doing so from "choice, but through the sense of duty to carry into execution the law of our land."[155] Reporters seemed irritated that Loyd was apparently unmoved by Snyder's words, being more interested in his surroundings, including the hanging rope that he glanced at from time to time.

When Snyder concluded his prayer, Loyd spoke again: "Good bye, friends, I hope to meet you in heaven. I ask God to take me[,] a poor sinner." While McFeron and Probst placed a black cap over his head, three straps around his limbs, and pulled the noose tight around his neck, Loyd exclaimed, "God have mercy on me[,] a sinner. Take me as I am." Newspapers remarked on Loyd's relative stoicism in these last moments. "The youthful murderer was brave to the last and did not flinch on the scaffold," the local *Weekly Herald-Disseminator* reported, "but stood erect, and having admitted the truth about the crime, seemed relieved."[156] Despite his weeks of boyish shenanigans, childish lies and deceits, and his bouts of unreserved weeping, Loyd had promised all along that he was no "coward" and would "go to the gallows and die like a man." And when standing on the scaffold, "I won't be a baby."[157] As such, to some of those who witnessed these end times, Loyd had at the last moments of his life become a man and possibly a saved one at that.

While the sheriff and his deputy completed final adjustments, Loyd exclaimed once again, "Kind friends, farewell, farewell."[158] And just as the final farewell rolled from his tongue, McFeron stepped on the trap's lever, setting the contraption into motion as if by the force of the invisible hand that had already compelled so much of what had transpired on that tattered agrarian landscape over the years.

It was then about 7:10 a.m. Loyd plummeted six feet, and all present heard the "sickening thud one will always remember." The force did its job, breaking his neck. Four physicians were on hand: Starr from Brownsville, Matthew Ellis from Albany, and William Davis and G. Watson Maston, who were in practice together in Albany. The foursome advanced toward the dangling boy. Starr felt the pulse, Ellis and Davis tracked the heartbeat, and Maston monitored the watch. At four minutes, Loyd's heart rate had climbed to 173. It then began to decrease. At six minutes it had fallen to 126. At eight minutes it dropped to 66, and the pulse was very weak. By nine minutes, Starr could detect no pulse, but at ten minutes there was a slight flutter. At eleven minutes the physicians reported ambiguous sounds. A minute later there was a slight movement, which continued for two more minutes. "At 14½ minutes his heart had ceased to beat."[159]

Two minutes later, at roughly 7:26 in the morning of 31 January 1896, the physicians declared the boy dead. The killing of Loyd was now complete.

EPILOGUE

# "The Case of Loyd Montgomery Does Not End with His Death"

*Burying a Boy and Digging Up the Past*

**AFTER OFFICIALS RELEASED LOYD'S BODY FROM THE** hangman's noose, they divided up the rope and distributed it to some of those who had witnessed the execution. By all reports, "among the first to secure a piece, and a good-sized one at that," was John McKercher. "Many followed suit, and the rope that hanged" Loyd, a newspaper added, was to be "exhibited in many places in Oregon." The gruesome display of souvenirs from executions, battles, and popular killings, legal or otherwise, was routine at this time in the United States. The items collected and presented ranged from pieces of the hanging rope, to postcards of the event, to parts of the victim's body, to the entire body itself. In the case of Loyd, and in addition to the dividing up of the rope, authorities placed his remains on a litter and transported them to the courthouse. There, over the next several hours, hundreds of the curious filtered through the building and viewed "the face of the perpetrator of one of the most coldblooded murders in the history of the Pacific Coast."[1]

Once the parade of spectators had diminished, the county turned the body over to a team of nine physicians, including Isaac Starr from Brownsville, for an autopsy.[2] The men confirmed that Loyd's plunge from the gallows had fractured his neck at the fourth cervical vertebra. This was "good" news in the sense that the goal in legal hangings was to render the victim unconscious through such a breakage high up in the nervous system and then the person would quietly succumb to asphyxiation. Given the autopsy's findings and the description of Loyd's last minutes, the plan seemed to have gone like clockwork. As such, Sheriff James McFeron, who had no firsthand experience in such matters, had done his research well. His practice sessions on the day before the execution and not far from Loyd's cell had helped tremendously. For his success, McFeron received praise. "His conduct throughout this crime," one news editor wrote, "has been that of a careful, faithful officer and he has executed good judgment both during the confinement of the condemned murderer in the jail and the trying ordeal in the last scene of the terrible tragedy. He performed his duty without flinching and in a manner which reflects credit on the sheriff's office of Linn county."[3]

The doctors who performed the autopsy were actually less interested in explaining the boy's death than they were in mining his body for what clues it might yield about his life. As such, they focused on the brain. Just as nineteenth-century medical science imagined that one could detect criminal instincts in the contours of one's face—and thus one of the reasons for the descriptions of Loyd's shady appearance in the days following the murders—it also held that criminality might be revealed in a diseased or malformed brain. Although there was some confusion in the press at first, in time the story was straightened out and the physicians' general agreement was reported: Loyd's brain was entirely healthy. This must have been something of a disappointment. On the brighter side, if that could be, the physicians also determined that Loyd's brain had not developed much of an intellect. The Albany Medical Club retained this piece of the boy's flesh— it weighed slightly more than forty-nine ounces—preserved it, and planned to examine it more thoroughly in the future.[4] Whether the club did and whatever became of the specimen is anyone's guess.

As for what remained of the boy, officials removed it to the jailhouse. Loyd had expressed a wish to be buried in McHargue Cemetery south of Brownsville and next to his parents. His surviving family, however, refused to have anything to do with his body, and the larger community did not favor burying it in the cemetery in Brownsville. So, Linn County took charge. On 1 February at 10:00 a.m., the morning after the execution and after the public viewing and the removal of the brain, the county hosted Loyd's funeral at the jail. The Reverends Riley Little (Albany United Presbyterian), Daniel Poling (Albany Congregational), and Charles McKee (Albany Baptist) conducted the service. Whether anyone else attended, other than perhaps Sheriff McFeron and the jail's inmates, is not to be found in surviving documents.[5] Curiously, Reverend J. E. Snyder from Brownsville, who had played such a prominent role during the last days of Loyd's life, appears not to have been present. But this was in no way an end to Snyder's relationship with the boy. Well into the twentieth century, he would be remembered for his farewell prayer on Loyd's scaffold, and he would even continue to draw material from the youth's life to add spice to his sermons.[6]

Whether Loyd's surviving family members even provided the boy a casket is unclear, but given their complete disinterest in his body, likely it did not. Records explain that the county paid Hugh Moyer fifteen dollars for a coffin "for [the] poor" at this time. Moyer operated a lumber mill that his father had founded years before in Brownsville (figure E.1). Hugh's mother was the sister of Eveline (Brown) Montgomery, which made the sawyer the first cousin to the slain John. It is likely, given that Loyd came from Brownsville, that officials chose to spread some of the financial rewards of his execution to that section of the county and to a member of the lad's extended family. They had, after all, suffered greatly from the event that ultimately led to the boy's hanging.[7]

The county also paid the Albany undertakers Irving & Fortmiller fifteen dollars for its work for the "poor" in the same period of time it executed Loyd. Perhaps that firm laid out his body, or what was left of it. We do know with certainty, however, who dug Loyd's grave. That was William Farley, whom Linn County had previously and subsequently engaged for the same sort of work and always for a fee of five dollars. Farley did his work for Loyd in the potter's field of Albany City Cemetery, which is today Riverside Cemetery (see map 7.1). It sits to the west of the central business district and is so named for its proximity to the Calapooia River. Farley likely assisted with the other particulars of the burial, namely filling in the grave with soil once the casket was lowered into place.[8] Loyd's grave is unmarked, and records of its exact location have not survived.

While most of the boy's remains were now at rest, during the eighteen years, five months, and five days of his life, Loyd's body and soul had

Figure E.1. Moyer Mill in Brownsville. Loyd's family refused to have anything to do with his body after his execution. Linn County stepped in to make final arrangements. Records indicate that the county purchased a coffin for the "poor" from Hugh B. Moyer, who operated a mill (founded by his father) in Brownsville at the time Loyd was executed. The coffin was likely the one Loyd was buried in. Moyer was a first cousin to Loyd's father, John. Source: *Illustrated Historical Atlas Map of Marion and Linn Counties, Oregon* (San Francisco: Edgar Williams, 1878).

endured a great deal. He was the product, agent, and victim of an extraordinary history. Neither a medical autopsy nor a psychological evaluation could present evidence of such a truth. The saga that Loyd participated in was one that saw some elevated to spectacular wealth and many others brought to their knees. It was a history of killing or subjugating some people and then appropriating their land and the bodies of the survivors for the benefit of others—and then celebrating that feat with race- and violence-charged memorials, monuments, theater, parades, written histories, and even carnival games. It was a world fast changing and that yet held out impossible expectations rooted in the myths of another time and place. And it asked lads like Loyd to live up to those illusory expectations, while at the same time it produced crushing inequities because of them. As the social and cultural expectations and ideals of that world escaped the grasp of more and more of its inhabitants, that world erected institutions of incarceration and opened graves in potter's fields for those who could not quite make a suitable adjustment to the want and dislocation that were now their lot. And then that world quickly filled those institutions and potter's fields to overflowing capacity. It was also a world that was rapidly expanding beyond the immediate horizons of an agrarian society that was never entirely contained, tethering it with ropes, lumber, hops, and other resources to industries, markets, and economies that spanned the globe and wherein the individual now seemed inconsequential. It was a world where the political hopes of many, born from vexation and desperation, remained unrealized. It was a world filled with illness, affliction, and violence. For all that world did to and failed to do for young people like Loyd, at the very least it was a world that could marshal an army of believers at the last minute and send it into battle for the lost souls who were staring into a fiery abyss—and doing so without a brain.

This is a pretty dark interpretation of the history that Loyd Montgomery lived through. I have argued throughout this study, however, that any explanation for why children kill their parents—a question that has haunted humanity since humanity has haunted the world—can come only from a full understanding of the history in which such an event takes place. Given the darkness of parricide, can a cheerier history be told?

Perhaps not cheerier, but the story of Loyd's parricide disconnected from the realities of a grim history has oft been told. It began before his body was cold in the grave and his brain pickled in a specimen jar. Harvey Scott, the editor of Portland's influential *Oregonian* newspaper, penned several opinion pieces about Loyd in the days following the boy's execution. In one of those, in which he presciently explained that "the case of Lloyd [sic] Montgomery does not end with his death," Scott derided editors from other newspapers, those who were able to view what had been going on in Linn County from a somewhat more objective vantage. Those more distantly situated people wanted to know how things like the environment in which Loyd grew up, the hardships he had endured, and the failures of his parents in his upbringing played a role in his story. In asking questions about such matters, these journalists clearly understood that life and thus history are both typically darker and more complicated than how they are officially portrayed. And they wanted to know Loyd's life through that history.[9]

Scott, on the other hand, would have none of it. First off, being in Oregon, he had a front-row seat to the painful events in Brownsville and Albany.

He sent his reporters to those places for in-depth coverage. And his newspaper often received angry letters from those who, having every right to be angry, suffered so terribly from what Loyd had done. With demonstrable and understandable sympathy for these aggrieved people, Scott held a hard editorial line against the boy and cruelly disparaged the women and men who had tried to intercede on the youth's behalf.

Second, Scott was a champion of all things Oregon, in particular its pioneer past. As a youngster (born in 1838), he had migrated with his family on the overland trails to Oregon Territory in 1852. As a young man he had fought in the Yakima (Indian) War of 1855–56 at the same time that he helped to support his natal family, bereft of its mother, who had died on the western trek. With enormous expenditure of energy, he put himself through college, and, as an admirer once explained, "he rose gradually from the level of association with the day laborer to regular companionship in his reading with the best minds of all ages." He became editor (for the first time) of the *Oregonian* in 1865, which in time and under his direction became the state's most influential newspaper. He was a member of the Indian War Veterans of the North Pacific Coast. A couple of years after the killing of Loyd, Scott cofounded and became the first president of the Oregon Historical Society. He presided over the planning of the Lewis and Clark Exposition, a 1905 event that announced Portland's entrance into the ranks of the world's leading cities. And he also served as president of the Sons and Daughters of the Oregon Pioneer Association. In later years, Scott's son compiled and edited a six-volume collection of his father's writings, entitling it *History of the Oregon Country*, which one critic described as "equal to the highest" narrative histories produced on the subject.[10]

Third, given his love of the past and his home state, as well as the privileged position he occupied, Scott also had an unsurprisingly upbeat view of the future. One of his postmortem editorials about Loyd, entitled "Wages of Sin," commented on that future. "Spring is coming on," he wrote the day following the execution, "and the sights of springing grass and budding trees will be unseen by Lloyd [sic] . . . who might, but for his rebelliousness and recklessness, have been spared to see this and many more bright springs. . . . The coming years have many things in store for the man today yet in his teens. The cause of human liberty, the amelioration of the common people, the evolution of popular comfort and attainment, will be making strides whose completion older ones will regret their inability to live long enough to see."[11]

Consumed by the unspeakable goings-on surrounding Loyd's bloody crime and his own love affair with his state, informed by romantic versions of the region's pioneer past, complicit in a cover-up of crimes against the region's indigenous people, and holding a progressive view of the future—all these prevented Scott from considering what life must have looked like from Loyd's perspective and from the real history, personal and otherwise, that the boy had actually lived. Claiming that distant editors' approach to Loyd's story was the stuff of nonsense, Scott instead parroted "the Oregon courts and healthy public opinion in Oregon," which "take very little interest in the origin of the murderous impulses which made it necessary to remove Lloyd [sic] Montgomery, as being dangerous to public order and human life." Rather, what was central in Scott's view was that Loyd had killed and, as a result, needed to be killed. Anything beyond that was of little social value. The title of Scott's editorial was actually "Penology and Justice." In more thoughtful hands, it might have been "Tragedy and Its Historic Causes."[12]

And so, since those early days and in the hands of Oregonians, Loyd's story has been merely the story of a bad boy, a story without broader social and cultural context, let alone worth. Loyd's uncle, Hugh Montgomery, put it this way in a 1937 interview: "One of the first tragedies of this region was the death of my oldest brother. He was killed by his own son. The boy was a spoiled, unruly youngster. He had been reproved by his father and in anger he took a gun, shot his mother, his father, and a neighbor . . . who happened to be passing."[13] Slightly more than a decade later, in 1948, E. M. Perfect, who claimed to have witnessed Loyd's hanging through holes whittled through the wooden enclosure, similarly recalled for interested reporters that the "boy, wouldn't do any work. . . . All he wanted to do was to hunt and fish." Perfect further explained that when Loyd returned from what would be his last hunting trip, when Daniel McKercher was at the Montgomery house, the miller supposedly said, "I wouldn't let this boy go hunting all of the time. I'd make him stay home and do some work." This, Perfect hinted, is what started Loyd down his deadly path. Portions of Perfect's story appeared again in the press four years later.[14] In 1977, Florence McKercher, recalling her memories and knowledge about the murders, explained that Loyd shot his parents and her uncle because he "was after his father's money."[15] An interview with Bessie Templeton, Loyd's cousin, carried in a 1978 publication, also stated rather matter-of-factly that, "in a fit of anger because his father forbid him to go on a hunting trip, [Loyd] murdered them" all.[16]

That the memory of Loyd and the awful thing he had done remained alive in Linn County is certainly evident in the above recollections, and there are many, many more such pieces than the few noted here. Why have these tellings of Loyd's story been less interested in his history and more focused on a few quick references to his depravity and selfishness? Partly the answer has to do with what Scott had argued back in 1896. Partly it has to do with a tradition that has dismissed children as historical actors. Partly the answer has to do with what is typically the approach to parricide—something explainable through the tools of psychology and criminology. This has rendered it more biographical than historical, more trivial and frivolous than structural.

In larger measure, it has to do with who has told Loyd's story. Because it was such an intensely personal affair, it has principally been family and others with local knowledge and a front-row seat who have shared and kept their recollections alive. Practically every reader of this volume will recognize the rather tired, though still profound observation that history is written by the victors. And so it has been in the case of Loyd. Many, many others also suffered through the same history that he did. Unlike him, they survived, adjusted to change, behaved in socially acceptable ways, carried on, and looked to a brighter future. Some among them then wrote their own history. In the hands of these sons and daughters of the pioneers, that narrative is one filled with triumphal and prideful stories of their stalwart, white American ancestors crossing the continent in ox-pulled wagons, defying and subduing hardship, setback, and enemy forces in human and environmental form along the way and in a new land. They built homes and farms, churches and schools, gristmills and lumber mills, and towns and courthouses. They cultivated wheatfields and hopyards. They produced and reproduced and died gracefully, quietly moving on to that distant shore. Such a story makes the "vanquished" people like Loyd into anomalies to expunge from histories and obituaries or, at most, explained away with simple phrases about personal defect. It is far easier and thus less painful to describe Loyd merely as a "spoiled, unruly youngster," a boy who "wouldn't do any work," who was "after his father's money," who did what he did just in a "fit of anger," and who was disposed to "rebelliousness and recklessness."

Such phrases, by the way, bear a striking resemblance to those filling the darkened registers that describe the boys who, in ever-increasing numbers, filed into the Oregon State Reform School in the 1890s. It is a far more difficult, challenging, heartbreaking, and self-reflective project to reopen those dusty ledgers and the unmarked graves of potter's fields—perhaps illuminated by the spirit of boys who once carried lanterns—and therein discover that what made Loyd Montgomery was something that made us all and our collective story.

Loyd Montgomery's hanging was the last state-sanctioned one in Linn County. Just after the turn of the century, Oregon's legislature moved all executions from the counties to the privacy of the state penitentiary in Salem. Although contained within enclosures at county courthouses for years, the hangings had simply become too much of a public spectacle.

Loyd's siblings, who lived through almost all the history he did, survived him. Taken in by their grandmother, a woman who had crossed the overland trails in 1846, they each lived well into the twentieth century, though none had an especially long life. The youngest, John, married and lived for some years in Oregon before moving on to Nevada in about 1928. He died from injuries sustained in a mining accident in 1930. In 1901, Orville moved eastward across the Cascades. He married and had children. He died in central Oregon in 1941. Eva married in 1903 in Albany and shortly thereafter moved with her husband to Portland. They had several children. She died from complications of diabetes in 1943. Robert Montgomery, who was the first of his siblings to discover the horrors visited upon their home by his eldest brother, survived all his siblings. He married, had two children, served in the military during the World War I era, and died in 1957. He was a resident of Wyoming for a number of years, but his remains are interred in a national cemetery in California.[17]

On 12 February 1896, less than two weeks after Loyd's execution, the Ancient Order of United Workmen in Brownsville held a program that consisted of "prayer, service, songs and addresses" conducted by the Reverends J. E. Snyder and William Sperry, both from that town, in celebration of the life of Daniel McKercher, now almost three months after his death. The financier's chair that he had occupied at the time of his murder was "neatly draped, and in a conspicuous place was a placard bearing the inscription, 'In memory of Brother D. B. McKercher, financier of Finley lodge, No. 41, A.O.U.W., died November 19, 1895.'" A "large crowd" was on hand to pay tribute to the miller's memory. In its headline, the *Oregonian* called the memorial service the "Last Chapter in Montgomery Tragedy." The graves of Daniel's father, mother, brother, sister-in-law, and niece—kin who all survived him—occupy the same row in the cemetery in Crawfordsville that he does. In August 1968, Linn County dedicated McKercher Park on the Calapooia River just east of the old Finley and later McKercher gristmill and just west of the town of Crawfordsville. Florence McKercher donated the land.[18]

Samuel Templeton, who owned and lived in the house where the Montgomery-McKercher murders occurred, survived until 1902. He was sixty-eight that year and doing what he loved best—mining, and in this case in the Blue River mining district high up the Calapooia southeast of Crawfordsville in the Cascades. Sometime in mid-June he came down with a case of the grippe. His brothers brought him home in a wagon. He died on 8 August and was also laid to rest in McHargue Cemetery, where so many others of his family and his one-time tenant-sharecroppers John and Elizabeth Montgomery were also interred.[19]

The Templeton-Montgomery house disappeared in time. Humble and forlorn, abject and haunting, it would have served as poignant reminder of the local, regional, and even national past—a monument quite different from so many of the historical markers and structures that we otherwise encounter along the highways and byways of this land. The Brownsville-Crawfordsville road, which once turned in sharp angles toward and away from that house's now largely forgotten location, today follows a more direct route and is somewhat set away from the location of its predecessor. But if one knows where to look, one can still find traces of its old pathway and the place where Loyd Montgomery momentarily stood all alone, just as history and future collided.

# NOTES

## PROLOGUE. "A SCENE OF WHOLESALE BUTCHERY"

1. "A Triple Murder," *Brownsville Times*, supplement, 20 November 1895, photocopy on file at the Linn County Historical Museum. Weather conditions are from *Oregonian* (Portland), 20 November 1895, 4.
2. Templeton, Templeton, and Breuer, *William T. Templeton*, 39–40, 68, 88; Genealogy Files: Montgomery family, Linn County Historical Museum; Family Files: Templeton family, Brownsville Community Library. On Samuel Templeton's farm: *Oregonian*, 22 November 1895, 1.
3. *Oregonian*, 26 November 1895, 1; *Weekly Herald-Disseminator* (Albany, OR), 19 December 1895, 4; Templeton, Templeton, and Breuer, *William T. Templeton*, 83.
4. This and the next paragraphs are based on *Oregonian*, 26 November 1895, 1; and *Weekly Herald-Disseminator*, 28 November 1895, 3.
5. The last three paragraphs are based on somewhat conflicting reports in the "Triple Murder" photocopy; and *Oregonian*, 26 November 1895, 1.
6. The scholarship and popular literature on Borden are daunting. One might want to start and (depending on one's stamina) stop with the exhaustive elevenhundred-page Martins and Binette, *Parallel Lives*.
7. *Inter Ocean* (Chicago), 21 November 1892, 3; *Trenton (NJ) Evening Times*, 13 December 1893, 7; *Oregonian*, 16 November 1893, 6; *Elkhart (IN) Daily Review*, 7 November 1893, 4; *Jackson (MS) Daily Citizen*, 30 December 1892, 3; *Trenton Evening Times*, 5 October 1895, 4; *Kansas Semi-Weekly Capital* (Topeka), 25 October 1895, 3; *Summerfield (KS) Sun*, 25 October 1895, 2.
8. Among more recent scholarly histories of American parricide, including infanticide, patricide, or matricide, other than in the case of Lizzie Borden, are Strange, "Unwritten Law of Executive Justice"; Bryan, "John Wesley Elkins, Boy Murderer, and His Struggle for Pardon"; Wheeler, "Infanticide in Nineteenth-Century Ohio"; and Pederson, "Gender, Justice, and a Wisconsin Lynching, 1889–1890." Though not analytical, Seagrave, *Parricide in the United States, 1840–1899*, provides a compendium of some one hundred nineteenth-century parricides.

9   The literature is vast. A useful overview of homicide, and more specifically why the United States has an exceptionally high rate of it compared to other industrialized nations, is the *American Historical Review*'s "AHA Forum: The Problem of American Homicide," from 2006. An excellent historical study on homicide in the United States for the era that this book considers is Adler, *First in Violence, Deepest in Dirt*. For a provocative study of why young men commit homicide in America, consider Courtwright, *Violent Land*. On serial murder, see Jenkins, "Serial Murder in the United States 1900–1940." Peterson del Mar, *Beaten Down*, looks more specifically at the Pacific Northwest.

10  Heide and Petee, "Weapons Used by Juvenile and Adult Offenders in U.S. Parricide Cases"; Heide, *Understanding Parricide*; Mones, *When a Child Kills*, 25; Ewing, *When Children Kill*, 5.

11  Heide, *Understanding Parricide*, 57. Heide also found that another fifty-eight people died annually at the hands of their stepchildren. On rates of parricide, see also Mones, *When a Child Kills*, 25; and Hillbrand and Cipriano, "Commentary: Parricides," 313. On the other hand, Shon and Targonski, "Declining Trends in US Parricides," 397–98, found a declining rate of parricide, though they included in their analysis some relatives other than parents.

12  Shon's work includes Shon and Barton-Bellessa, "Pre-Offense Characteristics of Nineteenth-Century American Parricide Offenders"; Shon, "Sources of Conflict between Parents and Their Offspring in Nineteenth-Century American Parricides"; Shon and Roberts, "Post-Offence Characteristics of 19th-Century American Parricides"; and Shon, "Weapon Usage in Attempted and Completed Parricides in Nineteenth-Century America." A slightly different version of the above discussion appeared in Boag, "Gender and Historicity of Parricide."

13  Foucault, *I, Pierre Rivière*, xiii, xiv (quotes).

14  This expands on an assertion made by some other historians of homicide. For example, Jeffrey Adler writes that "homicide is a 'social event.' It is the product of social relations and it is shaped and influenced by social conditions." Adler, *First in Violence, Deepest in Dirt*, 2.

15  Susman, foreword to *Wisconsin Death Trip*, by Lesy, n.p.

16  Goodall, "Upper Calapooia," 75; Works Progress Administration Writers' Program and the Linn County Pioneer Memorial Association, *History of Linn County*, 10; Gaston, *Centennial History of Oregon*, 3:125, 126; "McKercher Park Dedicated on Historic Site," *Brownsville Times*, 29 August 1968, 12; *Albany (OR) Democrat-Herald*, 15 January 1890, 3; *State Rights Democrat* (Albany), 27 May 1892, 3.

Biographical and genealogical details included throughout on the Montgomery, Templeton, and related families are drawn from various sources, including the Genealogical Files and Family Files held at Linn County Historical Museum and the Brownsville Community Library, respectively; research on Ancestry.com; various volumes of Miles and Milligan, *Linn County, Oregon Pioneer Settlers*; *Genealogical Material in Oregon Donation Land Claims*, vol. 1; the James Blakely Papers in the University of Oregon Libraries; and Templeton, Templeton, and Breuer, *William T. Templeton*. I provide specific citations only for direct quotations and more obscure references.

17  Unruh, *Plains Across*, 84–85.
18  Mackey, *Kalapuyans*, 10, 85–143; Boyd, "Another Look at the 'Fever and Ague' of Western Oregon."
19  US Department of the Interior, Census Office, *Report on the Population of the United States, 1890*, 1:448.
20  A useful synopsis of the DLCA is Robbins, "Oregon Donation Land Law." On the racial composition of Linn County, see US Department of the Interior, Census Office, *Report on the Population of the United States, 1890*, 1:426, 440, 442, 448.

PART 1. "AIDED BY BOYS UPON HORSEBACK"

1  "A Triple Murder," *Brownsville Times*, supplement, 20 November 1895, n.p., photocopy on file at the Linn County Historical Museum; *Oregon Mist* (St. Helens), 22 November 1895, 3 (quote); Turnbull, *History of Oregon Newspapers*, 297–98. Weather conditions come from *Oregonian* (Portland), 20 November 1895, 4; 5 December 1895, 6; 13 December 1895, 7; and *State Rights Democrat* (Albany), 22 November 1895, 1. For information on the sunset, which occurred at 4:41 p.m., I utilized Google, accessed 25 May 2017, www.google.com/search?q=Sunset+Brownsville+Oregon+November+19%2C+1895&ie=utf-8&oe=utf-8. The new moon had occurred only three nights before; see the calendar for 1895 at Time and Date, accessed 25 May 2017, www.timeanddate.com/calendar/?year=1895&country=1.
2  "Triple Murder" photocopy; Mintz, *Huck's Raft*, vii–viii.
3  "Triple Murder" photocopy; *Oregon Mist*, 22 November 1895, 3.
4  *Oregonian*, 9 January 1896, 4.
5  For a general summary, see Cashman, *America in the Gilded Age*, 135, 313–14, 323; and Danbom, *Born in the Country*, 131–34, 153–60.

CHAPTER 1. "THE HOPE AND LIFE OF THE NATION"

1  Jefferson, *Notes on the State of Virginia*, 84–85, 146–47, 164–65 (quote). For greater explication of the politics of early republicanism, consider McCoy,

*Elusive Republic*. On republicanism and agrarian expansion, see Danbom, *Born in the Country*, 65–85.

2   The Northwest Ordinance of the 1780s began the process of American expansion; it applied specifically to the region north of the Ohio River. See two classic studies: Rohrbaugh, *Land Office Business*; and Rohrbaugh, *Trans-Appalachian Frontier*.

3   Bergquist, "Oregon Donation Act and the National Land Policy," 29–30, 32. The use of funding for public schools that came from townships did not come to Oregon until the federal government granted the territory statehood in 1859.

4   Jefferson, *Notes on the State of Virginia*, 84–85n1, query 19, 292.

5   See Onuf, *Jefferson's Empire*. Slotkin, *Fatal Environment*, 52, explains that agrarian visionaries purposefully wished to explain away the violence in the reality of America's history.

6   On such issues, see Coleman, "'We'll All Start Even'"; Robbins, "Indian Question in Western Oregon"; and Bergquist, "Oregon Donation Act," 23–24.

7   On these topics, see, for example, Grandin, *End of the Myth*; and Slotkin, *Fatal Environment*.

8   Slotkin, *Fatal Environment*; Jennings, *Invasion of America*.

9   *Report of the Commission on Country Life*, 10–11.

10  In Oregon, the Commission on Country Life representatives explored the isolation and drudgery of farm life; poor sanitation, health, and the state of rural homes; migration of the rural population to the city; and the limitations of education for farmers' offspring. Each of these matters related to the experience and fate of children, a group that also occasionally came up for specific consideration in the meetings held in Oregon. See *Oregonian* (Portland), 3 December 1908, 10; 4 December 1908, 10, 14; and 6 December 1908, 6. On the Commission on Country Life, see Peters and Morgan, "Country Life Commission"; Bowers, *Country Life Movement in America*; and Ziegler, "'Burdens and the Narrow Life of Farm Women.'" On romanticization of rural life, including connections to the country life movement, see Danbom, *Born in the Country*, 168–75; and Danbom, "Romantic Agrarianism in Twentieth-Century America."

11  *Willamette Farmer* (Salem), 11 October 1873, 3. Similarly themed editorials appeared on other occasions, including 14 September 1872, 2; 7 April 1876, 9; and 17 March 1876, 9.

12  *Willamette Farmer* (Portland), 23 May 1879, 2.

13  *Willamette Farmer* (Salem), 2 June 1876, 2.

14  *Willamette Farmer* (Salem), 28 March 1884, 6.

15  *Willamette Farmer* (Salem), 2 February 1883, 6; 25 January 1873, 8. On the republican mother, see Kerber, "Republican Mother"; and Mintz and Kellogg,

*Domestic Revolutions*, 55–56. An overview of child-rearing literature of the antebellum era is Cott, "Notes toward an Interpretation of Antebellum Child-rearing." On the reality for women and girls in terms of child care and support of their husbands and men on western farms, see Handy-Marchello, *Women of the Northern Plains*, 63–68; and Jameson, "Women as Workers, Women as Civilizers."

16  *Willamette Farmer* (Salem), 14 September 1872, 2. On rural-urban migration, see, in addition to literature cited below, Riney-Kehrberg, *Childhood on the Farm*, 197–209. There is a long tradition of antiurbanism in the United States; a good introduction through the nineteenth century is Conn, *Americans against the City*, 11–24.

17  *Willamette Farmer* (Salem), 9 August 1878, 7 (quote); 27 August 1886, 3 (quote); *Willamette Farmer* (Portland), 2 February 1883, 6; 25 January 1873, 8; 3 August 1877, 5; 1 February 1884, 2.

18  See Lovoll, *Norwegians on the Prairie*, 152; Jensen, "Out of Wisconsin"; Alexander and Steidl, "Gender and the 'Laws of Migration.'"

19  *Willamette Farmer* (Salem), 14 September 1872, 2.

20  For example, *Willamette Farmer* (Portland and Salem), 19 March 1875, 2; 12 January 1883, 3 (quote); 1 August 1884, 3. Such advice was also provided elsewhere in the United States. See Riney-Kehrberg, *Childhood on the Farm*, 199–200.

21  *Willamette Farmer* (Salem), 7 November 1883, 3.

22  *Willamette Farmer* (Salem), 4 October 1873, 4.

23  On Gragg family members and their ages, see Joseph Gragg, Find a Grave, accessed 5 December 2020, www.findagrave.com/memorial/35739908/joseph-gragg.

24  Varied Gragg family correspondence, contained in the Joseph Gragg Papers.

25  For example, *Willamette Farmer* (Salem), January 1, 1875, 2; September 21, 1877, 6; November 30, 1877, 7; and June 13, 1884, 3.

26  Riney-Kehrberg, *Childhood on the Farm*, 36, 48; Mintz, *Huck's Raft*, 135–36.

27  See, for example, Mintz, *Huck's Raft*, 75–93; and Mintz and Kellogg, *Domestic Revolutions*, 43–60.

28  The sequence of quotations comes from *Willamette Farmer* (Salem), 20 June 1874, 2; 20 June 1884, 3; 25 July 1874, 2; 4 December 1874, 1; 18 July 1874, 2; and 14 September 1877, 2. For a general treatment of the role of sisters, the relationship between sisters and brothers, and alterations in family for a slightly earlier era, see Hemphill, *Siblings*, 155–85.

29  "Small Farms or Large," *Willamette Farmer* (Salem), 14 August 1874, 4 (quote); but see also L. B. Judson, "Small vs. Large Farms" (letter to the editor), *Willamette Farmer* (Salem), 24 January 1874, 4. On the social and economic effects

of the Donation Land Claim Act's largesse, see Prescott, *Gender and Generation on the Far Western Frontier*, 43; and Johansen, *Empire of the Columbia*, 232.

30  See Wiebe, *Search for Order, 1877–1920*; Slotkin, *Fatal Environment*; Trachtenberg, *Incorporation of America*; Chandler, *Visible Hand*; Foucault, *Discipline and Punish*; and Weber, *Economy and Society*.

31  On the atlas craze, see Conzen, "County Landownership Map in America"; and Conzen, "Landownership Maps and County Atlases."

32  *Illustrated Historical Atlas Map of Marion and Linn Counties*, 3. On the (in)accuracies of county atlas illustrations, see Swenson, "Illustrations of Material Culture in Nineteenth-Century County and State Atlases."

33  *State Rights Democrat* (Albany), 4 January 1878, 2; 11 January 1878, 2; *Weekly Mercury* (Salem), 26 March 1878, 4. In some instances, endorsements came from firms with partners. I counted such an endorsement as from two or more people, depending on the listing. This likewise influenced my tally of those who ultimately subscribed to the publication.

34  The $15 figure comes from later in 1878, when Edgar Williams advertised for a second, unrealized atlas, this one for some other counties. See *Oregon State Journal* (Eugene), 16 November 1878, 5. I have been unable to determine Williams's price scale for biographies, illustrations, and patron listings. Prices in other atlases at the time were, for biographies, 2.5¢ per word; a four-inch image, $28; a full-page illustration, $145, but with a listing in the patrons' section, only $9, which was less than in Oregon. See Swenson, "Illustrations of Material Culture in Nineteenth-Century County and State Atlases," 63; and Lyon-Jenness, "Picturing Progress," 198.

35  *State Rights Democrat*, 26 April 1878, 3; 3 May 1878, 3; *Illustrated Historical Atlas Map of Marion and Linn Counties*, 3.

36  *State Rights Democrat*, 26 April 1878, 3; 3 May 1878, 3; 17 May 1878, 3; and 13 September 1878 (quote). On Whiting, see US Department of the Interior, Census Office, Tenth Census, 1880, Manuscript Census, Linn County, Oregon, Enumeration District 69, page 19, line 18, and page 26, line 29; *Albany City Directory, 1878*, 17, 85; and Prince, *Standard History of Springfield and Clark County, Ohio*, 2:331–32. Whiting later illustrated for Portland's *West Shore* magazine; see Craghead, *Railway Palaces of Portland, Oregon*, 79–80; and Cleaver, "L. Samuel and the *West Shore*," 187–88.

37  *State Rights Democrat*, 7 June 1878, 3 (quote); 28 June 1878, 3.

38  *State Rights Democrat*, 13 December 1878, 3.

39  Conzen, "County Landownership Map in America," 20.

40  *Willamette Farmer* (Salem), 13 September 1878, 7.

41  Conzen, "Landownership Maps and County Atlases," 121.

42  Swenson, "Illustrations of Material Culture in Nineteenth-Century County and State Atlases," 63.
43  Lang, *History of the Willamette Valley*, 763; *Oregonian*, 15 August 1890, 4; *State Rights Democrat*, 15 August 1890, 3; Jeanette "Janet" Dalgleish Finlayson, Find a Grave, accessed 6 June 2020, www.findagrave.com/memorial/29571363/jeanette-finlayson; *Albany Register*, 10 December 1873, 3.
44  *State Rights Democrat*, 14 March 1873, 2.

## CHAPTER 2. "A CHILD, SICK WITH SCARLET FEVER"

1   *Oregonian* (Portland), 22 November 1895, 1; 24 November 1895, 4.
2   *San Francisco Examiner*, 2 February 1896, 4. In the mid-1890s, the *Examiner* was in fierce competition with the *San Francisco Chronicle*. Slightly earlier in the same year as the Montgomery parricide, the two newspapers printed all manner of dubious reports on the Theodore Durrant murders committed in San Francisco. See McConnell, *Sympathy for the Devil*, 140.
3   *Oregonian*, 29 December 1895, 10.
4   *Oregonian*, 24 November 1895, 4.
5   See, for example, Mok et al., "Family Income Inequalities and Trajectories through Childhood and Self-Harm and Violence in Young Adults."
6   A useful discussion of disease and illness and effects on the brain and development is contained in Keetley, *Making a Monster*, 180–88. The literature on the effects of childhood trauma is extensive. Works consulted include Mills et al., "Traumatic Events Are Associated with Diverse Psychological Symptoms in Typically-Developing Children"; Jakubovic and Drabick, "Community Violence Exposure and Youth Aggression"; Wall-Myers et al., "Understanding the Link between Exposure to Violence and Aggression in Justice-Involved Adolescents"; Jenness et al., "Association of Physical Injury and Mental Health"; Heide and Solomon, "Female Juvenile Murderers"; and Song, Singer, and Anglin, "Violence Exposure and Emotional Trauma as Contributors to Adolescents' Violent Behaviors."
7   The *Oregonian*, 11 February 1896, 4, reported this assessment that came from the *San Francisco Bulletin*.
8   On the violence of boyhood in nineteenth-century Oregon generally, see Peterson del Mar, *Beaten Down*, 66–68.
9   *San Francisco Examiner*, 2 February 1896, 4; US Department of the Interior, Census Office, *Report on the Population of the United States, 1890*, 286.
10  US Department of the Interior, Census Office, *Report on the Population of the United States, 1890*, 926.
11  Carlson, "Rural Family in the Nineteenth Century," 89–129.

12  A useful historical study is King, "Childhood Death."
13  *State Rights Democrat* (Albany), 22 December 1882, 2; 29 December 1882, 1. Reports on scarlet fever epidemics in eastern and southern Oregon at this time appear in *Oregonian*, 9 January 1883, 3; and 30 January 1883, 2. Other cases in Linn County are mentioned in *State Rights Democrat*, 15 December 1882, 4; and 29 December 1882, 3.
14  Analysis is based on data in Jackson, Winmill, and Zachrison, *Oregon 1880 Mortality Schedule*. Unless otherwise noted, information and statistics from the 1880 mortality schedule, which actually reports on the year 1879, come from this source.
15  US Department of the Interior, Census Office, *Report on the Mortality and Vital Statistics of the United States, 1880*, 382. Although in general agreement about the toll from these various diseases, this source and Jackson, Winmill, and Zachrison, *Oregon 1880 Mortality Schedule*, do have some specific differences when it comes to the exact number of deaths.
16  See, for example, *State Rights Democrat*, 25 November 1870, 2. On the reluctance of some in the American West to take the vaccine, see King, "Childhood Death," 30.
17  *Lebanon Express*, 30 November 1888, 3.
18  Various Gragg correspondence contained in Joseph Gragg Papers (hereafter, multiple letters are cited as Gragg correspondence).
19  *Willamette Farmer* (Portland), 9 February 1877, 1.
20  *New Northwest* (Portland), 19 November 1875, 2; Mary Irene Gragg, Find a Grave, accessed 3 December 2020, www.findagrave.com/memorial/35739912/mary-irene-gragg; George W. Gragg, Find a Grave, accessed 3 December 2020, www.findagrave.com/memorial/35739905/george-w-gragg; Cordelia G. Gragg, Find a Grave, accessed 3 December 2020, www.findagrave.com/memorial/35739902/cordelia-g-gragg.
21  *Willamette Farmer* (Portland), 17 December 1880, 3. For additional information on the Robertson family, I utilized public family trees available on Ancestry.com.
22  In 1895, 18 percent of children died before the age of five. Mintz, *Huck's Raft*, 134.
23  *Willamette Farmer* (Portland), 16 June 1882, 6.
24  *Oregonian*, 1 December 1895, 20.
25  *State Rights Democrat*, 20 December 1895, 3; *Oregonian*, 1 December 1895, 20; *Weekly Herald-Disseminator* (Albany), 19 December 1895, 4. On James Wallace, see *State Rights Democrat*, 25 April 1884, 3.
26  *State Rights Democrat*, 20 December 1895, 3. A brief overview of Charcot is Thorburn, "Jean Martin Charcot, 1825–1893." For Hurd, see his obituary in *Boston Medical and Surgical Journal*, 27 April 1899, 416. On Ellis and Starr,

see *Portrait and Biographical Record of the Willamette Valley, Oregon*, 2:834–35, 894–97. On eating epilepsy, see Yacubian et al., "Seizures Induced by Eating in a Family." A different version of this analysis appears in Boag, "Gender and Historicity of Parricide."

27  State of Oregon, *State of Oregon v. Lloyd [sic] Montgomery*, 12–13.
28  Gragg correspondence.
29  Gragg correspondence.
30  On drownings or near drownings related to boating accidents, see *Willamette Farmer* (Salem), 22 June 1872, 1; 28 May 1875, 8; and 21 June 1873, 1. For millraces and ponds, see *Willamette Farmer* (Salem), 28 June 1869, 1; 13 April 1872, 1; 18 June 1875, 11; 4 August 1876, 7; and 24 August 1872, 4. For fishing, see *Willamette Farmer* (Salem), 6 April 1872, 1; and 14 May 1875, 5.
31  *Willamette Farmer* (Salem), 24 August 1872, 1, 4, 7 (quote).
32  *Lebanon Express*, 7 August 1891, 1, 3.
33  *Willamette Farmer* (Salem) 9 June 1876, 1, 9.
34  *State Rights Democrat*, 15 July 1887, 3 (quote); 22 July 1887, 3 (quote); 5 August 1887, 3.
35  Examples of such accidents, injuries, and attacks, all from the *Willamette Farmer* (Salem), include those listed here. Wagons and carriages: 30 August 1878, 3; 10 November 1876, 8; 18 June 1875, 9; 12 March 1875, 11; 1 January 1875, 11; 25 December 1874, 1; 18 April 1874, 1; 5 July 1873, 3. Pocketknives, axes, miscellaneous cuttings, and amputations: 5 April 1878, 2; 14 September 1877, 5; 16 June 1876, 8; 2 July 1875, 10; 26 February 1875, 4; 25 September 1874, 9; 21 August 1874, 11; 18 September 1874, 9. Horses and other farm animals: 24 August 1877, 5, 7; 1 June 1877, 3; 2 February 1877, 6; 4 August 1876, 8; 30 June 1876, 1; 4 June 1875, 9; 14 May 1875, 9; 23 April 1875, 1; 4 July 1874, 4, 11; 28 March 1874, 11; 22 September 1876, 1. Gunpowder: 13 April 1877, 2; 6 July 1872, 1. Wild animal (bear): 26 May 1876, 9. Falls: 10 March 1876, 4; 4 June 1875, 9; 19 March 1875, 11; 11 December 1874, 10. Falling trees: 2 April 1875, 1. Water wells: 20 July 1872, 1; 28 July 1876, 5. Burns: 20 July 1877, 6.
36  Marcus Gragg to Mother, [Monroe, OR, 6 December 1889], Joseph Gragg Papers.
37  *State Rights Democrat*, 20 September 1894, 3.
38  *State Rights Democrat*, 23 October 1885, 3; *Oregon Daily Statesman* (Salem), 14 November 1885, 3.
39  *Willamette Farmer* (Salem), 8 June 1872, 1.
40  Bettie [Gragg], Monroe, OR, 4 March [18]87, to T. H. Gragg, Huntsville, W.T. [Washington Territory] (quote), Joseph Gragg Papers; Jeremiah "Jerry" Clark, Find a Grave, accessed 2 December 2020, www.findagrave.com/memorial

/131348752/jeremiah-clark; *Eugene Guard*, 6 January 1955, 23; *Statesman Journal* (Salem), 26 February 1887, 3; *Oregon Statesman* (Salem), 11 March 1887, 6 (quote).

41  Shon, "Weapon Usage in Attempted and Completed Parricides in Nineteenth-Century America," 234; Heide and Petee, "Weapons Used by Juveniles and Adult Offenders in U.S. Parricide Cases." The pervasiveness of gun ownership and the existence of gun "culture" in early America have been fiercely debated. A good overview is included in Crist, "Good, the Bad, and the Ugly." R. B. Blake Brown's "'Every Boy Ought to Learn to Shoot and to Obey Orders,'" 197, argues that guns became "a key part of boy and male youth culture in English Canada" starting in the 1890s and thus became linked to cultural ideas about manhood and growing imperialist sentiments. As my evidence from newspapers suggests, guns were a common item in Willamette Valley households in the late nineteenth century. In the 1930s, the Works Progress Administration undertook extensive oral histories with old-timers in Linn County. Those interviews make numerous references to guns and rifles. See Works Progress Administration, Federal Writers' Project, Oral History Interviews.

42  Gragg correspondence.
43  Gragg correspondence.
44  Gragg correspondence.
45  *Weekly Herald-Disseminator*, 19 December 1895, 5 (quote). A related article is in *Oregonian*, 1 December 1895, 20.
46  Examples, all from the Brownsville-Crawfordsville area, come from *State Rights Democrat*, 23 August 1889, 3; *Morning Daily Herald* (Albany), 28 July 1888, 3; 26 April, 1891, 4; 23 November 1888, 3; *Capital Journal* (Salem), 6 July 1893, 1; *Statesman Journal* (Salem), 15 August 1885, 3; and *Albany Daily Democrat*, 5 March 1892, 3; 20 September 1888, 3.
47  *Oregonian*, 21 November 1895, 1 (quote); 22 November 1895, 1 (quote); 24 November 1895, 4 (quote); 1 December 1895, 20; 3 December 1895, 4; 22 January 1896, 4 (quote); and *Weekly Herald-Disseminator*, 19 December 1895, 4 (quote).
48  *Willamette Farmer* (Salem), 25 January 1873, 8.
49  *Willamette Farmer* (Portland), 2 February 1883, 6.
50  *Willamette Farmer* (Salem), 25 January 1873, 8.

CHAPTER 3. "SPARE THE ROD AND SPOIL THE CHILD"

1  *Willamette Farmer* (Salem), 26 August 1887, 4.
2  *Oregonian* (Portland), 3 December 1887, 1; *Lebanon Express*, 9 December 1887, 3; *State Rights Democrat* (Albany), 6 December 1895, 3. The story of Loyd betting on his father's death comes from 1895. It explains that Loyd's deed took place

when he was ten years old and his father was ill. My research revealed the severe illness of both his father and mother in 1887, which is when Loyd was ten.

3   *Oregonian*, 4 December 1895, 3; *State Rights Democrat*, 6 December 1895, 3. Reverend Kelly gave his talk again on the fifth. On Kelly, see US Department of Commerce, Bureau of the Census, Twelfth Census, 1900, Manuscript Census, Benton County, Oregon, Enumeration District 3, sheet 8, line 77; US Department of the Interior, Census Office, Tenth Census, 1880, Manuscript Census, Multnomah County, Oregon, Enumeration District 89, p. 2, line 47; Bengal Joy Kelly, Find a Grave, accessed 12 June 2020, www.findagrave.com/memorial/15085695/bengal-joy-kelly. Kelly was the grandson of the famous Oregon pioneer and minister Clinton Kelly. Kelly also experienced his own horrible death, by incineration. See *Oregon Journal* (Portland), 31 July 1904, 1.

4   West, *Growing Up with the Country*, 83–84; Banks, *Oregon Boyhood*, 56.

5   Carlson, "Family in the Nineteenth Century," 327, 329.

6   *Oregonian*, 26 November 1895, 1. Days later, Loyd retracted this confession and told another story of the murders that, in the opinion of the press, "will not hold water." *State Rights Democrat*, 29 November 1895, 3.

7   *Oregonian*, 23 November 1895, 8.

8   *State Rights Democrat*, 20 December 1895, 3.

9   *Oregonian*, 1 December 1895, 20.

10  *Weekly Herald-Disseminator* (Albany), 9 January 1896, 4; *State Rights Democrat*, 22 November 1895, 3; *Oregonian*, 23 November 1895, 8; 26 November 1895, 1; 29 December 1895, 10.

11  *State Rights Democrat*, 22 November 1895, 3; *Oregonian*, 23 November 1895, 8.

12  Bloom, "'It's All for Your Own Good,'" 191–92; West, *Growing Up with the Country*, 148; Mintz, *Huck's Raft*, 11, 17–19, 190–91.

13  *Willamette Farmer* (Salem), 19 March 1875, 2.

14  *San Francisco Call*, 1 February 1896, 3.

15  Shon and Barton-Bellessa, "Pre-Offense Characteristics of Nineteenth-Century American Parricide Offenders"; Heide, *Understanding Parricide*, 14–17.

16  See, for example, *State Rights Democrat*, 22 November 1895, 3; *Oregonian*, 23 November 1895, 8; 26 November 1895, 1; and *Weekly Herald-Disseminator*, 6 February 1896, 3.

17  *Oregonian*, 23 November 1895, 8; *Weekly Herald-Disseminator*, 19 December 1895, 4 (quote).

18  *Oregonian*, 31 December 1895, 4.

19  *Oregonian*, 24 November 1895, 4.

20  *San Francisco Examiner*, 2 February 1896, 4.

21  *Oregonian*, 31 January 1896, 1.

22  *State Rights Democrat*, 22 November 1895, 3; 20 December 1895, 3.
23  *Oregonian*, 26 November 1895, 1.
24  This report from the *Lakeview Examiner* was printed and commented on in the *Oregonian*, 11 February 1896, 4.
25  Heide, *Why Kids Kill Parents*, 6. On the cultural context of abuse in American parricides, see Shon, "Sources of Conflict between Parents and Their Offspring in Nineteenth-Century American Parricides," 266–69; and Shon, "Existential Boundary Crossings," 450–51.
26  Peterson del Mar, *Beaten Down*; Peterson del Mar, *What Trouble I Have Seen*.
27  Nielsen, "Dr. Anna B. Ott, Patient #1763," 35. On patriarchy and the violence of settler-colonial society, see Arvin, Tuck, and Morrill, "Decolonizing Feminism." The literature on either side of the debate over whether patriarchy is a cause of domestic violence is vast. One useful summary that supports the patriarchy theory is Hunnicutt, "Varieties of Patriarchy and Violence against Women." See also Walker, *Battered Woman Syndrome*; and the historical works Pleck, *Domestic Tyranny*; and Gordon, *Heroes of Their Own Lives*.
28  Peterson del Mar, *Beaten Down*, 7, 63–66, 82; Gordon, "Family Violence as History and Politics," 24.
29  *Willamette Farmer* (Salem), 1 January 1875, 1.
30  *Willamette Farmer* (Portland), 27 April 1883, 3.
31  Knapp's letters to the editor of the *Willamette Farmer* (Portland): 26 January 1883, 1; 2 February 1883, 4; 13 April 1883, 3; and 4 May 1883, 1 (quote). Responses to him: 23 February 1883, 1; and 16 March 1883, 3. A slightly different version of this discussion appears in Boag, "Gender and Historicity of Parricide," 151–52, reproduced with permission of Palgrave Macmillan.
32  *Willamette Farmer* (Salem), 1 January 1875, 10.
33  Items 11573–11832, Reel 75, Oregon Provisional Government Records, 1841–59; *Oregon Statesman* (Salem), 27 September 1859, 2. Other facts about these people come from US Department of the Interior, Census Office, Ninth Census, 1870, Manuscript Census, Linn County, Albany Precinct, p. 47, lines 3–9, and Brownsville Precinct, p. 5, lines 19–23. For violence in the home and against wives in Oregon during this era, see Peterson del Mar, *What Trouble I Have Seen*, 9–46. On parents striking their children, see Peterson del Mar, *Beaten Down*, 63–64, 82–83. The Coueys' story appeared in a slightly different version in Boag, "Gender and Historicity of Parricide," 148–49, reproduced with permission of Palgrave Macmillan.
34  *Oregonian*, 6 January 1896, 6 (quote); 29 December 1895, 10 (quote); 3 December 1895, 4 (quote).

35  West, *Growing Up with the Country*, 149–56; Riney-Kehrberg, *Childhood on the Farm*, 56, 62, 76, 79, 188–90; Rotundo, *American Manhood*, 35, 42–49. A somewhat different version of this excerpt on boy culture appeared in Boag, "'He Took Up Arms against the Loins from Which He Sprang,'" 141.
36  For example, *Willamette Farmer* (Salem), 6 October 1876, 3; 30 November 1877, 7; 8 August 1884, 6; 30 April 1875, 2.
37  *State Rights Democrat*, 6 March 1891, 3; *Willamette Farmer* (Salem), 12 July 1873, 5; *Albany Daily Democrat*, 16 April 1895, 3; 25 April 1890, 3; 30 January 1890, 3; 26 July 1891, 1; *Willamette Farmer* (Salem), 19 January 1877, 8; *State Rights Democrat*, 7 June 1895, 2; *Willamette Farmer* (Salem), 9 August 1878, 2; *Evening Capital Journal* (Salem), 15 April 1892, 2; *The Dalles Times-Mountaineer*, 23 April 1892, 1.
38  *State Rights Democrat*, 8 March 1895, 2.
39  Bettie Gragg, Alpine, Oregon, to T. Herman Gragg, Huntsville, Washington Territory, 22 April 1887, 30 April 1887, Folder: Letters: 1886–1888, Joseph Gragg Papers.
40  "A Triple Murder," *Brownsville Times*, supplement, 20 November 1895, n.p., photocopy on file at the Linn County Historical Museum.
41  State of Oregon, State of Oregon v. Lloyd [sic] Montgomery, 12–13.
42  *Daily Oregon Statesman*, (Salem), 21 November 1895, 1.
43  *State Rights Democrat*, 7 February 1896, 1.
44  *Oregonian*, 23 November 1895, 8; 26 November 1895, 1.
45  *Oregonian*, 23 November 1895, 8; 29 December 1895, 10; *San Francisco Chronicle*, 6 January 1896, 3. On profanity and the cultural preoccupation with it, see *Albany Register*, 9 July 1875, 3; *State Rights Democrat*, 7 June 1895, 2; and *Corvallis Gazette Times*, 9 October 1885, 6.
46  *Weekly Herald-Disseminator*, 19 December 1895, 5 (quote); *State Rights Democrat*, 24 January 1896, 1 (quote).
47  State of Oregon, State of Oregon v. Lloyd [sic] Montgomery, 14.
48  *State Rights Democrat*, 27 December 1895, 1; 7 February 1896, 1.
49  *Weekly Herald-Disseminator*, 2 January 1896, 5 (quote); *Oregonian*, 1 January 1896, 2.
50  *Oregonian*, 13 November 1875, 3; 9 October 1884, 8.
51  Mrs. S. C. Adams, "Secretary's Report of the Oregon Childrens' [sic] Aid Society," Salem, Oregon, 8 October 1880, filed under call number 362.7 O66 1878/80, Oregon State Library, Salem; State of Oregon, *First Biennial Report of the State Board of Charities and Corrections*, 267; *Oregonian*, 14 October 1884, 8; 11 April 1888, 8; 25 May 1888, 4. On the national context, see Mintz, *Huck's Raft*, 154–84.
52  State of Oregon, State Penitentiary, Great Register, 1887–93.

53  State of Oregon, *First Biennial Report of the State Board of Charities and Corrections*, 268 (quote); State of Oregon, *Third Biennial Report of the Oregon State Reform School at Salem*, 12–13; State of Oregon, *Second Biennial Report of the Oregon State Reform School at Salem*, 7–9.

54  State of Oregon, *Second Biennial Report of the Oregon State Reform School*, 12; *Capital Journal* (Salem), 13 June 1894, 1.

55  State of Oregon, *Second Biennial Report of the Oregon State Reform School*, 8, 15. In my discussion of the reform school, I am also following the insights in Foucault, *Discipline and Punish*.

56  State of Oregon, *First Biennial Report of the State Board of Charities and Corrections*, 268–70.

57  State of Oregon, *First Biennial Report of the State Board of Charities and Corrections*, 21; State of Oregon, *Fourth Biennial Report of the State Reform School*, 8.

58  My ideas here are partly inspired by Slotkin, *Fatal Environment*, 310–11, where the author draws parallels between Indian removal and the late nineteenth-century reform endeavor that sent orphans and street boys from the American Northeast to western farms.

59  State of Oregon, Youth Authority, Admissions Registers, vol. 1, 1891–1900, 68, 52; *State Rights Democrat*, 6 May 1892, 4.

60  State of Oregon, Youth Authority, Admissions Registers, vol. 1, 1891–1900, 60 (quote); *Daily (Salem) Oregon Statesman*, 23 June 1892, 4; *Illustrated History of Central Oregon*, 390; *State Rights Democrat*, 30 December 1898, 1 (quote). McHargue had another brush with the law in Portland in 1905, when he impersonated a detective and passed forged checks. He died in Portland the following year from tuberculosis. *Oregonian*, 4 September 1905, 2; *Oregon Journal*, 7 June 1906, 14. See also *State Rights Democrat*, 12 November 1897, 1.

61  On the forgery episode, *Weekly Herald-Disseminator*, 21 November 1895; *Oregonian*, 22 November 1895, 1; 23 November 1895, 8. State of Oregon, *Second Biennial Report of the Oregon State Reform School*, 8, discusses the issue of changing the age restrictions at the reform school.

62  *Oregonian*, 4 December 1908, 14.

63  Cook, "Murders in Massachusetts." On the bad-boy problem elsewhere in rural America, see Riney-Kehrberg, *Childhood on the Farm*, 199–200.

64  *San Francisco Chronicle*, 2 January 1896, 6.

65  *Oregonian*, 9 January 1896, 4.

66  *Corvallis Times*, 8 January 1896, 3; *Weekly Herald-Disseminator*, 16 January 1896, 3.

67  *Weekly Herald Disseminator*, 28 November 1895, 4. Other references to Loyd in conjunction with Pomeroy and Durrant are *State Rights Democrat*, 29 November

1895, 4; and *Weekly Herald-Disseminator*, 9 January 1896, 5; 23 January 1896, 6. On Pomeroy, see Keetley, *Making a Monster*. On Durrant, see McConnell, *Sympathy for the Devil*.

68  The Finlayson episode that follows is reconstructed from varied sources, some of them telling slightly different versions and details: *Oregonian*, 6 November 1883, 1; *State Rights Democrat*, 9 November 1883; *Douglas Independent* (Roseburg), 10 November 1883, 3; *Oregonian*, 14 November 1883, 3; *State Rights Democrat*, 16 November 1883, 3; *Corvallis Gazette*, 16 November 1883, 4.

69  Weather comes from Sarah Jane (Savage) Cornett, Diary, 3 November 1883, in the possession of E. H. Margason, Shedd, Oregon.

70  *State Rights Democrat*, 16 November 1883, 3

71  *Oregonian*, 14 November 1883, 3; 6 November 1883, 3.

72  *State Rights Democrat*, 9 November 1883, 3.

73  *Oregon Sentinel* (Jacksonville), 5 April 1884, 3; *State Rights Democrat*, 18 April 1884, 3.

74  *State Rights Democrat*, 8 February 1884, 3; Lang, *History of the Willamette Valley*, 763; *Oregonian*, 15 August 1890, 4.

75  *Willamette Farmer* (Salem), 4 February 1876, 9; 30 November 1883, 3. See also *Willamette Farmer* (Salem), 30 November 1872, 6; 20 December 1873, 6; and *Willamette Farmer* (Portland), 24 August 1883, 3. On period concerns about the connection between Victorian novels and crime, particularly in the Pomeroy case, see Keetley, *Making a Monster*, 106–36.

76  *Oregonian*, 23 November 1895, 8.

77  *Oregonian*, 23 November 1895, 8.

78  *Daily Astorian* (Astoria, OR), 9 November 1883, 1.

79  *Oregonian*, 14 November 1883, 3.

80  *Oregonian*, 19 December 1895, 4.

81  *Oregonian*, 22 November 1895, 1; 23 November 1895, 8; *State Rights Democrat*, 29 November 1895, 1.

82  *Willamette Farmer* (Salem), 27 May 1887, 2; *Oregonian*, 1 December 1895, 20. A slightly different version of this excerpt on height and weight appears in Boag, "Gender and Historicity of Parricide," 160, reproduced with permission of Palgrave Macmillan.

83  *Lebanon Express*, 19 October 1894, 2; *State Rights Democrat*, 8 March 1895, 2; *Albany Daily Democrat*, 21 April 1892, 3.

84  The Warren School (no. 28), which operated between Brownsville and Crawfordsville in 1895, had at least eight boys between fifteen and twenty years old. Linn County, Oregon, School District 28 Records, 1894–95.

85   Carlson, "Rural Family in the Nineteenth Century," 293, 304–5; Prescott, *Gender and Generation on the Far Western Frontier*, 43; *Willamette Farmer* (Salem), 23 February 1883, 1.
86   Mintz and Kellogg, *Domestic Revolutions*, 60.
87   Carlson, "Rural Family in the Nineteenth Century," 327–28; Riney-Kehrberg, *Childhood on the Farm*, 42–44; Prescott, *Gender and Generation on the Far Western Frontier*, 49.
88   Streib, *Death Penalty for Juveniles*, 4.
89   Baxter, *Modern Age*, 3; Fuentes, "Cracking Down on Kids," 231.
90   *Weekly Herald-Disseminator*, 19 December 1895, 4.
91   *Weekly Herald-Disseminator*, 9 January 1896, 5; *Oregonian*, 1 December 1895, 20; 3 December 1895, 4.
92   *Oregonian*, 7 January 1896, 4.

## PART 2. "ONE BY ONE THEY ARE DROPPING LIKE THE AUTUMN LEAVES"

1   "A Triple Murder," *Brownsville Times*, supplement, 20 November 1895, photocopy on file at the Linn County Historical Museum.
2   *Oregonian* (Portland), 22 November 1895, 1; *Sunday Democrat* (Albany), 11 December 1921, 7.
3   *Morning Daily Herald* (Albany), 2 February 1888, 1 (quote); *State Rights Democrat* (Albany), 10 February 1888, 1.

## CHAPTER 4. "THE PINCHING ECONOMIES OF LIFE"

1   US Census Bureau, Seventh Census, 1850, Manuscript Agricultural Census, Linn County, Oregon; US Census Bureau, Seventh Census, 1850, Manuscript Census, Linn County, Oregon, p. 67, lines 29–36; Oliphant and Kendall, "Thomas S. Kendall's Letter on Oregon Agriculture, 1852," 193.
2   This and the next few paragraphs, unless otherwise noted, are based on Boag, *Environment and Experience*, 106–8, 113–15, 134–35; Johansen, *Empire of the Columbia*, 278–99, 306–10; L. Scott, "History of the Narrow Gauge Railroad in the Willamette Valley"; and Holtgrieve, "Effects of the Railroads on Small Town Population Changes."
3   *State Rights Democrat* (Albany), 9 December 1870, 3.
4   *State Rights Democrat*, 31 December 1880, 3.
5   US Department of the Interior, Census Office, *Report on the Production of Agriculture, Tenth Census, 1880, General Statistics*, 167, 202; US Department of the Interior, Superintendent of the Census, *Statistics of the Wealth and Industry of*

the United States, 1870, 230–31; Boag, *Environment and Experience*, 115, table 3; Blok, "Evolution of Agricultural Resource Use Strategies in the Willamette Valley," 71–83, 88.

6 US Department of the Interior, Census Office, Tenth Census, 1880, Manuscript Agricultural Census, Linn County, Oregon, Enumeration District 75, p. 14, line 4, and p. 211, lines 30–37.

7 US Department of the Interior, Census Office, *Report of the Population of the United States, 1890*, lxviii, lxx; US Census Office, *Twelfth Census of the United States, 1900*, lxxxii, 328; US Department of Commerce, Bureau of the Census, *Thirteenth Census of the United States, Population, 1910*, 3:486–88.

8 Johansen, *Empire of the Columbia*, 320; Danbom, *Born in the Country*, 133.

9 In 1870, Linn County had 747 farms, with the average size being 343 acres. By 1890, that number had increased to 1,711 and the average size had decreased to 244 acres. US Department of the Interior, Superintendent of the Census, *Statistics of the Wealth and Industry of the United States, 1870*, 230; US Department of the Interior, Census Office, *Report on the Statistics of Agriculture in the United States, Eleventh Census, 1890*, 224.

10 Kristin Hoganson found the very same processes at work among midwestern farmers in the same era. See Hoganson, "SHGAPE Presidential Address."

11 *Willamette Farmer* (Salem), 1 August 1884, 5. See also Danbom, *Born in the Country*, 133.

12 "Oregon Cities—Brownsville," Vertical Files, Oregon Historical Society Research Library.

13 Linn County, Oregon, Robert Montgomery, Probate Case No. 181, 48, 52–55, 60, 63, 66.

14 For example, *State Rights Democrat*, 3 April 1874, 4.

15 Danbom, *Born in the Country*, 134.

16 Hoganson, "SHGAPE Presidential Address," 177; Robbins, *Colony and Empire*, 91–93; White, *Railroaded*, 370–409.

17 US Department of Agriculture, Bureau of Statistics, *Wheat Crops of the United States, 1866–1906*, 39.

18 US Department of the Interior, Census Office, *Report on the Production of Agriculture, Tenth Census, 1880, General Statistics*, 202; US Department of the Interior, Census Office, *Report of the Statistics of Agriculture in the United States, Eleventh Census, 1890*, 381; US Department of Commerce, Bureau of the Census, *Census Reports, Volume VI: Twelfth Census, Agriculture, Part II, Crops and Irrigation*, 180; US Department of Commerce, Bureau of the Census, *Thirteenth Census for the United States Taken in the Year 1910, Volume VII: Agriculture, 1909 and 1910*, 420.

19  Kopp, *Hoptopia*, 35–38.
20  Templeton, Templeton, and Breuer, *William T. Templeton*, 43, 44, 61, 62, 84; Larsen, *Hop King*, 129; 225n11; *Capital Journal* (Salem), 28 August 1893, 1; *Daily (Salem) Oregon Statesman*, 1 September 1893, 4.
21  "United States Patent Office, Samuel R. Templeton, John C. Templeton, and Joseph H. Templeton, of Brownsville, Oregon. Improvement in Hop-Driers," accessed 31 August 2020, https://patentimages.storage.googleapis.com/75/e8/5f/3a49d9d52a838d/US190794.pdf.
22  "Your Father [William T. Templeton] & Mother and Brothers & Sisters, At Home by myself – March the 13th 1879," letter to "Robert," Templeton Family Papers.
23  US Department of the Interior, Census Office, Manuscript Agricultural Census for 1880, Linn County, Enumeration District 75, p. 14, lines 5, 6, 7.
24  US Department of the Interior, Census Office, *Report on the Production of Agriculture, Tenth Census, 1880, General Statistics*, 305, 307.
25  Linn County, Oregon, Agriculture Census, 1885 and 1895.
26  *State Rights Democrat*, 16 September 1881, 2; Kopp, *Hoptopia*, 64–68.
27  Templeton, Templeton, and Breuer, *William T. Templeton*, 53, 84–85, 96–97; *State Rights Democrat*, 21 August 1885, 3 (quote); 25 September 1885, 2 (quote); 27 August 1886, 3; 7 September 1888, 3 (quote). On Chinese laborers and racism in the hopyards, see Kopp, *Hoptopia*, 68–71.
28  *Morning Daily Herald* (Albany), 10 September 1890, 4; *Weekly Herald-Disseminator*, 14 September 1893, 3, 5; 7 September 1893, 3 (quote); *Oregon Populist* (Albany), 20 September 1893, 2. Templeton, Templeton, and Breuer, *William T. Templeton*, 85, mentions the leasing of fields to Suey Gee; *Albany Democrat*, 11 May 1906, 3, also mentions Suey Gee leasing Robert Templeton's hop farm. I have found news reports as early as 1902 mentioning Suey Gee in the hop business in Brownsville: *Albany Democrat*, 26 September 1902, 5.
29  US Department of Commerce, Bureau of the Census, *Census Reports, Volume VI: Twelfth Census, Agriculture, Part II, Crops and Irrigation*, 517, 518, 519, 586.
30  *Albany Weekly Herald*, 19 October 1893, 3.
31  *Albany Weekly Herald*, 30 August 1894, 5.
32  See *Morning Daily Herald*, 20 September 1888, 3.
33  See 1895 entries in "Account Books 1882–1902," Templeton Family Papers.
34  *State Rights Democrat*, 4 October 1895, 3; Larsen, *Hop King*, 183, 184–97; *Brownsville Times* fragment from 1893, on file at Linn County Historical Museum.
35  Linn County, Oregon, Tax Rolls, 1892 and 1895, reels 2 and 8.
36  US Department of Agriculture, Bureau of Statistics, *Wheat Crops of the United States, 1866–1906*, 35.

37  *Oregon Populist*, 30 August 1898, 1.
38  Johansen, *Empire of the Columbia*, 361.
39  *State Rights Democrat*, 20 January 1893, 3; 10 March 1893, 3; 23 June 1893, 3. T. L. Wallace & Co. advertisement in *Lebanon Express*, 6 January 1893, 5.
40  Linn County National Bank of Albany, Minutes, 1890–93, entry for 18 April 1890; Hines, *Illustrated History of the State of Oregon*, 1015–16; *Portrait and Biographical Record of the Willamette Valley, Oregon*, 1:39–41; Robbins, "George Chamberlain (1854–1928)."
41  Linn County, Oregon, Robert Montgomery, Probate Case; *Oregonian*, 23 November 1895, 8.
42  *State Rights Democrat*, 23 June 1893, 3 (quote); 2 June 1893, 3; US Department of Treasury, *Annual Report of the Controller of the Currency, December 4, 1893*, 1:75.
43  *State Rights Democrat*, 3 July 1893, 3; US Department of Treasury, *Annual Report of the Controller of the Currency, December 7, 1896*, 1:677; *Weekly Herald-Disseminator*, 7 September 1893, 5; *State Rights Democrat*, 10 November 1893, 3; 18 November 1893, 2; *Weekly Herald-Disseminator*, 28 December 1893, 5; *State Rights Democrat*, 8 March 1895, 4.
44  *Lebanon Express*, 5 April 1895, 3; *State Rights Democrat*, 22 March 1895, 3. On other flouring mill failures, see *State Rights Democrat*, 29 March 1895, 4; and 18 October 1895, 3.
45  *State Rights Democrat*, 18 October 1895, 3; 8 November 1895, 1; 15 November 1895, 1; 7 February 1896, 1; 19 December 1895, 4.
46  *Weekly Herald-Disseminator*, 28 November 1895, 5; entries for 1895 in "Account Books 1882–1902," Templeton Family Papers.
47  *Lebanon Express*, 12 April 1895, 2.
48  Minute book, Linn County Farmers' Union Records, 1871–85; "Farmer's Union Warehouse," *Albany Register*, 5 August 1871, 3.
49  E. Scott, "Grange Movement in Oregon," 6–7, 12; Masterson, "History of the Consumer's Cooperatives in Oregon Prior to 1900," 3; *Albany Register*, 14 February 1874, 3; *Oregon Cultivator* (Albany), 14 December 1876, 5 (quote); *State Rights Democrat*, 8 March 1874, 2.
50  E. Scott, "Grange Movement in Oregon," 12–13; Cashman, *America in the Gilded Age*, 29.
51  E. Scott, "Grange Movement in Oregon," 14 (quote).
52  E. Scott, "Grange Movement in Oregon," 33–35; Holden, "Rise and Fall of Oregon Populism," 96.
53  E. Scott, "Grange Movement in Oregon," 16; Holden, "Rise and Fall of Oregon Populism," 241, 247, 305; Dodds, *American Northwest*, 167.

54  Danbom, *Born in the Country*, 155–56; *State Rights Democrat*, 5 August 1887, 3; Holden, "Rise and Fall of Oregon Populism," 486; Oregon Farmers' State Alliance Industrial Union, *Constitution and By-Laws*; Griffiths, "Populism in the Far West," 93–95.

55  Holden, "Rise and Fall of Oregon Populism," 487 (quote), 488, 489 (quote).

56  Lipin, "Populism in Oregon." On Oregon populism, see in particular Holden, "Rise and Fall of Oregon Populism"; LaLande, "'Little Kansas' in Southern Oregon"; and Griffiths, "Populism in the Far West," 87–147.

57  Holden, "Rise and Fall of Oregon Populism," 509–11; Postel, *Populist Vision*.

58  Johansen, *Empire of the Columbia*, 262; Barber, "'We Were at Our Journey's End,'" 397; Pascoe, *What Comes Naturally*; Smith, "Oregon's Civil War." On the history of the anti-Black laws in Oregon, see Berwanger, *Frontier against Slavery*, 78–96; and McLagan, *Peculiar Paradise*. Although Oregon as a whole had been a Democratic stronghold through its early years, in the 1880s Republicans became the majority party. Robert E. Burton has attributed this to immigration from Wisconsin, Michigan, Minnesota, Sweden, Norway, and Germany. Burton, *Democrats of Oregon*, 3.

59  "Montgomery, Robert John," Early Oregonian Search, Oregon Secretary of State, accessed 9 July 2020, https://secure.sos.state.or.us/prs/personprofile.do?recordNumber=101034; US Department of the Interior, Census Office, Eighth Census, 1860, Manuscript Census, Linn County, Oregon, p. 674, lines 37 and 38; US Bureau of the Census, Fifth Census, 1830, Manuscript Census, Howard County, Missouri, 145; Catherine Louise (McHargue) Hume, interview by Leslie Haskins for the Works Progress Administration, 7 July 1939, Linn Genealogical Society, accessed 29 September 2011, http://www.lgsoregon.org/lgstng/showmedia.php?mediaID=22480; *1850 U.S. Federal Census – Slave Schedules* (Provo, UT: Ancestry.com), accessed 27 July 2020, www.ancestry.com/imageviewer/collections/8055/images/MOM432_422-0187?pId=91264357&backurl=https%3A%2F%2Fwww.ancestry.com%2Ffamily-tree%2Fperson%2Ftree%2F24658340%2Fperson%2F202210723087%2Ffacts%2Fcitation%2F702295817783%2Fedit%2Frecord; Everett Earle Stanard, "Old Stuff & New," *Sunday Democrat* (Albany), 15 July 1823, 5.

60  "Brown, Eveline Jane," Early Oregonian Search, Oregon Secretary of State, accessed 9 July 2020, https://secure.sos.state.or.us/prs/personprofile.do?recordNumber=107364; "Brown, Hugh Leeper," Early Oregonian Search, Oregon Secretary of State, accessed 9 July 2020, https://secure.sos.state.or.us/prs/profile.do?ancRecordNumber=7677; "Browning, Clarissa," Early Oregonian Search, Oregon Secretary of State, accessed 9 July 2020, https://secure.sos.state.or.us/prs/profile.do?recordNumber=17319; *State Rights Democrat*,

9 April 1886, 2; H. L. Brown to George L. Curry, June 15, 1856, item 10548, Oregon Provisional and Territorial Government Papers, 1843–59; "Couey, John B.," Early Oregonian Search, Oregon Secretary of State, accessed 29 September 2020, https://secure.sos.state.or.us/prs/profile.do?ancRecord Number=12349.

61 *Oregon Populist*, 30 August 1898, 1; *Evening Capital Journal* (Salem), 27 April 1893, 4; *Oregon Populist*, 11 October 1894, 4; *Lebanon Express*, 5 July 1895, 2; "Linn County Newspapers," accessed 2 July 2020, www.linncountyroots.com /Newspapers/MoreNews.htm.

62 Holden, "Rise and Fall of Oregon Populism," 508; *Morning Herald* (Albany), 9 November 1888, 3.

63 *Oregon Populist*, 20 September 1893, 3.

64 *State Rights Democrat*, 22 September 1893, 3.

65 *Oregon Populist*, 7 February 1894, 2; *Lebanon Express*, 9 March 1894, 3.

66 *Lebanon Express*, 25 May 1894, 4; *Oregonian*, 5 June 1894, 1–2; *State Rights Democrat*, 8 June 1894, 3.

67 *Portrait and Biographical Record of the Willamette Valley*, 2:1234–35; Templeton, Templeton, and Breuer, *William T. Templeton*, 20.

68 Legislative Committee Services, *Chronological List of Oregon's Legislatures*. Some of the party affiliations listed in this source are missing for a couple of assemblies, but I was able to identity their party affiliations in local newspapers.

69 Legislative Committee Services, *Chronological List of Oregon's Legislatures*; Holden, "Rise and Fall of Oregon Populism," 517; *State Rights Democrat*, 13 April 1900, 5; 20 April 1900, 5.

70 *State Rights Democrat*, 9 April 1886, 2; *Oregonian*, 24 November 1895, 4 (quote).

71 *Oregonian*, 22 November 1895, 1; *Weekly Herald-Disseminator*, 19 December 1895, 4.

72 *Oregonian*, 22 November 1895, 1.

73 *Oregonian*, 22 November 1895, 1.

74 Rotundo, *American Manhood*, 26, 55; Prescott, *Gender and Generation on the Far Western Frontier*, 39.

75 *Oregonian*, 1 December 1895, 20.

76 *Oregonian*, 10 January 1896, 3.

77 US Department of the Interior, Census Office, Tenth Census, 1880, Manuscript Agricultural Census, Linn County, Enumeration District 75, p. 14, Line 4.

78 US Department of the Interior, Census Office, *Report on the Production of Agriculture, Tenth Census, 1880, General Statistics*, 82–83; US Department of the

Interior, Census Office, *Report of the Statistics of Agriculture in the United States, Eleventh Census, 1890*, 174–75; US Department of Commerce, Bureau of the Census, *Agriculture*, part 1, 116–17.

79  Prescott, *Gender and Generation on the Far Western Frontier*, 43.
80  See, for example, Greven, *Four Generations*, 125–72.
81  Shon, "Sources of Conflict between Parents and Their Offspring in Nineteenth-Century American Parricides."
82  Linn County, Oregon, Robert Montgomery Probate Case.
83  *Oregonian*, 22 November 1895, 1; *Weekly Herald-Disseminator*, 19 December 1895, 4.
84  Prescott, *Gender and Generation on the Far Western Frontier*, 54.
85  Linn County, Oregon, Tax Rolls, 1890, reel 1, p. 190; 1893, reel 4, p. 173; 1894, reel 6, p. 233; 1895, reel 7, p. 258.
86  Linn County, Oregon, Tax Rolls, 1892, reel 3, p. 183; 1892, reel 2, p. 29; 1893, reel 5, p. 250; 1895, reel 7, p. 259; 1895, reel 8, pp. 392, 393.
87  Clark, *History of the Willamette Valley, Oregon*, 2:532.
88  Linn County, Oregon, Tax Rolls, 1895, reel 8, p. 393.
89  *Lebanon Express*, 21 November 1890, 3; Templeton, Templeton, and Breuer, *William T. Templeton*, 39 (quote).
90  "A Triple Murder," *Brownsville Times*, supplement, 20 November 1895, n.p., photocopy on file at the Linn County Historical Museum.
91  *Weekly Herald-Disseminator*, 28 November 1895, 3; *Oregonian*, 26 November 1895, 1; *State Rights Democrat*, 29 November 1895, 1.
92  *Oregonian*, 26 November 1895, 1.
93  *Oregonian*, 1 December 1895, 20. On the victims of parricide contributing to their own murders, see Shon, "Sources of Conflict between Parents and Their Offspring in Nineteenth-Century American Parricides," 259–63.
94  *Oregonian*, 26 November 1895, 1.
95  Shon, "Existential Boundary Crossings," 451 (quote); Shon, "Sources of Conflict between Parents and Their Offspring in Nineteenth-Century American Parricides," 259–63.
96  *New York Times*, 22 November 1895, 9. I have located no mention of the Montgomery parricide in the *Chicago Tribune*.
97  Shon, "Sources of Conflict between Parents and Their Offspring in Nineteenth-Century American Parricides," 259–63.
98  *Oregonian*, 26 November 1895, 1.
99  Shon and Roberts, "Post-Offence Characteristics of 19th-Century American Parricides," 155.

## CHAPTER 5. "HIS PEOPLE BEING PIONEERS"

1  The excerpt is from Minutes of the Linn County Pioneer Association, Book 1, 20 June 1895, 44–45, Linn County Pioneer Association Records (hereafter MLCPA). This chapter includes material originally appearing as part of Boag, "Death and Oregon's Settler Generation." It is utilized here with permission from the *Oregon Historical Quarterly*.

   The term *pioneer* is problematic for varied reasons, including that in the history of the American West it suggests that white Americans were the first people in the region who held any significance to the nation and its destiny. I use the term in this chapter because it was the term used regularly during the era that I consider, and I use it with all its problematic and nuanced meanings as a way to explore how Americans in Oregon thought about themselves and their ancestors, as well as the significance the "pioneer" concept held in their memorizing efforts.

2  Faust, *This Republic of Suffering*. Faust has argued that the early efforts in the South to erect monuments to the Confederacy's dead were focused primarily on their memory. Other historians, including Kirk Savage in his *Standing Soldiers, Kneeling Slaves*, explain that after Reconstruction, when white southerners extended Jim Crow laws in their region, the monuments and memorials took on another, darker meaning.

3  Historians have demonstrated the importance, even centrality, of the Civil War to the Pacific Northwest, however distant the region was from the actual conflagration. It tested loyalties, divided communities, renewed debates over race, and produced political turmoil. But considerably more distant from the region was the death of that war. Certainly, as relatively recent arrivals in Oregon, having come from all parts of the nation but especially the Upper South and Middle Border, the white American families in the Pacific Northwest still had close kin back East who stood in the midst of the war's onslaught. And after the war, thousands of its veterans migrated to Oregon. Civil War death and mourning touched Oregon in those ways, to be sure, but the state contributed the least of any state to the death toll of that conflict—fewer than 50 out of the 620,000. On the Civil War in Oregon, see Smith, "Oregon's Civil War"; Etulain, *Lincoln and Oregon Country Politics in the Civil War Era*; Edwards, "Six Oregon Leaders and the Far-Reaching Impact of America's Civil War"; and LaLande, "'Dixie' of the Pacific Northwest." The number of Oregonians who died in the Civil War comes from Fox, *Regimental Losses in the American Civil War*, 527.

4   Rees, "Oregon—Its Meaning, Origin and Application," 331.
5   Baker, "Oregon Pioneer Tradition in the Nineteenth Century," 48–55.
6   *Oregonian* (Portland), 1 January 1896, 26; 1 January 1, 1897, 6 (quote). The 1896 article specifically mentions Himes's record keeping. Although the 1897 article does not mention him, likely he supplied the information for the piece. On Himes, see Wexler, "George Himes (1844–1940)."
7   Baker, "Oregon Pioneer Tradition in the Nineteenth Century," 49–50.
8   *Constitution and Laws: Grand Cabin, Native Sons*, 4, Article II; *Constitution and Laws of the Grand Cabin, Native Daughters*, 39, Article II.
9   See, for example, various items in Native Daughters of Oregon Records, 1899–1901 and 1902–4.
10  "James Blakely's Cabin, No. 18," 283; *Oregonian*, 1 April 1894, 2.
11  *Constitution and Laws: Grand Cabin, Native Sons*, 1.
12  "Purple and Gold," 38.
13  "Purple and Gold," 38; "Native Daughters of Oregon," leaflet, folder 14, box 23, Associations and Institutions Collection.
14  Baker, "Oregon Pioneer Tradition," explores these themes. A couple of examples of these themes in the literature and meetings of the Native Sons and the Native Daughters can be found in "Pioneer Day and Pioneer Era"; and Minutes of the Elizabeth Thurston Odell Cabin, No. 8, Salem, Oregon, 25 February 1901, Native Daughters of Oregon Records, 1899–1901.
15  Works Progress Administration Writers' Program and the Linn County Pioneer Memorial Association, *History of Linn County*, foreword, n.p.; *Oregonian*, 26 November 1895, 1; *Weekly Herald-Disseminator*, 19 December 1895, 4; 6 February 1896, 3. Biographical information on Scott comes from various sources available through Ancestry.com.
16  *Lebanon Express*, 9 September 1887, 3.
17  The Cayuse view of events at Waiilatpu is naturally rather different from the version that American settlers in the Pacific Northwest told, and tribal members have also used the phrase "Whitman incident." The version of events that I describe and my sparing use of the term *massacre* are more in keeping with the American settlers' perspective, since I am emphasizing the meaning of those events to them. For a Cayuse perspective, see Minthorn, "Wars, Treaties, and the Beginning of Reservation Life."
18  This paragraph and the next are based on *Lebanon Express*, 9 September 1887, 3 (quote); Works Progress Administration Writers' Program and the Linn County Pioneer Memorial Association, *History of Linn County*, 15, 18; *History of the Pacific Northwest*, 2:621; and Carey and Hainline, *Brownsville*, 30–31.

19  On the Spaldings, see Drury, *Henry Harmon Spalding*. In 1916, Eliza Spalding Warren published her *Memoirs of the West*.
20  *Lebanon Express*, 9 September 1887, 3.
21  More recent studies that have examined the myths and memory of the Whitmans include Vaughn, "Killing Narcissa"; Addis, "Whitman Massacre"; and Grube, "'From Honeymoon to Massacre.'"
22  A good description of the actual events of the murders is contained in Jeffrey, *Converting the West*, 217–19.
23  Works Progress Administration Writers' Program and the Linn County Pioneer Memorial Association, *History of Linn County*, 96.
24  Varley, *Americans Recaptured*.
25  MLCPA, Book 1, 7 June 1894, 40; *Weekly Herald-Disseminator*, 24 May 1894, 1.
26  Warren, *Memoirs of the West*, 23–25. During this era, dime novels freely circulated. They typically detailed gruesome atrocities committed by Native Americans, and some protectors of social morality decried these popular works. See Keeting, *Making a Monster*, 112–15.
27  "Massacre in Oregon," 66–67. On the trial, see Lansing, "Whitman Massacre Trial."
28  Hugh Dunlap interview, 7 July 1939; Iva Templeton Galbraith interview, 21 October 1937; Bell (Gray) Gromley interview, 8 July 1940; Catherine Louise (McHargue) Hume interview, 7 July 1939, all by Leslie Haskins for the Works Progress Administration, Federal Writers' Project Oral History Interviews. Two early and later retellings of the Whitmans' story are Victor, *River of the West*, 410, 415–18; and Drury, *Marcus and Narcissa Whitman and the Opening of Old Oregon*. For an analysis of the (re)tellings of the Whitman incident, see Luce, "Excavating First-Person Accounts of the Whitman Massacre."
29  *Lebanon Express*, 9 September 1887, 3; Margaret Standish Carey, "Past Times," *Brownsville Times*, 25 March and 8 April 1987, "Past Times" clipping files.
30  Constitution of the Linn County Pioneer Association, contained within the MLCPA, Book 1, 1.
31  *Democrat Herald* (Albany), 18 January 1890, 3.
32  LCPA reunion programs, 1890, 1891, 1892, and 1893, Linn County Pioneer Association Records; Fred E. Harrison, "Early Day Linn County Pioneer Picnics" (quote) in Fred E. Harrison Histories of Linn County; MLCPA; and numerous newspaper reports, for example, *Brownsville Times*, 21 June 1907, 1; and 1 July 1910, 1.
33  MLCPA, Book 1, June 4, 1890, 18, 19.
34  *Brownsville Times*, 7 June 1901, 2.
35  *Brownsville Times*, 1 July 1910, 1.

36  *Brownsville Times*, 14 June 1901, 1.
37  MLCPA, Book 1, 78–79, 83–84, 87, 91, 95–96, 100, 103, 106–7.
38  Miles and Milligan, *Linn County, Oregon, Pioneer Settlers*, 1:5–6, 11:5–6.
39  *Lebanon Express*, 9 September 1887, 3; *Brownsville Times*, 23 June 1911, 1; *Oregonian*, 30 June 1912, 7; *Brownsville Times*, 29 June 1906, 1; "Pioneers in Attendance," 19.
40  *Oregonian*, 1 February 1913, 8.
41  *Oregonian*, 27 October 1912, 8 (quote); 27 November 1912, 1, 3.
42  Miles and Milligan, *Linn County, Oregon, Pioneer Settlers*, 1:5–6.
43  *Albany Evening Herald*, 25 May 1922, 3; *History of the Pacific Northwest*, 2:227; *Weekly Herald-Disseminator*, 28 January 1897, 3.
44  Whaley, "Reflection on Genocide in Southwestern Oregon"; Carpenter, "Pioneer Problems."
45  See Brown, *Civil War Monuments and the Militarization of America*.
46  *Statesman Journal* (Salem), 23 September 1885, 3.
47  On Blakely and other Linn County members, see *Weekly Herald-Disseminator*, 28 January 1897, 3; 27 May 1897, 5; *Semi-Weekly Democrat* (Albany), 23 June 1916, 1; 27 June 1916, 3; and *Oregon Journal* (Portland), 21 December 1910, 7. On Walker, see Gaston, *Centennial History of Oregon*, 2:494, 497; and *Oregonian*, 30 June 1912, 7.
48  Carpenter, "Pioneer Problems," 157 (quote); 168 (mentions Walker). On the Rogue River War, see especially Beckham, *Requiem for a People*; and Schwartz, *Rogue River Indian War and Its Aftermath*.
49  Riggs, "Lieut. T. A. Riggs on the Rogue River War," 158–59 (quote); *Brownsville Times*, 7 February 1913, 3.
50  *Albany Evening Herald*, 25 May 1922, 3; 16 June 1922, 1; *Brownsville Times*, 2 June 1922, 1; 9 June 1922, 1; *Greater Oregon* (Albany), 22 October 1965, 7; *Oregonian*, 17 February 1896, 7.
51  *Brownsville Times*, 16 June 1922, 7.
52  *Albany Democrat-Herald*, 7 August 1934, 1.
53  Stanard, "Pen Pictures of Pioneers of Linn County," 8.
54  T. A. Riggs to Mr. Geo. Goodall, 21 September 1901, reprinted in Goodall, "Upper Calapooia," 75.
55  Green, "Pocahontas Perplex." In Pacific Northwest history, see, for example, Cothran, *Remembering the Modoc War*.
56  Stanard, "Pen Pictures of Pioneers of Linn County," 8; Mrs. J. W. Moore interview, undated, by Leslie Haskins for the Works Progress Administration, Federal Writers' Project Oral History Interviews.

57  See, for example, Stanard's piece "Pen Pictures of Pioneers of Linn County"; and his "Lonely Old Squaw Last of Once Powerful Calapooias," *Oregon Journal*, 23 August 1906, 1; *Oregonian*, 30 June 1912, sec. 5, 7; *Semi-Weekly Democrat*, 22 April 1921, 1.
58  *Sunday Democrat* (Albany), 20 August 1922, 1.
59  Lewis, "Confederated Tribes of Grand Ronde." On the "Last of the Calapooia" issue, see Mackey, *Kalapuyans*, 147–51; and Lewis, "Four Deaths."
60  *Albany Democrat*, 28 June 1907, 4; MLCPA, Book 1, 12.
61  Dorissa Zoosman Miller, interview by Leslie Haskins, 20 March 1940, for the Works Progress Administration, Federal Writers' Project Oral History Interviews.
62  Templeton, Templeton, and Breuer, *William T. Templeton*, 98.
63  MLCPA, Book 1, 5 July 1889, 14; 4 June 1890, 18; 10 June 1896, 51; *Brownsville Times*, 16 June 1905, 1; "Souvenir Booklet and Program: Linn County Pioneer Association 56th Reunion, Brownsville, Oregon, June 17, 18, 19, 1943," 3–4, folder 4, box 20, Linn County Pioneer Association, 1943–48, Associations and Institutions Collection.
64  *Oregonian*, 8 October 1897, 3; MLCPA, Book 1, 1898, 70; 1897, 60 (quote); Hume interview.
65  Hume interview.
66  Hume interview; *Oregonian*, 8 October 1897, 3; "A Triple Murder," *Brownsville Times*, supplement, 20 November 1895, photostatic copy on file at the Linn County Historical Museum; *Oregonian*, February 1, 1896, 3.
67  *Oregonian*, 22 November 1895, 1.
68  *History of the Pacific Northwest*, 2:227.
69  *Brownsville Times*, 28 July 1911, 2.
70  MLCPA, Book 1, 11 June 1896, 53–55.
71  MLCPA, Book 1, 10 June 1896, 51.
72  MLCPA, Book 1, 10 June 1896, 50; *Oregonian*, 1 February 1896, 3.
73  MLCPA, Book 1, 11 June 1896, 52; *Weekly Herald-Disseminator*, 19 December 1895, 4.
74  For Orpha's obituary, see *Brownsville Times*, 26 January 1933, 3; for Samuel's, see *Oregonian*, 13 August 1902, 4; and for Clyde's (he died from "brain congestion"), see *Brownsville Times*, 8 March 1901, 2. Each of these individuals was interred at McHargue Cemetery.
75  *Brownsville Times*, 28 July 1911, 2.
76  *Semi-Weekly Democrat*, 4 February 1913, 2 (quote); *Oregon Journal*, 30 January 1913, 6 (quote). Also, see especially *Brownsville Times*, 7 February 1913, 3.

77  A few examples of news stories about her death (and life) are in *Oregon Journal*, 25 June 1919, 1; 29 June 1919, sec. 2, 16; *Statesman Journal*, 26 June 1919, 5; *Spokesman-Review* (Spokane, WA), 24 June 1919, 6; and *Butte (MT) Miner*, 6 July 1919, 12.

78  *Oregon Journal*, 29 June 1919, sec. 2, 16.

79  See Eliza Spalding Warren, Find a Grave, accessed 8 August 2020, www.findagrave.com/memorial/48899369/eliza-warren.

80  *Brownsville Times*, 27 June 1919, 1.

81  Stanard, "Pen Pictures of Pioneers of Linn County," 8 (quote); *Oregonian*, 21 August 1922, 5; *Oregon Journal*, 15 May 1921, sec. 2, 8; 19 April 1921, 2; 23 March 1919, sec. 3, 12, respectively; *Brownsville Times*, 25 August 1922, 1 (quote).

82  On the silencing of events that interfere with desired tellings of history, see Trouillot, *Silencing the Past*.

83  *Weekly Herald-Disseminator*, 19 December 1895, 4.

84  *Weekly Herald Disseminator*, 5 January 1896, 5.

85  *State Rights Democrat*, 29 November 1895, 3.

86  *Weekly Herald-Disseminator*, 19 December 1895, 4.

87  *Oregonian*, 16 December 1895, 3.

88  *Weekly Herald-Disseminator*, 26 December 1895, 3.

89  Bessie E. Leonard, "Family Historical Sketch" (unpublished manuscript, 1955–57), x, contained in Family Files: Templeton family; Templeton, Templeton, and Breuer, *William T. Templeton*, 83.

90  Thurston Pierce Hackleman Diary, 20 November 1895.

91  *Brownsville Times*, supplement, 20 November 1895.

92  *Weekly Herald-Disseminator*, 30 January 1896, 6.

93  *Oregonian*, 9 January 1896, 4.

94  In Oregon, a few monuments and memorials to the Civil War did appear around the turn of the twentieth century. In Washington State, even the Daughters of the Confederacy placed a commemorative marker to the Confederacy's president along the Jefferson Davis Highway, which was itself an early twentieth-century commemorative effort by the group. See, "GAR Plot," Eugene Pioneer Cemetery, accessed 7 May 2021, www.eugenepioneercemetery.org/gar-plot/; Hague and Sebesta, "Jefferson Davis Highway."

95  *Oregon Daily Journal* (Portland), 25 May 1919, 3 (quote). On these monuments and memorials, the efforts behind them, and the racial and nationalist meanings contained within them, see Larsen, *Missing Chapters*; Prescott, *Pioneer Mother Monuments*; Taber, "Sacagawea and the Suffragettes"; and Hanon, "Whitman Legend."

96  Baker, "Oregon Pioneer Tradition," 42–45; Miller, "Sons and Daughters of Oregon Pioneers."
97  Miscellaneous loose papers contained within MLCPA, Book 1.

PART 3. "WE'RE GOING TO HANG HIM RIGHT HERE"

1  Hainline, "1895 Triple Murder," 2.
2  Hainline, "1895 Triple Murder," 2 (quote); "A Triple Murder," *Brownsville Times*, supplement, 20 November 1895, n.p., photocopy on file at the Linn County Historical Museum (quote).
3  Hainline, "1895 Triple Murder," 2 (quote); "Triple Murder" photocopy.
4  *Oregonian* (Portland), 23 November 1895, 8.
5  *Weekly-Herald Disseminator* (Albany), 9 January 1896, 5.
6  R. M. Brown, "Western Violence," 6. Brown actually distinguishes between vigilantism and lynch mobs, something that historians have since critiqued. The literature on those topics is vast. A useful introduction to more recent scholarship, although now a few years old, is Belew, "Lynching and Power in the United States."
7  E. M. Beck, Stewart E. Tolnay, and Amy Kate Bailey pose such a thesis in their article "Contested Terrain."

CHAPTER 6. "THE SCAFFOLD IS ALL FRAMED AND READY"

1  According to an 1874 state law, executions had to take place on courthouse grounds. In 1879, Oregon adopted a new law requiring a high fence to surround gallows so as to keep crowds at bay. See Long, *Tortured History*, 24–25; and Goeres-Gardner, *Necktie Parties*, xvii–xviii. On executions as public spectacle, see Linders, "Execution Spectacle and State Legitimacy."
2  *San Francisco Examiner*, 2 February 1896, 4.
3  *State Rights Democrat* (Albany), 7 February 1896, 4.
4  Zucker, Hummel, and Høgfoss, *Oregon Indians*, 9–11, 14, 29, 36; Mackey, *Kalapuyans*; Lewis, "Four Deaths"; Lewis, "Molalla Tribal History."
5  Reinhardt, "Mill City"; *Albany Daily Democrat*, 20 January 1890, 3 (quote); 25 April 1888, 3; 1 August 1891, 3.
6  *Albany Daily Democrat*, 20 January 1890, 3; 6 June 1889, 3.
7  *Weekly Herald-Disseminator* (Albany), 9 January 1896, 3 (quote); Tattersall, "Economic Development of the Pacific Northwest to 1920," 65–67, 183, 186–87.
8  *Albany Daily Democrat*, 13 January 1893, 3; Gaston, *Centennial History of Oregon*, 3:225; *Weekly Herald-Disseminator*, 24 May 1900, 1. The first reference to a

donkey engine in the Santiam country that I can find is 1897. See *Daily Oregon Statesman* (Salem), 23 October 1897, 3. On the changing nature of Pacific Northwest lumber markets and production in the late nineteenth century, see Cox, *Mills and Markets*. On Chicago's dominance in the Great Lakes lumbering region, see Cronon, *Nature's Metropolis*, 159–206.

9    For example, *State Rights Democrat*, 28 August 1896, 3, mentions two accidents in logging and milling in the North Santiam country.

10   *Daily Oregon Statesman*, 10 July 1891, 3; 16 July 1891, 4.

11   *Weekly Herald-Disseminator*, 7 September 1893, 3; *Albany Daily Democrat*, 2 September 1893, 3. The former item, which explains that the fires began on Santiam Lumbering's stump lands, denied earlier reports that Santiam Lumbering lost property in the fire. The later report listed here does provide details of the losses. On the waste of logging and environmental change during this era, see Bunting, *Pacific Raincoast*, 147–51; and White, *Land Use, Environment, and Social Change*, 77–93. On fires, see White, *Land Use, Environment, and Social Change*, 89–91, 106–10; and Pyne, *Year of the Fires*.

12   *State Rights Democrat*, 14 February 1890, 3; 20 November 1896, 3.

13   *Albany Daily Democrat*, 2 April 1892, 1; *State Rights Democrat*, 8 July 1892, 1.

14   *Morning Daily Herald* (Albany), 9 August 1890, 4.

15   Bunting, *Pacific Raincoast*, 145; *Capital Journal* (Salem), 29 April 1892, 3; *State Rights Democrat*, 10 June 1892, 4 (quote); *Daily Oregon Statesman*, 2 December 1892, 4 (quote).

16   *Weekly Herald-Disseminator*, 1 October 1896, 1.

17   *State Rights Democrat*, 13 September 1895, 3.

18   The lumber sale to Linn County is recorded in *State Rights Democrat*, 14 February 1896, 1. This, plus other sales listed there, including payment to the scaffold builders and other news reports (cited later) explaining that the construction of the scaffold occurred at the Santiam Lumbering Company's lumberyard, leads to my conclusions here.

19   *Oregon Daily Statesman* (Salem), 24 December 1895, 7, explains that oxen teams were present on the Santiam, though utilized in road construction.

20   *State Rights Democrat*, 14 February 1896, 1. On Conn, see *Albany Evening Herald*, 19 May 1911, 3; and *Oregonian* (Portland), 23 May 1911, 7. On McChesney, see *Portrait and Biographical Record of the Willamette Valley*, 1:483–84; and *Albany Daily Democrat*, 1 January 1892, 3.

21   *Weekly Herald-Disseminator*, 6 February 1896, 3.

22   *Portrait and Biographical Record of the Willamette Valley*, 1:484.

23   *Oregonian*, 29 January 1896, 3; *Weekly Herald-Disseminator*, 30 January 1896, 5; *State Rights Democrat*, 31 January 1896, 3 (quote). Description of the gallows is

from "Tells of Murderer Hung in Albany," newspaper clipping from the *Benton County Herald*, 1970, contained in the Genealogy Files: Montgomery family, Linn County Historical Museum. The clipping explains that it is a reprint from the *Oregon Silver Imprint* (Albany), 31 January 1896.

24 *State Rights Democrat*, 7 February 1896, 1; "Tells of Murderer" clipping.

25 The seagrass reference appeared twice in the *State Rights Democrat*, 7 February 1896, 1; and 7 February 1896, 4. The latter read, "It is very proper for the sheriff to want to see some one stretch sea grass on that day." The *San Francisco Examiner*, 2 February 1896, described the rope as "hemp."

26 *Buffalo (NY) Commercial*, 27 April 1892, 8; *Buffalo Sunday Express*, 17 August 1884, 3; Wyllie-Echeverria and Cox, "Seagrass (*Zostera marina* [Zosteraceae]) Industry of Nova Scotia."

27 "The Mexican Hammock," *Atchison (KS) Daily Sun*, 29 October 1887, 7; "Ramie," *Pacific Commercial Advertiser*, 4 September 1869, 1; "A New Athletic Sport," *Inter Ocean* (Chicago), 26 September 1889, 6.

28 "A Sad Suicide," *Daily Arkansas Gazette* (Little Rock), 4 August 1883, 1; "Murdered and Thrown into the River," *St. Louis Globe-Democrat*, 1 July 1884, 3; "Caused by Dissipation," *St. Louis Globe-Democrat*, 9 October 1885, 3 (likely sisal); "Wildman Lynched," *St. Louis Globe-Democrat*, 15 October 1886, 3; *St. Louis Globe-Democrat*, 15 December 1886, 12 (likely sisal).

29 Dodge and US Department of Agriculture, *Descriptive Catalogue of Useful Fiber Plants of the World*, 31.

30 Davies and Matteoni, *Executing Magic in the Modern Era*, 70; *Freeman's Journal* (Dublin, Ireland), 23 January 1885, 5. Jack Shuler in *Thirteenth Turn*, 21, lists "manilla hemp," along with hemp and linen, as the type of rope used in nooses before artificial fiber, namely nylon, became common.

31 Davies and Matteoni, *Executing Magic*, 70; Bishop, *History of American Manufacturers from 1608 to 1860*, 88; MacFarlane, *Manufacturing in Philadelphia*, 32.

32 *San Francisco Examiner*, 2 February 1896, 4.

33 Ryder, *Men of Rope*, 61–62.

34 *Aberdeen (WA) Herald*, 14 July 1902, 7; *Oregonian*, 17 June 1893, 9; 12 September 1897, 10. On the history of henequen in agriculture during this era, see Evans, *Bound in Twine*.

35 *Oregonian*, 17 June 1893, 9, lists Portland Cordage's various products, including manila rope made in sizes from 1½ inches in circumference "and up." Its catalog for September 1905 lists a manila-hemp rope product ¾ inch in diameter. See Portland Cordage Co., *No. 4 Catalogue & Cipher Code: A Text Book for Buyers & Salesmen* (Portland, OR: Portland Cordage Company, 1905), 11, Portland Cordage Company Records.

36  Evans, "Force of Fiber," 107.
37  Edwards, *Abacá (Manila Hemp)*, 10; Hayase, "American Colonial Policy and the Japanese Abaca Industry," 506; Dolan, *Philippines*, 10.
38  Edwards, *Abacá (Manila Hemp)*, 26–27, 33; Hayase, "American Colonial Policy and the Japanese Abaca Industry," 508. The Bikol region was the center of the industry at the time. On Bikol, see Owen, *Prosperity without Progress*.
39  Dolan, *Philippines*, 120.
40  Ventura, "From Small Farms to Progressive Plantations," 463–64; Owen, *Prosperity without Progress*, 116–17, 134.
41  Edwards, *Abacá (Manila Hemp)*; Portland Cordage, *No. 4 Catalogue & Cipher Code*, 8 (quote). On the labor-intensive nature of the manila-hemp industry, see "Manila Hemp," 24.
42  *Oregonian*, 21 February 1888, 5; 4 August 1895, 7; 21 November 1895, 5; 10 June 1895, 1; *Morning Astorian* (Astoria), 25 June 1895, 1.
43  Varied sources provide weights of a bales that differ by a few pounds. I use Edwards, *Abacá (Manila Hemp)*, 32, which lists a bale's weight at 275 pounds.
44  See Andrews, *Killing for Coal*.
45  On rope manufacturing for this era, see Carter, *Spinning and Twisting of Long Vegetable Fibres*. Using Ancestry.com's search engine for the 1900 US manuscript population census of Portland and employing the keyword "cordage," I found at Portland Cordage eleven workers (most of them male) who were nineteen and younger: one was nineteen, two were seventeen, one was sixteen, three were fifteen, and four were fourteen.
46  *Oregon Journal*, 10 November 1912, 18.
47  On the environmental history of the Willamette Valley in the late nineteenth century, see Boag, *Environment and Experience*.

CHAPTER 7. "AT 14½ MINUTES HIS HEART CEASED TO BEAT"

1  "A Triple Murder," *Brownsville Times*, supplement, 20 November 1895, photocopy on file at the Linn County Historical Museum; *Weekly Herald-Disseminator* (Albany), 19 December 1895, 4; 28 November 1895, 4.
2  "Triple Murder" photocopy; *Weekly Herald-Disseminator*, 19 December 1895, 4; 28 November 1895, 4; *State Rights Democrat* (Albany), 29 November 1895, 4.
3  *State Rights Democrat*, 20 December 1895, 3; *Weekly Herald-Disseminator*, 19 December 1895, 4; *State Rights Democrat*, 29 May 1896, 3 (quote); US Department of Commerce, Bureau of the Census, Twelfth Census, 1900, Manuscript Census, Linn County, Oregon, Enumeration District 38, sheet 13, lines 95 and 96.

4   Attendance, 4 November to 29 November 1895, Linn County, Oregon, School District 28 Records, 1894–95, 1992-024-0005 [n.p.].

5   Attendance, 4 November to 29 November 1895, School District 28 Records, with data for Evans children and McCormack, n.p. (but page 83 lists Marshall Fox as a student in March 1895); *Weekly Herald-Disseminator*, 19 December 1895, 5.

6   On Robert A. Jayne, see *Weekly Herald-Disseminator*, 17 August 1893, 3; *State Rights Democrat*, 13 April 1894, 1; 5 October 1894, 3; and US Department of Commerce, Bureau of the Census, Twelfth Census, 1900, Manuscript Census, Linn County, Oregon, Enumeration District 46, sheet 12A, line 17. Jayne's other cases are mentioned in *State Rights Democrat*, 20 September 1894, 3; and *Weekly Herald-Disseminator*, 27 September 1894, 5.

7   *San Francisco Chronicle*, 21 November 1895, 4; "Triple Murder" photocopy. Sources on Joel Henry are from Ancestry.com, including the "Directory of Deceased American Physicians, 1804–1929"; Legislative Committee Services, comp., *Chronological List of Oregon's Legislatures*, 143. See also *State Rights Democrat*, 27 March 1885, 2; 16 January 1891, 4.

8   *Oregonian* (Portland), 22 November 1895, 1 (quote); "Triple Murder" photocopy (quote).

9   *State Rights Democrat*, 29 November 1895, 1; *Oregonian*, 22 November 1895, 1.

10  *Weekly Herald-Disseminator*, 28 November 1895, 3; *State Rights Democrat*, 29 November 1895, 1; *Oregonian*, 29 December 1895, 10.

11  US Department of the Interior, Census Office, *Report on the Population of the United States at the Eleventh Census, 1890*, 476, 549.

12  *Albany City Directory for 1892*; Works Progress Administration Writers' Program and the Linn County Pioneer Memorial Association, *History of Linn County*, 22–30; *Illustrated Historical Atlas Map of Marion and Linn Counties*, 26–26¼, 75, 82, 83.

13  For example, varied items in *State Rights Democrat*, 25 January 1895, 2 (quotes); and 29 March 1895, 2.

14  Abbott, "From Urban Frontier to Metropolitan Region," 80.

15  *Oregonian*, 1 December 1895, 20.

16  *Albany Register*, 28 January 1871, 3; *State Rights Democrat*, 7 June 1895, 3 (quote); *Weekly Herald-Disseminator*, 21 March 1895, 4; 25 April 1895, 3; 13 June 1895, 3. On the sewer system, see *State Rights Democrat*, 24 July 1891, 3; 7 February 1890, 1.

17  *State Rights Democrat*, 29 November 1895, 1.

18  *Weekly Herald-Disseminator*, 3 October 1895, 5; *Corvallis Times*, 16 October 1895, 1; *Lebanon Express*, 4 October 1895, 1; *Weekly Herald-Disseminator*,

28 November 1895, 5, 8; Goeres-Gardner, *Murder, Morality, and Madness*, 155–69.

19  *Illustrated Historical Atlas Map of Marion and Linn Counties*, 58–58¼; Hines, *Illustrated History of the State of Oregon*, 1269.

20  *Portrait and Biographical Record of the Willamette Valley*, 1:225–26; *History of the Bench and Bar of Oregon*, 198; Republican State Central Committee, *Republican League Register*, 255.

21  Clark, *History of the Willamette Valley*, 3:344–46; *Oregonian*, 22 November 1895, 1; State of Oregon, State of Oregon v. Lloyd [sic] Montgomery, 12–13.

22  *Oregonian*, 22 November 1895, 1 (quote); 29 December 1895, 10 (quote); 26 November 1895, 1; 1 December 1895, 1.

23  *Oregonian*, 26 November 1895, 1.

24  *Oregonian*, 3 December 1895, 4.

25  *Oregonian*, 26 November 1895, 1.

26  *Weekly Herald-Disseminator*, 19 December 1895, 4; Jury Book, Grand Jury Witnesses, Linn County, vol. 1 (n.p.).

27  *Weekly Herald-Disseminator*, 28 November 1895, 5, 8. Emma Hannah spent the rest of her life going back and forth between the state penitentiary and the state hospital. She died at the latter institution in 1933. Goeres-Gardner, *Murder, Morality, and Madness*, 169–70.

28  *Weekly Herald-Disseminator*, 28 November 1895, 8; State of Oregon, Circuit Court Journal, Linn County, 158–59.

29  *State Rights Democrat*, 29 November 1895, 3. Loyd began such a confession on 24 November before admitting to the three murders on the twenty-fifth.

30  *Oregonian*, 1 December 1895.

31  *Oregonian*, 1 December 1895, 20; *Capital Journal (Salem)*, 2 December 1895, 2.

32  *Oregonian*, 1 December 1895, 20.

33  *Oregonian*, 1 December 1895, 20 (quote); State of Oregon, State of Oregon v. Lloyd [sic] Montgomery, 12–16.

34  *State Rights Democrat*, 12 December 1895, 1.

35  *Oregonian*, 18 December 1895, 4.

36  *Oregonian*, 16 December 1895, 3.

37  *Statesman Journal* (Salem), 17 December 1895, 8; *Daily Eugene Guard*, 16 December 1895, 4.

38  These and subsequent references to the courthouse's architecture and furnishings come from *State Rights Democrat*, 25 November 1865, 3. Details on the older courthouse are from *Illustrated Historical Atlas Map of Marion and Linn Counties*, 26¼, which also states that the courthouse cost $35,000, not $25,000. Another publication, the *West Shore* 1, no. 3 (October 1875): 5, states that the

courthouse cost $40,000. I use the figure provided by the builder in the 25 November 1865 edition of the *State Rights Democrat* at the time when he completed his work.

39  *State Rights Democrat*, 1 July 1881, 5; *Illustrated Historical Atlas Map of Marion and Linn Counties*, 31.
40  *Weekly Herald-Disseminator*, 19 December 1895, 5.
41  On Kirkpatrick, see "Heroes of Battle Rock," 1. This article gives Kirkpatrick's name as "W. H.," but it was actually John M. See also Kirkpatrick and Dodge, *Heroes of Battle Rock*.
42  The first reference to him as a "boy" is in the "Triple Murder" photocopy. Examples of his age at sixteen are *Oregon Mist* (St. Helens), 22 November 1895, 3; and *Oregonian*, 21 November 1895, 1.
43  *Oregonian*, 23 November 1895, 8.
44  *Weekly Herald-Disseminator*, 28 November 1895, 5.
45  *State Rights Democrat*, 29 November 1895, 1.
46  *Oregonian*, 1 December 1895, 20.
47  *Oregonian*, 3 December 1895, 4.
48  *Oregonian*, 1 December 1895, 20.
49  Peter Boag, "'He Took Up Arms against the Loins from Which He Sprang,'" 148.
50  *Oregonian*, 27 November 1895, 3 (quote); 21 January 1896, 3; 22 November 1895, 1; *Statesman Journal*, 11 February 1943, 3; *Weekly Herald-Disseminator*, 16 January 1896, 3; Hainline, "1895 Triple Murder"; *Weekly Herald-Disseminator*, 16 January 1896, 3; *Albany Daily Democrat*, 25 July 1890, 3; *Oregonian*, 17 February 1896, 7.
51  *History of the Bench and Bar of Oregon*, 175; Hodgkin and Galvin, *Pen Pictures of Representative Men of Oregon*, 7; *Portrait and Biographical Record of the Willamette Valley*, 1:450–53.
52  Clark, *History of the Willamette Valley*, 3:5–6.
53  *Weekly Herald-Disseminator*, 19 December 1895, 5 (quote); State of Oregon, Linn County Circuit Court, Record of Trials, 1893–97.
54  Information on the jurors and those dismissed from duty reported here and subsequently comes from a variety of sources, including Ancestry.com; Linn County, Oregon, Tax Rolls; Linn County, Oregon, Agriculture Census, 1895; US Department of Commerce, Bureau of the Census, Twelfth Census, 1900, Manuscript Census, Linn County; and *Albany City Directory for 1892*. Although the *Weekly Herald-Disseminator*, 19 December 1895, 5, states that lawyers examined thirty-seven men, only thirty-five appear in State of Oregon, Linn County Circuit Court, Record of Trials, 1893–97.
55  I was unable to locate Truax in the 1895 tax assessments so used the figure

provided for him in 1896. I was able to determine the wealth of only seventeen of the twenty-three men excused from the jury pool.
56  *Oregonian*, 26 November 1895, 4.
57  Lockely, "Impressions and Observations of the *Journal Man*," 6.
58  *Weekly Herald-Disseminator*, 19 December 1895, 5.
59  *Weekly Herald-Disseminator*, 19 December 1895, 5.
60  *Weekly Herald-Disseminator*, 19 December 1895, 5.
61  *Weekly Herald-Disseminator*, 19 December 1895, 5; *Oregonian*, 19 December 1895, 3; State of Oregon, State of Oregon v. Lloyd [sic] Montgomery, 18–26.
62  *State Rights Democrat*, 27 December 1895, 1; *Oregonian*, 19 December 1895, 3. For specifics on the Russ House: *Albany City Directory for 1892*, 2; *State Rights Democrat*, 10 September 1886, 3 (a dinner party); 6 April 1888, 2 (electricity); and 24 April 1896, 3 (a wedding). Albany's *Weekly Herald-Disseminator* reported on 16 January 1896, 2, that the court allowed a bill of $13.50 for the jury from W. W. Rowell. Rowell was the proprietor of the Russ House. On menu prices, I compared the sum spent in Albany to menus contained in the University of Missouri Libraries, "Prices and Wages by Decade." For the weather: *Daily Oregon Statesman (Salem)*, 18 December 1895, 8.
63  *Oregonian*, 21 January 1896, 6 (quote); *San Francisco Call*, 1 February 1896, 3 (quote).
64  *State Rights Democrat*, 27 December 1895, 1; *Oregonian*, 19 December 1895, 3 (quote).
65  *Oregonian*, 20 December 1895, 3.
66  *Weekly Herald-Disseminator*, 26 December 1895, 3 (quote); 9 January 1895, 5; *Oregonian*, 30 January 1896, 3.
67  Gordon, "Family Violence as History and Politics," 24; Boag, "'He Took Up Arms,'" 152–55.
68  *Oregonian*, 31 January 1896, 1. None of these letters is preserved in the small William Paine Lord Papers collection at the Oregon State Archives.
69  *Oregonian*, 1 January 1896, 3.
70  *Oregonian*, 22 January 1896, 4.
71  *Oregonian*, 12 January 1896, 9 (quote). On Pritchard: Upton, *Proceedings of the Twenty-Seventh Annual Convention of the National-American Woman Suffrage Association*, 81; *Oregonian*, 16 July 1894, 5.
72  *Weekly Herald-Disseminator*, 30 January 1896, 6. See also *Oregonian*, 7 January 1896, 4; *Oregonian*, 9 January 1896, 4; and *Weekly Herald-Disseminator*, 16 January 1896, 3.
73  *Oregonian*, 7 January 1896, 6.

74  *Weekly Herald-Disseminator,* 9 January 1896, 5.
75  *Oregonian,* 22 January 1896, 4 (quote); 26 January 1896, 3 (quote).
76  *State Rights Democrat,* 24 January 1896, 3.
77  *Oregonian,* 9 January 1896, 4.
78  *Oregonian,* 7 January 1896, 6.
79  *Oregonian,* 22 January 1896, 4.
80  *Weekly Herald-Disseminator,* 6 February 1896, 3.
81  *Oregonian,* 6 January 1896, 6; *Weekly Herald-Disseminator,* 23 January 1896, 3.
82  *Oregonian,* 16 January 1896, 3.
83  *San Francisco Examiner,* 30 January 1896, 4.
84  *Weekly Herald-Disseminator,* 23 January 1896, 5 (quote); *Oregonian,* 9 January 1896, 4; 20 January 1896, 8; *Weekly Herald-Disseminator,* 30 January 1896, 6. Defense attorney Newport wrote a blistering response to "Witness," noting among other things that court-appointed counsel received no pay for their work. *Weekly Herald-Disseminator,* 30 January 1896, 3.
85  An especially notorious article on Loyd is *San Francisco Chronicle,* 6 January 1896, 3. This section on the media's relationship to Loyd is based in part on Boag, "'He Took Up Arms,'" 155–56.
86  *Oregonian,* 11 February 1896, 4.
87  *Oregonian,* 6 January 1896, 6 (quote). *State Rights Democrat,* 10 January 1896, 1, describes Loyd and George Piper's relationship. George's brother, Edgar, also was a famed journalist and worked at the *Oregonian* at the same time. Edgar had earlier worked for the *State Rights Democrat* in Albany, and he later, after Scott's passing in 1910, became the *Oregonian*'s editor. George's obituary, "Death Comes to George U. Piper," *Oregonian* (Portland), 11 March 1923, 10, explains that he worked for the *Oregonian* in the 1890s. George was also in time buried in Albany. On Edgar Piper, see "Death Summons Edgar B. Piper," *Oregonian,* 4 May 1928, 10; and Turnbull, *History of Oregon Newspapers,* 198–200.
88  *State Rights Democrat,* 10 January 1896, 3.
89  *Oregonian,* 29 December 1895, 10.
90  *Oregonian,* 31 December 1895, 4.
91  *Oregonian,* 29 December 1895, 10.
92  *Oregonian,* 6 January 1896, 6.
93  *Oregonian,* 9 January 1896, 6. Critical responses to Piper and the *Oregonian* from Albany newspapers include *State Rights Democrat,* 10 January 1896, 1, 3; and *Weekly Herald-Disseminator,* 9 January 1896, 5
94  *Oregonian,* 29 December 1895, 10.
95  *Oregonian,* 1 January 1896, 2.
96  *Oregonian,* 29 December 1895, 10.

97 *Weekly Herald-Disseminator*, 26 December 1895, 3.
98 *San Francisco Chronicle*, 6 January 1896, 3.
99 *Oregonian*, 1 January 1896, 2.
100 *Oregonian*, 29 December 1895, 10; 1 January 1896, 2; 30 January 1896, 3 (quote).
101 *Oregonian*, 6 January 1896, 6.
102 *Oregonian*, 9 January 1896, 4. This letter was later reprinted in the *Weekly Herald-Disseminator*, 16 January 1896, 3.
103 *Oregonian*, 10 January 1896, 4. Duncan McKercher's letter appeared the same day, on page 3.
104 *State Rights Democrat*, 13 March 1896, 4; *Oregonian*, 6 January 1896, 6; *San Francisco Chronicle*, 6 January 1896, 3 (quotes).
105 *San Francisco Examiner*, 2 February 1896, 4.
106 *State Rights Democrat*, 7 February 1896, 2, 3 (quotes).
107 *State Rights Democrat*, 13 December 1895, 3.
108 *Weekly Herald-Disseminator*, 26 December 1895, 3; *State Rights Democrat*, 27 December 1895, 4 (quote); 3 January 1896, 3 (quote).
109 I thank my colleague, Matthew Avery Sutton, historian of evangelicalism, for this language.
110 On the early history of churches in Linn County, see Works Progress Administration Writers' Program and the Linn County Pioneer Memorial Association, *History of Linn County*, 74–80; Oliphant, "Documents Illustrating the Beginnings of the Presbyterian Advance." On Protestant activism in the nineteenth-century Pacific Northwest more generally, see Soden, *Outsiders in a Promised Land*, 1–41.
111 Ward, "Lewis & Clark College"; Mercer, *Material Resources of Linn County*, 26, 51; *State Rights Democrat*, 10 January 1879, 1 (quote).
112 Carroll, *Report on Statistics of Churches in the United States at the Eleventh Census*, 77. In 1875, there were two towns: North Brownsville (the larger of the two) and Brownsville. They sat on opposite sides of the Calapooia River. In 1878, their combined populations reached six hundred, according to figures in *Illustrated Historical Atlas Map of Marion and Linn Counties*, 26½.
113 *Brownsville Times*, 28 July 1911, 2; Templeton, Templeton, and Breuer, *William T. Templeton*, 20–21, 24, 25, 30, 37, 43, 60, 73, 96; *State Rights Democrat*, 10 January 1879, 1; *Oregon Statesman*, 27 September 1859, 2.
114 Szasz, *Religion in the Modern American West*, 4; Carroll, *Report on Statistics of Churches in the United States at the Eleventh Census*.
115 Carroll, *Report on Statistics of Churches in the United States at the Eleventh Census*, 77; Killen and Shibley, with assistance from Boyer and Riley, "Surveying the Religious Landscape," 30.

116  *Lebanon Express*, 23 March 1894, 2; *Weekly Herald-Disseminator*, 21 March 1895, 7; *State Rights Democrat*, 1 June 1894, 1, 3.
117  McLoughlin, *Revivals, Awakenings, and Reform*, 141–78.
118  McLoughlin, *Revivals, Awakenings, and Reform*, 147–49, 150–62; Sutton, *American Apocalypse*, 8–9, 10–16.
119  Creech, *Righteous Indignation*. There are some references to connections between revivalism and populism in Linn and Marion Counties during this era. See the satirical and lengthy "Elder Wayback Heard from Again," *Lebanon Express*, 2 March 1894, 1; and a brief, local reference to "all those who were revived by religion have become Populists" in *Capital Journal*, 22 May 1894, 2.
120  *State Rights Democrat*, 18 January 1895, 1; 8 February 1895, 3; *Weekly Herald-Disseminator*, 25 April 1895, 3 (quote); *State Rights Democrat*, 15 February 1895, 3; 24 February 1895, 3; 14 June 1895, 3; *Weekly Herald-Disseminator*, 7 February 1895, 5; 14 February 1895, 4; *State Rights Democrat*, 8 February 1895, 1; *Weekly Herald-Disseminator*, 14 March 1895, 5; *State Rights Democrat*, 24 May 1895, 1; 28 June 1895, 3.
121  *State Rights Democrat*, 15 November 1895, 3; 22 November 1895, 3; 6 December 1895, 3.
122  *Oregonian*, 16 December 1895, 3. This article, as did a few others at the time, mistakenly rendered Dickson's name as Dixon.
123  *Oregonian*, 29 December 1895, 10.
124  See, for example, *Oregonian*, 1 January 1896, 2; *Weekly Herald-Disseminator*, 2 January 1896, 5.
125  *Oregonian*, 3 January 1896, 3, carries a story in which Loyd advises others. *Oregonian*, 30 January 1896, 3, mentions his advice to siblings and that his sister Eva joined the church. *Weekly Herald-Disseminator*, 20 February 1896, 3, carries the news that Orville was one of fifty who joined the church in Brownsville during a revival meeting.
126  *Weekly Herald-Disseminator*, 2 January 1896, 5.
127  *Oregonian*, 6 January 1896, 6.
128  Winston, *Red Hot and Righteous*, 23; *Oregonian*, 30 January 1896, 3 (quote).
129  On the Salvation Army's arrival in Portland: *Oregonian*, 17 October 1886, 8. On some early problems it encountered: *Morning Astorian* (Astoria, OR), 29 May 1887, 2; 28 September 1887, 3; *Albany Daily Democrat*, 14 March 1890, 3. On its early appearance in Scio: *Albany Daily Democrat*, 16 January 1890, 3; 14 February 1891, 3 (quote); 25 February 1890, 3; 29 May 1891, 3 (quote).
130  *State Rights Democrat*, 24 September 1894, 4.
131  *State Rights Democrat*, 14 February 1896, 1.

132  *State Rights Democrat*, 6 March 1896, 3; 13 March 1896, 3; 20 March 1896, 1. Mention of Loyd's conversion is in *State Rights Democrat*, 7 February 1896, 1. On the effects of the Salvation Army and Loyd's experiences on other inmates, see I. W. Rivers's lengthy letter to the editor of the *State Rights Democrat*, 13 March 1896, 3.

133  *Oregonian*, 29 January 1896, 3 (quote); *Weekly Herald-Disseminator*, 30 January 1896, 5.

134  *State Rights Democrat*, 13 March 1896, 4.

135  *State Rights Democrat*, 31 January 1896, 3.

136  *Oregonian*, 29 January 1896, 3; 30 January 1896, 3.

137  *Weekly Herald-Disseminator*, 30 January 1896, 5; *Oregonian*, 31 January 1896, 1; *San Francisco Examiner*, 2 February 1896, 4; *State Rights Democrat*, 7 February 1896, 1.

138  *State Rights Democrat*, 7 February 1896, 1. Weather details are from *Capital Journal*, 30 January 1896, 1.

139  *State Rights Democrat*, 7 February 1896, 1. Various newspapers carried his farewell, and they also differed on when he wrote it. The *State Rights Democrat* explained he did it during the day and turned it over in the evening for publication. Given that the letter does refer to his nerves at the time and he references it being morning, likely he wrote his farewell early in the day.

140  *Republican Weekly* (Fresno, CA), 7 February 1896, 2.

141  *Oregonian*, 31 January 1896, 1; *State Rights Democrat*, 7 February 1896, 1 (quote); *Weekly Herald Disseminator*, 6 February 1896, 3; *State Rights Democrat*, 13 March 1896, 4 (quote).

142  *Weekly Herald-Disseminator*, 6 February 1896, 3.

143  *Weekly Herald-Disseminator*, 6 February 1896, 3; *San Francisco Call*, 1 February 1896, 3.

144  *Weekly Herald Disseminator*, 6 February 1896, 3.

145  Catherine Louise (McHargue) Hume, interview by Leslie Haskins for the Works Progress Administration, Federal Writers' Project Oral History Interviews, 7 July 1939; Joseph Hume, Find a Grave, accessed 16 January 2021, www.findagrave.com/memorial/43745757/joseph-hume.

146  *Weekly Herald Disseminator*, 6 February 1896, 3.

147  *Weekly Herald Disseminator*, 6 February 1896, 3 (emphasis added).

148  *Weekly Herald Disseminator*, 6 February 1896, 3.

149  *Oregonian*, 1 February 1896, 3.

150  *Weekly Herald Disseminator*, 6 February 1896, 3.

151  *State Rights Democrat*, 7 February 1896, 1.

152  *State Rights Democrat*, 7 February 1896, 1.

153 *San Francisco Examiner*, 2 February 1896, 4. The details here and in the next few paragraphs are reconstructed from this article in the *Examiner* and from those printed in the *Weekly Herald Disseminator*, 6 February 1896, 3; *State Rights Democrat*, 7 February 1896, 1; and *San Francisco Call*, 1 February 1896, 3. I cite only direct quotations.
154 *Weekly Herald Disseminator*, 6 February 1896, 3.
155 *San Francisco Examiner*, 2 February 1896, 4; *Weekly Herald Disseminator*, 6 February 1896, 3.
156 *Weekly Herald-Disseminator*, 6 February 1896, 3.
157 *Oregonian*, 29 December 1895, 10; 30 January 1896, 3.
158 *State Rights Democrat*, 7 February 1896, 1.
159 *Weekly Herald Disseminator*, 6 February 1896, 3.

EPILOGUE

1 *San Francisco Call*, 1 February 1896, 3 (quote); *State Rights Democrat* (Albany), 7 February 1896, 1. On displaying bodies, body parts, and nooses, see Shuler, *Thirteenth Turn*, 127–56; Young, "Black Body as Souvenir in American Lynching"; Bender, "'Transgressive Objects' in America"; and Harrison, *Dark Trophies*.
2 *Weekly Herald-Disseminator* (Albany), 6 February 1896, 1.
3 *Daily (Salem) Oregon Statesman*, 2 February 1896, 8; *Weekly Herald-Disseminator*, 6 February 1896, 3 (quote).
4 *Daily Oregon Statesman*, 2 February 1896, 8; *State Rights Democrat*, 7 February 1896, 1. The *State Rights Democrat*, 7 February 1896, 3, explained that William A. Cusick, a physician who consulted at times for the Oregon Insane Asylum in Salem and who had traveled to Albany to participate in the autopsy, disagreed with the other physicians on the condition of Loyd's brain.
5 *Weekly Herald-Disseminator*, 6 February 1896, 3, 6; *State Rights Democrat*, 13 March 1896, 4; 7 February 1896, 1.
6 For example, *Albany Democrat*, 11 March 1904, 5; 14 May 1917, 2.
7 *State Rights Democrat*, 14 February 1896, 1.
8 *State Rights Democrat*, 14 February 1896, 1; *Weekly Herald-Disseminator*, 6 February 1896, 6 (quote); *Albany City Directory for 1892*, 63, 64, 78.
9 *Oregonian*, 11 February 1896, 4.
10 Nash, "Harvey Scott (1838–1910)"; "Harvey W. Scott," *Oregon Native Son*, 607; "Harvey W. Scott," *Oregon History Project*; H. Scott and L. Scott, *History of the Oregon Country*; "Harvey Whitefield Scott, II"; Young, review of *History of the Oregon Country*, 146 (quote).
11 *Oregonian*, 1 February 1896, 4.

12  *Oregonian*, 11 February 1896, 4.
13  Hugh L. Montgomery, interview by Leslie Haskins for the Works Progress Administration, Federal Writers' Project Oral History Interviews, November 1937.
14  *Greater (Albany) Oregon*, 27 August 1948, 9 (quote); 13 June 1952, 2.
15  Hainline, "1895 Triple Murder," 2.
16  Templeton, Templeton, and Breuer, *William T. Templeton*, 83.
17  The information in the paragraph is derived from research on Ancestry.com and from materials supplied to the author by Todd and Chris Cooper, descendants of Eva Montgomery Hunter.
18  *Oregonian*, 17 February 1896, 7 (quote); Linn County Cemeteries, Crawfordsville Union Cemetery, Lebanon Genealogical Society, accessed 11 December 20, www.usgennet.org/usa/or/town/lebanon/cems/craw3.html; "McKercher Park Dedicated on Historic Site," *Brownsville Times*, 29 August 1968, 12, clipping in Family Files: Templeton family.
19  *Oregonian* (Portland), 13 August 1902, 4; Templeton, Templeton, and Breuer, *William T. Templeton*, 39–40.

# BIBLIOGRAPHY

ABBREVIATIONS

OE     *Oregon Encyclopedia*
OHQ   *Oregon Historical Quarterly*
OHS   Oregon Historical Society Research Library, Portland
OSA   Oregon State Archives, Salem

PRIMARY SOURCES

*Unpublished*

Associations and Institutions Collection. Mss 1511. OHS.
Blakely, James. Papers. CA B583. Special Collections and University Archives, University of Oregon Libraries, Eugene.
Cornett, Sarah Jane (Savage). Diary. In the possession of E. H. Margason, Shedd, Oregon.
Family Files. Brownsville Community Library, Brownsville, Oregon.
Genealogy Files. Linn County Historical Museum, Brownsville, Oregon.
Gragg, Joseph. Papers. Ax 139. Special Collections and University Archives, University of Oregon Libraries, Eugene.
Hackleman, Thurston Pierce. Diary. Microfilm 32. OHS.
Harrison, Fred E. Histories of Linn County. Mss 633. OHS.
Linn County National Bank of Albany. Minutes, 1890–93. Mss 36. OHS.
Linn County Pioneer Association. Records. Pioneer Picture Gallery, Brownsville, Oregon.
Linn County Farmers' Union. Records, 1871–85. Mss 566. OHS.
Lord, William Paine. Papers. OSA.
Native Daughters of Oregon. Records, 1902–4. Mss 107. OHS.
Native Daughters of Oregon. Records, 1899–1901. Mss 772. OHS.
"Past Times" clipping files. Brownsville Community Library, Brownsville, Oregon.

Portland Cordage Company. Records. Mss 1744. OHS.
Templeton Family. Papers. Mss 1332. OHS.
Vertical Files. OHS.
Works Progress Administration. Federal Writers' Project. Oral History Interviews. Linn Genealogical Society. Accessed 29 September 2011. www.lgsoregon.org/lgswp/wpa-interviews.

*Published Works and Public Documents*

Adams, Mrs. S. C. "Secretary's Report of the Oregon Childrens' [sic] Aid Society." 8 October 1880. 362.7 O66 1878/80, State Library of Oregon, Salem.
*Albany City Directory, 1878.* Albany, OR: Mansfield & Monteith, 1878.
*Albany City Directory for 1892.* Albany, OR: William G. Obenauer, 1892.
Banks, Louis Albert. *An Oregon Boyhood.* Boston: Lee and Shepard, 1898.
Carroll, Henry K. *Report on Statistics of Churches in the United States at the Eleventh Census, 1890.* Washington, DC: Government Printing Office, 1894.
Clark, Robert Carlton. *History of the Willamette Valley, Oregon.* 3 vols. Chicago: S. J. Clarke, 1927.
*Constitution and Laws: Grand Cabin, Native Sons of Oregon and Constitution for Subordinate Cabins.* Portland, OR: W. A. Wheeler, 1899.
*Constitution and Laws of the Grand Cabin, Native Daughters of Oregon, and Constitution for Subordinate Cabins.* Portland, OR: W. A. Wheeler, 1899.
"Edward Payson Hurd." *Boston Medical and Surgical Journal,* 27 April 1899, 416.
Fox, William F. *Regimental Losses in the American Civil War, 1861–1865.* 1898. Dayton, OH: Morningside Bookshop, 1974.
Gaston, Joseph. *The Centennial History of Oregon, 1811–1912.* 3 vols. Chicago: S. J. Clark, 1912.
"Harvey W. Scott." *Oregon Native Son* 1, no. 1 (1899): 607.
"The Heroes of Battle Rock." *Coast Mail* (Marshfield, OR), 23 October 1880, 1.
Hines, H. K. *An Illustrated History of the State of Oregon.* Chicago: Lewis, 1893.
*History of the Bench and Bar of Oregon.* Portland, OR: Historical Publishing, 1910.
*History of the Pacific Northwest.* Volume 2. Portland, OR: North Pacific History Company, 1889.
Hodgkin, Frank E., and J. J. Galvin. *Pen Pictures of Representative Men of Oregon.* Portland, OR: Farmer and Dairyman Publishing House, 1882.
*Illustrated Historical Atlas Map of Marion and Linn Counties, Oregon.* San Francisco: Edgar Williams, 1878.
*An Illustrated History of Central Oregon.* Spokane, WA: Western Historical Publishing, 1905.
"James Blakely's Cabin, No. 18." *Oregon Native Son* 1, no. 5 (1899): 283.

Jefferson, Thomas. *Notes on the State of Virginia*. Edited with and introduction by William Peden. 1954. Chapel Hill: University of North Carolina Press, 1982.

Oliphant, J. Orin, and Thomas S. Kendall. "Thomas S. Kendall's Letter on Oregon Agriculture, 1852." *Agricultural History* 9, no. 4 (1935): 187–97.

Kirkpatrick, John M., and Orvil Dodge. *The Heroes of Battle Rock, or the Miners' Reward*. Myrtle Point, OR, 1904.

Lang, H. O., ed. *History of the Willamette Valley*. Portland, OR: Geo. H. Himes, 1885.

Linn County, Oregon. Agriculture Census, 1885. OSA.

———. Agriculture Census, 1895. OSA.

———. Jury Book, Grand Jury Witnesses. OSA.

———. Robert Montgomery, Probate Case No. 181. Records Clerk, Archive Department, Linn County Courthouse, Albany, Oregon.

———. School District 28 Records, 1894–95. Linn County Historical Museum, Brownsville, Oregon.

———. Tax Rolls. Linn County Tax Assessor's Office. Linn County Courthouse, Albany, Oregon.

Lockely, Fred. "Impressions and Observations of the *Journal* Man." *Oregon Journal*, 8 January 1924, 6.

MacFarlane, John J. *Manufacturing in Philadelphia, 1863–1912*. Philadelphia: Philadelphia Commercial Museum, 1912.

"The Massacre in Oregon." *Littell's Living Age* 19, no. 230 (14 October 1848): 66–67.

Mercer, A. S. *Material Resources of Linn County, Oregon*. Albany, OR: Brown & Stewart, 1875.

Oregon Farmers' State Alliance Industrial Union. *Constitution and By-Laws for the Government of the Farmers Alliance and Industrial Union of the State of Oregon*. Portland, OR: James A. Hines, 1891.

Oregon Provisional Government. Records, 1841–59. Manuscript 1226. OHS.

Oregon Provisional and Territorial Government. Papers, 1843–59. Knight Library, University of Oregon, Eugene.

"Pioneer Day and Pioneer Era." *Oregon Native Son* 2, no. 2 (1900): 97–98.

"Pioneers in Attendance." *Transactions of the Twenty-Third Annual Reunion of the Oregon Pioneer Association for 1895*. Portland, OR: George H. Himes, 1895.

*Portrait and Biographical Record of the Willamette Valley, Oregon*. Volumes 1 and 2. Chicago: Chapman, 1903.

Prince, Benjamin F., ed. *A Standard History of Springfield and Clark County, Ohio*. Volume 2. Chicago: American Historical Society, 1922.

"Purple and Gold." *Oregon Native Son* 1, no. 1 (1899): 38.

*Report of the Commission on Country Life*. With an Introduction by Theodore Roosevelt. New York: Sturgis & Walton, 1917.

Riggs, T. A. "Lieut. T. A. Riggs on the Rogue River War." *Oregon Native Son* 1, no. 3 (1899): 158–59.

Riggs, T. A. to Mrs. Geo. Goodall, 21 September 1901. Reprinted in George O. Goodall, "The Upper Calapooia." *Oregon Historical Quarterly* 4, no. 1 (1903): 70–77.

Stanard, Everett Earle. "Old Stuff & New." *Sunday Democrat* (Albany, OR), 15 July 1923, 5.

———. "Pen Pictures of Pioneers of Linn County—Article XXV: Aunt Eliza." *Sunday Democrat* (Albany, OR), 28 May 1922, 8.

State of Oregon. Circuit Court. Linn County, Journal. Volume 17, 1895–98. Albany Regional Museum, Albany, OR.

———. *First Biennial Report of the State Board of Charities and Corrections.* Portland, OR: F. W. Baltes and Company, 1892.

———. *Fourth Biennial Report of the State Reform School at Salem, Oregon.* Salem, OR: W. H. Leeds, 1899.

———. Linn County, Record of Trials, 1893–97 (14 March 1893–7 September 1897). Volume 1. OSA.

———. *Second Biennial Report of the Oregon State Reform School at Salem, Oregon, 1895.* Salem, OR: Frank C. Baker, 1894.

———. State of Oregon v. Lloyd [sic] Montgomery. Linn County Circuit Court Case #6600, 17 December 1895. Volume 17. OSA.

———. State Penitentiary. Great Register, 1887–93. OSA.

———. *Third Biennial Report of the Oregon State Reform School at Salem, Oregon.* Salem, OR: W. H. Leeds, 1896.

———. Youth Authority. Admissions Registers. Volume 1, 1891–1900. OSA.

Templeton, Dwight, Gladys Templeton, and Margaret Templeton Breuer, comps. *William T. Templeton: A Pioneer Family Geneology [sic] and History.* N.p.: by the compilers, 1978.

Upton, Harriet Taylor. *Proceedings of the Twenty-Seventh Annual Convention of the National-American Woman Suffrage Association, January 31st to February 5th, 1895.* Warren, OH: William Ritzel & Company, [1895].

US Bureau of the Census. Fifth Census, 1830. Manuscript Census, Howard County, Missouri.

US Census Bureau. Seventh Census, 1850. Manuscript Census, Linn County, Oregon.

US Census Office. *Twelfth Census of the United States, 1900: Population, 1900.* Part 1. Washington, DC: United States Census Office, 1901.

US Department of Agriculture. Bureau of Statistics. *Wheat Crops of the United States, 1866–1906.* Bulletin 57, rev. Washington, DC: Government Printing Office, 1908.

US Department of Commerce. Bureau of the Census. Tenth Census, 1880. Manuscript Census, Linn County, Oregon.

———. *Agriculture*. Part 1. Washington, DC: Government Printing Office, 1902.

———. *Census Reports, Volume VI: Agriculture. Part II. Crops and Irrigation*. Washington, DC: Government Printing Office, 1902.

———. *Thirteenth Census of the United States Taken in the Year 1910, Volume VII: Agriculture, 1909 and 1910*. Washington, DC: Government Printing Office, 1913.

———. *Thirteenth Census of the United States, Population, 1910*. Volume 3. Washington, DC: Government Printing Office, 1913.

———. Twelfth Census, 1900. Manuscript Census, Benton County, Oregon.

———. Twelfth Census, 1900. Manuscript Census, Linn County, Oregon.

US Department of the Interior. Census Office. Eighth Census, 1860. Manuscript Census, Linn County, Oregon.

———. Ninth Census, 1870. Manuscript Census, Linn County, Oregon.

———. *Report on the Mortality and Vital Statistics of the United States, 1880*. Part 1. Washington, DC: Government Printing Office, 1885.

———. *Report on the Population of the United States, 1890: Part I*. Washington, DC: Government Printing Office, 1895.

———. *Report on the Population of the United States, 1890*. Part 1. Washington, DC: Government Printing Office, 1895.

———. *Report on the Production of Agriculture, Tenth Census, 1880, General Statistics*. Washington, DC: Government Printing Office, 1883.

———. *Report on the Statistics of Agriculture in the United States, Eleventh Census, 1890*. Washington, DC: Government Printing Office, 1895.

———. Seventh Census, 1850. Manuscript Agricultural Census, Linn County, Oregon.

———. Tenth Census, 1880. Manuscript Agricultural Census, Linn County, Oregon.

———. Tenth Census, 1880. Manuscript Census, Multnomah County, Oregon.

———. Superintendent of the Census. *The Statistics of the Wealth and Industry of the United States, 1870*. Washington, DC: Government Printing Office, 1872.

US Department of Treasury. *Annual Report of the Controller of the Currency, December 7, 1896*. Volume 1. Washington, DC: Government Printing Office, 1896.

———. *Annual Report of the Controller of the Currency, December 4, 1893*. Volume 1. Washington, DC: Government Printing Office, 1893.

US Patent Office. "Samuel R. Templeton, John C. Templeton, and Joseph H. Templeton, of Brownsville, Oregon. Improvement in Hop-Driers." Accessed 31 August 2020. https://patentimages.storage.googleapis.com/75/e8/5f/3a49d9d52a838d/US190794.pdf.

Victor, Frances Fuller. *The River of the West: Life and Adventure in the Rocky Mountains and Oregon*. Hartford, CT: Columbian Book Company, 1870.

Warren, Eliza Spalding. *Memoirs of the West: The Spaldings*. Walla Walla, WA: the author, 1916.

SECONDARY SOURCES

Abbott, Carl. "From Urban Frontier to Metropolitan Region: Oregon's Cities from 1870 to 2008." *OHQ* 110, no. 1 (2009): 74–95.

Addis, Cameron. "The Whitman Massacre: Religion and Manifest Destiny on the Columbia Plateau, 1809–1858." *Journal of the Early Republic* 25, no. 1 (2005): 221–58.

Adler, Jeffrey S. *First in Violence, Deepest in Dirt: Homicide in Chicago, 1875–1920.* Cambridge, MA: Harvard University Press, 2006.

"AHA Forum: The Problem of American Homicide." *American Historical Review* 111, no. 1 (February 2006): 75–114.

Alexander, J. Trent, and Annemarie Steidl. "Gender and the 'Laws of Migration': A Reconsideration of Nineteenth-Century Patterns." *Social Science History* 36, no. 2 (2012): 223–41.

Andrews, Thomas G. *Killing for Coal: America's Deadliest Labor War.* Cambridge, MA: Harvard University Press, 2008.

Arvin, Maile, Eve Tuck, and Angie Morrill. "Decolonizing Feminism: Challenging Connections between Settler Colonialism and Heteropatriarchy." *Feminist Formations* 25, no. 1 (2013): 8–34.

Baker, Abner Sylvester. "The Oregon Pioneer Tradition in the Nineteenth Century: A Study of Recollection and Self-Definition." PhD diss., University of Oregon, 1968.

Barber, Katrine. "'We Were at Our Journey's End': Settler Sovereignty Formation in Oregon." *OHQ* 120, no. 4 (2019): 382–413.

Baxter, Kent. *The Modern Age: Turn-of-the-Century American Culture and the Invention of Adolescence.* Tuscaloosa: University of Alabama Press, 2008.

Beck, E. M., Stewart E. Tolnay, and Amy Kate Bailey. "Contested Terrain: The State versus Threatened Lynch Mob Violence." *American Journal of Sociology* 121, no. 6 (2016): 1856–84.

Beckham, Stephen Dow. *Requiem for a People: The Rogue Indians and the Frontiersmen.* Norman: University of Oklahoma Press, 1971.

Belew, Kathleen. "Lynching and Power in the United States: Southern, Western, and National Vigilante Violence." *History Compass* 12, no. 1 (2014): 84–99.

Bender, Cora. "'Transgressive Objects' in America: Mimesis and Violence in the Collection of Trophies during the Nineteenth Century Indian Wars." *Civil Wars* 11, no. 4 (2009): 502–13.

Bergquist, James M. "The Oregon Donation Act and the National Land Policy." *OHQ* 58, no. 1 (1957): 17–35.

Berwanger, Eugene H. *Frontier against Slavery: Western Anti-Negro Prejudice and the Slavery Extension Controversy.* Urbana: University of Illinois Press, 1967.

Bishop, J. Leander. *A History of American Manufacturers from 1608 to 1860.* Volume 3. Philadelphia: Edward Young, 1868.

Blok, Jack H. "The Evolution of Agricultural Resource Use Strategies in the Willamette Valley." PhD diss., Oregon State University, 1973.

Bloom, Lynn Z. "'It's All for Your Own Good': Parent-Child Relationships in Popular American Child Rearing Literature, 1820–1970." *Journal of Popular Culture* 10, no. 1 (1976): 191–98.

Boag, Peter. "Death and Oregon's Settler Generation: Connecting Parricide, Agricultural Decline, and Dying Pioneers at the Turn of the Twentieth Century." *OHQ* 115, no. 3 (2014): 344–79.

———. "Gender and Historicity of Parricide: A Case Study from the Nineteenth-Century North American West." In *Parricide and Violence against Parents throughout History: (De)Constructing Family and Authority?*, edited by Marianna Muravyeva and Raisa Maria Toivo, 139–68. London: Palgrave Macmillan, 2018.

———. "'He Took Up Arms against the Loins from Which He Sprang and the Womb That Bore Him': Gender and Parricide during the American Agrarian Crisis—A Case Study." *OHQ* 113, no. 2 (2012): 134–63.

Boag, Peter G. *Environment and Experience: Settlement Culture in Nineteenth-Century Oregon.* Berkeley: University of California Press, 1992.

Bowers, William L. *The Country Life Movement in America, 1900–1920.* Port Washington, NY: Kennikat Press, 1974.

Boyd, Robert T. "Another Look at the 'Fever and Ague' of Western Oregon." *Ethnohistory* 22, no. 2 (1975): 135–54.

Brown, R. Blake. "'Every Boy Ought to Learn to Shoot and to Obey Orders': Guns, Boys, and the Law in English Canada from the Late Nineteenth Century to the Great War." *Canadian Historical Review* 93, no. 2 (2012): 196–226.

Brown, Richard Maxwell. "Western Violence: Structure, Values, Myth." *Western Historical Quarterly* 24, no. 1 (1993): 5–20.

Brown, Thomas J. *Civil War Monuments and the Militarization of America.* Chapel Hill: University of North Carolina Press, 2019.

Bryan, Patricia L. "John Wesley Elkins, Boy Murderer, and His Struggle for Pardon." *Annals of Iowa* 69, no. 3 (2010): 261–307.

Bunting, Robert. *The Pacific Raincoast: Environment and Culture in an American Eden, 1778–1900.* Lawrence: University Press of Kansas, 1997.

Burton, Robert E. *Democrats of Oregon: The Pattern of Minority Politics, 1900–1968.* Eugene: University of Oregon Press, 1970.

Carey, Margaret Standish, and Patricia Hoy Hainline. *Brownsville: Linn County's Oldest Town.* Brownsville, OR: Calapooia Publications, 1976.

Carlson, Christopher Dean. "The Rural Family in the Nineteenth Century: A Case Study in Oregon's Willamette Valley." PhD diss., University of Oregon, 1980.

Carpenter, Marc James. "Pioneer Problems: 'Wanton Murder,' Indian War Veterans, and Oregon's Violent History." *OHQ* 121, no. 2 (2020): 156–85.

Carter, Herbert R. *The Spinning and Twisting of Long Vegetable Fibres (Flax, Hemp, Hute, Tow, & Ramie): A Practical Guide.* London: Charles Griffin and Company, 1904.

Cashman, Sean Dennis. *America in the Gilded Age: From the Death of Lincoln to the Rise of Theodore Roosevelt.* 3rd ed. New York: New York University Press, 1993.

Chandler, Alfred D., Jr. *The Visible Hand: The Managerial Revolution in American Business.* Cambridge, MA: Belknap Press of Harvard University Press, 1977.

Cleaver, J. D. "L. Samuel and the *West Shore*: Images of a Changing Pacific Northwest." *OHQ* 94, no. 2–3 (1993): 166–224.

Coleman, Kenneth R. "'We'll All Start Even': White Egalitarianism and the Oregon Donation Land Claim Act." *OHQ* 120, no. 4 (2019): 414–37.

Conn, Steven. *Americans against the City: Anti-Urbanism in the Twentieth Century.* Oxford: Oxford University Press, 2014.

Conzen, Michael P. "The County Landownership Map in America: Its Commercial Development and Social Transformation 1814–1939." *Imago Mundi* 36, no. 1 (1984): 9–31.

———. "Landownership Maps and County Atlases." *Agricultural History* 58, no. 1 (1984): 118–22.

Cook, Waldo L. "Murders in Massachusetts." *Publications of the American Statistical Association* 3, no. 23 (1893): 357–78.

Cothran, Boyd. *Remembering the Modoc War: Redemption Violence and the Making of American Innocence.* Chapel Hill: University of North Carolina Press, 2014.

Cott, Nancy F. "Notes toward an Interpretation of Antebellum Childrearing." *Psychohistory Review* 6, no. 4 (1978): 4–20.

Courtwright, David T. *Violent Land: Single Men and Social Disorder from the Frontier to the Inner City.* Cambridge, MA: Harvard University Press, 1996.

Cox, Thomas R. *Mills and Markets: A History of the West Coast Lumber Industry to 1900.* Seattle: University of Washington Press, 1975.

Craghead, Alexander Benjamin. *Railway Palaces of Portland, Oregon: The Architectural Legacy of Henry Villard.* Charleston, SC: History Press, 2016.

Creech, Joe. *Righteous Indignation: Religion and the Populist Revolution.* Urbana: University of Illinois Press, 2006.

Crist, Thomas A. "The Good, the Bad, and the Ugly: Bioarchaeology and the Modern Gun Culture Debate." *Historical Archaeology* 40, no. 3 (2006): 109–30.

Cronon, William. *Nature's Metropolis: Chicago and the Great West*. New York: Norton, 1991.

Danbom, David B. *Born in the Country: A History of Rural America*. 2nd ed. Baltimore, MD: Johns Hopkins University Press, 2006.

———. "Romantic Agrarianism in Twentieth-Century America." *Agricultural History* 65, no. 4 (1991): 1–12.

Davies, Owen, and Francesca Matteoni. *Executing Magic in the Modern Era: Criminal Bodies and the Gallows in Popular Medicine*. Cham, Switzerland: Springer International Publishing, an imprint of Palgrave Macmillan, 2017.

Dodds, Gordon B. *The American Northwest: A History of Oregon and Washington*. Arlington Heights, IL: Forum Press, 1986.

Dodge, Charles Richards, and US Department of Agriculture. *A Descriptive Catalogue of Useful Fiber Plants of the World*. Washington, DC: Government Printing Office, 1897.

Dolan, Ronald E. *Philippines: A Country Study*. 4th ed. Washington, DC: Federal Research Division, Library of Congress, 1993.

Drury, Clifford Merrill. *Henry Harmon Spalding*. Caldwell, ID: Caxton Printers, 1936.

———. *Marcus and Narcissa Whitman and the Opening of Old Oregon*. Glendale, CA: Arthur H. Clark, 1973.

Edwards, G. Thomas. "Six Oregon Leaders and the Far-Reaching Impact of America's Civil War." *OHQ* 100, no. 1 (1999): 4–31.

Edwards, Harry Taylor. *Abacá (Manila Hemp)*. Manila, Philippines: Bureau of Print, 1910.

Etulain, Richard W. *Lincoln and Oregon Country Politics in the Civil War Era*. Corvallis: Oregon State University Press, 2013.

Evans, Sterling. *Bound in Twine: A History and Ecology of the Henequen-Wheat Complex for Mexico and the American and Canadian Plains, 1880–1950*. College Station: Texas A&M University Press, 2007.

———. "The Force of Fiber: Reconnecting the Philippines with Latin America and the American West via Transnational Environmental History." In *A Field on Fire: The Future of Environmental History*, edited by Mark D. Hersey and Ted Steinberg, 101–15. Tuscaloosa: University of Alabama Press, 2019.

Ewing, Charles Patrick. *When Children Kill: The Dynamics of Juvenile Homicide*. Lexington, MA: Lexington Books, 1990.

Faust, Drew Gilpin. *This Republic of Suffering: Death and the American Civil War*. New York: Vintage, 2008.

Foucault, Michel. *Discipline and Punish: The Birth of the Prison*. New York: Pantheon Books, 1977.

———, ed. *I, Pierre Rivière, Having Slaughtered My Mother, My Sister, and My Brother . . . : A Case of Parricide in the 19th Century*. Translated by Frank Jellinek. 1973. Lincoln: University of Nebraska Press, 1982.

Fuentes, Annette. "Cracking Down on Kids." In *Childhood in America*, edited by Paula S. Fass and Mary Ann Mason, 229–32. New York: New York University Press, 2000.

"GAR Plot." Eugene Pioneer Cemetery. Accessed 7 May 2021. https://www.eugene-pioneercemetery.org/gar-plot/.

*Genealogical Material in Oregon Donation Land Claims*. Volume 1. Portland: Genealogical Forum of Portland, Oregon.

Goeres-Gardner, Diane L. *Murder, Morality, and Madness: Women Criminals in Early Oregon*. Caldwell, ID: Caxton Press, 2009.

———. *Necktie Parties: Legal Executions in Oregon, 1851–1905*. Caldwell, ID: Caxton Press, 2005.

Goodall, George O. "The Upper Calapooia." *OHQ* 4, no. 1 (1903): 70–77.

Gordon, Linda. "Family Violence as History and Politics." *Radical America* 21, no. 4 (1987): 21–32.

———. *Heroes of Their Own Lives: The Politics and History of Family Violence, Boston 1880–1960*. Urbana: University of Illinois Press, 2002.

Grandin, Greg. *The End of the Myth: From the Frontier to the Border Wall in the Mind of America*. New York: Metropolitan Books, 2019.

Green, Rayna. "The Pocahontas Perplex: The Image of Indian Women in American Culture." *Massachusetts Review* 16, no. 4 (1975): 698–714.

Greven, Philip J., Jr. *Four Generations: Population, Land, and Family in Colonial Andover, Massachusetts*. Ithaca, NY: Cornell University Press, 1970.

Griffiths, David B. "Populism in the Far West, 1890–1900." PhD diss., University of Washington, 1967.

Grube, April Mae. "'From Honeymoon to Massacre': Memory and Remembrance of Marcus Whitman, 1847–1962." MA thesis, Washington State University, 2014.

Hague, Euan, and Edward H. Sebesta. "The Jefferson Davis Highway: Contesting the Confederacy in the Pacific Northwest." *Journal of American Studies* 45, no. 2 (2011): 281–301.

Hainline, Patricia. "An 1895 Triple Murder." *Northwest Passages: Historical Newsletter* 10, no. 4 (1995): 1–3.

Handy-Marchello, Barbara. *Women of the Northern Plains: Gender and Settlement on the Homestead Frontier*. St. Paul: Minnesota Historical Society Press, 2005.

Hanon, Delaney Hardin. "The Whitman Legend: The Intertwining of History and Memorial in the Narrative of Marcus and Narcissa Whitman." Honors thesis, Whitman College, 2017.

Harrison, Simon. *Dark Trophies: Hunting and the Enemy Body in Modern War.* New York: Berghahn Books, 2012.

"Harvey W. Scott." *Oregon History Project.* Accessed 24 January 2021. https://www.oregonhistoryproject.org/articles/biographies/harvey-w-scott-biography/#.YA2aXOCIaXo.

"Harvey Whitefield Scott, II." *OregonLive.* Accessed 24 January 2021. https://obits.oregonlive.com/obituaries/oregon/obituary.aspx?n=harvey-whitefield-scott&pid=2752178.

Hayase, Shinzo. "American Colonial Policy and the Japanese Abaca Industry in Davao, 1898–1941." *Philippine Studies* 33, no. 4 (1985): 505–17.

Heide, Kathleen M. *Understanding Parricide: When Sons and Daughters Kill Parents.* Oxford: Oxford University Press, 2014.

———. *Why Kids Kill Parents: Child Abuse and Adolescent Homicide.* Thousand Oaks, CA: SAGE, 1995.

Heide, Kathleen M., and Eldra P. Solomon. "Female Juvenile Murderers: Biological and Psychological Dynamics Leading to Homicide." *International Journal of Law and Psychiatry* 32, no. 4 (2009): 244–52.

Heide, Kathleen M., and Thomas A. Petee. "Weapons Used by Juvenile and Adult Offenders in U.S. Parricide Cases." *Journal of Interpersonal Violence* 22, no. 11 (2007): 1400–1414.

Hemphill, C. Dallett. *Siblings: Brothers and Sisters in American History.* New York: Oxford University Press, 2011.

Hillbrand, Marc, and Traci Cipriano. "Commentary: Parricides—Unanswered Questions, Methodological Obstacles, and Legal Considerations." *Journal of the American Academy of Psychiatry and the Law* 35, no. 7 (2007): 313–16.

Hoganson, Kristin. "SHGAPE Presidential Address: Mind the GAPE; Globality and the Rural Midwest." *Journal of the Gilded Age and Progressive Era* 19, no. 2 (2020): 176–90.

Holden, Margaret Kolb. "The Rise and Fall of Oregon Populism: Legal Theory, Political Culture and Public Policy, 1868–1895." PhD diss., University of Virginia, 1993.

Holtgrieve, Donald G. "The Effects of the Railroads on Small Town Population Changes: Linn County, Oregon." *Yearbook of the Association of Pacific Coast Geographers* 35 (1973): 87–102.

Hunnicutt, Gwen. "Varieties of Patriarchy and Violence against Women: Resurrecting 'Patriarchy' as a Theoretical Tool." *Violence against Women* 15, no. 5 (2009): 553–73.

Jackson, Ronald Vern, Wylma Winmill, and Shirley P. Zachrison, eds. *Oregon 1880 Mortality Schedule.* Bountiful, UT: Accelerated Indexing Systems, 1981.

Jakubovic, Rafaella J., and Deborah A. G. Drabick. "Community Violence Exposure and Youth Aggression: The Moderating Role of Working Memory." *Journal of Abnormal Child Psychology* 48, no. 11 (2020): 1471–84.

Jameson, Elizabeth. "Women as Workers, Women as Civilizers: The True Womanhood in the American West." In *The Women's West*, edited by Susan Armitage and Elizabeth Jameson, 145–67. Norman: University of Oklahoma Press, 1987.

Jeffrey, Julie Roy. *Converting the West: A Biography of Narcissa Whitman*. Norman: University of Oklahoma Press, 1991.

Jenkins, Philip. "Serial Murder in the United States 1900–1940: A Historical Perspective." *Journal of Criminal Justice* 17, no. 5 (1989): 377–92.

Jenness, Jessica L., Cordelie E. Witt, D. Alex Quistberg, Brian D. Johnston, Ali Rowhani-Rahbar, Jessica L. Mackelprang, Katie A. McLaughlin, Monica S. Vavilala, and Frederick P. Rivara. "Association of Physical Injury and Mental Health: Results from the National Comorbidity Survey—Adolescent Supplement." *Journal of Psychiatric Research* 92 (September 2017): 101–7.

Jennings, Francis. *The Invasion of America: Indians, Colonialism, and the Cant of Conquest*. Chapel Hill: University of North Carolina Press, 1975.

Jensen, Joan M. "Out of Wisconsin: Country Daughters in the City, 1910–1925." *Minnesota History* 59, no. 2 (2004): 48–61.

Johansen, Dorothy O. *Empire of the Columbia: A History of the Pacific Northwest*. 2nd ed. New York: Harper & Row, 1967.

Keetley, Dawn. *Making a Monster: Jesse Pomeroy, the Boy Murderer of 1870s Boston*. Amherst: University of Massachusetts Press, 2017.

Kerber, Linda. "The Republican Mother: Women and the Enlightenment—An American Perspective." *American Quarterly* 28, no. 2 (1976): 187–205.

Killen, Patricia O'Connell, Mark A. Shibley, Kellee Boyer, and Kellie A. Riley. "Surveying the Religious Landscape: Historical Trends and Current Patterns in Oregon, Washington, and Alaska." In *Religion and Public Life in the Pacific Northwest: The None Zone*, edited by Patricia O'Connell Killen and Mark Silk, 25–50. Walnut Creek, CA: AltaMira Press, 2004.

King, Charles R. "Childhood Death: The Health Care of Children on the Kansas Frontier." *Kansas History* 14, no. 1 (1991): 26–36.

Kopp, Peter A. *Hoptopia: A World of Agriculture and Beer in Oregon's Willamette Valley*. Oakland: University of California Press, 2016.

LaLande, Jeff. "'Dixie' of the Pacific Northwest: Southern Oregon's Civil War." *OHQ* 100, no. 1 (1999): 32–81.

———. "A 'Little Kansas' in Southern Oregon: The Course and Character of Populism in Jackson County, 1890–1900." *Pacific Historical Review* 63, no. 2 (1994): 149–76.

Lansing, Ronald B. "Whitman Massacre Trial." *OE*. Accessed 7 August 2020. https://oregonencyclopedia.org/articles/whitman_massacre_trial/.

Larsen, Dennis M. *Hop King: Ezra Meeker's Boom Years*. Pullman: Washington State University Press, 2016.

———. *The Missing Chapters: The Untold Story of Ezra Meeker's Old Oregon Trail Monument Expedition, January 1906 to July 1908*. Puyallup, WA: Ezra Meeker Historical Society, 2006.

Legislative Committee Services, comp. *Chronological List of Oregon's Legislatures*. Salem: Oregon State Legislature, 2008. Accessed 23 June 2020. https://www.oregonlegislature.gov/citizen_engagement/Reports/Chronological.pdf.

Lesy, Michael. *Wisconsin Death Trip*. With a foreword by Warren I. Susman. Albuquerque: University of New Mexico Press, 1973.

Lewis, David. "Confederated Tribes of Grande Ronde." *OE*. Accessed 2 August 2020. https://oregonencyclopedia.org/articles/confederated_tribes_of_grand_ronde/.

Lewis, David G. "Four Deaths: The Near Destruction of Western Oregon Tribes and Native Lifeways, Removal to the Reservation, and Erasure from History." *OHQ* 115, no. 3 (2014): 414–37.

———. "Molalla Tribal History." *Quartux*. Accessed 8 January 2021. https://ndnhistoryresearch.com/tribal-regions/molalla-ethnohistory/.

Linders, Annulla. "The Execution Spectacle and State Legitimacy: The Changing Nature of the American Execution Audience, 1833–1937." *Law and Society Review* 36, no. 3 (2002): 607–56.

Lipin, Lawrence. "Populism in Oregon." *OE*. Accessed 10 August 2020. https://oregonencyclopedia.org/articles/populism_in_oregon/.

Long, William R. *A Tortured History: The Story of Capital Punishment in Oregon*. Eugene: Oregon Criminal Defense Lawyers Association, 2001.

Lovoll, Odd S. *Norwegians on the Prairie: Ethnicity and the Development of the Country Town*. St. Paul: Minnesota Historical Society Press, 2006.

Luce, Tamar J. "Excavating First-Person Accounts of the Whitman Massacre." *Nebraska Anthropologist*, 2012. Accessed 6 August 2020. https://digitalcommons.unl.edu/cgi/viewcontent.cgi?article=1176&context=nebanthro.

Lyon-Jenness, Cheryl. "Picturing Progress: Assessing the Nineteenth-Century Atlas-Map Bonanza." *Michigan Historical Review* 30, no. 2 (2004): 167–210.

Mackey, Harold. *The Kalapuyans: A Sourcebook on the Indians of the Willamette Valley*. Salem, OR: Mission Mill Museum Association, 1974.

"Manila Hemp." *Scientific American* 82, no. 2 (13 January 1900): 24.

Martins, Michael, and Dennis A. Binette. *Parallel Lives: A Social History of Lizzie A. Borden and Her Fall River*. Fall River, MA: Fall River Historical Society, 2010.

Masterson, Iver Willis. "A History of the Consumer's Co-operatives in Oregon Prior to 1900." MA thesis, University of Oregon, 1939.

McConnell, Virginia A. McConnell. *Sympathy for the Devil: The Emmanuel Baptist Murders of Old San Francisco*. Westport, CT: Praeger, 2001.

McCoy, Drew R. *The Elusive Republic: Political Economy in Jeffersonian America*. Chapel Hill: University of North Carolina Press, 1980.

McLagan, Elizabeth. *A Peculiar Paradise: A History of Blacks in Oregon, 1788–1940*. Portland, OR: Georgian Press, 1980.

McLoughlin, William G. *Revivals, Awakenings, and Reform: An Essay on Religion and Social Change in America, 1607–1977*. Chicago: University of Chicago Press, 1978.

Miles, John, and Richard R. Milligan, comps. *Linn County, Oregon Pioneer Settlers: Oregon Territory Donation Land Claim Families to 1855*. Vols. 1–40. Albany, OR: by the compilers, 1983–94.

Miller, Merle. "Sons and Daughters of Oregon Pioneers." *OE*. Accessed 13 August 2020. http://oregonencyclopedia.org/articles/sons_and_daughters_of_oregon_pioneers.

Mills, Mackenzie S., Christine M. Embury, Alicia K. Klaneky, Maya M. Khanna, Vince D. Calhoun, Julia M. Stephen, Yu-Ping Wang, Tony W. Wilson, and Amy S. Badura-Brack. "Traumatic Events Are Associated with Diverse Psychological Symptoms in Typically-Developing Children." *Journal of Child and Adolescent Trauma* 13, no. 4 (2020): 381–88.

Minthorn, Antone. "Wars, Treaties, and the Beginning of Reservation Life." In *Wiyaxayxt/Wiyáakaa'awn/As Days Go By: Our History, Our Land, Our People—the Cayuse, Umatilla, and Walla Walla*, edited by Jennifer Karson, 61–89. Pendleton, OR: Tamástslikt Cultural Institute; Portland: Oregon Historical Society, 2006.

Mintz, Steven. *Huck's Raft: A History of American Childhood*. Cambridge, MA: Belknap Press of Harvard University Press, 2004.

Mintz, Steven, and Susan Kellogg. *Domestic Revolutions: A Social History of American Family Life*. New York: Free Press, 1988.

Mok, Pearl L. H., Sussie Antonsen, Carsten B. Pederson, Matthew J. Carr, Nav Kapur, James Nazroo, and Roger T. Webb. "Family Income Inequalities and Trajectories through Childhood and Self-Harm and Violence in Young Adults: A Population-Based, Nested Case-Control Study." *Lancet Public Health* 3, no. 10 (2018): e498–507.

Mones, Paul A. *When a Child Kills: Abused Children Who Kill Their Parents*. New York: Pocket Books, 1991.

Nash, Lee. "Havey Scott (1838–1910)." *OE*. Accessed 1 December 2020. https://www.oregonencyclopedia.org/articles/scott_harvey_1838_1910_/#.YA2JMOCIaXo.

Nielsen, Kim E. "Dr. Anna B. Ott, Patient #1763: The Messiness of Authority, Diagnosis, Gender, and Insanity in Nineteenth-Century America." *Signs: Journal of Women in Culture and Society* 45, no. 1 (2019): 27–49.
Oliphant, J. Orin. "Documents Illustrating the Beginnings of the Presbyterian Advance into the Oregon Country." *Washington Historical Quarterly* 26, no. 2 (1935): 123–28; and no. 3 (1935): 202–24.
Onuf, Peter S. *Jefferson's Empire: The Language of American Nationhood*. Charlottesville: University Press of Virginia, 1999.
Owen, Norman G. *Prosperity without Progress: Manila Hemp and Material Life in the Colonial Philippines*. Berkeley: University of California Press, 1984.
Pascoe, Peggy. *What Comes Naturally: Miscegenation Law and the Making of Race in America*. New York: Oxford University Press, 2009.
Pederson, Jane M. "Gender, Justice, and a Wisconsin Lynching, 1889–1890." *Agricultural History* 67, no. 2 (1993): 65–82.
Peters, Scott J., and Paul A. Morgan. "The Country Life Commission: Reconsidering a Milestone in American Agricultural History." *Agricultural History* 78, no. 3 (2004): 289–316.
Peterson del Mar, David. *Beaten Down: A History of Interpersonal Violence in the West*. Seattle: University of Washington Press, 2002.
———. *What Trouble I Have Seen: A History of Violence against Wives*. Cambridge, MA: Harvard University Press, 1996.
Pleck, Elizabeth. *Domestic Tyranny: The Making of American Social Policy against Family Violence from Colonial Times to the Present*. Urbana: University of Illinois Press, 2004.
Postel, Charles. *The Populist Vision*. New York: Oxford University Press, 2007.
Prescott, Cynthia Culver. *Gender and Generation on the Far Western Frontier*. Tucson: University of Arizona Press, 2007.
———. *Pioneer Mother Monuments: Constructing Cultural Memory*. Norman: University of Oklahoma Press, 2019.
Pyne, Stephen. *Year of the Fires: The Story of the Great Fires of 1910*. New York: Viking, 2001.
Rees, John E. "Oregon—Its Meaning, Origin and Application." *OHQ* 21, no. 4 (1920): 317–31.
Reinhardt, Bob. "Mill City." *OE*. Accessed 5 November 2020. https://www.oregonencyclopedia.org/articles/mill_city/#.X_OQuF6IZm8.
Republican State Central Committee, comp. *Republican League Register: A Record of the Republican Party in the State of Oregon*. Portland, OR: Register Publishing, 1896.
Riney-Kehrberg, Pamela. *Childhood on the Farm: Work, Play, and Coming of Age in the Midwest*. Lawrence: University Press of Kansas, 2005.

Robbins, William G. *Colony and Empire: The Capitalist Transformation of the American West*. Lawrence: University Press of Kansas, 1994.

———. "George Chamberlain (1854–1928)." *OE*. Accessed 22 July 2020. https://oregonencyclopedia.org/articles/chamberlain_george_1854_1928_/#.WzmQk9gzaV4.

———. "The Indian Question in Western Oregon: The Making of a Colonial People." In *Experiences in a Promised Land: Essays in Pacific Northwest History*, edited by G. Thomas Edwards and Carlos A. Schwantes, 51–67. Seattle: University of Washington Press, 1986.

———. "Oregon Donation Land Law." *OE*. Accessed July 22, 2020. https://oregonencyclopedia.org/articles/oregon_donation_land_act/.

Rohrbaugh, Malcolm J. *The Land Office Business: The Settlement and Administration of American Public Lands, 1789–1837*. 3rd ed. Bloomington: Indiana University Press, 2008.

———. *The Trans-Appalachian Frontier: People, Societies, and Institutions, 1775–1850*. 3rd ed. Bloomington: Indiana University Press, 2008.

Rotundo, E. Anthony. *American Manhood: Transformations in Masculinity from the Revolution to the Modern Era*. New York: Basic Books, 1993.

Savage, Kirk. *Standing Soldiers, Kneeling Slaves: Race, War, and Monument in Nineteenth Century America*. Princeton, NJ: Princeton University Press, 1997.

Schwartz, E. A. *The Rogue River Indian War and Its Aftermath, 1850–1980*. Norman: University of Oklahoma Press, 1997.

Scott, Edna A. "The Grange Movement in Oregon, 1873–1900." MA thesis, University of Oregon, 1923.

Scott, Harvey W., and Leslie M. Scott. *History of the Oregon Country*. 6 vols. Cambridge, MA: Riverside Press, 1924.

Scott, Leslie. "History of the Narrow Gauge Railroad in the Willamette Valley." *OHQ* 20, no. 2 (1919): 141–58.

Seagrave, Kerry. *Parricide in the United States, 1840–1899*. Jefferson, NC: McFarland, 2009.

Shon, Phillip C. H. "Weapon Usage in Attempted and Completed Parricides in Nineteenth-Century America: An Archival Exploration of the Physical Strength Hypothesis." *Journal of Forensic Sciences* 55, no. 1 (2010): 233–36.

Shon, Phillip Chong Ho. "Existential Boundary Crossings: An Archival Exploration of Identity Projects in Nineteenth-Century American Parricides." *Human Studies* 35, no. 3 (2012): 445–57.

———. "Sources of Conflict between Parents and Their Offspring in Nineteenth-Century American Parricides: An Archival Exploration." *Journal of Forensic Psychology Practice* 9, no. 4 (2009): 249–79.

Shon, Phillip C., and Michael A. Roberts. "Post-Offence Characteristics of 19th-Century American Parricides: An Archival Exploration." *Journal of Investigative Psychology and Offender Profiling* 5, no. 3 (2008): 147–69.

Shon, Phillip C. H., and Joseph R. Targonski. "Declining Trends in US Parricides, 1976–1998: Testing the Freudian Assumptions." *International Journal of Law and Psychiatry* 26, no. 4 (2003): 387–402.

Shon, Phillip Chong Ho, and Shannon M. Barton-Bellessa. "Pre-Offense Characteristics of Nineteenth-Century American Parricide Offenders: An Archival Exploration." *Journal of Criminal Psychology* 2, no. 1 (2012): 51–66.

Shuler, Jack. *The Thirteenth Turn: A History of the Noose*. New York: Public Affairs, 2014.

Slotkin, Richard. *The Fatal Environment: The Myth of the Frontier in the Age of Industrialization, 1800–1890*. New York: Atheneum, 1985.

Smith, Stacey L. "Oregon's Civil War: The Troubled Legacy of Emancipation in the Pacific Northwest." *OHQ* 115, no. 2 (2014): 154–73.

Soden, Dale E. *Outsiders in a Promised Land: Religious Activists in Pacific Northwest History*. Corvallis: Oregon State University Press, 2015.

Song, Li-yu, Mark I. Singer, and Trina M. Anglin. "Violence Exposure and Emotional Trauma as Contributors to Adolescents' Violent Behaviors." *Archives of Pediatrics and Adolescent Medicine* 152, no. 6 (1998): 531–36.

Strange, Carolyn. "The Unwritten Law of Executive Justice: Pardoning Patricide in Reconstruction-Era New York." *Law and History Review* 28, no. 4 (2010): 891–930.

Streib, Victor L. *Death Penalty for Juveniles*. Bloomington: Indiana University Press, 1987.

Susman, Warren I. Foreword to *Wisconsin Death Trip*, by Michael Lesy. Albuquerque: University of New Mexico Press, 1973.

Sutton, Matthew Avery. *American Apocalypse: A History of Modern Evangelicalism*. Cambridge, MA: Belknap Press of Harvard University Press, 2014.

Swenson, Russell. "Illustrations of Material Culture in Nineteenth-Century County and State Atlases." *Pioneer America Society Transactions* 5 (1982): 63–70.

Szasz, Ferenc Morton. *Religion in the Modern American West*. Tucson: University of Arizona Press, 2000.

Taber, Ronald W. "Sacagawea and the Suffragettes." *Pacific Northwest Quarterly* 58, no. 1 (1967): 7–13.

Tattersall, James Neville. "The Economic Development of the Pacific Northwest to 1920." PhD diss., University of Washington, 1960.

Thorburn, A. Lennox. "Jean Martin Charcot, 1825–1893: An Appreciation." *British Journal of Venereal Diseases* 43, no. 2 (1967): 77–80.

Trachtenberg, Alan. *The Incorporation of America: Culture and Society in the Gilded Age*. New York: Hill and Wang, 1982.

Trouillot, Michel-Rolph. *Silencing the Past: Power and the Production of History*. Boston: Beacon Press, 1995.

Turnbull, George S. *History of Oregon Newspapers*. Portland, OR: Binfords & Mort, 1939.

University of Missouri Libraries. "Prices and Wages by Decade: 1890–1899." Accessed 2 January 2021. https://libraryguides.missouri.edu/pricesandwages/1890-1899.

Unruh, John D., Jr. *The Plains Across: The Overland Emigrants and the Trans-Mississippi West, 1840–60*. Urbana: University of Illinois Press, 1979.

Varley, Molly K. *Americans Recaptured: Progressive Era Memory of Frontier Captivity*. Norman: University of Oklahoma Press, 2014.

Vaughn, Chelsea. "Killing Narcissa: Race, Gender, and Violence in Recreations of the Whitman Incident." *OHQ* 115, no. 3 (2014): 380–413.

Ventura, Theresa. "From Small Farms to Progressive Plantations: The Trajectory of Land Reform in the American Colonial Philippines, 1900–1916." *Agricultural History* 90, no. 4 (2016): 459–83.

Walker, Lenore E. A. *The Battered Woman Syndrome*. 4th ed. New York: Springer, 2017.

Wall-Myers, Tina D., Abigail Salcedo, Paul J. Frick, James V. Ray, Laura C. Thornton, Laurence Steinberg, and Elizabeth Cauffman. "Understanding the Link between Exposure to Violence and Aggression in Justice-Involved Adolescents." *Development and Psychopathology* 30, no. 2 (2018): 593–603.

Ward, Jean M. "Lewis & Clark College." *OE*. Accessed 14 January 2021. https://www.oregonencyclopedia.org/articles/lewis_and_clark_college/#.YADZieCIaXo.

Warren Ryder, David. *Men of Rope: Being the History of Tubbs Cordage Company; Together with an Account of Some of the Collateral Activities in Which Its Pioneer Founders Engaged*. San Francisco, CA: Historical Publications, 1954.

Weber, Max. *Economy and Society: An Outline of Interpretive Sociology*. 3 vols. New York: Bedminster Press, 1968.

West, Elliott. *Growing Up with the Country: Childhood on the Far Western Frontier*. Albuquerque: University of New Mexico Press, 1989.

Wexler, Geoffrey. "George Himes (1844–1940)." *OE*. Accessed 11 August 2020. https://oregonencyclopedia.org/articles/himes_george_1844_1940.

Whaley, Gray H. "A Reflection on Genocide in Southwestern Oregon in Honor of George Bundy Wasson, Jr." *OHQ* 115, no. 3 (2014): 438–40, 446.

Wheeler, Kenneth H. "Infanticide in Nineteenth-Century Ohio." *Journal of Social History* 31, no. 2 (1997): 407–18.

White, Richard. *Land Use, Environment, and Social Change: The Shaping of Island County, Washington*. Seattle: University of Washington Press, 1980.

———. *Railroaded: The Transcontinentals and the Making of Modern America*. New York: Norton, 2011.

Wiebe, Robert H. *The Search for Order, 1877–1920*. New York: Hill and Wang, 1967.

Winston, Diane. *Red Hot and Righteous: The Urban Religion of the Salvation Army*. Cambridge, MA: Harvard University Press, 1999.

Works Progress Administration Writers' Program and the Linn County Pioneer Memorial Association, comps. *History of Linn County*. 1941. Portland, OR: Boyce-Wheeler, 1982.

Wyllie-Echeverria, Sandy, and Paul Alan Cox. "The Seagrass (*Zostera marina* [Zosteraceae]) Industry of Nova Scotia (1907–1960)." *Economic Botany* 53, no. 4 (1999): 419–26.

Yacubian, E. M., R. Skaff, E. Garzon, N. I. O. Braga, A. C. Sakamoto, and H. Carrete. "Seizures Induced by Eating in a Family." In *Reflex Epilepsies: Progress in Understanding*, edited by Peter Wolf, Yushi Inoue, and Benjamin Zifkin, 123–34. Esher, UK: John Libbey Eurotext, 2004.

Young, F. G. Review of *History of the Oregon Country*, by Harvey W. Scott and Leslie M. Scott. *Washington Historical Quarterly* 16, no. 2 (1925): 146–48.

Young, Harvey. "The Black Body as Souvenir in American Lynching." *Theatre Journal* 57, no. 4 (2005): 639–57.

Ziegler, Edith M. "'The Burdens and the Narrow Life of Farm Women': Women, Gender, and Theodore Roosevelt's Commission on Country Life." *Agricultural History* 86, no. 3 (2012): 77–103.

Zucker, Jeff, Kay Hummel, and Bob Høgfoss. *Oregon Indians: Culture, History & Current Affairs; An Atlas & Introduction*. Portland, OR: Western Imprints, the Press of the Oregon Historical Society, 1983.

NEWSPAPERS AND PERIODICALS

*Albany Daily Democrat*
*Albany Democrat*
*Albany Democrat-Herald*
*Albany Evening Herald*
*Albany Register*
*Albany Weekly Herald*
*Brownsville Times*
*Capital Journal* (Salem)
*Corvallis Gazette*
*Corvallis Gazette-Times*
*Corvallis Times*

*Daily Astorian*
*Daily Oregon Statesman* (Salem)
*Eugene Guard*
*Evening Capital Journal* (Salem)
*Examiner* (San Francisco)
*Greater Oregon* (Albany)
*Lebanon Express*
*Morning Daily Herald* (Albany)
*Morning Democrat Herald* (Albany)
*Morning Herald* (Albany)
*New Northwest* (Portland)
*New York Times*
*Oregon Cultivator* (Albany)
*Oregonian* (Portland)
*Oregon Journal* (Portland)
*Oregon Mist* (St. Helens)
*Oregon Populist* (Albany)
*Oregon State Journal* (Eugene)
*Oregon Statesman* (Salem)
*San Francisco Call*
*San Francisco Chronicle*
*Semi-Weekly Democrat* (Albany)
*State Rights Democrat* (Albany)
*Statesman Journal* (Salem)
*Sunday Democrat* (Albany)
*The Dalles Times-Mountaineer*
*Weekly Herald-Disseminator* (Albany)
*Weekly Mercury* (Salem)
*West Shore* (Portland)
*Willamette Farmer* (Portland and Salem)

# INDEX

*fig* denotes figure; *map* denotes map

## A

abaca, 165–66. *See also* manila hemp
abuse, child, 68–71, 189; Charles Finlayson and, 83; childhood development and, 46; Loyd and, 68–69, 70–71, 75; parricide and, 8, 69. *See also* corporal punishment
abuse, domestic, 70–71; patriarchy and, 69
accidents and injuries, childhood, 53–56; boys compared to girls, 53–54; childhood development and, 46; guns, 55–56; Loyd and, 58
Ackerman, Feicke, 184
African Americans, 15, 172; racism and, 111, 134; republicanism and, 26; slavery and, 26, 111
agrarian protest: in Linn County, 41–42, 108–13. *See also* populist movement; Populist Party
agriculture, Willamette Valley: depression (1873–97) and, 99–100, 102–5, 107–8; environmental change and, 167; expansion of in nineteenth century, 95–97; globalization and, 98, 99; market produce, 97; Oregon State Reform School and, 77; wheat, 11, 96, 97, 100. *See also* hop industry
Albany City Cemetery, 173*map*, 215
Albany Iron Works, 174
Albany Medical Club: Loyd's brain and, 214
Albany, OR, 2*map*, 13*map*, 11, 14, 41, 45, 52, 61, 83, 84, 87, 92, 102, 112, 158, 161, 162, 170, 172–73, 173*map*, 174, 176, 180, 182, 184, 187, 193, 196, 197, 200–201, 202, 215; agrarian revolt and, 112; bad-boy problem in, 72,
73, 79–80; depression of the 1890s and, 105–8, 161, 164, 173–74; railroad and, 96; religious revivals in, 203–4; Salvation Army and, 206
American Legion, 138
Ancient Order of United Workmen, 182, 221
Arthurs, John, 172
Aunt Eliza. *See* Lize

## B

bad-boy problem, 18, 36, 59, 72–73, 76, 78, 79–80, 81, 82, 85, 89, 122, 186; Loyd and, 45, 81–82, 85–86, 89; rural-urban migration and, 80, 81
Battle of Big Meadows (1856), 138; reenactment of (1922), 138, 139, 140
Black, David, 206
Blain, Wilson, 201
Blakely, James, 2, 98, 127, 130, 135, 137; as "Indian" fighter, 136–37, 138, 147–48; Linn County Pioneer Association and, 134, 136–37, 146; Lize and, 139; tributes to, 147–48
Blakely, Sarah, 135, 136
Blakely Cabin of the Native Sons of Oregon (Brownsville), 127
Borden, Lizzie, 7, 8
boy culture, 72–76; Loyd and, 88
boys, incarceration: in Oregon State Penitentiary, 76–77; in Oregon State Reform School, 77, 80–81, 88, 221
boys, rural: accidents and, 53–56; city and, 30, 31, 32, 36; concern over, 23, 24, 67; credit

boys, rural (*continued*)
system and, 98; drownings of, 53–55; farm labor of, 32–33, 63, 77, 87–88; guns and, 56–57; hunting by, 1, 56, 63; idealized relationships with father, 33, 34; idealized relationships with mother, 30, 34–35; idealized relationships with sisters, 34–35; idealized view of, 28, 29, 35; keeping on the farm, 30, 32; killing and torturing animals by, 57–58; mundane life of, 30, 32, 33, 45; republicanism and, 29, 35; school and, 33, 73, 83, 87, 92, 171; slaughtering animals by, 57; transition to manhood by, 59, 86–88, 116; violence against others by, 55, 72–73. *See also* bad-boy problem; boy culture; children

Boys and Girls Aid Society of Oregon, 76

Brown, Clarissa (Browning), 12, 130, 136, 144

Brown, Hugh, 12, 93, 95, 98, 111, 130, 136, 137, 143–44

Brown, Richard Maxwell, 155

Brownsville, OR, 1, 2*map*, 6*map*, 11, 12*fig.*, 13*map*, 14, 21, 47, 52, 55, 61, 91, 93, 98, 114, 117, 130, 136, 143, 148, 152, 154, 170, 171, 172, 176, 177, 182, 209, 210, 212, 213, 214, 215; agrarian protest and, 112, 113; bad-boy problem and, 72, 79–80; depression of 1890s and, 104, 105; hops and, 103–4, 105; Linn County Pioneer Association and, 123, 127, 132, 134, 135, 138–39, 140, 145–46; railroad and, 96; religion and revivalism in, 201–2, 203, 205, 208

Brownsville Cemetery, 14*map*, 130, 214

Brownsville Grange, 109

*Brownsville Times*, 21, 62, 91, 135, 139, 144, 151; silencing the Montgomery parricide by, 147, 148, 149

Bryan, William Jennings, 113

Burkhart, Jonathan W., 184

Burnett, George: bad boys and, 186; biographical details of, 184, 186; as judge at Loyd's trial, 184, 186, 187, 188–89

## C

Caldwell, John H., 184

Carpenter, Marc James, 137

Cavender, Albert, 21, 22, 23, 62, 91, 92, 154, 171

Cayuse people, 130, 131, 133; perspective on Whitman "massacre" by, 246n17

Cayuse War (1857–55), 137

Chamberlain, George, 106

Champoeg, OR, 125

Charcot, Jean-Martin, 52

childhood: invention of, 33

children: accidents and injuries of, 53–55; age of culpability, 88; changing conceptions of, 33–34, 35, 76, 88; city and, 29, 30–32; corporal punishment and abuse of, 68–71; death of, 48, 49–50, 53–56; debate over nature of, 45, 65–66; depicted in *Illustrated Historical Atlas Map of Marion and Linn Counties, Oregon*, 38, 40*fig.*; disease and illness of, 48–51; Donation Land Claim Act and, 26; educational requirements for, 87; history and, 22; as hope of the nation, 29, 35; idealized relationships with fathers, 34; idealized relationships with mothers, 30, 34–35; imagined effects of dime novels and Victorian literature on, 85, 133–34; Montgomery parricide and, 22–23; parental responsibility for raising, 61, 66, 67–68; parricide and, 8, 22, 121; poverty and, 45–46; republican landscape and, 26, 28–36; violence and trauma in the lives of, 46, 55–57. *See also* boys, rural; child-welfare movement; girls, rural

child-welfare movement, 76, 88, 189–90

Chinese, 15, 172, 202; hops and, 102–3; racism and, 72, 102–3, 110, 111

Chinook Jargon, 141

*Chittagong*, 166

cholera, 48

churches. *See* religion and revivalism, Linn County

Commission on Country Life, 28, 81, 226n10

Compton, Lawrence, 79
Conn, Isaac, 161, 162, 166, 207, 211
Conzen, Michael P., 38
Cooke, Jay, 109
Cooley, George, 98, 99
coroner's jury in Loyd Montgomery's case, 62, 113, 171, 177, 178; determination of, 23; Loyd and, 68, 172; men empaneled for, 172; proceedings of, 172
corporal punishment: debate over, 69–70; Loyd and, 69, 70, 74–75; Oregon State Reform School and, 77. *See also* abuse, child
corporate society: creation of in late nineteenth century, 36–37, 155
Couey, John, 70, 71, 111
Couey, Mary (Griffith), 70–71
country life movement, 28
Courtney, Agnes, 12–13
Cowan, James L., 106
Craft, Adniram D., 184
Crawfordsville, OR, 4, 6*map*, 11, 13, 13*map*, 47, 55, 73, 75, 81, 210, 222; agrarian revolt and, 112, 113; Linn County Pioneer Association and, 129, 130, 131, 134
Crawfordsville Cemetery, 222
Crossmeier, Ralph, 7
Curtis Lumbering Company, 159
Cusick, William A., 263n4

## D

Danbom, David B., 99
Davis, William, 212
Dawes Act, 79
death: American culture and, 11, 124; boys by guns, 56; childhood accidents and, 53–56; childhood development and, 46; childhood disease and illness and, 48, 49–50; of children from murder, 73; impact of Daniel McKercher's, 182–83 221–22; Loyd's, 15, 89, 155, 156, 168, 211–14; neonatal and early childhood, 50–51; and pioneer culture of Oregon, 19, 42, 122, 123–25, 127; of pioneers, 93, 126–27, 135–36, 143–45, 147–48; republican landscape as a site of, 27, 28. *See also* genocide; killing
depression (1873–97), 4, 10–11, 24, 79, 92, 93–94, 99–100, 101*fig*., 103–8, 109, 110, 116–17, 118, 122, 125, 157, 159, 160–61, 173–74, 203. *See also* panic of 1873
Dickson, Frank, 201, 203–4
diphtheria, 48, 49–50
disease and illness, 48–53
Donation Land Claim Act, 14–15, 125; impeding agricultural expansion in the Willamette Valley, 35–36, 115; race and, 14–15, 26; republican landscape and, 26, 35–36
Donation Land Claims, 37, 40, 111, 143, 180, 184, 201; along the upper Calapooia River, 14*map*
drownings, 53–55
Dr. S. A. Richmond & Company, 52
Duniway, Abigail Scott, 96, 191
Durrant, Theodore, 82, 85, 191

## E

Edgar Williams Company, 37
Ellis, Matthew, 52, 212
epilepsy: Loyd and, 51–52, 178–79; prevalence of in Willamette Valley, 50–51
Evans, Edmond, 171, 172
execution of Loyd Montgomery: crowds assembled for, 156, 211; expanding state apparatus and, 154–55, 156, 168; final minutes before, 211–12; globalization and, 156–68; justification for (real and imagined), 157; news coverage of, 211–12; preparations for, 162–63, 164, 166, 207–8; rope and noose for, 156, 157, 162–63, 164, 166, 211, 213; scaffold for, 156, 157, 161–62, 207, 208, 211, 213–14; success of, 213–14; those invited to, 207–8, 211

## F

Farley, William, 215
Farmers' Alliance, 108, 110

INDEX 287

farmers and farming, Willamette Valley: credit system and, 98–99; local issues confronting, 11, 35–36, 41–42, 87, 95, 96–97, 98, 100–105, 107–12, 115, 116, 170; romanticization of, 28–35, 37, 38–39, 41–42. *See also* agrarian protest; agriculture, Willamette Valley; republican landscape

fathers: idealized relationships with sons, 33, 34; role played in Loyd's trial, 184–86, 188; and tensions with sons on Oregon farms, 35–36, 87, 115, 116; as victims of parricide, 7–8, 57, 71. *See also* Montgomery, John B.

Faust, Drew Gilpin, 124–25

Findley, John, 12

Findley, William, 12

Finlayson, Charles, 40, 82–85, 86, 89, 153; bad-boy problem and, 89; body of, 86; compared to Loyd, 82; influence of trashy Victorian literature on, 85; violent behavior of, 83

Finlayson, Colon, 40

Finlayson, James, 39–40, 41–42, 49, 82, 83, 84; residence of, 40*fig.*

Finlayson, Janet (Dalgleish), 40, 83

Finlayson parricide: story of, 83–85; recalled locally, 85, 86, 153

Finley, Richard, 13

Finley-McKercher gristmill, 4, 11, 13, 114, 182, 222

Foucault, Michel, 9

Fox, John, 74*fig.*, 75, 76, 81, 194, 205, 206

Fox, Marshall, 74*fig.*, 75, 76, 81, 171, 194, 205, 206, 209

Freud, Sigmund, 7

Fruit, Martin, 172

## G

Gee, Suey, 103, 240n28

gender: Daniel McKercher and, 195–96; Donation Land Claim Act and, 14; changing roles of farm women, 34–35; childhood accidents and, 53–54; childhood disease and, 50; children's farm labor and, 32–33, 57, 63; guns and, 57; hunting and, 63; idealization of farm boys and girls, 29–30, 32–33; *Illustrated Historical Atlas Map of Marion and Linn Counties, Oregon* and, 38, 39, 40; Loyd's case and, 189–92; Loyd's trial and, 184–86; manhood in early Oregon, 22, 36, 59, 86–89, 184–86; Montgomery parricide and, 71, 120, 121, 180–83; patriarchy in early Oregon, 69; parricide and, 8, 121; pioneer obituaries and, 147–48; raising of farm children and, 33–35; republicanism and, 25–26, 35; roles in farming and, 32, 33, 97; rural-urban migration and, 30–32. *See also* bad-boy problem; boy culture; boys, rural; girls, rural; manhood and manliness; Montgomery, John B.; Montgomery, Loyal "Loyd" Bryson

genocide, 137, 140, 147. *See also* death; killing

Gilkey, Edgar, 4, 119

girls, rural, 29–30; accidents and drownings of, 53–54; city and, 30–32; corporal punishment and, 70; relationships to brothers, 35; relationships to young men, 32

Githens, William E., 184

Gleason, William A., 184–85

Gragg, Bettie, 56, 57, 58; as teacher, 73

Gragg, Cordelia, 49

Gragg, George, 49

Gragg, Herman, 53

Gragg, Joseph, 33, 49, 53

Gragg, Lovina, 33, 49

Gragg, Marcus, 33, 49, 53, 55, 58

Gragg, Mary, 49

Gragg, Philo, 33, 49, 53, 58

Gragg, Vernon, 33, 49, 53

Gragg boys, 33, 57–58

grand jury in Loyd Montgomery's case, 177–78

Grand Ronde Reservation, 141, 158

Griffith, Elisha, 12

Griffith, Elizabeth, 12
guns: accidental death of boys and young men and, 56–57; availability of in Willamette Valley, 57; manliness and, 57; parricide and, 8, 57

## H

Hackleman, Thurston Pierce, 151
Halsey, OR, 13*map*, 203
Hannah, Emma, 175–76, 178–79, 182, 188, 189, 207, 256n27
Haskins, Leslie, 133
Hearst, William Randolph, 44
Heide, Kathleen M., 9
hemp (Cannabis), 163, 164
henequen (sisal), 163, 164
Henry, Joel, 170, 172
Hiatt, Lottie, 175–76
Hill, J. L., 208
Himes, George H., 126–27
Holcomb, Ella, 207
Holden, Margaret Kolb, 110, 112
Holdridge, Earl, 203
Holladay, Ben, 96
hop industry, 3, 4, 11, 91, 98, 100–105, 129, 164; Chinese labor and, 102–3; Linn County economy and, 11, 100, 102–5; Native American labor and, 102–3, 103*fig.*, 141; Templeton family and, 11, 12, 100–102, 117; violence and, 56, 102–3
Hume, Catherine (McHargue), 143, 210
Hume, Joseph, 143, 209–10
Humphrey, Napoleon, 183, 184, 187
Humphreys, Thomas N., 185
hunting, 1, 56, 57, 63; accidents, 56

## I

Idaho, 130, 148, 176; gold rush in, 96
*Illustrated Historical Atlas Map of Marion and Linn Counties, Oregon* (1878): 37, 118, 149, 176, 180, 216*fig.*, 228n34; colonialism and, 39; contents of, 37, 38; illustrations in, 37, 38; images of farms in, 38, 39, 40*fig.*, 42, 119*fig.*; promotion of, 37; republican landscape and, 38, 39; subscriptions to, 38
Indian Wars, Pacific Northwest, 137, 138; national belonging and, 125, 149. *See also* Battle of Big Meadows (1856); Cayuse War (1857–55); Rogue River War (1855–56); Yakima War (1855–56)
Indian War Veterans of the North Pacific Coast (IWV-NPC), 137–38, 148, 149, 218
Irvine, Elijah, 178
Irving & Fortmiller undertakers, 215
Isom, John, 108
Isom, Thomas "Crock," 108

## J

Jayne, Robert A., 171–72
Jefferson, OR, 83
Jefferson, Thomas, 25–26, 29, 36
Jenkins or Judkin, D. E., 200
Jennings, Francis, 27
Jordan, OR, 13*map*, 175

## K

Kalapuya people, 2, 13–14, 141, 149, 157–58, 167. *See also* Lize
Keeney, Jonathan, 137, 140
Kellogg, A. B., 207
Kelly, Bengal Joy, 61–62, 88, 200, 204; sermon on Loyd, 62, 67, 70, 72, 88, 204, 233n3
Kendall, Thomas, 95, 201
killing: animals, 33, 57–58; Oregon's culture of, 122, 123–24, 132, 138, 147–48, 149; republican landscape and, 27, 149, 171. *See also* death; genocide
Kirkpatrick, John, 180
Klamath Reservation, 158
Knapp, J. B., 70
Knee, Henry, 51
Know Nothings, 111

## L

labor, child: advice on boys and farming, 32–33; boy's versus men's, 63, 87–88;

labor, child (*continued*)
  changing nature of on farms, 34; farms and, 33, 72, 87–88, 97; hop industry and, 104; Oregon State Reform School and, 77, 79; rope industry and, 166; social importance of, 63
Ladd, William S., 106, 164
Lafollet, Bryant, 32–33
Lapwai (Spalding) Mission, 130, 201
Leonard, Bessie E. (Templeton): on day of Montgomery parricide, 3; and memory of the Montgomery parricide, 150–51, 220
Lewis and Clark Exposition (1905), 218
Linn County, OR, 2*map*, 13*map*; agrarian protest in, 41–42, 109–13; agriculture in, 95, 96, 100, 102–5, 115; bad-boy problem in, 81–82, 89; demographics of 15, 47; depression (1873–97) and, 105–8, 160–61; logging in, 158; Loyd's burial and, 214–15; Loyd's execution and, 129, 161, 210; provides pension for Lize, 140; religion and revivalism in, 201–4, 206; schools in, 87; white settlement of, 12
Linn County Courthouse: 173*map*, 174, 175*fig.*, 181*fig.*, 187, 188; agrarian protest and, 41; construction and architecture of, 179–80; display's Loyd's body, 213; Loyd and, 178, 179–80
Linn County Farmers Union, 109
Linn County Jail, 15, 19, 75, 108, 161, 162, 173*map*, 174–75; 175*fig*, 197, 201, 206–7, 208, 209, 210, 211, 215; remodel of, 174–75
Linn County National Bank, 106–7, 164
Linn County Pioneer Association (LCPA), 123–24, 127, 132, 136, 137, 149, 177; becomes the Linn County Pioneer Memorial Association, 152; commemoration of violence against indigenous people by, 138–39; Committee on Death of, 123, 124; founding of, 129–30, 131, 134; Montgomery parricide and, 144–46; objectives of, 134–35; racial exclusion of, 131; reunions of (1887) 134, (1890) 135, (1894) 132, (1896) 144–45, (1913) 141, (1922) 138; Templeton family and, 141, 142, 152

Little, Riley, 201, 209, 211, 215
Lize, 139–40, 141, 148; as last of the Calapooia, 140–41, 148; Linn County Pioneer Association reunion and, 141; pension from Linn County for, 140; Pocahontas trope and, 140
logging and lumber industry, Linn County, 157–61; depression of the 1890s and, 160–61; environmental change and, 159–60, 167
Lord, William Paine, 67; manhood and, 190, 191

# M

Malone, Wade, 56
manhood and manliness: age and, 86–87; body and, 86; defenders of Daniel McKercher and, 195; defenders of Loyd and, 190–91; dependence on fathers and, 87; farm labor and, 87–88; justice for Loyd and, 184; republican farmer and, 29, 59, 114; school attendance and, 87. *See also* gender; Montgomery, John B.; Montgomery, Loyal "Loyd" Bryson
manila hemp, 163–66, 168; agricultural uses of, 164; environmental change in the Philippines and, 165; industry in the Philippines, 165–66; preferred for hangman's noose, 163. *See also* abaca
Marion County, OR, 2*map*, 37–38, 39, 79, 102
Marshall, Miss Orlena, 51
Martin, Barney, 176, 177
Martin, Egbert, 73, 176–77
Martin, Ernest, 73, 176–77
Martin, Robert, 146
Marwood, William, 163
Maston, G. Watson, 212
McCain, James, 183–84, 186, 187
McChesney, John, 161, 162, 166, 207, 211

McCormack, Fred, 171, 178, 187
McFeron, Elizabeth (McHargue), 65, 170, 208; providing Loyd a Bible, 204
McFeron, James Andrew, 65*fig.*, 76, 143, 174, 178, 179, 180, 183, 188, 194; arrest of Loyd by, 172; arrival at scene of the Montgomery parricide by, 170; biographical details of, 164, 170; criticized for conduct in Loyd's case, 170; defense of John Montgomery by, 114; Emma Hannah case and, 176; explains John Montgomery's fears of Loyd, 114, 182; insights into Loyd's childhood by, 64, 70, 120; Loyd's confessions and, 88, 178; Loyd's funeral and, 215; praised for conduct in Loyd's case, 214; preparation of Loyd's execution by, 162–63, 164, 166, 207–8, 209, 210–11, 212, 214; relationship to Montgomery family, 170
McHargue, James, Jr., 80
McHargue, James, Sr., 12, 111, 141, 143
McHargue, Sarah (Montgomery), 12, 111, 141, 143
McHargue, William, 111
McHargue, William Claud, 80, 81, 170
McHargue Cemetery, 14*map*, 143, 144*fig.*, 214, 222
McKee, Charles, 201, 215
McKenzie, A. S., 207
McKercher, Daniel, 183*fig.*; biography of, 182–83; dog of, 6, 183*fig.*; final resting place of, 222; funeral and memorial services for, 138–39, 182–83, 221–22; Loyd's accusations against, 15, 178, 194–95, 204, 207; manhood of defended, 195–96; murder of, 5; role in the Montgomery parricide, 4, 64, 120, 121, 219; support of Montgomery family by, 114, 119–20
McKercher, Duncan, 195
McKercher, Florence: donates land for McKercher Park in Crawfordsville, 222; and memory of parricide, 153–54, 219–20
McKercher, John, 153, 168, 182, 222; Loyd's execution and, 154, 207, 211; receives a piece of the hangman's noose, 207–8; role in preventing Loyd's lynching, 154
McKinney, John, 201
Meeker, Ella, 101, 113
Meeker, Ezra: depression of the 1890s and, 105; hops and, 100, 101; Oregon Trail commemoration and, 151
migration, rural-urban, 29, 30, 31*fig.*, 32, 92, 116; bad-boy problem and, 80, 81; fears concerning, 29, 30–32
Mill City, OR, 13*map*, 153, 160, 161
Mintz, Steven, 22
Molalla people, 158
Montgomery, Canada, 12
Montgomery, Clara, 71
Montgomery, Elizabeth Ann (Couey), 3, 4–5, 47, 48, 61, 92, 93, 111, 116, 117, 118, 119, 122; blamed for Loyd's murderous actions, 67; burial of, 143, 222; domestic violence and child abuse and, 70–71; funeral of, 172; infantilization of Loyd and, 88–89; Linn County Pioneer Association reunion and, 145; murder of, 4–6, 121; relationship with Loyd, 71; silenced in the parricide, 71
Montgomery, Ellen, 12, 111
Montgomery, Eveline (Brown), 3, 12, 97, 111, 115, 116, 130, 136, 169, 202, 215; death and obituary of, 144, 147, 149, 150–51; monument to, 143, 144*fig.*, 151; relationship to the Montgomery parricide, 149–50; relationship with grandson Loyd, 150, 189; silencing of Montgomery parricide in memory of, 147, 149
Montgomery, Eveline "Eva," 1, 47, 48, 207, 221, 261n125
Montgomery, Hugh, 219
Montgomery, John (great-grandfather of Loyd), 12, 111
Montgomery, John B. (father of Loyd), 3, 4, 47–48, 80, 91, 92, 93, 98, 113, 121–22, 130, 144, 145, 146, 147, 170, 183, 210, 215; argument with Loyd, 4, 64, 119, 120, 121; blamed for Loyd's murderous actions,

Montgomery, John B. (father of Loyd) (*continued*)
67; burial of, 143, 222; depression of the 1890s and, 114, 116–17, 118, 119, 120, 182; child abuse and corporal punishment and, 68–69, 71, 120; farming failure of, 92, 114, 115–16, 117; fear of Loyd, 120; funeral of, 172; illness of, 61; Linn County Pioneer Association reunion and, 145; manhood of, 114, 116, 118, 120; mining attempt by, 117; murder of, 4, 5*map*; politics of, 114, 118; relationship with Loyd, 4, 62, 63–64, 65, 66, 68, 70, 71, 74, 80, 81, 116, 120, 121; reliance on Loyd, 81, 115–16; renting Samuel Templeton's hop farm by, 87, 104–5, 114, 115–16; role in his own murder, 120; role in Loyd's trial, 184–86

Montgomery, John Clarence (brother of Loyd), 1, 47, 221

Montgomery, Loyal "Loyd" Bryson, 3*fig.*, 198*fig.*, 199*fig.*; abuse and corporal punishment of, 46, 68–69, 70–71, 75; accusations against Daniel McKercher by, 15, 178, 194–95, 204, 207; argument with father, 4, 64, 119; arrest of, 15, 143, 172; autopsy of, 214; bad-boy problem and, 76, 81–82, 85–86, 89; behavioral problems of, 44, 53, 74–75; betting on father's death, 61, 66; biography of, 47; body of (when living), 86, 88–89, 120, 180–81, 193, 214; body of (when dead), 157, 213–14; boy culture and, 73–74, 88; brain of, 214, 215, 217; burial and grave of, 152, 215; casket for, 215; character and temper of, 44–45, 58–59, 64, 73, 149; cognitive issues of, 75; commission of murders by, 4–6, 5*fig.*, 120, 121; compared to Charles Finlayson, 82, 85; compared to Jesse Pomeroy, 82; compared to Orville Montgomery, 64; compared to other boys, 45, 67, 73; compared to Theodore Durrant, 82; confession of (attempts to get), 88, 143, 170, 196, 197, 200, 205, 207, 209, 210; confession of (fabricated version of), 45, 67, 196–97; confession of (version from 25 November 1895), 15, 53, 63, 68, 71, 120, 177, 194–95, 196; confession of (version from 28 November 1895), 178; confession of (final version on 31 January 1896), 143, 210, 212; corporal punishment and, 64, 69, 70, 74–75; death of, 15, 89, 155, 156, 168, 211–14; demeanor at trial of, 186; Emma Hannah and, 175, 178–79, 182; epileptic seizures and spells of, 51–53, 178–79, 187; father's dependence on, 81, 115–16; father's fear of, 120; favorable views of, 44–45, 73, 192; funeral of, 214–15; gender issues and, 18, 63–64, 86–88, 89, 120–21, 180–84, 210, 212; globalization and, 157; hunting by, 3, 4, 51, 63, 64, 65, 73, 119; immediately following his parricide, 169–70; indictments of, 178; infantilization of, 88–89; insanity defense and, 179, 187; jail time of, 51–52, 75–76, 172, 175, 177, 178–79, 194–95, 198*fig.*, 199*fig.*, 200, 201, 204–6, 207–12; labor of, 33, 63, 87–88, 104; lawyers of, 176–77, 183, 187, 192; legal pleas of, 179; Linn County Pioneer Association reunion and, 145–46; memory of, 153, 219–21; musical instrument playing by, 71, 162, 194, 200, 205, 207, 209; post-trial news coverage of, 192, 193, 195–97, 211–12, 217–19; post-trial social reaction to, 189–92, 193–96; pranks while in jail, 75–76; profanity and, 65, 74; relationships with other youths, 75–76; relationship to history, 149, 215–17; relationship with father, 4, 61, 62, 63–64, 65, 66, 68, 70, 74, 71, 80, 81, 116, 120, 121; relationship with fellow inmates, 75–76, 175, 178–79, 182, 194, 196, 197; relationship with grandmother, 150, 189; relationship with mother, 71; relationship with news reporters, 177, 179, 193; religion and revivalism and, 200–201, 204–5, 207, 208; reputation of, 44–45, 62, 64, 66, 73, 177, 218–19;

request to see model of the scaffold by, 209; running away by, 66, 74, 80; on the scaffold, 211–12; scarlet fever and, 48; school difficulties of, 74–75; schooling of, 75, 86; stealing by, 66–67, 73–74, 80, 129; as subject of sermons, 61–62, 72, 215; suicide fears and, 207, 208–9; threatened lynching of, 154; threats of violence by, 58, 74; trauma and, 46–47, 58–59; visits with siblings in jail, 150, 189, 207. *See also* coroner's jury in Loyd Montgomery's case; execution of Loyd Montgomery; grand jury in Loyd Montgomery's case; Montgomery parricide; trial of Loyd Montgomery

Montgomery, Orville Ernest, 3, 33, 47, 48, 63, 87, 115, 169, 178, 187, 207, 221; comparison with Loyd, 64; reputation of 3, 64; witness at brother's trial, 187; witness for Loyd's grand jury, 178

Montgomery, Robert (grandfather of Loyd), 12, 97, 98–99, 106, 111, 115, 141; as Indian fighter, 137, 138; monument to, 143, 144*fig.*, 151

Montgomery, Robert C. (brother of Loyd), 1, 6, 47, 178, 221; discovers murder scene, 169; witness at brother's trial, 187; witness for Loyd's grand jury, 178

Montgomery family: credit system and, 98–99; depression (1873–97) and, 104–5, 116–17; corporal punishment, abuse, and violence in, 64, 68–69, 70–71; farming history of, 97; genealogy of, 16–17*chart*; household size in 1890, 47–48; illness and, 48, 50, 61; memory of parricide and, 150–51, 219–20; pioneer history of, 12, 92–93, 151; political affiliation of, 111, 113, 114; poverty of, 4, 48, 91–92, 114–17, 118–20; prosecution of Loyd and, 182, 183, 188; religion of, 202; silencing of parricide and, 146–47, 148, 149; southern roots of, 111; subsequent to the parricide, 150–51, 221

Montgomery parricide: bad-boy problem and, 81–82, 89; Daniel McKercher's role in, 120, 121; depression (1873–97) and, 66–67, 92, 119–20; domestic violence or physical abuse and, 69, 70–71, 120, 121; events described, 1, 2–6, 119–20; farm life as a cause of, 67; gender issues and, 71, 120, 121; Linn County Pioneer Association reunion and, 144–46; Loyd's parents blamed for, 67–68; Loyd's trial and conviction for, 182–83, 188; meaning of, 9–10, 11, 41–42, 45, 85–86, 149; memory of, 150–51, 152, 153, 217–21; news coverage of, 7, 23, 92–93; popular understandings of, 61–62, 217–21; poverty and, 46, 119–20; relationship to history, 27, 93–94, 122, 125, 149, 152, 155, 168; religious revivalism and, 61–62, 202, 205; silencing of in history, 146–48, 149; sociopathy of Loyd and, 66; trivialization of, 121, 220; Whitman incident and, 151. *See also* Montgomery, Elizabeth Ann (Couey); Montgomery, John B.; Montgomery, Eveline (Brown); Montgomery, Loyal "Loyd" Bryson

Montgomery-Templeton house, 4, 5, 5*map*, 6, 6*map*, 52, 67, 91, 103, 118, 154, 168, 170, 195, 222

Montieth & Seitenbach, 83

Moore, John, 140

Moyer, Hugh B., 215

*Musa textilis*. *See* abaca; manila hemp

# N

Native Daughters of Oregon, 127, 129, 131, 149, 152; Margurite Tuff's Cabin of, 128*fig.*; racial exclusion of, 127, 128

Native Sons of Oregon, 127, 129, 131, 149, 152; James Blakely Cabin of in Brownsville, 127; magazine of, 128; racial exclusion of, 127, 128

Newport, N. Monroe, 176, 179, 187, 192, 259n84

Nez Perce people, 130, 131
Noble, Willie, 56
Northern Pacific Railroad, 96, 109

**O**

Oakville, OR, 13*map*, 200, 201
Obermeyer, William J., 185
Oregon and California Railroad (O&C), 96, 109
Oregon Children's Aid Society, 76
Oregon Fisheries Commission, 106
Oregon Historical Society (OHS), 127, 129, 218
*Oregonian* and Loyd Montgomery. *See* Piper, George; Scott, Harvey W.
Oregonian Railway Company, 96
Oregon Pioneer Association (OPA), 125–26, 126*fig.*, 127, 129, 134, 135, 136, 137, 149, 152, 218; founding of, 125
Oregon State Grange, 28, 109–10; anti-Chinese nature of, 110; *Willamette Farmer* as mouthpiece of, 28
Oregon State Insane Asylum, 178
Oregon State Penitentiary, 80, 148, 157, 179, 207, 221; boys and youths confined to, 76–77
Oregon State Reform School, 77, 78*fig.*, 79, 221; advocacy for, 76; boys in purview of, 77, 88; depression of the 1890s and, 79; Linn County boys in 79–80; as a modern institution, 77–79
Oregon State Woman Suffrage Association, 190
Oregon Supreme Court, 184; Loyd's case and, 191, 192
Oregon Trail, 13, 151
Osborn, Josiah, 133, 134, 143, 144; Whitman "massacre" story by, 133–34
Osborn, Margaret (Findley), 133, 143, 144

**P**

Palouse wheat growing region, 100
panic of 1873, 18, 24, 41–42, 94, 96, 99, 100, 109, 125. *See also* depression (1873–97)

parricide: causes of, 8, 115, 121; child abuse and, 69; and children as historical actors, 22; ethnology of, 9–10; historiography and, 8, 9; limitations of sociological studies of, 8–9, 220; Lizzie Borden and, 7; masculinity and, 121; modern rates of, 9; rural America and in 1890s, 7–8; sociopathic tendencies of perpetrators of, 66; victims of, 8; weapons used in, 8, 57; Western culture and, 7. *See also* Montgomery parricide
Patrons of Husbandry (Grange), 108. *See also* Oregon State Grange
Pearl, Jode, 113, 172
People's Party. *See* Populist Party
Perfect, E. M., 219
Peterson del Mar, David, 69
Philliber, Clyde, 73
pioneer(s), Oregon: celebration of the racial violence of, 124–25, 136–39; commemoration of, 123–29, 134, 135, 136–37, 138–39, 143–44, 152; death of, 93, 126–27, 135–36, 143–45, 147–48; Montgomery parricide and, 92–93, 125. *See also* Linn County Pioneer Association; Native Daughters of Oregon; Native Sons of Oregon; Oregon Pioneer Association
Piper, George: and *Oregonian* reporting on Loyd, 193–94, 195, 196, 204
Poling, Daniel, 201, 215
political motherhood, 189
Pomeroy, Jesse, 82, 85
Pool, William "Harry," 75*fig.*, 75–76, 81, 194, 205, 206
populist movement, 110, 112, 203. *See also* agrarian protest
Populist Party, 110, 124; in Linn County, 111–13; in Oregon, 112. *See also* agrarian protest
Portland Cordage Company, 164, 165–66, 167
Pritchard, Jennie, 190
Prohibition Party in Linn County, 113
Propst, Quincy, 162, 166, 194

**R**

race and racism: agrarian protest and, 110; exclusionary laws and, 111; framing of Oregon history and, 128, 129, 131, 132*fig.*, 133, 137, 147–48, 149, 220; indigenous people and, 13, 27, 138, 139–40, 148; labor in hop fields and, 102–3, 104; land law and, 14–15, 26; pioneer memory and, 148, 220; in pioneer organizations and celebrations, 127, 128, 131, 134, 137, 138, 216; religious revivalism and, 203; republican landscape and, 26, 27; silencing of the Montgomery parricide and, 149

Rader, A. J., 105

Red Crown Roller Mill, 107*fig.*, 107–8

Reese, Orlando, 49

religion and revivalism, Linn County, 200–207

republican landscape: agrarian protest and, 110; bad-boy problem and, 89; childhood trauma and, 46; children and, 26, 28–36; death and, 27, 28; domestic violence and, 69; *Illustrated Historical Atlas Map of Marion and Linn Counties*' depiction of, 37–43; imperiled nature of, 27–28, 79; Montgomery parricide and, 168; racial violence and, 26, 27; Thomas Jefferson and, 25–27; *Willamette Farmer* as monument to, 28; Willamette Valley and limits to expansion of, 35–36; Willamette Valley as, 26, 27

republican motherhood, 30

Richardson, James H., 185

Riggs, Timothy, 138, 139–40

Rivers, I. W., 196, 197*fig.*, 206, 207, 209, 262n132

Rivière, Pierre, 9

Roberts, Edwin C., 185

Robertson family of Marion County, 49–50

Rogue River War (1855–56), 137, 138, 149, 180; genocide and, 137; Linn County volunteers and, 136–37, 138, 139, 140, 147–48

Roosevelt, Theodore, 28, 151

Rounds, Albert, 79–80, 81

rural reform, 28, 35–36

Russ House, 173*map*, 187, 206

**S**

Sacagawea monument, 152

Salvation Army, 187, 205–7; Linn County and, 206; Loyd's conversion and, 201, 205, 207, 209

Santiam Lumbering Company, 158, 159–61, 164, 207; location of Albany lumberyard, 173*map*

scarlet fever, 48, 49–50; Loyd and, 48

schools: Albany and Linn County in 1890s, 87; bullies at, 73, 186; Charles Finlayson and, 83; Linn County's religious affiliated, 55, 201; Loyd and, 74–75, 87, 118, 171; republican landscape and, 26. *See also* Oregon State Reform School; Warren School

Schulmerich, William, 81

Scio, OR, 13*map*; Salvation Army and, 206

Scott, Harvey W.: attacks the California press's view of Loyd, 192–93; attacks women and men who defended Loyd, 190–91; biography of, 218; as champion of Oregon, 218; editorial policy on Loyd of, 45, 92, 192, 185–96, 217–18, 219; Montgomery parricide and, 217–19; women's rights and, 191. *See also* Piper, George

Scott, James: execution of Loyd and, 129; Linn County Pioneer Association founding and, 129–30; questionable testimony in Loyd's case by, 129

seagrass rope, 163, 164, 253n25

Seminole War (1816–58), 137

Shanks, Elmer, 55

Shaw, John, 158, 159, 160, 164, 167

Shedd, OR, 13*map*, 109, 171, 201, 209

Shon, Phillip Chong Ho, 9, 121

Shulse, John, 201, 209, 211

sisal (henequen), 163, 164

Sky tus, 102

INDEX 295

Slotkin, Richard, 27
smallpox, 48–49; vaccine for, 48, 49
Smith, Adam, 99, 157
Snyder, J. E., 146, 201, 205, 209, 210, 211, 215, 221; Loyd's execution and, 146, 211
Sodaville, OR, 13*map*, 203
Sons and Daughters of Oregon Pioneers, 152, 218
Sons and Daughters of the Linn County Pioneer Association, 141, 145, 177
Southern Pacific Railroad, 96
Spalding, Amelia, 130
Spalding, Eliza. *See* Warren, Eliza (Spalding)
Spalding, Eliza (Hart), 130, 201; death of, 130
Spalding, Henry, 130, 137, 201
Sperry, Carpus, 201
Sperry, William "Jim," 138–39, 221
Stanard, Alphonso, 139
Stanard, Everett Earle, 139, 141; and biography of Lize, "the last of the Calapooia," 139–40
Starr, Isaac: Loyd's autopsy and, 213–14; Loyd's epilepsy and, 52; Loyd's execution and, 212; smallpox vaccines and, 49; visits Loyd in jail, 208
Stockman, J. R., 108
Susman, Warren, 10–11
Swarthout, Ernest, 8
Swarthout, John, 8

## T

T. L. Wallace & Company, 105–6
Templeton, Albert, 3, 116, 117, 127, 141, 142*fig.*, 145, 152
Templeton, Bessie. *See* Leonard, Bessie E. (Templeton)
Templeton, Charles, 92
Templeton, Clyde, 1, 3, 92, 150, 178; death of, 146; Montgomery parricide silenced in the memory of, 146; witness at Loyd's trial, 187; witness for Loyd's grand jury, 178
Templeton, David, 142*fig.*
Templeton family, 142*fig.*; depression of 1890s and, 116–17; Ezra Meeker and, 101, 105; hop industry and, 11, 12, 100–102, 117; laborers employed by, 102; leasing hopyard to Suey Gee, 103; Linn County Pioneer Association and, 141, 142, 152; local reputation of, 114, 117; McHargue cemetery and, 143
Templeton, James, 101, 118, 142*fig.*, 145, 146; home of, 119*fig.*
Templeton, John, 101, 142*fig.*
Templeton, Joseph H. 142*fig.*; photograph of Brownsville by, 12*fig.*
Templeton, Matilda, 142*fig.*
Templeton, Orpha (Montgomery), 116–17, 150; on day of Montgomery parricide, 3, 146, 169; Montgomery parricide silenced in the memory of, 146; witness at Loyd's trial, 187; witness for Loyd's grand jury, 178
Templeton, Robert, 3, 116–17, 142*fig.*, 150, 169; witness for Loyd's grand jury, 178
Templeton, Samuel, 3, 11, 21, 87, 91, 92, 108, 129, 138, 142*fig.*, 146, 154, 164, 178, 222; death of, 103, 222; financial status of, 104, 117–18; hop industry and, 101–2; as Indian fighter, 137, 138; mining activities of, 117, 222; relationship to Warm Springs people, 102; renting farm to Montgomery family, 87, 104–5, 114, 115–16; story about Loyd stealing by, 66–67; witness for Loyd's grand jury, 178. *See also* Montgomery-Templeton house
Templeton, Sarah (Montgomery), 3, 116
Templeton, William A., 101, 113, 142*fig.*
Templeton, William T.: quoted, 101
Thompson, Mr. and Mrs. W. L., 201, 207
trauma: boyhood and, 58–59; effect on personality development, 46; Elizabeth (Couey) Montgomery's childhood and, 71; Loyd and, 46–47, 58–59, 118
trial of Loyd Montgomery, 179–80, 182, 183–84, 186–87; death sentence delivered at,

188–89; defense at, 187; gender issues and, 180, 184–86; Judge George Burnett and, 184, 186, 188–89; jury and, 184–86, 187–88; prosecution at, 187–88; relationship to parricide and, 188; verdict in, 188
Trites, Frank, 185
Truax, Elias, 185
Tubbs Cordage Company, 164
typhoid, 48

## U
U'Ren, William S., 112

## V
Victor, Frances Fuller, 131, 132
violence: against animals, 57–58; against history, 43; against indigenous people and its celebration in Oregon, 122, 124–25, 136–39, 140–41; Charles Finlayson and, 83; childhood and, 46, 47, 55, 56, 57, 58, 69–70, 72, 73, 83; child on child, 55–56; dime novels and trashy Victorian literature and, 85, 133–34; domestic, 69, 70–71; effects of ignored in nineteenth-century Oregon, 46; in Loyd's life, 58, 68–69, 70, 71, 74, 75, 118; personality development and, 46; pioneer stories of, 131, 132–34; poverty and, 45–46; racial in Oregon, 26, 27, 28, 69, 72, 102–3, 134, 139–40; republican landscape and, 26, 27, 28; transformed in pioneer obituaries, 147–49

## W
Waiilatpu (Whitman) Mission, 130, 131, 133, 137, 148
Walker, Cyrus, 137, 148
Wallace, James, 52
Warm Springs people, 141; as hop pickers, 102
Warm Springs Reservation, 102, 158
Warren, Andrew, 130, 171
Warren, Eliza (Spalding): birth of, 130; death of, 148; Linn County Pioneer Association and, 131, 132–33; memory of, 148; monument to, 148, 151; stories of Whitman "massacre" by, 131–33, 149; Warren School and, 171; whiteness and, 131, 137; Whitman "massacre" and, 130 131, 148
Warren School (Linn County School No. 28): attendance and, 237n84; Montgomery parricide and, 171, 178
Washburn Park (Brownsville), 138, 140
Watson, Perry, 180
Weaver, Fitler & Company, 163
Weaver, James B., 112
Whiting, Junius, 38, 39, 119
Whitman, Marcus, 130, 131, 132, 133
Whitman, Narcissa (Prentiss), 130, 131, 132–33
Whitman "massacre," 130, 131, 132, 132*fig.*, 148, 149; Cayuse perspectives on, 246n17; relationship to Montgomery parricide, 151; stories of, 132–34, 137
Whitman National Monument, 152
Whitney, John, 176, 178, 179, 186, 187, 188, 192
*Willamette Farmer*: advice on raising rural children by, 30–33, 34, 36, 65–66, 70, 98; boy culture and, 59–60; ceases publication, 61; Charles Finlayson parricide and, 85; drownings and, 54; gender bias of, 29, 30; globalism and, 98; linking dime novels and trashy Victorian literature to bad boys by, 85; prescriptions for rural children, 29–35; promotion of bourgeois family ideal in the countryside by, 35; republican landscape and, 28–37; rural reform and, 28, 30, 35–37, 39; view of children by, 29; views on city by, 29, 30; views on corporal punishment by, 69–70
Willamette Valley, OR: agrarian protest and, 108–9; childhood accidents in, 55; childhood disease and illness in, 48, 50–51; childhood drownings in, 53–54; contradictory views of rural life depicted in, 42; environmental change in, 167; family size

Willamette Valley, OR (*continued*)
in 1890s, 47; hunting tradition in, 63; infrastructure expands in, 95–96; logging and lumber industry in, 158. *See also* agriculture, Willamette Valley; farmers and farming, Willamette Valley

Williams, Edgar, 37, 38, 43

Wilson, James, 170, 172, 175

Windes, W. J., 172

Writers' Project of the Works Progress Administration, 133

**Y**

Yakama Reservation, 103

Yakima War (1855–56), 218

Yost, Robert, 54

EMIL AND KATHLEEN SICK SERIES IN WESTERN HISTORY AND BIOGRAPHY

*The Great Columbia Plain: A Historical Geography, 1805–1910*, by Donald W. Meinig

*Mills and Markets: A History of the Pacific Coast Lumber Industry to 1900*, by Thomas R. Cox

*Radical Heritage: Labor, Socialism, and Reform in Washington and British Columbia, 1885–1917*, by Carlos A. Schwantes

*The Battle for Butte: Mining and Politics on the Northern Frontier, 1864–1906*, by Michael P. Malone

*The Forging of a Black Community: Seattle's Central District from 1870 through the Civil Rights Era*, by Quintard Taylor

*Warren G. Magnuson and the Shaping of Twentieth-Century America*, by Shelby Scates

*The Atomic West*, edited by Bruce Hevly and John M. Findlay

*Power and Place in the North American West*, edited by Richard White and John M. Findlay

*Henry M. Jackson: A Life in Politics*, by Robert G. Kaufman

*Parallel Destinies: Canadian-American Relations West of the Rockies*, edited by John M. Findlay and Ken S. Coates

*Nikkei in the Pacific Northwest: Japanese Americans and Japanese Canadians in the Twentieth Century*, edited by Louis Fiset and Gail M. Nomura

*Bringing Indians to the Book*, by Albert Furtwangler

*Death of Celilo Falls*, by Katrine Barber

*The Power of Promises: Perspectives on Indian Treaties of the Pacific Northwest*, edited by Alexandra Harmon

*Warship under Sail: The USS* Decatur *in the Pacific West*, by Lorraine McConaghy

*Shadow Tribe: The Making of Columbia River Indian Identity*, by Andrew H. Fisher

*A Home for Every Child: Relinquishment, Adoption, and the Washington Children's Home Society, 1896–1915*, by Patricia Susan Hart

*Atomic Frontier Days: Hanford and the American West*, by John M. Findlay and Bruce Hevly

*The Nature of Borders: Salmon, Boundaries, and Bandits on the Salish Sea*, by Lissa K. Wadewitz

*Encounters in Avalanche Country: A History of Survival in the Mountain West, 1820–1920*, by Diana L. Di Stefano

*The Rising Tide of Color: Race, State Violence, and Radical Movements across the Pacific*, edited by Moon-Ho Jung

*Trout Culture: How Fly Fishing Forever Changed the Rocky Mountain West*, by Jen Corrinne Brown

*Japanese Prostitutes in the North American West, 1887–1920*, by Kazuhiro Oharazeki

*In Defense of Wyam: Native-White Alliances and the Struggle for Celilo Village*, by Katrine Barber

*Gold Rush Manliness: Race and Gender on the Pacific Slope*, by Christopher Herbert

*Reclaiming the Reservation: Histories of Indian Sovereignty Suppressed and Renewed*, by Alexandra Harmon

*Pioneering Death: The Violence of Boyhood in Turn-of-the-Century Oregon*, by Peter Boag

www.ingramcontent.com/pod-product-compliance
Lightning Source LLC
Chambersburg PA
CBHW030523230426
43665CB00010B/750